Poetics of Contemporary Dance

LANCHESTER LIBRARY, Coventry University
Gosford Street, Coventry CVI 5DD Telephone 024 7688 7555

Laurence Louppe   Photo: Jorge Leon

You must be strong enough to admit vulnerability
Helen McGehee

Poetics of Contemporary Dance

Laurence Louppe

Translated by Sally Gardner

DANCE BOOKS
ALTON

First published in 2010 by Dance Books Ltd
The Old Bakery
4 Lenten Street
Alton
Hampshire GU34 1HG

First published as *Poétique de la Danse Contemporaine* by Contredanse,
Brussels, Belgium in 1997

ISBN: 978-1852731403

A CIP catalogue record for this book is available from the British Library

Printed and bound in Great Britain by Lightning Source

Contents

Introduction to the English translation

I first met Laurence Louppe through her writings in the Belgian journal *Nouvelles de Danse* in the mid-1990s. At that time I obtained her permission to have some of her articles published in translation in the journal *Writings on Dance*. Subsequently, I had the pleasure of meeting Louppe in person and on several occasions enjoyed her hospitality and great personal warmth. My decision to translate *Poétique de la danse contemporaine* took shape slowly as I did not initially see myself as a translator in any professional sense (although it could be said that 'translation' is central to the work of a dancer). Nevertheless, I realised that through undertaking a translation I might comprehend the book more fully, while at the same time making it available to a wider readership. I am grateful to Laurence Louppe for allowing me to undertake this project and to David Leonard at Dance Books for supporting its publication in English.

This introduction is intended to provide Anglophone readers with a brief background to the book. It does not attempt to summarise the ideas contained in the text as these are too numerous and complex to be treated summarily, and because Louppe herself admirably orients the reader to her approach in her own Preface and Introduction. Here, I have tried to provide some coordinates to guide readers new to Louppe's work and to give some background to the book's genesis. I also use the opportunity to raise some issues regarding Louppe's critical writing and its poetics and, more broadly, the respective poetic and conceptual resources of the French and English languages.

While it differs from it in many respects (and draws on a vastly expanded field of works and commentary), *Poétique de la Danse Contemporaine* was predated by John Martin's *The Modern Dance*, published in 1933.[1] *Poétique* emerged from the 'round tables' that took place at le Cratère, Théâtre d'Alès, Cevennes, France, in the early 1990s. These colloquia were organised by Marie-Claire Gelly with Louppe and numerous artists as key interlocutors, and they addressed questions from the general public and other practitioners in fields ranging from psychoanalysis to kinesiology. They prompted an examination of contemporary dance principles and values while, according to Louppe, at the same time precipitated a deep reflection on how to 'read' the dance. Similarly, Martin's earlier book, the text of a series of lectures he had given the previous year at the New School for Social Research in New York City, was attempting to educate a local contemporary art-interested audience about *a largely unfamiliar subject*, namely, the distinct nature of new dance developments at the time.[2] While Martin's book was *one of the first attempts to analyze the American modern dance* (Martin's Foreword), Louppe's later *Poétique*, written for a francophone audience and from a French perspective, discusses a broader field now called (perhaps uncomfortably in English) 'contemporary dance'.[3] Louppe, in fact, argues in her book that '*la danse contemporaine*' belongs more to the field of contemporary art (where each artist's work is singular) than to 'dance,' given that until the twentieth century dance had always been 'social' or traditional – in other words embodying not individual or iconoclastic values but those of the social group. The field called contemporary dance (including what Louppe calls '*la grande modernité*' – see below), Louppe argues, has few historical roots in dance itself.

Louppe's opting for the term contemporary dance might also be seen as a response to the need for precisely that inclusivity which Martin had earlier rejected. Such inclusivity makes it possible to connect late 20th century developments in French dance with the major currents and influences of modern dance from which it had earlier been isolated, for reasons that Louppe herself does not discuss here.[4] Indeed, it is important to note what was at stake for Louppe in undertaking the major task represented by her book. In the introduction to a 'sequel,' *poétique de la danse contemporaine: la suite*, published in 2007, which surveys mainly French dance production of the late 1990s, Louppe acknowledges that *between 1991 and 1995 (she had) despaired of contemporary dance*.[5] She admits to having turned back nostalgically to her earlier *Art Press* articles on minimalism and Black Mountain College. *Poétique de la Danse Contemporaine*, first published in 1997 – its writing therefore undertaken at the time of her 'despair' – is both an action and an intervention, a call to recognise a set of fundamental values in a field at risk of complete capitulation to 'the market' and reduction to pure spectacle. In this sense, her project has a utopian more than nostalgic edge: it imagines how this unprecedented art might live up to the promises embodied in the resources that are identified, affirmed and critically discussed in detail in the book. These are the resources that were elaborated in and are the legacy of what Louppe calls *la grande modernité*, that period in which *the choreographer, dancer, thinker* (invented) *not only a performance aesthetic but a body, a practice, a theory, a movement language.*

Louppe's terminological choices also reflect important theoretical considerations. True to the project of contemporary dance itself, she is concerned to avoid positivistic, naturalistic and biologistic notions of bodies and their 'lineages'. For her, 'body states' (an important concept) and body matter (which includes corporeal energies, intensities, presences, auras, ghosts, doublings and multiples) can circulate or resonate transubjectively in ways not bounded by literal bodily or even temporal borders: *the body in dance is not limited to a factual architecture and still less to a closed volume whose ultimate contours would be defined by an epidermis.* This has implications for understanding the ways corporeal values have been transmitted historically and geographically. 'Transubjective resonances' are more diffuse and mysterious than literal 'body-to-body' influences but they certainly do not exclude or negate the importance of such processes: rather, they enable dance lineages to be questioned, complicated, multiplied and extended; and linear, progressivist versions of dance history to be avoided. On the other hand (and, here again, Louppe conceptualises an irreducibly social and cultural body-agent), she argues that contemporary dance is part of an 'anthropological continuum' of human gesture: contemporary dance can both draw upon and maintain all the movements that have ever been made or imagined. It is potentially a vast archive containing all the bodies and moves that have ever existed. It is also an imaginative repository for infinitely new bodies to come.

Poetics of Contemporary Dance is based in and integrates an impressive knowledge of English, French and other language dance sources. Louppe's familiarity with the archive of actual contemporary dance works and practices is also extensive, marked by her proximity to Germany and Belgium and to North American dance through those US choreographers and dancers who, for various reasons, have had a presence and influence in France. The traces of these transatlantic crossings mark her thought. She is committed to the knowledges and poetic resources internal to and inherited from dance modernity and from dance practices – even while bringing to this project her own extensive knowledge beyond dance. Her intellectual resources include the philosophical works of Agamben, Barthes, Bataille, Benjamin, Deleuze, Derrida, Foucault and many others, as well as a deep knowledge of art and literary history. This command of intellectual and philosophical resources is never brandished, however, and while it informs and extends never dominates the dance thought. The approach of *Poetics of Contemporary Dance* is consistent with Louppe's participation during the 1990s in the Département Danse at the Université de Paris VIII, St Denis, where she was involved with others in wanting *to see emerge a speech that comes out of the experience of the choreographic artist and the perception of work... theory indissolubly linked with practice... not imposing epistemological categories from other knowledges....*[6] Louppe's literacy in numerous fields does mean that the text vibrates with multiple levels of meaning, even though not all these levels necessarily 'translate'. It could be said that her critical approach is that of an alchemist who is concerned to transmute dance and dance works so that, across the potential ravages of time and forgetting, they can retain the 'flame' of their liveness.[7]

Louppe's approach to contemporary dance poetics is neither a method nor a set of rules or prescriptions: it is 'interpretive' of dancing and dances, with all of the suggestions across languages that can be drawn out of this word.[8] In French, the '*interprète*' is the dancer/performer (any single performance or version of a work being an 'interpretation'). The apprehension of a dance by a spectator/critic is a '*lecture*' or reading. If we were able to retain a foot in both language camps the translation of *lecture* as 'interpretation' would give the spectator (not to mention the dance commentator or theorist) a role as a dancer (*interprète*) which is exactly one of Louppe's points: that in apprehending dance the spectator must be open to being caught up in and therefore being changed by it: *The art of movement can only be understood by implicating one's knowledges in it.* Poétique de la Danse Contemporaine is an invitation to a dance's audience to read dancing with their bodies – to become a dancer – to allow the dance and the performer to 'work' (on) them and thus to understand something of what is at work in the dance and for the dancer. The hermeneutic task to 'understand' (a) dance involves the dance reader in learning to dance to the extent of allowing her/his body to be moved in watching the dancer. Similarly, a critic cannot simply approach the dance through a process of stabilisation (such as a scientific approach might require).[9] Louppe makes herself and her body available as a kind of channel or mechanism of thought – a thought that moves and is moved, and is both an agent and recipient of kinespheric resonances. Her own writing, then, is of necessity poetic and metaphorical, for the ideas have to vibrate and summon up responses from the reader's own 'body matter' – another dance in fact.

The question of 'interpretation' can serve to introduce a reflection on this book's translation from French into English. From my point of view as translator, re-visiting the experiential and empirical 'here and now' of dance practices (such as I have personally encountered them as a dancer) through the metaphysically oriented mediation of the French language has been revealing of new terms, experiences, resonances and questions.[10] The stylistic differences between French and English languages have been widely discussed. For example, Vinay and Darbelnet note English's preference for the *plane of the real* and for *concrete verbs attached to particular concepts, expressing actions taking place before our eyes and seeming to have value only in the present.*[11] French on the other hand tends to operate on *the plane of meaning/understanding* ('entendement'), *that is, on a level of abstraction to which the mind rises to consider reality from a more general angle.* French language is *less encumbered with the details of reality.*[12] This characterisation of French as more generalising than English is worth discussing a little further: how can the potential singularity of dance experience (*a unique dancer in relation to a unique spectator* as Louppe's colleague, Hubert Godard, has said) be rendered in French when singularity itself *comes into being as that which resists an attempt to see something as a particular instance of a general idea?*[13] Between English and French, however, there may be no simple distinction to be made on this point concerning degrees of generality and concreteness/abstractness. Samuel Weber, comparing English to German in a philosophical context, has pointed out that what characterises English is more that it *does not tolerate the notion that what is nearest at hand may in fact be most abstract.*[14] He goes on to argue that, in the case of English, *the tyranny of empiricism is far more effective in estranging the entire speculative dimension from the realm of ordinary discourse.*

If English *demands empirical concreteness from the outset* the important thing for the dancer is therefore, as the post-modern dancers of the 1960s showed, not to attend less to this necessary concreteness but to understand that it, too, *has a speculative dimension*, that the concrete 'here and now' resonates and 'vectorises', to use Isabelle Stengers' expression.[15] Further, despite its 'abstractness', French can be closer to its underlying bodily metaphorics than English. French concepts often resonate more actively with their anthropological roots or with what Weber calls *the concreteness words have...as abstractions from the language of everyday activity.*[16] Thus, in French, a concept's own 'poietics' may be more accessible: the word for knowledge/familiarity/understanding – *connaissance* – for example, still tangibly resonates with its literal meaning of 'being born with', while the English 'knowledge' seems more 'stillborn', lacking a directly perceivable heritage in fundamental human life activity.[17] Similarly, Louppe draws on ordinary concepts that in French resonate not as finished actions or objects but as events or becomings: *'surgissement'*, *'développement'*, and *'connaissance'* are some of these. In other words, while French is more 'nominalising' than English, French nouns themselves can be more processual, giving more space to the idea of something as it takes shape or emerges into appearance. Finally, there are other everyday 'abstractions', also used habitually in dance practice, that in French already have an inherently practical dimension (not necessarily the case in English). An example here is the word *expérience* which in French contains no clear distinction between the (English) ideas of 'experience' and 'experiment'.[18] Thus, in French any experience is also an experiment and vice versa. This is very pertinent, suggestive and valid in the setting of contemporary dance with its founding experiential/experimental orientation in which any compositional experiment is of the order of experience for the dancer (and vice versa) since, potentially, it is 'undergone' and brings about unanticipated transformations.

While it is not my intention to provide a comprehensive glossary, it is worth mentioning Louppe's extensive use of the term *matière* (matter), a term whose resonances (including archaic ones) Louppe uses for their peculiar relation to dance. In the physical sciences, *matière* as 'matter', in all of its energetic potential and potential to change states, is not to be confused with *matériau*, which is a particular kind or form of matter seen as relatively passive or inert. In discourses on art the *matériau* is the material out of which an artwork is made. In dance, however, a dance is made not just from *matériau corporel* but from body *matière*, the live unstable 'body states' of the dancer which are her/his primary materials. This idea can be linked to the ancient Greek '*poiein*' or 'making/forming' (the root of our 'poetics') – a making that entails the formation and transformation of matter/material and which harkens back to pregnancy and childbirth.[19] Dance-*making* (a pragmatic term in English – often used as a way to avoid the more balletic 'choreography'), is a kind of limit case of *poiein* because the dance is made from *the power of the body to exude aliveness out of its own matter.* Indeed there is, subtly, a maternal metaphorics in Louppe's book – with movement as the mid-wife or 'maieutic' accompanying and facilitating the birth of new bodies; and the idea that the *interprète*, whether dancer or spectator, must in the first instance allow themselves to be in a relation of affective 'attachment' (*adhésion*) to, rather than one of critical 'judgement' upon, a dance work. But to return to *matière*, it is a term that is crucial conceptually in terms of avoiding any positivism with regard to 'the body' and the oppositions that accompany positivism, such as that between 'the body' and 'space'. In dance, our matter/material works and is worked: it does not exist positivistically in space, but spatialises. Grammatical as well as semantic issues are also pertinent here, as French can use its reflexive constructions or 'middle voice' to suggest that an entity is both the subject and object of its own action – a body-subject, in effect, works her/himself into and as the dance.

Louppe's knowledge of linguistics is extensive. Through her terminology she often draws analogies or distinctions, implicitly or explicitly, between dance/movement and language. She attributes Dalcroze with having first articulated that the body is not simply a support for verbal language or language's double: if the body conveys messages it can do so in its own way and differently. In this regard, it is useful to consider Louppe's frequent use of the linguistic term '*propos*' ('intention' or, literally, 'predicate'), that is, as what is 'put forward' in an act of dancing. The word 'propos' here relates dance and language while enabling their differences as communication to be clarified. As in language, the particular *propos*/intention of a dance or dance 'utterance' may be retained through different actualisations, while, alternatively, across different apparently convergent actualisations, deep, unintended divergences of intention might arise (such as in re-constructions of dance works). The use of *propos*/intention as a dance term can, in turn, serve as a reminder of the underlying intransitive and 'forceful' qualities of 'speech acts' – unearthing their power to *do* as well as mean. Furthermore, *predication is not an act that can occur alone* but only in conjunction with the grammatical subject.[20] This is radically the case in dance where there is no distinction between the 'speaking' and the grammatical subject so that the *intertwining and interplay of the functions of identification (the subject which gives force to the predicate) and predication in one and the same sentence* are irreducible.[21] The idea of *propos*/intention in dance, then, links dancing to 'action' in the intransitive, ancient Greek sense with its political overtones.[22] Indeed, Louppe notes in her book that, according to Bartenieff, Laban's concept of 'effort' (*antrieb*) contained this intransitive sense of action as *the organism's urge to make itself known.*[23]

There is, as always in translation, a category of terms that are more strictly 'untranslatable'. An example of such a word is '*écriture*', which is an everyday French word for writing and 'hand-writing' and may be familiar to English readers as a concept in post-structuralist and feminist thought (see, for example, Barthes and Cixous respectively).[24] Louppe, after Barthes, discusses *écriture* as closely related to dance 'style' and 'composition'.[25] The concept of *écriture* carries the necessary idea of an active writing of and through the body itself where the body is not simply the transparent vehicle for a transcendent idea.[26] The idea of *écriture* is also important because contemporary dance is not simply 'self-expression' or 'interpretive': that is, although it is 'individual' it is not simply personal. Discussing literary authorship Foucault says that, *écriture creates a space into which the writing subject constantly disappears.*[27] The dancing author/subject, however, cannot finally disappear, and *écriture* is that which prevents the performer from being simply what Louppe calls a 'presenter', or one who 'shows', rather than one who 'writes'. *Ecriture* arises in the relation between the choreographer and the dancer (even if they are one and the same person) and in the work they do to define, as they compose, the dance: *écriture* inscribes the values of the movement 'style' insofar as these are particular, communicable and apprehendable but are not a (universal) code. Louppe also notes that in purely 'spectacular' dance creations the deployment of elements external to the movement substitutes for the work on the dance *écriture*.

Trans-linguistic and trans-cultural work and reflection can contribute to ongoing debate around questions of dance discourses and terminologies.

Such debate responds to the need for precise terms to share complex move-ment experiences, threads and ideas created in the often intimate spaces and relationships of dance creation and spectatorship, and in view of the fact that the historical works and processes out of which terms have emerged are no longer fully available to us (as a result of which we lack their full range of referents). Further, as Louppe points out, there are many aspects of contemporary dance processes (including its historical begin-nings) that are 'invisible', as they take place in regions 'upstream' of what is usually recognised as visible or they *come from a place other than the one where legitimated conducts of thought and knowledge usually recognise them-selves.* In *Poetics of Contemporary Dance* Louppe undertakes a process of re-discovering the terms she discusses through her 'attachment' to prac-tices and works and does not assume ready-made definitions. In a similar manner, for me, the process of translation has been a process of re-discov-ery and a means of reading English language dance terms with new interest.

I hope this translation does justice to Louppe's thought. While taking full responsibility for any errors or misunderstandings in the text, I would like to acknowledge the assistance of numerous others who have supported me in this work. I would like to thank, in particular, Cathy de Plee of Contredanse who has been so generous with her time, her fine perceptions and her willingness to further engage, beyond her mother tongue and ear-lier editorial work with Louppe on her book, with its many ideas. I would like to thank Michel Cheval, also from Contredanse, who has enthusiasti-cally supported me in this venture, particularly in my successful application to the Centre National du Livre, France, for a translator's grant which ena-bled me to spend time working on this project at Bibliothèque of the Centre National de la Danse, Pantin, in 2008. I would like to acknowledge the School of Communication and Creative Arts at Deakin University for grant-ing me study leave to undertake the main part of the translation. I thank Russell Dumas, Paul Komesaroff and Philipa Rothfield for their valuable comments on and discussion of the manuscript.

Sally Gardner
Melbourne, 2009

1 One of the most important differences is the very different intellectual milieux within which the two books were conceived – although these differences may not be as great as first appears given that the New School for Social Research in New York, where Martin gave the lectures on which his book was based, was and is a centre for continental philosophy.

2 Note that in this book quotations are indicated by italics.

3 In the chapter 'Why a Poetics?' Louppe notes that she may be reproached for not making a distinction between 'modern dance' and 'contemporary dance'. Martin argued that the term modern *is obviously an inadequate one. It is not synonymous with contemporary dance, for it is by no means that inclusive.* In *The Modern Dance.* New York: Dance Horizons, 1933, p.3.

4 I thank Russell Dumas for pointing out that *danse contemporaine* does not necessarily translate unproblematically as 'contemporary dance'. At the very least the resonances and meanings of the terms used for identifying and periodising art and other movements are not necessarily translatable, and this is the case across both cultures and disciplines. For example, in the discipline of History the term 'modern' in English can refer to 'after 1500' or the time since the Middle Ages, just as in French '*contemporain*' can refer to the period since the Revolution. In his 'The Task of the Translator: Introduction to the Translation of Baudelaire's *Tableaux Parisiens*' in *Illuminations,* new York: Shocken Books, 1969, Walter Benjamin noted that: *The words* Brot *and* pain *'intend' the same object but the modes of intention are not the same. It is owing to these modes that the word* Brot *means something different to a German than the word* pain *to a Frenchman that these words are not interchangeable for them, that, in fact they strive to exclude each other.*

5 *poétique de la danse contemporaine : la suite.* Brussels: Contredanse, 2007, p. 7.

6 Handbook for U.F.R. 1 Arts, Philosophie, Esthétique: Formation Arts du Spectacle.

7 In 'Walter Benjamin' in *Men in Dark Times,* (Penguin 1968) Hannah Arendt quotes Kant discussing the relationship between the 'critic' and the 'commentator': *Critique is concerned with the truth content of a work of art, the commentary with its subject matter....If...one views the growing work as a funeral pyre, its commentator can be likened to the chemist, its critic to an alchemist. While the former is left with wood and ashes as the sole objects of his analysis, the latter is concerned only with the enigma of the flame itself: the enigma of being alive.* p. 155.

8 Excluding perhaps the sense of 'interpretive dance' which in English is associated with an amateur 'expressive' practice.

9 John Dewey's concern and caution that *(w)hen artistic objects are separated from both conditions of origin and operation in experience a wall is built around them that renders almost opaque their general significance...*is pertinent to Louppe's own concern. Dewey, J. *Art as Experience.* New York: Paragon Books, 1934, p.3.

10 Louppe herself makes several comments in her book about the place of languages in relation to different movement/dance values – without of course proposing any causality. For example, she notes the unaccented nature of the French language in relation to French dancers' almost universal use of very accented dance phrasing.

11 Vinay, J.P. and Darbelnet, J. *Stylistique comparée du français et de l'anglais.* Paris: Dider, 1958, p.18

12 Ibid., p.59.

13 See Chakrabarty, Dipesh *Provincialising Europe: Postcolonial Thought and Historical Difference.* Princeton: Princeton UP, 2000, p.83. Facing the singular, writes Chakrabarty, *might be a question of straining against language itself.* The Godard quotation is from 'Singular, Moving Geographies: an interview with Hubert Godard by Laurence Louppe' in *Writings on Dance,* volume 15: The French Issue, Winter 1996, p. 21, first published as 'Le déséquilibre fondateur' in *Artpress,* Spécial hors série, No.13, October 1992.

14 Weber, L. Translator's Preface to Adorno, T. *Prisms.* UK: Neville Spearman, 1967, p.12.

15 Stengers, I. 'A Constructivist Reading of Process and Reality' in *Theory, Culture and Society,* volume 25(4), 2008, p.96.

16 Weber, op.cit., p.12.

17 Weber, op.cit. says that, *German sentences have a history; sentences in English tend to be stillborn.*

p.13.

18 See Stengers op.cit.

19 See also Benveniste, E. 'The notion of "Rhythm" in its Linguistic Expression' in *Problems in General Linguistics*. Florida: University of Miami Press, 1971. Here is another important archaic reference for contemporary dance. Benveniste says that *ruthmos* (rhythm) originally meant form, but form *in the instant that it is assumed by what is moving, mobile, fluid, the form of that which does not have organic consistency; it fits the pattern of a fluid element, of a letter arbitrarily shaped, of a robe which one arranges at one's will, of a particular state of character or mood. It is the form as improvised, momentary, changeable.* Rhythm is the *particular manner of flowing* and of the changeable 'dispositions' of things and moods. pp. 285-6.

20 Searle, J.R. *Speech Acts: An essay in the philosophy of language.* Cambridge UP, 1969, p.126.

21 Ricoeur, Paul *Interpretation Theory: Discourse and the Surplus of Meaning.* Texas: The Texas Christian University, 1976, p.11. In language, the subject of the sentence or *énoncé* is not necessarily the 'speaking subject' (the subject of the *énonciation*).

22 See Arendt, Hannah *The Human Condition.* Chicago and London: University of Chicago Press, 1958.

23 Bartenieff, I. with Lewis, D. *Body Movement: coping with the environment.* New York: Gordon and Brach, 1980, p.51. The dance's 'propos' or intention should not be confused with the dancer's or a mover's 'intent' in Laban's terms i.e. in terms of the inner impulses. However, the dancer's intent will always be a question in relation to choreographic intention and vice versa.

24 See Barthes' seminal text *Writing Degree Zero* in *Writing Degree Zero and Elements of Semiology*, translated by Annette Lavers and Colin Smith and with a Preface by Susan Sontag. Boston: Beacon Press, 1970; and Cixous's *The Laugh of the Medusa* (1975) in *Laughing with Medusa*. Oxford UP, 2006.

25 In their footnote to Barthes 'Introduction' to *Writing Degree Zero*, Lavers and Smith note that *écriture is now more and more frequently used as a substantive corresponding to all senses of the verb écrire, generally to mean the style, the fact of composing a work, or the actions which properly belong to a writer...and is translated as 'writing', 'mode of writing'.* p. 1. *Ecriture* is related to 'idiolect' as Barthes discusses in *Elements of Semiology: the 'style' of a writer, although this is always pervaded by certain verbal patterns coming from tradition that is, from the community.* Op.cit., p.21.

26 See Koritz, A. *Gendering Bodies/Performing Art: Dance and Literature in Early Twentieth Century British Culture.* Ann Arbor: University of Michigan Press, 1995 for a discussion of Symbolist ideas of the dance trace.

27 Foucault, M. 'What is an author?' in *Modern Criticism and Theory: A Reader* edited by David Lodge. London and New York: Longman.

Preface

The development of contemporary dance is one of the major artistic phenomena of the twentieth century. In some European countries such as

France where it has really only existed since the Second World War, this dance phenomenon has expanded to become one of the great cultural developments of the contemporary era. Better recognised and supported both by the public and institutionally since the '80s, contemporary dance is present in all cultural arenas. Amongst artists and intellectuals it can compete with the more elaborated and advanced expressions of contemporary art-making; amongst the age- and other groups with a taste for mediatised culture it easily holds its own within that vast machinery; and it is not afraid of allying itself with rock music or television. In the space of several decades it has become an exemplary force for integrating and expressing the consciousness of our time.

But its important presence in quantitative terms – its exposability or 'exhibition value' (a term of Benjamin's that I will make further use of) – has never really led to an accompanying 'knowledge' ('*connaissance*'), or at least to a sensibility specific to its intention. The contemporary dance spectator is destined to wander from one performance to another mostly without any threads to connect him or her to a permanent field of references or, better still, to an artistic field capable of producing and awakening specific sensations, thoughts, body states and states of awareness that the other arts cannot provide. Hence, each contemporary dance choreographer and sometimes each choreographic work is approached according to the contingencies of the theatrical calendar as an isolated event, a fleeting spectacle amongst others. Singularity is rendered banal and profits only the simple consumption of a cultural 'moment' whose newness itself, reiterated as such, puts it at risk of self-erasure.

Our purpose in these pages is to develop some ideas regarding the whole field of contemporary choreography, its elaboration, its resources, its modalities of creation; and at the same time to suggest the kinds of sensations and perceptions towards which it aims to lead the spectator, to what threshold of aesthetic (*sensorielle*) listening and autonomous aesthetic awareness a dancing body can lead whomever allows her/himself to be touched by the experience and the experiment of movement.

To many, this undertaking will seem rather futile. Dance, and contemporary dance in particular, can speak to one's imagination without having to be explained. The perception of a moving body sets in motion each individual's own imaginary possibilities and inner journeys which it would be inappropriate to try to control or even direct. The success of contemporary dance performances in itself attests to the intensity of the dialogue between the body of the observer and that of the dancer, and demonstrates how a common fund of preoccupations and desires flows from one to the other.

Furthermore, beyond the fact of being labelled 'dance', contemporary choreographic practice belongs to the art of today. It is above all a contemporary response to a contemporary field of questions. For most spectators and probably for the youngest and most passionate, the actual conditions of this art are of little importance in comparison with its power to stir up the imaginative and emotive issues of the present time: a time which we know to be particularly susceptible to whatever can superficially play on emotions without having to answer for the way this game is played. Everything concerning the terms with which contemporary dance might be elaborated or inscribed in a given discipline could be considered offensive because it assigns a specialised territory to this 'dance' which is often only a desired object because it seems to escape any precise genre or limits.

But contemporary dance owes this power of 'present-ing' the world, of making it emerge out of its own shadow, to a formidable set of theoretical and practical tools which were set in place at the beginning of the twentieth century. To ignore this, by regarding contemporary dance as epiphanic or as the spontaneous outburst of artistic invention, hides two important elements: firstly, an immense foundation of work (*travail*), body work, dancing work, to make visible a body's imaginary and to make it readable. And then, no less important, its foundation in a thought that has been elaborated over the course of the century (from poorly recognised and very marginal sources), not parasitic on any other science and which, in our view, represents one of the major forms of the epistemological rupture which, in the human sciences and in politics and philosophy, has shaken all the currents of thought of our time. Of course, the epistemological rupture exercised by contemporary dance is still not well recognised. This rupture, as we will see, makes of the body, and especially the moving body, at once the subject, the object, and the tool of its own knowledge out of which another perception, another consciousness of the world and above all a new way of sensing and creating, can be awakened. But this renewal of perception involves the contemporary dance spectator as much as the dancer. That is why occasional attendance at a performance, despite the liveliness of the perceptions it might arouse, risks leaving the subject cut off from the riches that are more deeply buried. Far from burdening the spectator with useless information this deeper knowledge can help them to identify their own reactions, to understand the acuity of certain propositions and to feel the aesthetic experience resonating more deeply.

Besides, it is in fact the public which has often expressed a wish to gain access to the implicit zones which a dance performance activates without always revealing the process. I have often been asked to present the work of a choreographer and have been confronted with the desire of this or that cultural community to know more, to go beyond the limited horizon of an isolated presentation. They want to understand all of the references upon which the field of contemporary choreography is based and within which the work in question has been elaborated. They often want a deeper knowledge of its history. Far from making the reception of the work less poetic, such knowledge increases a public's interest and heightens its desires.

For me, more than anywhere, it has been at the Cratère Théâtre d'Alès that these kinds of exchanges have taken place. Credit goes to the team there and especially to Marie-Claire Gelly who organises the dance activities. I went to Alès for the first time in January 1993 when I was invited to give an historical perspective on the birth of contemporary dance. I had the joy of meeting a first small group of spectators who were as open to as surprised by an unknown current of thought which they had just discovered. The collaboration continued and I was able to appreciate, even at the time of the performances which occasioned my interventions, how much the latter immediately became a sharing of reflections, ideas, and inter-subjective experiences. Gradually, until 1996, I was able to observe in this community of spectators the birth of a new sensibility and shared parameters upon which a real dialogue could take place between the artists, the work, and the audience. And the topics of more structured encounters proposed by Marie-Claire Gelly and sometimes by the choreographers themselves have always exceeded the purely promotional aims to which discourses on dance are all too often subject. In the course of genuine colloquia or 'round tables', as well as in the simple presentation of a work, there was always an authentic and deep reflection (even if sometimes it could not avoid a ritually 'learned' form of speech) on, for example, dance notation (autumn 1993); choreographic *écriture* (in November 1993 with Christian Bourigault); and dance memory, remembering dances, body memory (March 1994 with the Carnets Bagouet and Odile Duboc). This book, it could be said, has been constructed around these exchanges and takes up the themes in order to develop and document them more systematically. A number of ideas considered here have been inspired by the propositions, the questions and dialogues which were articulated during these exchanges.

It was at Alès following these experiences that, on the initiative of Marie-Claire Gelly, without whom it wouldn't have existed, the project of this book was born. It was Alès that welcomed me as writer-in-residence for a large part of the book's drafting. It thus owes its origin, direction and vision to the team at the Cratère Théâtre. I would like to thank this team and especially Marie-Claire Gelly whose presence in the field of contemporary dance, well beyond her formal institutional responsibilities, is so precious – as ally, inspiration and spirit. I would also like to thank the faithful Alès audiences who witnessed my interventions and who have often amazed me by the acuity of their perceptions of a choreographic work and the sensitivity of their approaches.

I also want to thank the choreographers and dancers whom I have met, whose works or teaching I have observed, with whom I have dialogued and who have given me their presence, their movements, their voices, their conversation and the story of their experiences which have been my most precious inspiration. I also thank my History of Dance students who are today now well-known dancers, creators, researchers, teachers in their own right. Their lucid awareness of inheriting the extraordinary achievements of modernity, but also their wonderful anticipation of a dance still to come and of which they know themselves to be the vehicles, have often illuminated my research and sustained and nourished my own hopes.

And amongst the dancers who surround us today in France, I thank the first, the oldest (who by force of their dynamism and determination are the youngest), those to whom we owe the existence of a singular and innovative current of contemporary dance which has grown prodigiously over several successive generations of sensibility. They will be cited frequently in these pages. They were the first, here, to teach dancers the modernity of the free body which invents its own movement. They have also given local root to contemporary dance which was born under other cultural skies. Their names are those of a cosmopolitan family, dear, kind, diverse, who come together through the contingency of migrations and chance alliances: Françoise and Dominique Dupuy, Jacqueline Robinson, Karin Waehner and the late Jerome Andrews. From them we have in one and the same apprenticeship the dance and also its discourse; the freedom of movement and what the movement has to say. While working, I often think of this double support: it is to them that I owe the power to think and to write contemporary dance in my own language. A language in which I hope it will finally find all of its words...[1]

1 In the original French language editions (1997, 2000, 2004) the author also thanked Contredanse, the Belgian publishers of *Poétique de la Danse Contemporaine*: *My gratitude goes to Patricia Kuypers and Claire Destrée not only because they have included me in their collection 'Thinking through Movement' but because the numerous dialogues that we have had around the editing of* Nouvelles de Danse *have always been rich, illuminating and full of vitality, knowledge and rigour.*

Introduction

Why a Poetics?

A work of art is both the means and the act of an understanding.
Henri Maldiney[1]

Only in the active meeting between an intention and an attention is there a work of art. Art is for everyone also a practice.
Gerard Genette[2]

A poetics seeks to define and uncover in a work of art what touches us, animates our sensibility, and resonates in our imagination. Thus, poetics is the ensemble of creative conducts that give birth, meaning and sensuous existence to a work. Its goal is to observe not only a field where sensing is foremost in the ensemble of experiences but the very transformations of this field. The object of a poetics, like that of art itself, is at one and the same time knowledge, affect and action. But poetics also has a more particular mission: it does not only tell us what a work of art does to us, it teaches us how it is made.

In other words, what path does the artist follow to reach the point where the artistic act is available to perception, there where our consciousness can discover it and begin to resonate with it? Yet the work's journey does not end there: it is in (re-)turn transformed and enriched as it resonates. For poetics includes the process of perception itself. As we will discuss further, it breaks with the dichotomy that opposes the actor and the receiver: it 'devectorises' (to use Genette's expression) the traditional one-way conception of communication and places the work of art at the heart of a shared 'work'. ³

Poetics has been defined as the study of the factors that elicit affective responses to a system of signification or expression. Roman Jakobson applied the term in a linguistic context by studying the elements that constitute the emotive function of language (as opposed to its denotative or referential functions). The poetic function is specific in that it immanently involves the intervention of a double artistic point of view: a subject (whether hypothetical or not) of the creative act in close relation with an interlocutor whose sensibility the former seeks to touch at the threshold of an aesthetic response (what I will call 'aesthesias' or the factor of sensing which acts before any conceptualisation). Every work of art is a dialogue. *Focused on the addresser the so-called EMOTIVE or 'expressive' function aims at a direct expression of the speaker's attitude toward what he is speaking about.*⁴ This 'expression' of the subject's attitude in language does not necessarily pass through the grammatical subject of an utterance (*énoncé*), but through choices whose emotive appeal dynamises the 'attitudes of the subject' whose referent is the common fund of experience with an Other proposed by the work of art. Which means that all verbal poetics opens in language the space of a presence. For stronger reasons, the situation is essentially no different for dance (and more generally for the movement of the human body, as we will see). It is simply exacerbated and, as it were, exposed: the subject is in her/his movement directly. S/he does not have an instrument to substitute for her/his own presence, as s/he does in language. 'The attitude of the subject' coincides with the subject her/himself and is given completely in her/his movement.⁵ All movement is thus automatically expressive even if it does not have 'expression' as its aim.[6] Any movement, even when it accomplishes a 'survival activity' (the expression that Labanists use to define functional movement) is thus tied all the more closely to a body symbolics which it puts into play through its action. So we can understand how an art such as dance which, like poetry in language, tends to develop activity in the affective movement factors, is, more than in verbal poetics, connected to all of the deepest roots of the individual and that these are able to 'colour' a gesture (*énoncé gestuel*). Dance, which can be considered the body's poetry, intensifies and exemplifies this connection. Here, more than elsewhere the double presence, dancer-spectator – also a corporeal encounter – actualises itself in an intensified dialogue. This dialogue is even more able to awaken aesthesias because it takes place as an encounter in time and space. This encounter cannot be 'postponed' (*différé*). It involves, in itself, an experience/experiment of perceiving in space and time, an undergoing of this experience – on both sides. A poetics of dance, and especially of contemporary dance where the theoretical principles are extremely rich, has an advantage in that it explores the mechanisms of this exceptional situation. As the term indicates, it enters the realm of forming/ transforming (in Greek, *poiein*).[7]

It is a way of studying shared experiments/experiences and, through them, transformations in the sensed – as much for the dancer as for the dance's witness. Which means that dance poetics has no limits to its field of investigation. In dance, because of the engagement of the dancer in her/his movements, the work of art itself is predicated on the matter/material of the self. This is so even if particular aesthetics work on the territories of exchange or resonance, of depersonalisation even, which is often the case in contemporary dance, in order to avoid the straightjacket of classical 'mimesis' and awaken zones where the subject 'circulates', is doubled, de-centred or aleatory. In an expressive field that is still obscure and poorly explored by the science of aesthetics, dance affects the ontology as much as the philosophy of art. It concerns all the human sciences. And by virtue of this, what is essential in dance poetics comes less from an aesthetic approach (which is mine) than from sciences of movement and methods of functional analysis. Kinesiology and the different kinds of movement analysis are even more indispensable to the study of dance art than linguistics is to literary studies. Thus, this 'poetic' undertaking can occupy only a small place in the ensemble of choreographic knowledges. In other words, the present author is not an expert in these rich approaches even if on occasion she utilises some of their ideas. I wish to signal in advance the modest limits of this essay on the poetics of contemporary dance. In order to be understood, contemporary dance must not only be the object of deep and reflexive approaches in the movement sciences, but the dance itself, in its thinking and artistic aims, must be seen to have been elaborated on the ground prepared by them, sometimes at the very heart of their investigations. Mostly, these pages will only gather traces of this history as so many gestural fragments of the perpetually fermenting macrocosm that the world of contemporary dance has become. Their ambition is simply to trace a rapid itinerary through a few foundational or seminal elements of this art, to sketch the principles of a perspective that might serve to make the works intelligible. The approach will be poetic because understanding dance involves knowledge not only of its products but also of its practices. The art of movement can only be understood by implicating one's knowledges in it, and usually by involving oneself in its activity, in its *poiein/* making, where creative processes are already charged with the artistic complexity that they are employed to make visible.

In dance commentary, as elsewhere, there are appropriate approaches that take up a critical position outside the making of dance. These define its reception, analyse its forms, identify the codes and their circumstances and undertake comparisons. This approach, which is illustrated by some excellent contemporary studies, has been productive particularly following the work of Susan Leigh Foster.[8] She is essentially an aesthetician and, even more, a semotician. Her's are the responses of an isolated individual analysing her perceptions at one end of the traditional mechanism: 'emitter – signal – receptor'. The poetic approach implies another division of labour. The analysing subject is not assigned a fixed point: s/he is invited to move between discourse and practice, sensing and doing, perception and implementation. This is really the only way to touch an art's thought; to observe not only the finished product but the production at work in the work. Henri Meschonnic, after Valéry, reminds us that *theory only exists in and through practice*.[9] Critical reception of the work involves us in a temporality which, even if it comes after the work's creation, revisits it via a long meditation starting with the work's premises: its hidden design, the birth of its material, the choice of tools, its processes of elaboration. For the subject this is an imaginary journey which is often reconstituted after the event as the work is analysed, but it is a journey in which the subject is invested if only because, far from being simple receptacles, her/his own aesthesias are themselves active at the very heart of the process of understanding. Aesthetics, as the thought of sensuous and emotional experience, becomes an act of 'taking with' (*comprendre*), as Maldiney says, where 'listening' to the work gives access to the paths along which it has come into existence.[10]

Thus poetics implies what Meschonnic discussing the place of the observer calls the *dissemination of the subject* as the agent of circulation between levels and not simply a subject lying passively in the path of a trajectory of signs.[11] The listening subject is, therefore, 'corporealised' as much as, in being studied, the work is materialised.

The analytical or poetic gaze, then, is not only a scopic one. The whole body is involved. What Meschonnic says of literary or artistic critical perception in general applies even more to choreographic analysis. For, in the latter case, the body of the listener is explicitly solicited as such, well beyond the scopic, because a much more diverse sensorium is addressed. But this, perhaps, more literal corporealisation in the case of dance interests us in the first place to the extent that it allows us to penetrate further into what precedes the establishment of any poetics: the processes of a sensibility directly touched by the object of its study, involved in the different phases of its sensing, reworking this sensing through experience of the work, and constituting itself in reading the work. Commenting on Paul Valéry's famous *Introduction to the Course on Poetics*, Dominique Dupuy has evoked this poetic reading of movement as *an event which is a becoming*.[12] Critical perception of a work will thus be caught up in this becoming, which means that the work of movement is a becoming as much for the maker-performer as for the spectator: *to dance is to show what the dance makes (of)/does to me*, says Stephanie Aubin.[13] Bodies are traversed or touched by what they do or by what they perceive. In dance, in an exemplary way, the dissemination of any possible reading (and probably of the subject of that reading) will pass through all the dimensions of experience. The danced movement will inscribe itself in the body which creates and sustains it, and in the body which receives or perceives it. A dance poetics, therefore, will be located at the intersection of these different polarities. It should itself be that point of intersection, the fluid interstice where these corporeal exchanges are negotiated. Hubert Godard speaks eloquently of *a unique dancer for a unique spectator*.[14] In this sense, in the extreme of the situations to which it gives rise and their exemplary character, a poetics of dance can become the model for all poetics. We are talking here of poetics in the sense that the reading of a work encourages, as the object of its labour (*travail*), the mobility of the aesthesias. But such a reading can also involve a more cognitive approach and an interpretation in terms of meaning. It goes without saying that as regards 'meaning', especially for contemporary dance, we are a long way from a narrativity content to identify an explicit referent. The meaning or 'sense' is rather an unnamed objective that the dance interrogates without describing. Sally Gardner has proposed, in similar terms, a 'hermeneutics' of dance – not because the traditional definition of hermeneutics is the interpretation or translation into a universal language of an arcane or enigmatic text unintelligible because it belongs to a sacred or esoteric code, but hermeneutics in the post-Heideggerian sense which *acknowledges the central position of the subject in the creation of meanings* and where there is a dialogical process and *not the application of an interpretative method*.[15] This dialogue takes place along the conjunctive tissue of sensuous relations between the dancer and her or his witness; it is changeable, fluctuating and deeply circumstantial and is part of an experience that is not at all generalisable.

We can see therefore that an aesthetic or poetic approach to dance is complex. It is also relatively rare. Indeed, most of the authoritative discourses on dance come from cognitive approaches: even if these come from within the field of so-called 'dance-specific' knowledges. Amongst these there are the choreographic analyses local to contemporary dance which include the different types of movement analysis or analyses of choreography according to different artists' schools and their theoretical and practical methods for constructing a dance – where, in making their dances, artists have at the same time conceived ways of analysing them. Wigman, D'Houbler, Humphrey, Nikolais, Cunningham, Rainer, are amongst those theorists of dance composition, whose number is ever growing as today's choreographers seek to continue to communicate their ideas and describe their processes; or as theoreticians analyse in various ways what constitutes a compositional school. Let us note that, for the present, the interruption in the development of dance theory (in favour of a massive explosion in dance spectacle and the promotional material that sustains it) is at risk of exhausting dance resources, or of simply continuing to exploit the same analytical tools without renewing them: we must evolve and move on.

There are also other perspectives borrowed by analogy or by application from disciplines outside the field of dance – the human sciences, philosophy, semiotics – and which are often able to yield important insights. The most interesting studies on dance today are strongly informed by this last type of discourse. The most compelling draw on phenomenology and structuralist or post-structuralist perspectives (to which Anglo-Saxon critics freely refer), or from Kleinian or Lacanian psychoanalysis which are precious keys to another body-thought. But this does not resolve the difficult question of knowing to what extent tools of thought exterior to the theory and practice of dance can be applied to it. For us the answer is by no means clear: the field in which contemporary dance has been elaborated, including the historical one, strikes us above all by its character, if not of impermeability at

least of extreme singularity. It involves a whole mass of experiences foreign
to all others, and whose very propositions come from a place other than the
one where legitimated conducts of thought and knowledge usually recognise themselves.

There are, of course, very close connections between contemporary
dance and the other artistic practices – and historical research continues to
uncover the importance of the dialogue between the modern dancers and
the avant-gardes. Similar connections exist between the evolution of dance
and the human sciences which are concerned with the place of the subject
in experience, and with the question of the very status of that subject. All
of these aesthetic or anthropological approaches can intersect with dance
thought. But none can substitute for it. They can clarify, enrich and expand
it in the same way that dance thought, in return, can clarify them or reveal
entire areas of body knowledge. But any attempt to occlude or subordinate
the ideas elaborated in the choreographic field ends by seriously diluting the
thought of the moving body, making it into a parasitic discipline. When in
fact its originality and autonomy are profound.

The most formidable of all these 'hijackings' comes from an anthropology ignorant of the strength of anthropological analyses produced by
dance itself, an anthropology whose cognitive field is being considerably
enriched thanks to dance anthropologists or movement analysts. Dance, or
more particularly the dancing body, is usually subordinated to socio-cultural and historical contexts, as an emanation or product of an
environment that shapes it and assigns it the role of witness in the reproduction of dominant representations. This family of analysis is more useful
for works of the past or works that are outside the contemporary domain.
They become dangerous when a creative act escaping traditional precepts is
regarded as a simple reflection of the broader issues of a period; and the
body's inscription in discourses of social conduct or wider pathological phenomena invites dance commentary to slide ever more easily into a
neo-positivist discourse in which the dancing body is reduced to a symptom. In fact, for the contemporary dancing body the tendency (especially
amongst the best Anglo-Saxon commentators) is the opposite. There, on
the contrary, it is considered as itself interpreting the world, as a structure
for conscious information and as an instrument revealing the contemporary conscience, sometimes even a weapon in the struggle against injustice
or stereotypes, the manifestation of a consciousness that opposes these and
is engaged in a project of resistance, if not of denunciation. In any case,
happily, by no means an epiphenomenon linked causally to a society of

which it is the immediate product, blinded in respect of its own objectives by
a momentary ideology or by the models that would enslave it.

Two important facts about today's dance have been particularly
favorable to this approach: firstly, a certain narrative aspect of dance which
allows for a rather facile interpretation of discursive themes, and more or
less metaphorical forms and treatments of opinion. Then, the fact that,
sociologically, especially outside France and Belgium which are somewhat
isolated in this respect, dancers are engaged alongside other university, cultural, artistic or para-artistic movements, in militant struggles on behalf of
racial or sexual minorities and so on. The slightest thing then, as soon as
this critical perspective is at work, involves that one duly note, analyse,
interpret, and especially appraise in order to evaluate, the ideological and
artistic efficacity and pertinence of the artistic means used.

Henceforth, a critical-theoretical approach to dance, as Gay Morris has
justifiably noted, will go beyond the question of knowing *how dance might be
studied and analysed* to *the place of dance in culture and history.*[16] In other
words, not what it is that is at work in dance, but what dance itself can work
on, the human milieu in which it unfolds its potential and of which it, itself,
proposes a form of knowledge (and interpretation). Susan L. Foster presents
dance, even more clearly, as an active means of decipherment. *Choreography is psychic. It is critical and historicising. It is deployed in these pages as a tool
of thought, a physics of the mind.*[17] Foster notes that for her and for the other
contributors to *Corporealities* the approach to the body and physicality takes
place through a search for what it is in this body that makes sense.[18] So that
despite different points of view and the different methodologies, the dancing body that we find in these excellent writings still remains an instrument
for cultural and historical readings. Often coming from theorist-practition-
ers like Foster and Franko, these approaches show a determination to make
of dance not only an object but a tool of thought in/of the world, and more
particularly of the political and social context within which the dancing
body intervenes.

Our quest is different. Undoubtedly because our field of observation is
also different and, in part, determines our gaze. As in the analysis of any
art, a dance analysis is called to work on the problems posed in and by the
work of art itself. In dance, the invitation goes further: the kind of perception proposed by choreographic performance is both multiple and intimate:
multiple, because, beyond the gaze and to a greater extent, it is kinesthetic
sensations which put us in touch with a work, its means of creation, its
objectives and its meanings; intimate, because as soon as a tactile sensibility
is involved, the relation of the analysis to the perceptual registers that are

addressed is assimilated more to what is most secret and closest to the sen-suous and emotional in us than what is directly translatable in habitually rational terms. And when an apparently broader 'context' (cultural, artis-tic) can clarify the long corporal path taken by the movement in its emergence, this 'context' is indebted to the very matter that it colours or stirs up.[19]

Of course this point of view should be re-visited and re-examined. Since Laban and those who, like Bonnie Bainbridge-Cohen (an indirect link), have extended his work we have known that our comprehension of the world is activated by means of our sensory channels, and our critical awareness heightened by them as much as, if not more than, by the discursive paths of denotative communication.[20] This means that the very body of anyone who writes on dance is worked on by the dance; that all of the movements, the choreographic processes seen, integrated, approached also through practice, end up woven into the very frame of our perception. The vast receptive 'activity' of the critic's body (what Deleuze calls in *The Logic of Sensation* the 'constitutive passivity') will determine in large part the more or less controlled play of his/her aesthesias and the manner in which they will be translated into verbal expressions; like the overflowing of a wave loaded with its impressions, like the journey of a body that arrives on the banks of its own 'saying', the clumsy saying whose blindness the writer will doubtless need to recognise. The presentness of the experience is too destabilising for anything said about dance to really be regarded with any certainty as legitimate. This is why I feel charged with the task of speaking of dance from out of the milieu in which I live, from out of the problematic field of which it is the theatre, and out of the diverse tensions, exaltations or ruptures that I experience. Thus, I must warn from the start that I will not be able to abstract myself from my own speech, nor from the choice of works studied which are of necessity linked to the arbitrariness of my own life in dance, nor from the relativity out of which a discourse on dance justifies itself as the coming and going of cognitive and sensuous exchanges between two or more experiences of the body. That is why I cannot align my point of view and still less the particulars of my approach (which may be the weaker for this) on the model of Anglo-Saxon critics however much I might admire and read them with fervour. This is for two reasons, one of which relates to a position that I hold unconditionally: that is, to grasp the 'sense' (*sens*) of the choreographic only from its material and the body states that are its instrument and score – much more than from the sym-bolic articulation of choreographic 'images' or the mechanisms of an ideology at work solely through the figural elements which emerge from it.

This first reason rests fundamentally on the second which has to do with the necessities of cultural, social, and university contexts which are scarcely aware of the real contents of dance theory and of the immensity of the conceptual and practical tools that it has brought to light during the last one hundred years and more.

It seems to us indispensable to compile and put forward these ideas of a contemporary dance poetics as a reminder of what is at stake. Besides, the very idea of a poetics invites us to focus upon the resources that the practice itself has chosen. Dance itself, therefore, will dictate the orientations of this poetics through the work that it never stops renewing. It will often involve the question of the 'work of dance', the word 'work' (*travail*) being used here in its original sense, not of suffering, nor of an ascetic voluntarism (nothing is less part of the philosophy of contemporary dance than these two attitudes) but of the body's capacity to produce out of its own material the sources of its profound energy. As in the labour of childbirth it is the power of the body to exude aliveness out of its own matter/material that interests us.

Limiting this analysis to the perceptual field – where a dialogue with the dancer's body is effectively engaged – automatically affects the gamut of references upon which the reader will be invited to share numerous perceptions. A large part will be devoted to French contemporary dance and, even in this field, a personal selection based in the responses of the author has been at work – sometimes unconsciously, which proves how much the perception of dance depends upon the engagement of the whole person in the presence of the choreographic event. And in the plethora of contemporary dance as we know it today, the most important element is undoubtedly the polymorphously prismatic character of its luminous moments. Of the hundred flowers blossoming in the wake of the new dance and giving voice to today's body it is very difficult to choose an emblematic example without putting into the shade all the others. A complete panorama of contemporary dance is impossible unless as an encyclopedia or index requiring continual updating. It has not been possible here to cite all the names worthy of mention and I hope that it will be immediately understood that no rejection or contempt is intended. Nor have I been persuaded by the hierarchies and preferences of institutions or the media. Works of modest notoriety, danced without the need to create a sensation (but often more conducive to perceptual discoveries) sometimes reveal whole vistas of what is most enigmatic in dance, while works that gain the attention and support of the media may only furnish mechanically the vision of a well-managed spectacle. In dance aesthetics the value of the successful performance is often secondary to that of a vanishing luminosity which, like a meteorite, traverses a danced moment carrying its charge of what has been lit up in the bodies of the dancer and the spectator. We are all in search of these brilliant moments and of the indelible mark they make on us despite the elusive transience of their passing. I write on behalf of a poetics of these transsubjective resonances. It will thus be readily understood that certain works will be absent from such a diverse study. Taken together, the notoriety of these works will serve to guarantee them against a silence which in no way compromises the value and esteem that they deserve. On the other hand, those works and their authors that I have privileged are those with whom I have been able to entertain a dialogue: in conversation and exchange of ideas in situations favoured by life circumstances, but also by friendship, esteem and a shared sensibility. The most important dialogue remains, of course, what happens between dance and its perception: the thought which transmits itself in a movement to the awareness of a witness. But ideas, experiences and conversations inflect and enrich this moved dialogue with a multitude of still finer sensations.

Can a poetics be neutral? No: the vocation of poetics is no longer governed by the necessity to provide a *collection of rules, recommendations and precepts* (as in Aristotle's or Horace's time), an approach already denounced by Valéry who proposed a 'poietics' thus insisting on the Greek etymology related to 'forming/transforming'.[21] We need to understand this forming as a vibrant project that is much more activating than regulative. Contemporary dance does not, any more than does Valéry, envisage a normalising or censuring poetics; and tying it to a canonical foundation would be a gross misunderstanding. For the contemporary dance work and its interpretation there exist no precedent for imposing a single reference point, or for situating a work within a long historical succession against which it could be judged, as is the case in music or theatre. Sally Banes rightly notes that this kind of evaluative approach is most common with balletomanes who always judge a particular performance in relation to an image of previous interpretations.[22] I hope that nothing of this kind will be found here: firstly, the idea of evaluation (so important in our culture of 'experts') is foreign to the dynamics of contemporary dance. Does this mean that any qualitative approach to this field is unthinkable? Certainly not. Works, languages, movements are appraised in so far as they question, enrich, unsettle; and to this end coherence, engagement, and a very great mastery of process are required. One can be more or less persuaded, more or less carried away. But this is not arbitration: it is rather an (eventual) 'attachment' (*adhésion*) – for not every proposition succeeds in eliciting one. A given movement may not be compatible with our anticipation that a body will spring forth; an excessive overlaying of processes or effects may not satisfy the silent dialogue between my body-consciousness and the dancer. From one side or other a block or rigidity may prevent this dialogue. But this movement between us is not invasive: it should never use shock value or other mechanisms that subject the other's imagination/imaginary, the palpitating threshold where kinesthesias and what they allow us to comprehend are awakened. There is nothing fusional here even if in contemporary dance we are invited to join the dancer at the heart of the experience that s/he is undergoing. It is a question of an empathy. It has nothing to do with 'communication'. We know for example that Merce Cunningham's dance does not communicate. It does not require the approval of the spectator. Its relevance lies in the force of an art without mystification, all of whose parameters are freely and openly 'given', and where the dancer's investment in the complexity of an always unforeseeable (even to itself) effect is real. And if we are in tune with this it is enough to awaken our interest without our consent ever being forced. As a result, Cunningham's art leaves no one indifferent, even a public that is barely initiated into the more arcane aspects of contemporary art. In fact, contemporary dance has never really subscribed to a homogenous artistic programme in relation to questions of form. On the contrary, and it is here that its poetics brings it into proximity with other areas of thought and judgment, it has always upheld 'values.' These values can easily be turned in a militant direction. In itself militantism, which was one of the resources of the artistic avant gardes, has not been completely exhausted. Poetics, however, demands something beyond this: that we grant values the possibility of making art, that is, of engendering unknown values upon which our shallow provisional judgments would have no power of appraisal. But a poetics does not choose its own situation, still less the place from which its statements are made historically. *A poetics is critical*, remarks Meschonnic, *because its situation is critical.*[23] The critique to which a poetics exposes itself because it proposes its own vision of its times is what propels it beyond these times into the field of a 'becoming-event', to use Dominique Dupuy's term, of which the present or past work is only an initial spark – an opening towards which its speech is oriented, without this in the least changing or determining its genesis. It does not propose norms or canons as classical poetics does, but interrogates indefinitely the field of the possible. *There is thus something of the utopian in the poetic* (this is Meschonnic again). In the name of this utopia, of this contemporary dance-to-come, I may perhaps be excused for sometimes being normative – not in terms of formal criteria or esthetic preferences but in the name of the very values which draw me to this art, and which sustain my hope in its evolution and for its recognition within the art and thought of today.

Certain anti-historical preferences on my part can also be explained by the enduring nature of these values and the impossibility of being able to anticipate their still latent modes of appearance and visibility. Since the beginning of the century, contemporary dance 'schools' and currents have followed one upon the other. Each of these, from one generation to the next, at least as long as contemporary dance originated in the avant gardes, has manifested a more or less communally shared point of view, albeit with different degrees of polemic and more or less visible platforms of debate. In certain generations, the aesthetic and ideological confrontations were overt: like the opposition in the 1930s between the introverted, expressionist aesthetic of Mary Wigman and the dance of Kurt Jooss which was a platform for a public and objective art. Similarly, with the ruptures between American generations around the refusal of Modern Dance and its institutionalised models and dance-making processes between the '40s and '50s. (A debate that we would do well to transfer to current issues: the cult of product-spectacle and its codification, for example). The creative currents of the century are quite accessible to us today through film, in written documentation and especially in the repertoire or in the body-work that such an art has required. But it is no longer possible to project ourselves into history, still less to choose to settle down in the past and make its postulates exclusively ours. The immense wealth put forward by each movement, each current of modernity, forbids us to reject one in favour of another. In the following pages the reader will be invited to travel in space and time amongst the different schools always looking to gather from them their thought and their contribution, gleaning the infinite resources, the sometimes half forgotten fragments bequeathed to us by modernity. And this bequest is not one of goods amassed, but on the contrary, of a dialectical heritage where each contribution is questioned, taken up again, displaced, rejected, sometimes effaced, revisited and finally brought forward to where it is least expected. It is striking, for example, to see how the current infatuation of European dancers with Trisha Brown has put back into circulation hitherto forgotten values essential to contemporary dance: the experience of weight, the fluidity of continuous movement, a non-anticipation of the movement to come, etc. But this time, the choreographer's thought and her aesthetic determination give these values a much wider resonance, a credibility and a vast artistic and reflexive dimension. They are a summons, an ideal, an infinite threshold of transcendence.

The other reason for this journey through body states is to break with a

linear, often naively progressivist, and today no longer sustainable, vision
of the history of dance – a teleological history where enlightenment is attained through successive rejection of impurities (such as narrative) and
where contemporary perfection triumphs...[24] A vision (one of the most dis-
puted) conceived by Clement Greenberg when he represented the US art of
the '50s as the manifest pinnacle of avant garde achievement. Even if, today, the progressivism of this modernist idea might be given some
consideration, it is barely tenable – neither as an idealising theory, nor still
less in times like these when the radicality of the original aims are obscured
by a world of images and fictions. We know that, today, each phase or each
diverging branch of the art reveals new material or new questions which
imply or often involve the more or less irretrievable loss of other qualities.
Cunningham's decentred space abandons (deliberately, in his quest for a
'planar presence' analogous to non-illusionism in painting) the poetics of
volume that is so powerful in Graham and Limón. In dance there are premonitory flashes as well as regressions, minor reworkings and complete
abdications. Genuine choices as well, as in the example above, where to
choose is often to reject and sometimes to destroy or to re-discover with
astonishment what was repressed in a preceding era. Everyone has noticed
the deep relation between the '20s and '30s and the radicality of the '60s in
the United States. (The conquest of modernity in France at the same time
might well be connected.) Cynthia Novack has made links between the
emergence of Contact Improvisation and the beginnings of modern dance
in Germany, as these moments are *experimental currents which are basically
not formal and which consist essentially of a range of principles or movement
ideas for exploration...*[25] And there is the (very considered and deliberate)
periodic return to the pure moment of a 'degree zero' of the body where
everything remains to be invented anew. These, amongst others, are the
moments which lead us to abandon the impoverished vision of a continuous thread and invite us to steer our way among states of the body as so
many incarnations of history much more profound than would be allowed
by the apparent stages of a chronology. This sense of history must be applied to all fluctuations and all resonances. Dominique Dupuy's idea of
linkages (*reliement*) comes to mind in the sense that this linkage is not only
historical.[26] At work on possibly secret 'filiations', the linkage can advance
in time and space through co-presences, sudden alliances between bodies
that have never met each other. Something echoes from one body to another, not so much in terms of what they do but in terms of a body state to
be read and deciphered. This reverse side of movement, this invisible of the
body that is at one and the same time its genesis and seed and which, even

when I am amongst my contemporaries, is a latent power which approaches me and takes hold of me, but escapes me without my being able always to distinguish its hazy identity. Here, history is no longer in play. Except to be re-invented as another history, perhaps the only true one, of these underground passings and resurgences.

Some readers will reproach me for not making a distinction between the various stages in dance modernity up to the present – for example, for not distinguishing what is modern from what is contemporary or of the present time, perhaps. Some dancers whom I know and love will hold this against me: Merce Cunningham and Trisha Brown for example, for whom any rapprochement with modern dance is unthinkable when they themselves have fought against its overbearing influence. Their whole work is one long process of disconnecting from the earlier elements that they continue to question. I am more sensitive to this kind of reproach than to that of historiographers. Nevertheless, I must be excused for persisting in this. For me, contemporary dance only exists from the moment that the idea of a 'non-transmitted' movement language first appeared at the beginning of the century. Furthermore, within all the 'schools', I have found perhaps not the same aesthetic preferences (which have, as I write this, little by little lost their importance) but the same 'values.' These values (what Françoise Dupuy aptly calls *the fundamentals of contemporary dance*) sometimes undergo opposite treatments but are nevertheless always recognisable: the individualisation of the body and original movement expressing a non-transferable identity or project; the production, and not reproduction, of movement (from out of the sensible sphere of each person – or from a deep and willing commitment to the another's choices); work on the matter/material of the body, of the self (in a subjective way or, by contrast, through working on alterity); the non-anticipation of form (even if the choreographic maps/plans can be decided in advance as in the case of Bagouet or Lucinda Childs); the importance of gravity as a spring for movement (whether through playing with it or giving oneself up to it). There are also moral values such as personal authenticity, respect for the other's body, non-arrogance, the need for a solution that is right and not simply spectacular, the transparency of and respect for processes engaged. All of these categories which I can only introduce here will be developed in more depth in the following pages. What is important is to know that these 'values' have not changed, that when they are missing something of the contemporary evaporates or is lost and, up till now, has not been replaced by anything else unless by a formalism or by reproducing past models. The works and approaches that interest us today in one way or another revisit these funda-

mentals. One could even go so far as to affirm that their artistic accomplishment resides in the way these returns are effected (even when their
objectives are apparently displaced).

Nevertheless, despite this non-linear vision of dance modernity in the
20th century I propose a distinction which is not strictly historical even
though it establishes a certain diachrony: namely that between what I call
'*la grande modernité*' and the present period. The '*grande modernité*' refers to a
creative framework where the choreographer, dancer, thinker invents not
only a performance aesthetic but a body, a practice, a theory, a movement
language. This includes the family of 'founders' (which Anglo-Saxons call
'the originals') beginning with Isadora Duncan and whose last representa-
tives could be those of the generation of the '60s in the United States – at
the famous Judson Church; and in France, in the transmission by some bold
innovators of a language which, while they may not have created it, was
taken on by them, perilously, at first hand. They did so in relation to theoretical ideas that were strong enough to legitimate and ground the slightest
choice. In contrast to this *grande modernité* there is the current abundance
of work which is extremely rich in possibilities but which is usually limited
to adjusting a formula without re-inventing a language or the tools that
would allow its elaboration: generations which some schools of criticism
have baptised more or less approximately 'new dance' (a term which has
resurfaced at least three times since the 1920s). While maintaining this
historical and artistic distinction at least in an implicit way, I will also be
intertwining data, ideas and perceptions in view of the fact that innovations, similarities and corporealities, as they echo one another, allow me to
bring together, in relation to a choreographic question, historicities that are
apparently disparate but active around a shared preoccupation.

This study does not propose a new methodology for understanding the
dancing body. Mostly, I will be using concepts that have already been employed by dancers themselves, particularly in the wake of Laban and his
school. This is evident, for example, in the use of the Laban movement
factors as an analytic basis. There is a double reason for this. Firstly, we are
in a 'poetics'. It is right that the analysis of contemporary dance should
proceed from the very sources that have given it body and thought. In this
way the non-initiated reader will be able to measure the practical and theoretical work through which modernity in dance has been elaborated over
the course of the century. Then, because the dance is to be read primarily in
the very body which gives it birth and in which it grows: the intention more
or less clear of the poetic act in dance passes by way of movement as the
generative process both of body states and states of thought. In approach-

ing the corporal basis of an inexhaustible poetics no-one has ever gone as far (to be better informed) as Laban in his description of the modalities of 'effort' – the qualitative distribution of the movement elements and their mobilisation, the 'inner attitudes' and the inter-subjective circulation by means of which a poetics of both the act and its reading are woven – which his disciples have in particular enriched and completed. It might be asked what kind of innovation is offered here when the frames of analysis or the methods of reading the dancing body refer to well-worn concepts in the history of choreographic modernity. The choice, despite its limits, is dictated by several imperatives. One, as I have said, is to make known to the non-dance reader the immense theoretical wealth and the painstaking labour necessary to make possible (and credible) the epiphany of a body's action that the impact and appearance of dance performance hides from them. The other imperative is that the resources of contemporary dance, which are little known or sometimes depreciated in the choreographic world itself, are often re-experimented or rediscovered in each generation on a theoretical as well as a practical level, without ever being able to spring from or take root in a heritage; and consequently they remain underdeveloped. It is clear that evolution in dance thinking can only occur by recognising the heritage of modern dance and the bodies of knowledge it furnishes, including in its rupturing processes. Without these, neither the dancer nor the theoretician breaks with anything, especially not with the said heritage which he or she often reiterates without any knowledge of what has already been given shape, and without re-tracing the great disruptive forces which could give real substance to further ruptures. But it is important to recognise that the methods of analysis here are not definitive. Many things in bodies have changed and, today, it is time to establish perspectives that are more connected to current sensibilities. It is time to explore new modes of perception and new paths of analysis on a deeper level. Unfortunately, such a project can only be realised to the extent that the theoretical and practical heritage of dance are themselves identified and understood. In France, a lot of time has been lost, and the unconscious use of concepts which have already been explored over a long period, or even the impoverished nature of the approaches that substitute for these, demonstrate the scale of the loss. Here, therefore, we will have to be satisfied with indicating some landmarks, even while we ought to be moving forward, thinking in movement as dance thought does, evolving on the basis of the practices and the works. Of course, today there are other perspectives at work and homage will be paid to numerous Anglo-Saxon theoreticians who have already been mentioned above. But as I have already noted, their observation takes place in another field, and especially with different objectives: perhaps for historical reasons their vision is linked more to what there is in choreographic creation that structures, signifies, metaphorises. We, however, prefer to remain within the intimacy of movement and the genesis of the work's components, there, where it works to make itself, where it is exposed and takes risks. But also where it touches us and sometimes where it leads us. I dare to hope that at the end of this journey through new states of the body a new poetics will have emerged and of which I will simply have been the humble announcer.

And it is also because I speak from a place that is at once both modest and painstaking that the sources I invoke are diverse. Beyond my own observations there are testimonies from or citations of texts by great choreographers or theoreticians – mostly theoretician-dancers who are by far the most *au fait* with their concerns – and the most clear-sighted theoreticians who are non-dancers. I draw as well, of course, upon any ideas able to clarify and nourish the experience/experiment of dance: sometimes upon reference books (few of which are available in French), but also upon the whole gamut of 'dance talk' circulating in forms that are more or less elevated, more or less perennial, more or less accessible to collective visibility: interviews with dancers, extracts from video commentary, concert programmes, periodicals which are often so enlightening, other documents and tracts... a body of material that is 'poor' in inverse proportion to the wealth of sensations and desires that it reveals, and the multitude of movements and presences that it presumes. This democratisation of sources also bears witness to the paucity of sites where the dancing body can inscribe its thought. Thus, what dance does/makes/forms (*le faire de la danse*) is elaborated across a thousand sparse resonances which a diffuse plan can take hold of, here and there, without law or limit like a conglomeration of different consciousnesses and imaginations. To this image might be added, a 'listening' to/for dance out of gathered shreds, brief sightings, felt densities, perceptual imprints. These do not produce explanation, and still less the definitive keys or recipes that might give direct access to the work but, instead, voices, the rustle of bodies, and the elaboration of an alive and multiple text a few bright threads of which I have tried, here, to assemble.

1 Maldiney, Henri *L'Art, l'éclair de l'être*, 1992.
2 Genette, Gerard *Esthétique et poétique* (Introduction), 1992.

3 Ibid., p. 8.
4 Jakobson, Roman 'Linguistics and Poetics' in *Style in Language*, 1960.
5 The author uses *'le geste'* here which I have chosen, as elsewhere in the text, to translate as 'movement'. See the author's discussion of the two terms *geste* and *mouvement* in the chapter 'Poetics of Movement'. (Transl.)
6 'Expressive' here relates to the idea of 'expression' rather than 'expressivity'. Expression might generally be understood as an intransitive use of a signifying material, without seeking a concrete result or semantic application.
7 *Poiein* (Gk.) – the art of shaping, forming/transforming matter: the work of creation/ destruction. Reference to the term (in modernity) is often a way of raising the issue of the role of the artist (and artistic force) as an 'actor' in the public sphere. Stathis Gourgouris writes that: *The transformative power of* poiein, *first of all as a social imaginary but also as artistic (poetic, strictly speaking) force, is consistently underplayed in favor of a certain analytic relation to knowledge...*See 'Poiein – Political Infinitive' in *PMLA*, Vol.128(1), January 2008, Special Issue on *The New Lyric Studies*, Yopie Prins and Virginia Jackson eds. (Transl.)
8 Susan Leigh Foster. Her work, *Reading Dancing, Bodies and Subjects in American Modern Dance*, 1986, will often be referred to. See also Judith Lynne Hanna, *The Performance–Audience Connection*, 1983.
9 Meschonnic, Henri *Les états de la poétique*, 1985.
10 *Comprendre* – (literally to take with) means 'to understand'. (Transl.)
11 Ibid. See also Jacques Derrida, *Dissemination*, 1981.
12 Dupuy, D. 'La mesure des choses' in *Marsyas*, No. 26, Juin 1993, pp. 59-60.
13 Oral source: Stéphanie Aubin, text delivered at 'Signature, Dance(d) Conference': 'L'art en scène' by the Cie Larsen, Paris, Cité Internationale, 1994.
14 Godard, H. 'Singular Moving Geographies' in *Writings on Dance*, 15, Winter 1996, pp.12-21. Originally published as 'Le déséquilibre fondateur' in *Artpress*, #Hors Série, 'Les vingt ans d'Art Press', Autumn, 1992.
15 Gardner, S. 'Hermeneutics and Dancing' in *Writings on Dance*, No.10, Autumn 1994, p. 37.
16 Morris, G. *Moving Words: Re-writing Dance* (Introduction), 1996, p.12.
17 Foster, S. 'Introduction' to *Corporealities: Dancing, Knowledge, Culture and Power*, 1996, p.xi.
18 Ibid., p. 11.
19 Cf. Roger Copeland, 'Beyond Expressionism, Merce Cunningham's Critique of the Natural' in *Dance History an Introduction*, 1983, pp. 182-197. Copeland rightly notes that knowledge of 20th century art history is indispensable to understanding Cunninghan's thought and work.
20 See Laban, Rudolf *The Mastery of Movement*, 1971; and Bainbridge-Cohen, Bonnie. *Sensing, Feeling and Action*, 1993.
21 Valéry, Paul *Variété II*. Paris: Gallimard, 1928, p. 61.
22 Banes, S. 'On your Fingertips: Writings on Dance Criticism', in *Writing Dancing in the Age of Postmodernism*, 1994, pp. 269-283.
23 Meschonnic, Henri. *Les états de la poétique*, 1985.
24 Cf. Schulmann, Nathalie, *Réflexion sur l'Histoire de la Danse*, dossier pour l'UV Histoire de la Danse, Univ. Paris VIII, 1991-92 (unpublished).
25 Novack, Cynthia J. *Sharing the Dance, Contact Improvisation and American Culture*, 1990, p. 23.
26 Dupuy, Dominique 'Le Maître et la Mémoire' in *Saisons de la danse*, No. 241, December 1992, pp. 43-44.

Contemporary Dance: The Birth of a Project

Modern dance is the individual quest for an individual vision.
Anna Sokolow[1]

What is contemporary dance (since we refuse to make too rigorous a distinction between 'modern' and 'contemporary')? Certainly not simply a mutation of movement codes in relation to other dance forms even if, as has been claimed, there are certain intended or unintended constants.[2] In any case, there is certainly no question of an externally recognisable vocabulary or form even if, since the beginning of the 20th century, the treatment of movement has sometimes produced similarities in corporeal 'colouring'. The question of contemporary dance is elsewhere. The great dance critic, John Martin, who witnessed the emergence of modern dance from the 1920s saw it immediately: what counted in the 'new dance' (a term used in Germany as well as in the United States) was not 'What does it look like?' but 'What does it say?'[3] This was not to condemn dance to deliver a message but rather to void it of pure spectacle. But what did this new dance say? Something that was at once enormous and delicate: action is the consciousness of a subject in the world. This is an objective, certainly, of all the arts but is also the extreme limit where they can dematerialise. The dancer, however, has no other support at her/his disposal than what shows and above all localises her/him as this subject in the world: a body and this body's movement created from an extreme 'nearness', without any other projection in an already instituted (verbal) code. The dancer has nothing exterior or supplementary to the matter/material of the self with which to build a signifying universe, an intelligible imaginary.[4] S/he does not modify or take hold of any of the world's objects even if s/he enters into relationship with them.

Modern dance is this essentially and voluntarily divested art, and is so the more for having no tradition, or at least only a very recent one. Indeed, it was by refusing any tradition that for the first time in history a non-transmitted movement, and one that does not realise the exemplary values of the (social) group, was elaborated. This refusal marks not only the artistic but also the anthropological aspect of the body's contemporary revolution. One tradition, the only real one, says Carolyn Brown, a long-time dance collaborator with Cunningham, *is to begin everything again from out of one's own resources.*[5] In contemporary dance there is only one true dance: the dance of each individual. (In *The Art of Dance* Isadora Duncan wrote that, *the same dance cannot belong to two people.*) Contemporary techniques, no matter how scientific, no matter how long it takes to acquire them, are before anything else the instruments of a knowledge leading the dancer to this singularity. The modern and contemporary dancer owes her theory, thought and vitality to her own forces. Even if certain avant-garde practices (including 'performance art') have joined dance in this pure 'co-substance' of the subject with her/his work, contemporary dance has this in particular: that it secretes its matter and the qualities of this matter from the 'expenditure' that gives it birth. Here, there is no precedence, no law already in place.

But there is a history, one that is inseparable from that of our century, and not only from a chronological point of view: dance has shared the 20th century's currents of ideas, questions and disasters. In retracing this history as if returning to a source, we are always brought back, not to a point of sustenance, to a permanent energy supply, but on the contrary to a pole of profound letting go – like an empty space through which the body must always pass in order to reinvent itself. This epicentre of deprivation is not, as we will see, amnesia. On the contrary, a consciousness of contemporary dance heritage is what frustrates possible strategies of recovery. During our meetings at Arles in 1989, Dominique Dupuy brought the terms 'memory and forgetting' together. It is essential to connect these two ideas. Memory is in fact not valuable per se but needs to be thought and weighed at each instant. Memory is only valuable against an ideology of forgetting, as dialectic and questioning, because forgetting covers things with its ash, with a debris of disavowed submission and easy formalisms. It petrifies in secret abdications the hope of a freedom to come. Forgetting is one of the forces that systematically dominates the body: it imposes the 'models' of the moment making them appear inevitable and rendering other possibilities invisible. Memory (if it is worth anything) opposes the hypostatisation of empty forms: it can act to break up specular identifications in favour of a body that never assumes an origin or conforms to a mould but constructs or de-constructs itself in history. It is a body-history, evolving, taken up and transported by historicity through its own time. That is why the theme of memory, as we will see, has a place in the poetics of dance as one of the instruments of that poetics – as the resource of a body poetics severed from all established authority. Memory as the articulation of knowledges specific to the contemporary dance body can also confer existential and cognitive dimensions on memories of movements and bodies. All the bodies which have made contemporary dance are still with us, and these reflections arise as though thanks to the aliveness of their movements. Rather than memory, we could use, as I have already suggested, the Deleuzian concept of 'co-presence' – a permanent reverberation in us which comes from another time the better to question our own.[6] *The past is always present and, besides, there is no past,* affirmed Martha Graham.[7] We are grateful to dancers for their work in this regard: for members of the Quatuor Knust and the Company Icosaèdre, re-doing works from the '20s to the '60s constitutes, not a patrimonial celebration of the artistic order one is trying to found, but an urgently needed reactivation and renewal of modernist invention.

Contemporary dance, like the cinema, was born at the end of the 19th century. Like the cinema it was a new art even if the oldest of supports – the human body – was its vehicle. Loie Fuller announced, emblematically, the common emergence of body movement and the movement of light (the body's mobility lit by projections), sometimes from out of the same prefiguring: the birth of bio-mechanics, and the way phases of movement and their dynamics were made visible through chromophotography, for example. New movements which had not yet been registered arose because the intermittence that had enclosed an enigma in its rapid beating finally opened its folds. Marey wrote that, *the strangeness of the images comes from their having stilled fleeting states of the face and movement which in nature unfold by gradual transition with none appearing in isolation.*[8] These were mysterious images that remained at the blurred edges of the visible: they were inadmissible even, because the moving body resists so strongly its own imaging and, even more, the traditional norms of that image-construction. Marey: *Could ugliness be what we do not know? And would the truth hurt our eyes when we saw it for the first time?*[9] New body states multiplied and, even today, still no classification of them is possible: take a certain Madeleine G, a Frenchwoman whose surname is unknown and who even before the coming of Duncan performed in Germany in a state of hypnosis. Eugenia Casini-Ropa sees her as one of the precursors of contemporary dance: a body-abyss, a subject who allows the other to perceive only her own letting go. [10] In fact, we can rest assured that the history of the origins of contemporary dance are not to be found in dance history: existing at the limit of any identifiable representation it lies in the margins of that history. That is why it is worth avoiding an approach in terms of the body's social visibility as this is described in the history of representations or other related scenographies – even if serious and enlightening studies have dealt with this aspect. Great progress has been accomplished, of course, concerning the sources, methodologies, and history of movement in general, and it is possible to follow a socio-anthropologist of dance as credible as Judith Lynne Hanna when she analyses the evolution of corporal codes in the 19th century, despite the inevitable recurrence of a North American obsession with gender which, in the event, given the masculine-feminine conflicts for which academic ballet was a battlefield appears completely relevant to her aims.[11] But the scene to which Hanna turns her gaze does not belong to the history nor even the genealogy of contemporary dance which has had only an incidental and belated relationship with so-called classical dance. At the beginning there was no relation, no conflict: simply another place.

Besides, there are many other enigmas concerning the origins of contemporary dance to resolve. It did not grow out of dance but from an
absence of dance. Its tutelary figures, at least those to whom we have historical access like Dalcroze, were not even dancers but visionaries who
discovered dance along the path of their own researches. Nietzsche, displacing Schopenhauer's binary opposition, foresaw a non-representational
art like music which would be more like a 'will', a pure desire without image: *a baseless will*, says *The Birth of Tragedy*. At this moment in Western
thought dance appeared fantasmatically, an absolute dance without reference to an existing style, like a possible body becoming sedimented in the
imaginary or, in what amounts to the same thing, the image of a
(Dionysiac) body that had been lost since the dawn of civilisation. It is
worth rereading the chapter, 'The Dance', in Wagner's *The art-work of the
future*. Dance is viewed as the subject's total engagement in its action. It is
the dramaturgy of being, the art of arts. But, as Wagner knows, this dance
did not exist. In the decadent and pathetically gallant ballet stage he saw
only a ridiculous caricature not even worthy of his concept of 'musical
drama'.[12] Hence his conclusion: *Dance, admirable art, pitiful art*. It is thus
from this double representation of an absence and an emergence, simultaneously impossible and hoped for, that an imaginary and sympathetic
milieu is elaborated but cannot serve as a crucible, still less a genealogical
point of reference, for contemporary dance. It is more like the dawn of an
unthought where the body might reinvent its own history.

No other artistic modernity lacks, thus, a heritage in the continuity (*filiation*) of a given discipline – even if it only refutes it. This is the singular
destiny of an orphan art which has no birthplace and is obliged to find itself
and perhaps invent a distant, erratic origin. It is, first of all, in the history of
body-subjects in the sense proposed by Michel Foucault that we must look
to find not so much signs but symptoms: the history of the subject in its
articulation of knowledge categories and its 'practices of the self' as *The
History of Sexuality* showed. But also in the history of a body-object as it
appears in the interstices of diverse medical, and punitive jurisdictions. A
body which has no proper visibility and is not projected in any
'spectacularisation' of individual or social relations. Oppression and disci-
plinary regulation, recalls Foucault, work more on 'forces' than on 'signs'.
(And it is just these forces that are the unnamed material upon which the
whole work of contemporary dance takes place).[13] Out of 'force' contemporary dance makes a fundamental aesthetic resource to surpass and
overcome the sign's power of visibility: it was to give this force, which had
been held back in a non-signifying limbo, its own access to the symbolic.

The great nineteenth-century machine of oppression, and the cracks in a body in the process of being lost were necessary for this unseen force to implode. *From the end of the Nineteenth Century the western bourgeoisie had lost its gestures*, claims Georgio Agamben.[14] And in this dispossession, we might echo him, the dominant class took with it through the stages of production all the bodies at its disposal, mutilated bodies whose movements rampant industrialisation was to fragment into discrete, repetitive modules, sealing the end of a global body-subject rich in multiple relational networks with the world and itself. It was out of this field of loss that reforming, often vitalistic currents were born in the United States and Germany – the first homes of an industrial hypertrophy. These currents were to serve as a frame and sometimes support for the theoretical and practical elaboration of contemporary dance whose many early figures were close to therapy. Being close also in this regard to the cinema, at least as Agamben conceives of it, dance sought to repare the loss of gesture but also to record this loss.

A very important figure, Francois Delsarte, however, emerged well before this in the middle of the nineteenth century. It is not within the scope of the current approach which is not an historical exegesis to question the 'real' importance of Delsarte: we know of him in effect through a series of founding stories which attribute to him an important role in the genesis of modern dance. From Genevieve Stebbins to Ted Shawn, these convincing accounts and the theoretical relevance to which they attest contribute to this figure's importance.[15] Elsewhere, several extant texts of Delsarte's recently republished in their original (French) language bear witness to the power of his intuition and his thought on the body.[16] A singer, actor and teacher of public speaking and music, he was a theatrical reformer under Louis-Philippe. Although he is amongst the pantheon of theatre theorists he enjoys today only a modest notoriety. The apparent vagueness of his thought (for those who don't know movement) and the esotericism of his discourse have discredited what many refuse to call a thought. Delsarte's theory of performance or vocal art will not be examined here. That has already been done in a number of studies, but we can perhaps revisit something of the original project which is so buried that it still largely eludes our modern references.[17] Indeed, the whole of modern dance, or almost, draws a large part of its existence from these domains exiled from history, these fringes of thought where nameless bodies wander – bodies which have not found a legitimate or legitimating sign to index them in the great directory of ideas.

Delsarte was by no means a dancer (at age thirty when *Giselle* was created did he know only the state of the art at this time?). The questions that

Delsarte posed had nothing to do with the usual field of dance. On the other hand, he radically questioned the role of the body and movement in relation to the symbolic function of the subject. A perfectly incongruous or even anachronistic question for someone living in the period of a citizen-king and then a citizen-emperor. But discursive ahistoricity is integral to the question of dance much more than are certain performances. Today, discourse on dance retains this character of exteriority and foreignness with respect to other discourses, otherwise it is submitting itself to borrowed axioms. Francois Delsarte was out of time: and another body can only emerge in these fringes of recognised thought or historicity. He was led by his great religiosity towards a very old conceptual territory which allowed him a distance from his own century and access to an atemporality where our own problems, too, can resonate. In relation to a number of questions, the science of movement – a reading of the moving body as expression – belonged to another, earlier era while other questions were for an era to come. Delsarte, perhaps without knowing it, made the link. Today, classical rhetoric and movement practices in the arts of oratory and representation since the era of the Carrache have been the subject of several studies, most importantly by Marc Fumaroli.[18] We should also mention Dene Barnett, an actor-dancer-researcher who has 'embodied' these old knowledges. And we know how much this still mysterious movement language (*gestuelle*) was important in the dance spectacles of the 17th and 18th centuries. The treatises on *The Eloquence of the Body*, to cite the beautiful title of Abbé Dinard's 1715 treatise, have been the subject of an excellent study by the semiotician Marc Angenot.[19] These are so many fascinating testimonies to the corporeal technics permanently deployed in almost all the liberal arts and carried down to us by painting. Today's theatre historians have essentially retained the form and work of the Berliner, Johan Jacob Engel whose *Thoughts on Gesture and Theatrical Action*, in posthumous translation, synthesises in many respects everything that had been elaborated previously from the rhetoric of declamatory movements and the eloquence of the abbés Barry and le Faucheur, to the treatise on pantomime by dancing master, John Weaver, and the 'actions' of Noverre. And it ought not be forgotten that the very term 'actio' is none other than an important part of rhetoric – a concept which was certainly transferred by Noverre to a naturalistic context, but was not strictly speaking transformed. Noverre, like Diderot and Lessing, must be situated in the historical and aesthetic frame of 'mimesis'. Delsarte was to move out of this frame. But it is essential to recall (here all too briefly) the kind of very traditional if not already obsolete field of resonances and references that the problem of 'expression,' to use Stebbins's term, posed for Delsarte. Without such an understanding, the extent of the Delsartian revolution cannot be grasped and we cannot understand what he unglues in thinking movement. But before we continue it must be noted that it is through the expedient of 'expression' or rather to use a more precise terminology, of the communication of a signified, that a new thought of the body was elaborated, that is, within the signifier itself – a transformation all the more remarkable in that the question is no longer tied to the body's expressivity but to meaning itself whose function the body can displace. Engel's treatise, with the help of images and commentaries (which are also of extreme interest) examines each 'disposition' according to a theory of the 'passions' in keeping with classical mimesis and its imitative mechanisms: in the same way that Weaver, some fifty years earlier, had described for each passion the gestural sequence which 'declines' it.[20] These are so many descriptions of a 'kinesics' in which there is a central referent: the verbal *énoncé*. Such is the founding syntagm where a pantomimic movement and also its motor set-up – the least directly translatable into verbal terms – retain an enunciative organisation: this because, initially, in numerous expressive practices from eloquence to singing and probably to dance, they accompany spoken or sung discourse but do not substitute for it. Which to us significantly dramatises the rapport between dance, and probably the other arts, and the inexpressible, that limit of language which poetry can always touch but which human movement exceeds by soliciting other levels of awareness. Then, in the classical era when in certain silent arts – painting and pantomime – there is only corporal expression, speech/language is even more present as though incarnated, forever imprinted in a movement unable to free itself from language. Foster, in a recent study and before her the already cited Angenot, have shown this point of irreversible rupture in our culture between motor activity and verbal language, the one excluding the other.[21] The body in all cases no longer participating in the elocutive function is condemned to reproduce it from a distance. Does this moment of the Enlightenment, where the function of the body is cast far from the verbal frontiers of rationality, predispose not only movement but also the anthropological orientation towards it to assign it another place, a different level of consciousness outside the closure of the logos? Thus awakening the very essence of danced movement, namely a flight from the universe of the verbal? Delsarte's thought, in fact, has to do with these two problematics: the one very old and linked to classical ideas on the teaching of expressivity; the other new but obscure and poorly articulated, where movement is something else, a world which has taken the side of silence, as Laban was to describe it. From one to the other there is this double movement which can be found again and again in contemporary dance: the will to break with conventions, but more still the will to cleave to what has, consciously or unconsciously always existed, the underlying continuum of the human beyond established codes.[22]

Let us return to this first series of questions. It was in taking these into account but lifting them from the context in which they had been formulated that Delsarte (and this was his genius) was to respond. What then did he discover? That the body has its language unknown to language: a zone of sign production that he names in a strangely premonitory fashion, 'semiotic'. A language coming from poorly identified depths to which neither words nor habitual codes of human knowledge have access. Thus, the body as 'another scene' where an existential drama plays itself out in which movement is no longer the mimetic support of an already structured referent, but on the contrary an emanation (if not a constituent) of that very scene of which it is at one and the same time both the agent and the reader. Amongst the few existing writings of Delsarte the extraordinary 'revealing episodes' show how, through a purely empirical investigation, (which still has neither model nor theory) he was led to the threshold of this mysterious reading. The role of the shoulders for example as the 'pathic' zone or complex emotional nexus where the slightest and barely perceptible 'movement towards' is inscribed and the affective subject not only expresses itself but is constituted. *The shoulder is in effect literally the thermometer of passion and sensibility. It is the measure of their vehemence, and indicates the degree of heat and intensity.*[23] But these changes in temperature, like the interstices of the body shown by Marey, are for the present at the extreme limit of social visibility. *How much there is in these light oscillations that escapes vulgarity.* The shoulder not only gives the real degree of affective mobilisation which is more readable in other parts of the body (in facial expression, for example, but doesn't the face already react according to a repertoire of expressions?) but above all governs the corporal response by leading the torso into concavity (an element which is to be found in the curving of contemporary dance and which goes deeper than a simple question of vocabulary). Even more enigmatic is the abduction of the thumb when the body senses the proximity of death. It is the sign of an extreme prescience that Delsarte was to notice even in cadavers. Can bodies that the 'spirit' has left still speak from the same unfathomable force that animates our gestural sphere?

It is along this path and not as a too simple 'reform' or even 'revolt' in the modes of movement 'treatment' that we must look for the roots of the contemporary project of dance: the discovery of a body concealing a singular mode of symbolisation foreign to every pre-constituted framework. Contemporary dance owes its existence to a new conception of the body and movement (of the body in movement) to which all theoreticians starting with Laban will return. The discovery of an 'untoward movement' to use an expression of Hubert Godard's, owing its conditions of existence only to itself, is inconceivable without this transformation in the vision of the body at the dawn of modernity in dance.[24] But well beyond a movement's nature is the conception of an 'underworld', to use Nietzsche's expression,[25] that this movement could, if not illuminate, at least signal as a threshold, at once so close but unattainable – a universe whose uncertain surface human movement alone could touch, even if certain poets have been able to sense in the body the presence of 'nameless forces' (Novalis).

What we retain of the 'founding stories', the texts of dancers who bear witness to Delsarte's heritage, particularly those by the important choreographer, teacher and theoretician Ted Shawn is, firstly, this relation of the world to symbolic as opposed to mimetic movement unknown to analytic awareness: this world requiring us to explore it through a radically singular process. Delsarte left a system and even a 'method' with very interesting practical exercises of observation and investigation which were astonishingly premonitory in their quest for a listening to the body by the body itself. Furthermore, it is regrettable that the majority of commentators on Delsarte focus on the few written texts and not on the rich fund of exercises left by Delsartist, Genevieve Stebbins.[26] In reading her and Shawn's 'The application of the science of Delsarte to the art of dance' one realises that these Delsartist accounts attribute to this great mythical figure what might be considered the fundamentals of contemporary dance: firstly the importance of the torso. The centre of the body as the prime mover in preference to segmented movement is not only a question of the displacement of corporal zones, even if this displacement would go on to have an extreme importance in practice. It is primarily the valuing of an asemic place, a new fund of sense deeper than that of the extremities or that movement's connection with the verbal (to signification at least) can expose. This torso inhabited by the viscera and barely articulated visibly is, in terms of deeper sensing, not assigned a directly readable semic production. In this way it is the poetic organ par excellence. *The torso must become the most sensitive and the most expressive part of the body.*[27] In order to multiply its revelatory possibilities it is necessary to open all of its compartments, and to hear their diaphragmatic pulsation; and, especially, to follow the path of the vertebral column which is the 'chain' of our constitution and our continuity, not only on the skeletal but also on the emotional and expressive planes. This is

where the importance of freedom in the back comes from – from the cervi-
cal to the lumbar spine *so that no blocking opposes the flow of pure succession
along the vertebral column.* This astonishing phrase on the importance of
'succession' as the opening to continuous flow, announces Trisha Brown's
continuous dorsal movement as we are able to admire it today.[28] It also
signals the supremacy for Delsartists of the pathic over the semic. Also important is their bringing to light the body's weight, not only as the factor of
displacement, but also as the qualitative agent of a new poetics of weight
with which the whole gravitational system (body and earth) is associated,
*in order to put into play profound dynamics of sensing, of the sensation of great
mass and weight.* And here Shawn evokes Isadora Duncan for whom the
most beautiful movements were always close to the ground. Finally, and not
surprisingly, Shawn evokes Stebbins's 'exercises in de-composition' which
go from high tensile to none at all and which he likens to the German
'*Spannung*' such as it can be deciphered in Dalcroze's exercises.[29] Our intention here is certainly not to verify the truth of these attributions, still less to
suspect an a posteriori doctrinal projection in Shawn's references. But to
reveal the quasi-immediate force of transposition within a project where
the whole matter/material of being becomes a language. That the body
might find its own poetics in its texture, its flows, its supports has to do with
the very invention of contemporary dance. To invent a language, in fact, is
not to manipulate a pre-existing material but to give birth to this very material, while justifying artistically its genesis and by implicating the subject in
the undertaking as producer and interpreter of her/his own matter.

1 In Cohen, Selma-Jeanne *Modern Dance: Seven Statements of Belief,* 1968.
2 In particular by Laban in one of his first works, *Choreographie,* 1926. Cf. Vera Maletic's analysis
in *Body, Space, Expression,* 1984. The articulation of these correspondences can be found in recent
studies which re-examine historically and geographically all choreographic manifestations and
among which are Janet Adshead's *Dance Analysis, Theory and Practice,* 1988, as well as the extensive corpus used by Susan L. Foster in *Reading Dancing,* 1986.
3 Martin, John. *The Modern Dance,* 1933.
4 We will always use this term in its Saussurian linguistic sense of the material support of a
signified.
5 Brown, Carolyn in *Dance Perspective,* special issue devoted to Merce Cunningham, Winter 1968.
Reprinted in *Merce Cunningham,* 1975.
6 Gilles Deleuze: a concept developed especially in *The Time-Image,* 1989.
7 Cited in M. Horosko (ed.) *Martha Graham: the Evolution of her Dance Theory,* 1982.
8 Marey, E-J. *Le mouvement.* 1894, republished 1994. p. 194.
9 Ibid., p. 195.
10 Casini-Ropa, Eugenia *La danza e l'agitprop,* 1981, pp.9-18.
11 Hanna, J. L. *Dance, Sex and Gender,* 1990. For a work that deciphers the history of movement
and the body refer also to *A Cultural History of Gesture* edited by Jan Bremmer and Hermann

Roodenburg, 1992. This volume brings together work of the French school of body historians (Jean Claude Schmitt, for example) and the excellent current of Anglo-Saxon dance anthropology.

12 Wagner, Richard. *The art-work of the future, and other works*, 1993. See also Duncan, I. *The Art of the Dance*, 1928.

13 Foucault, M. *Discipline and Punish: the birth of the prison*, 1977, and the recurrent Foucauldian idea of 'body discipline' (*prise sur le corps*).

14 Agamben, G. 'Notes on Gesture' in *Theory out of bounds, volume 20. Means without ends: notes on Politics*, edited by S. Buckley, M. Hardt, B. Massumi, 2000, pp.50-60.

15 Cf. Stebbins, G. *Delsarte's System of Expression*, 1885, republished 1977; and Shawn, T. *Every Little Movement, a Book about Delsarte*, 1954, republished, 1974.

16 Cf. Porte, Alain *François Delsarte, une anthologie*, 1992.

17 Amongst others: *Beyond Stanislavski, les fondements du mouvement scénique*, papers from the Saintes conference, 1991, edited by Jean-Marie Pradier. Saintes: Rumeur des Ages-Maison de Polichinelle, 1992.

18 Fumaroli, Marc *L'école de silence*, 1993.

19 Angenot, Marc 'Traités de l'éloquence du corps' in *Semiotica*, No. 8, 1973, pp. 60-78.

20 Weaver, John 'The History of the Mimes and Pantomimes', London, 1727, in *The life and works of John Weaver*, 1985, pp. 754-755 and 762.

21 Foster, Susan L. 'Textual Evidances' (sic) in *Bodies of the Text*, edited by Ellen Goellner and Jacqueline Shea Murphy, 1995, p. 231-246.

22 Duncan, Isadora *The Art of the Dance*, 1928, p. 62: *The dance of the future will be a new movement, a consequence of the entire evolution which mankind has passed through.*

23 Francois Delsarte in Porte, Alain *François Delsarte, une anthologie*, 1992, pp. 80-83.

24 Godard, Hubert. 'Le geste inouï' in *Dansons*, January, 1993.

25 Nietzsche, F. *Thus Spake Zarathustra*, 1958.

26 Genevieve Stebbins, 1885, op. cit. Stebbins's 'line' is worth re-examining today. Outside the importance of her own work we note the influence that she has had on the Munich school of movement analysis through her pupil Hedwig Kallmeyer, subsequently a teacher in her own right, and on Elsa Gindler and Laban. Interesting information on this line are given in the *Cahiers de l'Association des Elèves du Dr. Ehrenfried*. Thanks to Nathalie Schulmann for having alerted me to their existence.

27 Shawn, T. *Every Little Movement*, 1974, chapter 4, pp. 79-90.

28 'Succession' which is very important in certain German practices, in particular that of the Hellerau-Laxenburg school such as it is still taught by Françoise Dupuy, has often been neglected in spite of its poetic and existential importance. It is an essential element that has been developed in all contemporary dance techniques especially in that of Humphrey-Limoó.

29 Shawn, T. *Every Little Movement*, 1974, p. 34 and 85.

The Tools

The Poetic Body

The dancer is fortunate indeed for he has for his instrument the most eloquent and miraculous of all instruments, the human body.
José Limón[1]

Behind your thoughts and feelings, my brother, there is a powerful master and an unknown guide and who is called: self. He lives in your body, he is your body.
F. Nietzsche[2]

To be a dancer is to choose the body and its movement as one's relational field, as one's instrument of knowledge, thought and expression. It is also to

trust in the 'lyric' character of the organic, without at the same time ascrib-
ing to a precise aesthetic or form: neutral movements or body states
(expressly unaccented and without 'design') have their own lyrical quality
as much as any overtly spatialised and musicalised movement. The main
thing is to work first of all on the organic conditions of this poetic emergence. Once this fertile choice is made the body becomes a formidable tool
of consciousness and sensation.

But this cannot be taken for granted: the corporal material (*matériau*),
'the carcass' as Jerome Andrews called it, is complex, difficult to know and
to integrate into a global awareness of the self.[3] Dance requires infinite
work in order to move forward in this awareness. Along the way, areas of
knowledge are illuminated, possible orientations are revealed, and preferences are established. In dance, a great artist is one who has chosen a
particular body state autonomously and consciously. That is why the 'great
moderns' from Duncan to Wigman, Hawkins or Cunningham seem so powerful to us. They invented their own corporeality, outside of any model or
without following any score given in advance. Today, of course, the dancer
works much more with a gamut of pathways (at best with a problematic)
that has already been traced and from which it would be naïve to claim to
invent or even invest a new body. But the vast reserves of the modern dance
heritage remain, the infinite wealth of practices, corporeal philosophies,
diverse and evolving pedagogies by means of which, more modestly perhaps, today's dancer will not invent a body but rather seek to work,
understand, refine and above all make of it a lucid and singular project.
And out of it to invent her/his own poetics for 'playing upon' an intention
for which the body and its movement will furnish, primarily, the texture
without this being necessarily questioned or even perceived, unless sublimi-
nally.

It is this subliminal level underlying the corporal text that interests us. It
is in these implicit zones that the whole 'sense' of a choreographic act takes
place. How to approach and understand the body? One's own or another's?
There are of course methods of investigation and analysis. I have already
mentioned Jerome Andrews. His knowledge of the body was infinite and
drew on multiple currents. He was, however, in defiance of the body as if it
were an unfathomable or alarming stranger. To understand the mysteries
of 'the carcass' he drew upon the Pilates technique in which the body discovers and constructs itself using supports – the static or moving plates and
levers of machines with sliding parts.[4] Dominique Dupuy has remarked
that in this work with the machine, as in other methods of apprenticeship
of the body-self,....*the body is put in a situation close to the void: it is not pre-*

constructed and set in place. It is in a sort of absence and silence in which any-thing can happen.[5] Any investigation of the body demands this meditative and concentrated silence, where the body-subject goes looking for itself: for the other in the self or the self in the other (here, the machine suggests this other body which waits and asks). Observational practices in the studio often take place in pairs. The other's body with its supports, its contacts or even its own tactile or visual observation shows me my own. This research rarely uses images or anatomical figures, but more often sensations and intensities.

Contemporary dance, however, and numerous techniques which are associated with it, 'en-vision' (or 'in-vision') the moving body. This en-visioning is either a body's own or comes through the 'eyes' of another. For example, in a therapeutic and investigative technique such as Ida Rolf's method, the 'contour' of the body is very important. For 'ideokinesis', a body thought whose resonances are felt in the body itself, visualisation generates a 'being-body'. This visualisation is not a directly optical one: an inner vision must be activated where the organic and the imaginary, the body and the mind intermingle. As the name indicates, ideokinesis links movement to idea – an eminently poetic meeting between an interiorised body state and 'Idea' in an almost Mallarmian sense: a 'becoming idea' of the body, which opens (its) awareness. Irene Dowd, one of the seminal figures of this approach which is highly developed at the forefront of dance developments in the United States, notes that *...all postural alignment patterns, all muscle use and development, all human body movement is directed and coordinated by the activity of our nervous system, in other words, our thinking. Therefore, in order to change our body shape or our movement patterns we must change our neurological activity...The plasticity of the mind is what makes a movement possible. If you can conceive the possibility of a movement of the human body then you can learn to do it.*[6] In 'learning to do it' the main aim is certainly not to achieve some kind of 'peak' or acrobatic performance even if the complexity of a movement can be followed and resolved by visualisation. Contemporary techniques propose more subtle criteria which must be apprehended qualitatively and, above all, in their singularity. Irene Dowd: *There is no right image or right posture, nor even right movement. There is a way of working which at any moment leads you simultaneously towards unity and openness.* The deepest goal of Dowd's thought is a transformation wherein the moving body can enter into its becoming. Contemporary dance has divested itself of the studio mirror so as not to work on the old specular ground where our bodies reproduce indefinitely the fantasmatic appearance of the same. But also so that the corporal schema might escape the direct and deadly power of the scopic 'plan'.

Even if these kinds of 'vision' can reconstruct and transform the body they must be combined with other sensory fields and developed with them. In order to understand the corporal architecture, vision here (even in Irene Dowd's thought where it becomes an interior vision of the body's alignment) is allied with the sense most developed in contemporary dance: the tactile. The hand then, or any other part of the body, can be an eye. The palpating palm can see. An important exercise, used particularly by Trisha Brown, consists of 'tracing': the dancer explores by touching all the parts of her/his body as though to revisit its supporting structure, the location of the organs, but also the contours and the boundary of the skin. It is an exercise in the order of seeing but also of drawing. As if in traversing my body with my hand, at once seeing and blind, I could trace and read the score: the cavities, hollows, gaps, slopes and curves, at once landscape and text which already contains in being laid out in the visible-tactile, touching-touched, seeing-seen (to use the dual categories of Merleau-Ponty in *Eye and Mind*) all its lyrical potential whose imperceptible advent can be generated by the slightest movement.

Visiting the structure of the body thus must remind us of all that modernity in dance has 'displaced' in this very body, knowing that these displacements were multiple, sometimes divergent and always dictated by the urgent necessity of creating or recreating a singular body out of which a physical identity can make sense. In order to reinvent bodies, contemporary dance began by rethinking and redistributing its anatomy and anatomical functions. This leads us straight away, even historically, to the essential idea of a body which is not given but discovered, even invented. We have seen that, from the beginning, primacy was given to the torso as the supreme site of expression: the torso, the site of functions, of the viscera, trunk, the animal in us which had for too long been kept in a sense limbo. Modernity in dance was to allow this torso to express itself, to sing, even to cry from out of the dark aphasia to which the history of the body had confined it; even to the detriment of the extremities which had previously been considered the privileged expressive machinery. They were to be banished: firstly, because they are para- or post-linguistic doubles; and, second, because our extremities and the organs of communication situated in the face constitute our instruments of 'captation' and thus of power over objects or bodies. This is especially so for the hands and arms. The human thumb, in symmetrical opposition allows us to take hold of matter and thus makes possible its transformation.

Indeed, all these evolutionary factors described by Leroi-Gourhan have long been valued – at the level of modes of production as much as of representation.[7] The mimetic or plainly expressive possibilities of the face or the extremities have been widely exploited in acting (theatre, cinema, pantomime) – in a naturalist or non-naturalist aesthetics. But contemporary dance has drawn attention, as we have said, to the non-semic zones of homo sapiens: in other words, the zones which have not mastered a discourse. It so happens that these zones are also 'disarmed' surfaces or body parts, divested of the power to interfere, incapable of manipulating (the chest, the thorax, back and shoulders...). Historically, the contemporary dance body is marked by its letting go the power over things. It is freed into its own incapacity, a parcel of immanence that does not allow itself an operational hold on reality or to be part of a mechanics of meaning. This double choice for the a-semic and for renouncing 'power over' did not lead to the abandonment of hitherto privileged zones, but rather to their diversion. They became caught up in a great reversal, a great work to de-hierarchise the role of the limbs: beginning with the head – at least as the support for the face which was no longer to be the imperial and immovable throne of expression, meaning or utterance. Firstly, it had to allow the body to take the expressive role that facial expression had hitherto monopolised. *The face is of course the mirror of all that goes on, but it should not be more prominent than is intended and must not substitute for all that which isn't going on in the body,* remarked Hanya Holm.[8] And when the head is not substituted for the body as a whole it *becomes* body, weight, matter. In Kreutzberg's solos it can roll like a ball, an object given up to its own destiny or, masked, as in a famous photograph of Sophie Tauber taken at the gallery Dada in 1916 (the mask was by Marcel Janco) it can become dislocated like an appendage about to become detached from the body, a grimacing trinket that the dancer hardly holds on to as she almost tips over backwards.[9] The head itself can also become a character: it can become a body and, in a grimacing dance of facial expressions, can carry the whole of the choreographic project. We can see this throughout German expressionist dance and particularly intensely in Valeska Gert.[10]

The upper or lower limbs can also lose their functions, becoming atrophied or disappearing altogether: arms are claws in Sophie Tauber or stumps in Dore Hoyer, and legs trail or slither in the numerous floor dances familiar in contemporary choreography where the feet no longer have a supporting function. This principle is recalled and taken to an extreme in Contact Improvisation where the supporting function is distributed over the entire body. In Japanese butoh a recurrent motif appears: the legs in the foetal position are delivered from their ambulatory function and freed of their instrumentality, like those of a helpless baby. Human anatomy and even elementary body functions have been re-visited, broken off or transformed by contemporary dance in order to summon, beyond recognisable and admissible forms, all these other possible, poetic bodies with the potential to transform the world through the transformation of their own matter/material. For other possible bodies are effaced by an anatomical body obedient to the canons of the single ideal glorified in classical aesthetics. From Rodin (and his teeming *Doors of Hell*), to expressionism in painting and dance, to Nijinsky who reinvented a whole gamut of deviants (*dérives*), the whole of modern art opened doors to a multitude of corporeities that had been reduced to invisibility. From out of the roots of the unseen, Nijinsky's dance reorganised matter/material otherwise. Nijinsky's individual inspiration and solitary genius was able to give fleeting form to an eruption of the unseen from out of its corporeal limbo. Contemporary dance's value and labour will be to form techniques and processes to reach into the living body itself and like Harald Kreutzberg in *The infinite circle* and Meredith Monk, in voice and movement, to bring into appearance all the other weak, ridiculous, mad bodies that history and the world have removed from our perception and even sometimes thrown onto the scrap-heap of existence. In the same way that the simple exploration of corporeal landscapes, or the limitless textuality concealing within us its own sensible mutations, lead us to be able to read in ourselves the presence of 'another body' that, through the slightest movement, might suddenly appear. Thus are often born the transparent 'characters', the furtive passengers of certain choreographic languages (Wigman, Kreutzberg, Linke, Monk, Bagouet, Brown), light shadows to which the choreography sometimes does not even allow the time needed to really exist, nor the consistency or mimetic thickness to enable them to be really 'told'. Their appearing is tied only to the metaphor that is necessarily present in movement or a body state. Thus can a body, even anatomically defined, allow a glimpse of the multiple layers of possibility that the so-called 'proper' or self-identical body does not contain.[11]

In fact, the body in dance is not limited to a factual architecture, however subtle, and still less to a closed volume whose epidermis would define the ultimate contour – *the frontier between the me and the not-me* to use Didier Anzieu's expression.[12] Even if the skin constitutes an important interface between the subject and the world, for the dancer it does not just enclose the self topically. Firstly because, as Bonnie Bainbridge-Cohen notes (with her famous formula: *By my weight, I know where I am*), the self is primordially located in relation to gravity. Then, because the skin also contains a wealth of information which exceeds any simple idea of 'property/ownership' (*propriété*): citing the No master Zeami, Hubert Godard recalls that there are dances of the skin, just as there are of the bones and flesh. The skin is a perceptual milieu which puts the body into relation with all points in space. It does not enclose like an organic packaging but, on the contrary, it opens and makes volumes. The practice of Contact Improvisation teaches us that the skin through its unfolding and its tactile faculties holds within it the sources of three-dimensionality. In fact, this voluminosity which is essential in contemporary dance is what opens the body to the world from within its own movement. In 'sculpting space' as Laban terms it, the body immediately inscribes its own reliefs in a sphere of influence (*mouvance*). These reliefs are engraved according to the relays between tensions and counter tensions: it is these which sculpt the folds of corporeal matter/material in dynamic trajectories. More important than the idea of the anatomical body is, in the first instance, what Laban called the 'kinesphere' or 'gestural sphere' – the space of proximity whose edges the limbs can touch. The kinesphere circumscribes the sphere of movement that is possible without moving from the spot. It is here that a body's being is elaborated. For the body is neither a centralised nor isolated matter/material: it is born in the medium that enables it to find its own identity. For Hubert Godard, *movement makes the body at each instant*.[13] It is thus from out of its own movement sphere (*la sphère gestuelle*) that a body can perhaps re-invent itself, ceaselessly re-engender itself. In which case, a poetics of the body would only be a sub-clause to the movement analysis that gives it life. What makes the body poetic is neither a morphological presence nor even a given volume emanating from this morphology across a constant and smooth sphere of movement: this sphere only exists by its turbulence, through the incisive effects of the 'tensions' which develop there and the directions that are engaged. It is a moving, trembling, flashing sphere, a 'dynamosphere' to use Laban's term, where each tension inscribes the outcome of a motor impulse. Thus in *Point and Line to Plane* Kandinsky defines a point in relation to the sparks that Grete Palucca's stretched fingers can light up in space, as if at the junction of two opposing energies. But even here something is circumscribed: a volume, perhaps magnetic, always folds around an interior space. Can the body and its kinespheric space be limited to a measurable sphere at the edges of which tensions will come to their end and die? No. What choreographic space teaches us is the limitlessness of the kinespheric body whose existence exceeds in every direction any simple dimensional evaluation. Or, more exactly, the kinesphere in its expansive

nature can open out to infinity (or retract just as far) the poetic communication of a body state. Phenomenologists, too, have seen that experience of
the world and the fabric of relations that we maintain with it cannot be
enclosed, since it is through the infinity opened up by movement itself that
the body exists and situates itself. This recalls Laban's idea of the
kinesphere. The body does not come before its own movement: there is no
initial prior body-substance, but a network of interferences and tensions
through which the subject is constituted by its own medium. We owe to
Vera Maletic an illuminating comparison between Laban and three great
figures of phenomenology, Straus, Buytendijck, Merleau-Ponty:[14,15] *A com-
parative study of (their) approaches to spatiality and temporality is hereby
proposed from the point of view of selected topics. All four authors share a view of
the interdependency of body, movement and space...The concern with spatial orientation rooted in the existential foundations of man, such as the gravitational
field, the body structure and the centre of gravity, and the movement organization
and movement possibilities is common to the four authors.*[16] Maletic has seen a
relationship between two visions of the kinesphere as an open body which
makes the infinite vibrations of its tactility resound in space. One in which
Straus evokes...*the 'three-mile zone' of the sphere surrounding our body as a
border with fluctuating frontiers which expand or shrink... the space itself loses
its static character, opens endlessly before us, and expands or represses*; and
Laban's conception *of a kinesphere which shrinks or grows with respect to the
normal kinesphere* making it possible to describe *innumerable variations of
trace-forms.* Maletic concludes that dance is the terrain where body-space is
verified and emblematised: *Dancing, of course, is a true model in which the
expressive body-movement-space is most obvious.* This very expansiveness can
generate a choreographic project: the sensuous and lyrical qualities of the
body-space are conveyed by the choreographer who elaborates the
compositional frame in relation to the kinesphere of the dancers. For it is
always in the between-two of a relation, the intercorporeal emphasised by
Cunningham, that a choreographic 'text' is made. It is in the between-two
of his or her body and that of the dancer, at the intersection of what below
will be called 'the personal spheres,' that the choreographer becomes the
visionary reader of the other's kinesphere and can read in it the lines of
tension, the secret inscriptions, the different shades of the imaginary; and
with movement as the (legitimate and mysterious) midwife (*la maieutique*),
can precipitate them, and free them from the invisible.[17] Neither the movement nor choreographic inspiration exists unless in this interstice of bodies
which gives frame and substance to choreographic material.
    What body is in play? It is essential to ask this primordial question before

any choreographic project can be 'read'. When this dimension is not taken into account, either in the creation of choreography or in its interpretation (*lecture*), an important 'unthought' zone is created, seriously compromising the credibility of a choreographic intention and obstructing its perception. It goes against the whole project of contemporary dance to assume that there is a neutral body from which any choreographic motif at all might be articulated. Worse still, such an assumption means that any process will be ideologically and aesthetically blind and will lead to very serious misunderstandings regarding a work's intention, supposing there is one. However, today as before, a choreographic work is often approached and, alas, evaluated from an undifferentiated perception of the body. Mostly, in fact, observation of dance is limited to analysing only the explicit forms or propositions: sometimes even only the accessories or the accompanying arts which frame it, forgetting that it is the body, understood as 'underneath', which makes the whole choreographic project (even if this project includes other ingredients). And it seems as if today's choreographer has adapted to this kind of perception with styles which play only with effects and impressions, the figurative shadows that can inhabit a movement and give it a sense/direction that, elsewhere, would arise in the body itself and in the imaginaries that it produces.

It is a curiously archaic approach, for it recalls a moment when the knowledges that have been accumulated during the whole history of modernity in dance could not yet be taken into consideration. What wasn't seen was precisely that the modern bodies were multiple and that their identity was decided by the aesthetic and even philosophical choices of their author. In the first third of the century, in fact, modern dance astonished so much with its continual ruptures from accepted movements that it was seen globally as a 'one'. It is interesting to learn from Martha Graham herself that, before the Bennington Summer Schools in the thirties, the different corporeities set in motion by the different players in the choreographic revolution (Humphrey, Holm, Graham herself) had not been recognised.[18] The Summer Schools which juxtaposed the teaching and the different corporeal approaches (sometimes in the same half-day) put an end to this blindness. The immense number of students who participated in the classes, whether or not they were dancers, were able to confirm from within their own bodies how much the purposes and commitments of each choreographer were different, how much each of them founded a 'body' in which their whole art originated. Modern dance no longer appeared as a homogenous field of expression but on the contrary as a heterogenous and profoundly individual vision, always beginning with the invention of a sin-

gular and irreducible body, what Selma Jean Cohen was to express thirty
years later with the phrase *modern dance is a point of view*: a multitude of
points of view, each of which proposes a different corporeal thinking.[19] To
return to the Bennington era: there was the Humphrey-body which worked
on instability and the limitless letting go of a thorax invited to fall; the tense
and willful Graham-body with its powerful variations of energy in the
systolic phase of the breath; the Holm-body which already had its centre
moving throughout the whole body, and its shifting points of intensity, later
to be found more clearly in her pupil, Alwin Nikolais.

Susan Foster has also proposed a grid for reading the body according to
the 'sense' that each great modern, from Martha Graham to the Judson
generation (here represented by Deborah Hay), confers on the body: as pure
articulation of motor powers for Cunningham, as the medium between the
self and the world for Graham.[20] This indispensable analysis can be taken
still further: for it is no longer adequate today to simply consider the body as
a vehicle of meaning and to decode it. We need to observe the organic
terrain where this semantics is elaborated – the implicit prerequisites out of
which the realm of appearances opens up; and how the spectator's perceptions are entangled with the body of the dancer in the same way that the
self's body is constructed through the apprehension of the other's – meaning that a dance aesthetics is contained within the very matter/material of
its elaboration. Not only dance aesthetics, but also the history of the art of
choreography have, in fact, evolved less in terms of formal choices or apparent creative decisions than in choices (recognised or not) of body states.
Thus Cynthia Novack (who pays homage to Foster's grid mentioned above)
locates a fault line between a 'voluntarist' and intentional body in the first
part of the century (a body that Novack describes as 'expressive' not because it refers to some form of narration external to itself but because, even
as a non-figurative aesthetic, it tries to communicate a desire, a quality that
is intensifying), and the body discovered by Erick Hawkins in the philosophical context of 'kinetic awareness', a phenomenological and objectal
body which became a basis for whole avant-garde of the sixties.[21] For, indeed, Cunningham's neutral body, a non-judging, non-affective passenger/
spectator to the world, and the task- oriented body of the Judson Church
needed for their work, or at least as an affirmation of their principles, the
corporeal foundation of Hawkins's philosophy. Here, we are a long way
from stipulating an aesthetic language or of formally encoding one, but
instead at the base of what is a real 'choice' in dance. Today, bodies often
change from one state to another; and it seems that the historical breach is
overcome or levelled out in favour of a poetics of 'indifference' where know-

ing about the historical fractures between bodies is no longer important. Is this a reconciliation or a suppression of the question, 'which body?' It is far from clear – and most of the time different corporealities circulate visibly or invisibly within dancing bodies like mysterious waves whose corporeal references become mixed or superimposed. What is most important, then, in terms of a 'poetic' reading is to illuminate the inscription of 'marks' (indices), and not of 'signs' based on purely formal criteria. Nor should the approach be in terms of mechanistic, linear or causalist genealogies or lines of descent but, instead, of borrowings or traces, reflections of a body that has passed our way and set in motion a state or sudden surprise. Amongst the most credible are those who can be recognised as having travelled paths which, if not new, have been at least conscious and inventive, where the technical means are visible, (almost) like a mode of referencing or citation. The greatest artists allow the body of the dancer to speak as a textuality reflecting the ideas and debates which, within a choreographic project, can reconcile different corporeal preferences and choices. It is impossible, for example, not to perceive in Trisha Brown's aesthetic what the dancers have brought with them from contact improvisation, enabling this choreographer to work with an astonishing multi-directionality. 'Style,' then, is engaged in and through the body of the dancer, through her/his knowledges and convictions regarding the philosophy of the body. Here, once again, the idea of a performer (*interprète*) as someone who simply 'relays' the work founders. For choreographic creation cannot be the unique and originary deed of an 'author' in the way it is in most works of art. Many bodies circulate and are summoned up in the choreographer's body and sensibility. And in dialogue with dancers' bodies, themselves traversed by multiple personal histories, they multiply. In a different way, in Dominique Bagouet's work there is a kind of 'phantom-memory' or half-erased memory of the 'body parts' familiar from Nikolais' practice, making the dancer's extremities undulate, alternately tensing and letting go. Except that Carolyn Carlson's teaching (from which Bagouet learned a great deal) vehemently insists that the centre can move around (Nikolais' 'travelling centre') which makes each limb into a whole body, or rather concentrates the intensity of the whole body in the extremity. With Bagouet, however, the frequent distal movements are attentively and precisely executed, or performed with a relaxed casualness as if the gesture was, enigmatically, a question without answer – sometimes rising to a suspension, which is no less interrogative. In both cases it is a question less, perhaps, of a journey of the centre than of a journey of the soul. But in the very quality of buoyancy, albeit changed and re-oriented, Bagouet's movement was 'given' to the dancer who mostly treated it according to what we will call the personal 'style' (or the corporal signature).[22] In contemporary dance, then, there is a kind of 'setting/nesting' (*enchâssement*) where several bodies encounter one another at the intersection of a gestural moment. What was initially transmitted is displaced, dissolves or remains like a shadow, not in the bodies but between them, just as the interpretation of a corporal text must be effaced or suppressed in order for it to be renewed. It is all legible even in being lost, including in the distortions that ignorance (or merely 'spectacular' processes) can impose on the different trainings or creative resources. Our perception is activated, made alert by powerful tools for reading the body that were elaborated simultaneously with the development of contemporary dance, and which have given us access to deep resources. These have multiplied the interpretive stages as well as the great wealth of sensuous experience that can be got from them. But with contemporary dance, where body-to-body relations are constantly intensified, the dancer's body touches the spectator's even without their realising it, and dialogues with their kinesphere enriching it with an ever-renewed experience – as long as the receptive space where these contacts occur is not blocked or fixed. These bodily contagions are diffused delicately and almost imperceptibly, for not all of the body is evident or apparent. There are very active zones which are more like halos or auras through which the dancer touches the Other's kinesphere. Among these vivid latencies, what has been most discussed – either in the human sciences or by the sciences of choreography – is the postural element whose existence and functioning, even when recognised, nevertheless remains very difficult to grasp. At the same time as the kinesthetic sense is affected by the perception of weight transfer, postural tone speaks to the spectator's awareness and awakens lively echoes within it. *Dance reinforces the postural preferences of the group*, notes Martha Davies referring to the traditional dances practised within societies which still share common values.[23] In contemporary dance where there has been an individualisation of preferences, the postural relation is established, either in fusion or conflict, between an individual dancer and an individual spectator. It is not strictly transferred through movement but rather by means of the diffuse and inexplicable contact which, in the interstice between two perceptions, stirs up the poetic grain.

The question, 'Which body?' posed by any choreographic work, is important well beyond the field of dance. In the first place, historically, rather than *the* body, it has shown us *bodies*, each of which has proposed a thought on/of the body. The question relativises and frees us from the presence of an absolute, universal and univocal body – a conceptual fantasy – whose essentialism, curiously, certain writings on dance maintain. The whole direction (*sens*) of contemporary dance, on the contrary, consists in letting go of the fantasy of an original body; and we have understood how much the work of dance implies a long search for a becoming-body. In this self-becoming-in-its-body (*ce devenir du soi au corps*) numerous techniques of movement intelligence (Alexander, Feldenkrais, Pilates, etc., already mentioned) can help anyone engaged in this search, whether or not they are dancers. Nevertheless, often in the name of the opposition 'nature-culture', the conception of a primitive animality endures. The binary pair nature–culture is in danger of proposing, amongst other things, a definitive relation where the former is anterior to the latter. It is no surprise to find the neo-classicist André Levinson, in the '30s, taking up the nature-artifice opposition in the name of a certain vision of western classical dance. Here, the academic dancer was to be at once the emblem and the illustration of artifice, a vision which many classical dancers vigorously reject today and not without good reason: as if the body's organic character, maintaining within us some wild matter, was fatally subjected to the human – and, in consequence, to the symbolic. The theory of an original body still gives rise to several approaches all of which are untenable. There is the 'naïve fetishisation' of the proposition 'THE body' which the dancer Christophe Wavelet rightly condemns – as if on the one hand there were a mixture of uncontrollable chaotic immanence and on the other a platonic, archetypal and immutable entity.[24] In both cases, a barrier strangely forbids touching the body reflectively or through any cognitive, practical or theoretical practices. A true analysis of body states involving a specific set of principles would thus be useless if 'the' body is seen as a universal, perfectly knowable if not masterable notion – at any rate, 'given'. To this body different apprenticeships in training or modes of performance would bring in a supplementary way the seal of civilisation and creativity. In fact, what we have instead is an economy of the body as a matter/material that must be worked, thought and lived in acknowledgement of the need for permanent experience/experiment. The 'carcass' discussed by Jerome Andrews is a complex but rich material and the extraordinary tool of our awareness and sensibility. It cannot be differentiated from thought, let alone be opposed to it, because it constitutes a fertile terrain of discovery and research.

Contemporary dance has explicitly worked on avoiding these traditional dualisms. For this dance, the body thinks and produces meanings. Or rather, in the vision that took hold after the holistic teachings of Kallmeyer and Dalcroze's inner musicality, the body, reflection, and poetics sweep each other up along the same journey and support each other in a permanent give and take. Twenty years after the beginning of contemporary dance, dancers' explorations were joined, on a less synthetic plane (and certainly without the intention of being applied) in anthropology. In Marcel Mauss's *'corps montage'*, for example, physiological factors constitute only one set of corporeal determinants and Mauss regards what we think of as the body's 'functions' as so many 'techniques' already containing systems of representation.[25] In discovering Mauss's ideas, a posteriori, after the translation of his works into English around 1973, American dancers and theorists were struck by the convergence between his ideas and the thinking that Laban's successors had initiated. For, at the level of thought and material elaboration, dance works on becoming a body which is not given in advance. Or rather it works a multitude of bodies each of which contains, like a secret score, the immense gamut of its possibilities and poetic tonalities, what Laban calls the 'corporeal signature'. In fact more than bodies, there are body states, 'corporeal moments' as Hubert Godard would say.[26] These transmute across eras, cultures and individuals, from one situation or one response to another, according to individual mechanisms: not only a field of interference but a field capable of organising this interference. Dancing consists, then, in making readable the sensory network that the movement at each instant brings forth and works on. Here again the order of meaning is not a value to be added but a semiotic function residing within the body as a permanent potential. Michel Bernard sees this very semioticity (and not some organic given that is before or underlying it) as that which gives rise to the existential experience of the body: *The reality of the human body comes as much from its semiotic function as from its form or motor capacity.*[27] Or we might say from its 'lyrical function' which originates with the very presence of the body, in the mutation of its textures and its fluids.

Concern at seeing corporeality along with its knowledges and poetics submitted to a mechanical or purely biological vision (or at least inscribed in modes of representation that are more or less determinist) is doubtless what led a whole branch of thinking in dance to look for ways to free the body–self from any dependence on causality. This quest has always haunted dance modernity, especially through the work of the great Nietzscheans (Laban, Humphrey...) who aspired to unchain motor powers in order to direct the body into a uniquely symbolic dimension. Contrary to what one might think, this undertaking did not lead to a negation of the body's organic depths but, instead, it was in deeply exploring the most intimate sources of weight transfer that both discovered something of this buried poetics. Matthias Alexander's uncovering of a proximity to the 'self' that enables inhibition of unproductive automatic patterns, for example, provided a means for a new and serene autonomy of corporeal awareness.[28] But it is to Cunningham and the American rebels of the '60s that we must look to find the most convincing – and also the most expansive – forms of this aspiration: initially, in the wake of the ideas of John Cage, through their use of aleatory processes to find the body's indetermination.

Even before choosing 'indeterminacy,' Cunningham's *Untitled Solo* which was made in the radical and influential environment of Black Mountain College, dissociates rather than sequences movements as if the body, escaping the Law, could reinvent a new order to preserve it from the traditional view of a fatal body. Gradually, Cunningham was to make his system less demonstrative and also less painful. As if the defiance of *Untitled Solo* once it had to be shared with others, obliged him to spare them the wounds of these first ruptures. As Cunningham has noted, the dissociation embodied in his technique (the top of the body from the bottom, for example) never goes against the body's wholeness with its spine as the source from which the movements radiate.[29] For in freeing the 'being-body' (*l'être corps*) to its own anti-fatalism, the organism is not an enemy; it is, on the contrary, an ally which helps (if only in the willing suppleness of the vertebrae) to find stronger and more inventive means to be free. We can see the same (apparent) contradiction in the first experiments of the Judson Church rebellion where the use of different inhibiting procedures (tasks, mechanical constraints) in turn isolated the *corps-destin* from any hereditary, biological or psychological overcoding. Pre-determining movement even in anatomical terms, was anathema to this wild and desperate attempt to have done with the causalism incarcerating the 'biological' part of the self. The generations of dancers of the '60s fought against a determinism which was, after all, only a form of the juridical more or less imposed by obsolete modes of representation. *We began to explore systems which knocked out the relationship of cause and effect*, wrote Halprin... *We used objects and accessories, we used space in a determining way. I wanted to isolate these elements, to work with a system where all that could be free from a relationship of cause and effect.*[30] And how could such a programme be accomplished without first working on the body as a terrain for the elimination of causality? Halprin began by isolating body parts which she moved without sequencing them in a pre-determined pathway. Then she made lists of movements on pieces of paper and used chance methods to select them. The body as a score not programmed by biology already, in itself, becomes a writing both of the indeterminacy inherited from Cage and Cunningham, but also of the 'unpredictable' – an important idea for the generations of dancers of the '60s:

because the unpredictable is in fact highly determined by the history of the 'me' who improvises, and allows an already inscribed movement memory to appear. At the same time, however, the practices of indeterminacy displaced the intervention of the subject so as to obliterate this memory. Halprin's scores, her improvisations under conditions of restraint, her endless exhausting repetitions of the one action which gave rise to unexpected movement states as she progressively let go control, are tools for combining the two concepts. And for making the body less a break with the subject than the site of another search *for* the subject.

Nothing of this free, non-determined body would have been possible without the corporal knowledges instituted at the beginning of the century – without the observation of different tissue states, different insertions of the musculature, without the teaching of Feldenkrais learned by Halprin and others. That is, without the signposts along innumerable possible paths through which an errant awareness explores in depth its organic circuits the better to extract from them a promise of freedom, not submission. The body is firstly what one thinks of it, what it itself thinks, and where we accept it will lead us. Even if today we are far from these enlightening processes, even if the dancing body today plays with its shadows, opacities and (in the form of metaphor) its forgettings, in the practices and the thought of contemporary dance, it remains nevertheless the great guide announced by Nietzsche.

1 Cited in Lewis, Daniel *The Illustrated Technique of José Limón*, 1989, p.53.

2 Nietzsche, F. *Thus Spake Zarathustra*, 1958.

3 Jerome Andrews in *Forward and Backward*, video-portrait of N. and N. Corsino, 1992. The word 'carcass', often used by Andrews, appears in the text of his numerous essays, unfortunately unpublished except for one in *Marsyas*, No. 26, June 1993, pp.45-48.

4 Cf Dominique Dupuy's description of the Pilates 'machine' in 'Faire machine avant' with drawings by J-P. Schneider in *Nouvelles de Danse*, No. 17, October, 1993, pp.36-37.

5 Dupuy, D. 'Le corps émerveillée' in *Marsyas*, No. 16, December 1990, p.32.

6 Dowd, Irene. *Taking Root to Fly: ten articles on functional anatomy*, 1981, re-ed. *Articles on Functional Anatomy*, 1995, p.3 and 5.

7 See Leroi-Gourhan, A. *Le geste et la parole*, 1964.

8 Holm, Hanya. 'Hanya Speaks' in *The Vision of Modern Dance*, 1998 (second edition), p.81.

9 Sophie Tauber, exhibition catalogue, MNAM, Paris, Nov./Dec., 1990, p.32.

10 For the 'faces' of Valeska Gert, cf. Maïté Fossen's study in *Empreintes, écrits sur la danse*, No.5, March 1983. It will be noted that the face and in particular the mouth had already been given a choreographic place by the German dadaists whether or not the mouth uttered anything. See the exaggerated mimicries of Schwitters when he was reciting the 'Ursonate' (*cahiers Merz*, No. 22, Dresden, 1932) or the grimace dances of Raoul Houssmann. Read in relation to the latter: 'Dans l'antre chaotique de la Bouche' in *Raoul Haussmann* exhibition catalogue, Musée Chateau de

Rochechouart, 1995, pp.79-89.

11 Godard, Hubert. 'La Peau et les Os', *Bulletin of the CNDC*, No. 4, July, 1989, p.8.

12 Anzieu, D. *The skin ego*, 1989.

13 Godard, H. 'A propos des théories d'analyse du mouvement' in *Marsyas*, No. 16, December, 1990, pp.19-23.

14 Maletic, Vera 'Appendix I: The lived body-space-expression' in *Body Space Expression*, 1987, pp. 195-196.

15 To recall: Straus, E. *Phenomenology and Psychology*; Merleau-Ponty, M. *Phenomenology of Perception* and *The Visible and the Invisible*; Buytendijk, F. *Algemeine Theorie der Menschlichen Haltung und Bewegung*, 1956.

16 Ibid. The connections are made by Maletic, 1987. The citations are from Straus, E. 1956, p. 154, and Laban, *Choreutics*, posthumous publication by Lisa Ullmann, 1996, p. 42.

17 Maieutic refers to a Socratic mode of enquiry or *serving to bring out a person's latent idea into clear consciousness* (Concise OED, Sixth Edition, 1976, edited by J.B.Sykes.). The Greek root is *maia* or midwife and thus, here, movement serves the birth of bodies. The metaphorics of knowledge as *co-naissance* (being born with) is thus made tangible – and connects us back to the origins of the idea of poetics (Gk. *poiein*) in the making/forming/transforming of material from out of itself and its own energies. (Transl.)

18 Graham in *Martha Graham: her theory and training* edited by Marianne Horosko, 1989.

19 Cohen, S-J. *Modern Dance: Seven Statements of Belief*, 1969, p.14.

20 Foster, S. L. *Reading Dancing*, 1986, pp.42-3.

21 Novack, C. *Sharing the Dance*, 1990, p.31.

22 Ginot, I. 'Fissures, petites fissures' in *La danse, naissance d'un mouvement de pensée*, 1989, pp.152-3.

23 Bartenieff, I., Davis, M., et al. *Four adaptations of the Effort Theory*, 1972, p.44.

24 Wavelet, C. 'Quel corps, quelle transmission, quel enseignement?' in *Marsyas*, No. 34, Summer 1995, pp. 39-44.

25 Cf. Mauss, Marcel. *Sociology and Psychology: essays*. Translation of Mauss's *Sociologie et Anthropologie* by Ben Brewster, 1979. (see especially Chapter 6: 'Techniques of the body')

26 Godard, H. 'Singular Moving Geographies', 1996.

27 Bernard, M. *L'expressivité du corps, recherche sur les fondements de la théâtralité*, 1976.

28 Caplan, D. 'The Alexander Technique' in *Contact Quarterly*, Vol. 3, No. 10, 1985.

29 Cunningham, Merce. 'The Function of a Technique for Dance' in Walter Sorrell, *The Dance has Many Faces*, 1952.

30 Rainer, Y. 'Some retrospective notes: Anna Halprin' in *TDR*, No. 10 (T-30), Vol. 2, Winter 1965.

Breath

Down through the workings of his own throat to that place where breath comes from, where breath has its beginnings, where drama has to come from, where the coincidence is, all act springs.
Charles Olson[1]

For the breath is the mysterious great master who reigns unknown and unnamed behind all and everything – who silently commands the function of muscles and joints – who knows how to fire with passions and to relax, how to whip up and restrain – who puts the breaks in the rhythmic structure and dictates the phrasing of the flowing passages – who above all this regulates the temper of expression in its interplay with the colourfulness of rhythm and melody.
Mary Wigman [2]

There is nothing so extraordinary as to observe, in stillness, the deep involuntary movements going on inside us: the diaphragm rising and falling like a wave alternately dilating and contracting the thoracic cage. If I am more attentive and follow the path of my breath to the final point of exhalation I can feel the whole torso become infused right down to the sacral region, while on the in-breath my head is filled with air. In fact my whole body is ventilated by the continual passage of breath. Breath reveals only spaces; in breathing we touch and know our inner cavities. The body thus revealed is a net, not a mass. It is empty, not full. It refers us, beyond physical sensations, to the geography of the body's landscapes, to a space that connects outside and inside, a global space whose conjugal luminosities the body only diffracts: the body as a passage, a porous screen between two states of the world, and not an opaque, full, impenetrable mass. Thanks to the breath a dancer's body becomes this 'sieve-body' through which sensations are filtered and essential threads of knowledge are gradually deposited. Breath is the sensation of a mechanism for beginning and becoming, leading us ceaselessly from letting our weight go to suspending it, from the before to the after, from the empty to the full. It is a mechanism for taking hold of the outside, and for returning to the world the air that our body has extracted from it, at the same time resonating with the elemental currents, the winds and waves that make things flow and sweep the whole universe along with them. We know that through their myths and practices the oldest cultures have given breath a primordial role. The sail flapping in the wind, says Michel Serres, exteriorises a pneumatic corporality in terms of which the boat's ropes represent muscle fibres.[3] Once again, contemporary dance has sought to establish a continuum (lost for dance in an arid formalism which has become merely frivolous) rather than break with the great forces that nourished ancient Mediterranean and Oriental civilisations; and also an 'anthropological continuum' of different body functions whose equivalences the breath maintains. Once more, it is the dancer who reveals the powerful source of an imaginary. In the same way that breath produces in us a vocal vibration, it also sets movement reverberating. And if one wanted to distinguish the two it would only be, says Maldiney, in terms of their spatialisation.[4] In her/his poetic experience of the body, the dancer is inspired by respiration. The phrasing of movement is aerated in its unfolding, its quality, its 'grain'; and, in turn, movement and its expression play with the flow of the breath. Wigman, again, regards the breath as a diffracted but equally expressive treatment of space-time: *When the dancer crosses through space with solemnly measured steps, his deep and calm breathing gives his carriage and movement an appearance of innermost composure and completion in itself; and when – by incessantly springing up and down – he throws himself into a condition of flickering agitation which not only takes possession of his body but of the entire being, then there no longer exists a moment of quiet breathing for him. He breathes, rather, with the same vibration that fills and shakes his whole being.*[5]

It is, of course, in jumping that the necessity of breathing in and out appears fundamental, as it is in any movement that has an explosive quality. Here, breath's power helps to get us into the air, with movements of elevation carrying the dancer upward in consonance with the pneumatic changes orchestrated by his/her body. From the moment of suspension at the end of the out breath to the new inhalation that brings it back down towards the underworld, the body becomes, from within, a meteor. *When a dancer starts to jump, he chases the stream of his breath like lightning from below to the top, from the feet upward through the body, to be able to hold his breath from the instant of leaving the ground until he has reached the height of his leap and has almost gone beyond it. In these few seconds of his utmost exertion, holding his breath, he actually defies all gravity, becomes a creature of the air, and seems to fly or float through space. At the downcurve only his breath flows back into the relaxing body and returns the dancer to the earth after his short soaring flight.*[6] From Wigman's description we can imagine Nijinsky's leap as Paul Claudel saw it when they met in Brazil: an electric meeting between the dancer and the poet of the *Five Great Odes*. The meeting led to one of the most beautiful texts ever written on dance – often cited by Dominique Dupuy: *He brought us the leap, that is, the victory of respiration over weight.*[7]

In fact, contemporary dance has never had a fixed 'breathing method' as such. In Wigman's (essential) text we can see how the moving body lives with its breathing according the terms of a spontaneous contract without the need for specific rules. A scepticism regarding aspects of breathing disciplines that are too systematised and not oriented poetically has been influential here. Jacques Garros, whose research and teaching on the act of breathing are well known in French dance, has also questioned mechanistic or dissociative techniques.[8] In this regard, Hubert Godard cites Matthias Alexander, *who was against any direct breathing work, but for a more precise awareness of proprioception.* Which, continues Godard, does not prevent his method from effecting significant improvements in breathing.[9]

In fact, the awareness of breath and of its resources is more important for the contemporary dancer than any ritualised study. An informed practice of breath should be inextricable from the necessities and qualities of movement. Sometimes it is the movement that reveals the internal respiration whose visible aspect it is: throwing (objects, scarves), in which an impetus becomes functional, enabled Dalcroze, and Humphrey in *Soaring* (1924), to make the impulse of an in-breath visible. Here, again, is the celebrated concern for an 'anthropological continuum' linking the contemporary dancer across the body's memory to fundamental movements. All the work movements founded on this type of accentuation, in particular the use of throwing tools (to use ethnological jargon) – the scythe, the sickle, boomerang, etc. – find their force in the breath. In this fundamental sense, throwing actions in Régine Chopinot's *Végétal* (1995) gain their poetics as much from the dancers' breathing as from the scattering and fluttering of the leaves that the sculptor Andy Goldsworthy piled up on the stage.

But this awareness of the breath needs to be revisited, thought, felt. That is why in all phases of its history contemporary dance has, in a reflexive or remedial way, called upon the great Eastern or Mediterranean techniques in which breathing represents, physically and metaphorically, the source of any search for the self. The heritage of a long tradition, the wealth of sensory and intellectual awareness developed in oriental body knowledges were very quickly perceived within the modern currents of movement research. From Steiner's 'Eurhythmy' in Germany, to the yoga techniques imported to California by Denishawn, the pneumatic thought of the East has had its influence on bodies, has hollowed out inner spaces and has infused thought undoubtedly much more than the visibly oriental forms adopted by Ruth St Denis in her dance. And it is probably through breathing exercises that the East, infiltrating our bronchia and our larynxes and even our nasal passages through the practice of '*pranayama*', has most marked the Western dancer deep in the pneumatic architecture of her/his body.

The history of these relations can be traced: they take us from the dawn of the century when Indian techniques were first encountered, and the arrival of the great Asian practitioners like Miro Ito, to the later discovery of martial arts and the influence of aikido in the sixties, or of Sufism and Mevlana ideas of the whirling breath on certain American dancers like Laura Dean or French ones like Alain Buffard, a longtime dancer with Larrieu on whose sense of breath Buffard's influence was considerable. The commitment of Denishawn students to breath and to the spirit of yoga in particular was evident: especially in Graham for whom breathing action determined the two alternating phases of movement and its expression. Breath 'designs' this founding alternation through real changes in body material. Gertrud Shurr, who was one of Graham's first dancers, describes how they came progressively to understand this bodily enigma in very clear terms: *We found that upon the exhaling of breath, the skeleton or bones of the body moved: the pelvic bone tipped forward, the cartilage of the spine allowed the spine to stretch and curve backward, and the shoulders moved forward, always*

*retaining the alignment of shoulder over hip, while never lowering the level of the
seated position. When the breath was inhaled, the skeleton resumed its original
position moving to that position in the same order: pelvis, spine, shoulders...The
muscles return to their original position upon release.*[10] The foundations of
Graham technique are thus drawn from *a new approach to physicality based
on the processes of respiration.* Breathing plays a very different role in Doris
Humphrey's work. Its poetics of alternating states where movement arises
from the instability between fall and recovery allows a greater role for the
fluctuations of weight. The deeply melodic character of her work coming
from her modulation of breath and weight, is lovingly described by her
disciple José Limón as a succession of breaths which together give line to the
body: *Fall and recovery. Breath. Suspension. Tension and relaxation. Breath
phrase. Breath rhythm. Always the breath. She moved like a gazelle.*[11] There is
the same metaphysics of breath in Cunningham for whom the flux of
things, water, air and the shimmering of being form the weft of a 'passage'
where the breath's coming and going is made palpable. Here we find the
double influence of a relativist materialism, whose roots can be found as
much in Democritus and Lucretius as in Zen philosophy, with its openness
to a possible multiplicity. For Cunningham, the many dimensions of time
are exchanged in breathing. Breathing is by definition the very experience
of this many-faced time in the body, emblematising the unceasing work of
the dancer between past and future *renewing daily the old experiences and
searching for new ones.*[12]

The 'diaphragmatic body' approach practised in the thought and teaching of Jerome Andrews and carried on today by Dominique Dupuy goes still
deeper. The three horizontal diaphragms – pelvic, thoracic and cranial –
function simultaneously, remarks Dupuy, as irrigators and filters, as frontiers and 'relays'. To this list of major diaphragms can be added other
filtering tissues, the skin, and the plantar epidermis, called by dancers, 'the
belly of the foot'.[13] Work on 'sites of transit' drives a practice of bodily
mobility that brings about permanent functional changes; and an experience strongly suggestive of the 'body without organs,' an image which we
should remember Gilles Deleuze and Felix Guattari took from the breath-
oriented body of Antonin Artaud.[14] Among the phases of respiration,
Dupuy gives particular attention to exhalation, not only because it supports
movement but because it has to do with the sensation of air as pure passing
and thus with loss: air is not an acquisition, it is taken but not kept. It is
restored, given back in the process of elimination and in the accent we give
to it.[15] (To bring accent into a poetics of breath is to recall the link between
the diaphragms and weight. Weight lifting, pressing, condensing in torsion,

so many actions that lower, fold and retract the interior filters.) In this loss of air, there is loss of breath, out-of-breath, breathing out-of-control. *For in breathlessness there is an internal passion,* writes Dominique Dupuy, *which it would be interesting to deliberately provoke,* so much does this state of exhaustion drive the body to a deep, drunken shaking.[16] The power of the pneumatic machine is always revealed to us in the state of breathlessness with its spasms, chaotically agitated thorax, body and mind mobilised by the irrepressible wave and perturbation of the diaphragm. That intense experiences leading to breathlessness (fast or violent movements and emotions, etc.) are linked to the high points of life brings us back to dance as the experimental/experiential scene of being.

More meditative is the experience of the phases between dilatation and contraction of the diaphragm with their more or less prolonged apneas (with lungs full or empty according to the desired quality). It is in this in-between place at the crossroads of opposing currents that the Mâ of Japanese Zen is awakened. The breath is abolished or released more than controlled. Dominique Dupuy again: *Finally expiration leads us to emptiness, to the Mâ of breathing. This moment of emptiness has nothing to do with an arrest or breathlessness. It is an instant of intense awareness when time is suspended and one waits to live one more instant.*[17] The respiratory act is without doubt one of the rare situations in which the duality of full and empty can be approached experimentally, and where this duality can become one of the body's choices in dance. In his quest to teach Mâ, Hideyuki Yano was able to make this approach to emptiness into a poetics which, grounded nevertheless in corporal experience, transcended it, almost effaced it in order to retain only its impalpable change. Yano made emptiness a frame for the elaboration of an imaginary where each dancer was summoned to find her/his own break-through, her/his own unreachable point. Or using mythically charged texts, as he liked to do, he would search for a 'character' to light up an errant awareness.

Meredith Monk, too, invents or rather discovers in her breath a whole world of characters of whom, to begin with, she is unaware while they sleep or are buried in the mysterious geographies of body states. Monk came from dance and the Judson Church experiments. From within the presence of body, voice and song she invented new states of space-time. Hers is a narrative art but one which totally escapes (any hasty) distinctions between on the one hand the non-figurative arts born of the avant-gardes and on the other a 'return' to theatricality. What Monk reveals to us is a theatre of open composition without climax or moment of 'recentring', proving that what is important in dance is less the relation to narrative

than the way it organises regimes of tension. Monk's group pieces, like
Education of a Girl Child (1972) which are often constructed according to an
aesthetics of 'character', are movement compositions which draw on an
impressive art of presence in the (singer-dancer) performers. But the performers' roles, and the formal organisation play essentially on an
instrument of singing voices, whose timbres range from sharp to velvety or
dry and which themselves gain their artistic force in large part from the
body's profound presence, and a quasi static evolution of space, time and
atmosphere. The breath work is not only in the singing. It becomes visible. It
weaves its very dramaturgy from the bodies in their appearing. For Monk,
the voice is constructed with and within the whole empty-fullness of the
body, the whole being, however simple or relaxed, without the one dominating the other. For Monk the voice is part of movement and is engendered in
the first instance in a body awareness proper to the dancer; a *dancing voice,
supple like the spine.*[18] This breath suffuses movements which alternate or
join with moments of a cappella singing. Song and movement evoke an
illegible 'de-referenced' text but nevertheless the glossolalia that serve as
speech seem to harken very quickly to meaning. Vocalisations, use of the
throat and vibrato are as many elements of 'language' through which actions, emotions, characters are drawn. But, above all, they make even more
manifest in her work breath's passing through the body's interior. The work
is not a spectacular *mise en scène* of the voice but a 'theatre' constructed out
of it. It emanates the different qualities of each voice, including those
within the voice of each of the performer-characters. Monk's theatre which
lies on the border between concert and drama (*action scénique*), between
dance and installation is a diaphragmatic theatre in which a strange
memory of beings and things seems to body forth. It is an archaeology of
body states as in her film *Book of Days,* (1987) about a Jewish community
living in Occitain in the Middle Ages or *Dolmen Music* (1979) a dreamlike
evocation of ancient materials, objects, bodies which seem to enter a time
beyond time. Voice leads them there, like a pre-verbal memory in which
movement gradually finds its place.[19]

   With the new Eastern influences, particularly the martial arts, the use of
the breath was able to play more or less spectacularly on the percussive
aspects of a movement or to emphasise the unvarying astringency of a state
of resistance. There are some very clear examples in Japanese butoh-de-
rived dance where the oriental influence is accentuated well beyond what
the geographical and cultural origin of the dancers might justify. The ath-
leticism of the dancers from Shankai Juku is based on complex breathing
techniques. Dominique Dupuy cites Amagatsu's 'onstage fall', a *fall back*

along his whole length as a particularly poignant moment, a fall co-ordinated with the rise of the diaphragm illustrating, *the violent letting go of an extremely precise internal movement,* what Dupuy describes later as the 'true fall' linked to the rising and falling of the breath. Sometimes using breath energy has given these impulsive movements something like the intentional quality found in Eastern combat arts. The body empties itself through an aesthetic of exasperation as if to evacuate all finality or signifying elaboration. This was, amongst other things, one of the deeply nihilistic roots of François Verret's work, particularly in the memorable duet *Tabula Rasa* with Alain de Raucourt – a dance of men driven to exhaust their own movement in the breathless energy of an unfinished gesture: an organic excess from which there could be no reverberation beyond expelling its own spasms. All Verret's works and that of others who were for a time inspired by it (from Diverrès to Monnier) arose from this act of rupture. Tools provided by the martial arts, their heightened use of breath directed into the thrust of movements and into confrontation, played a significant role in the elaboration of a French dance aesthetic at the beginning of the '80s.[20]

Here, we can see once again how a resource patiently brought to light and applied by modern dance, became in the course of the late '70s, and even more in the '80s, a directly expressive material. Dramatised, used for its auditory or visual effect, the breath now appears in the raw. The prudishly hidden breathlessness of the academic dancer who had always had to obscure the workings of her/his body was refused. But there was also a willingness to explore breath's wild or animal character, as a sonorous analogy with the sighs or inner voices of strong emotions: pain, rage, fear, sexual pleasure. Perhaps, as was the case with Joëlle Bouvier-Régis Obadia, a desire to resuscitate a 'primal scene' where the body works on a forbidden threshold which dance can permanently transgress. All these choices are apposite and have made the dance of the '80s resound with the raucous symphony of breath music. The relationship of dance and the body to sound would be marked by it, as we will see. 'Upstream' of these examples of breath semantics there remains its role as an existential practice, as a way of constructing a body. In fact, to interpret a dancer's breath, whatever its goal or use, is to be carried away by that same breath, to allow oneself to breathe as though with lungs that engage all bodies in the same expending or the same suspension. In this regard, the impression of apnea shared with the performers of Larrieu's *Waterproof,* danced in a swimming pool, causes a powerful empathy to circulate between the breath of the spectators, and the empty lungs of a dancer, suspended between high and low water like a floating pocket devoid of organic contents. The non-breath, then, whether

of empty or full lungs, creates a sort of ballast which plays on sensations of
weight and works the gravitational tissue of the spectator producing transformations in perception and state. Time within a non-breath becomes a
line of tension as fine as it is continuous. *Waterproof* which was a great
work of the '80s changed the experience of duration: it created an amphibi-
ous duration shared between air and water, between the crystalline cold of
the depths and the humid warmth of an indoor pool. From out of the profound disjunction between states of breath whose forms escape vision to
become pure sensation of the unrepresentable, a sovereign aesthetics can
be born.

1 In 'Projective Verse' cited by L. Steinman in *The Knowing Body: Elements of Contemporary Performance and Dance*. 1986.
2 In Wigman, Mary *The Language of Dance*, 1966.
3 Serres, Michel *Le contrat naturel*, 1990.
4 Maldiney, Henri *L'art, l'éclair de être*. 1993, pp. 45 and 153.
5 Wigman, 1966, p. 11.
6 Ibid.
7 Paul Claudel. 'Art Poétique' in *Oeuvres Complètes*. La Pléiade, Gallimard, cited in Dupuy, D.
'L'alchimie du souffle' in *Marsyas*, No. 32, December 1994.
8 Garros, J. 'L'acte respiratoire est le chemin' in *Marsyas*, No.32, op.cit.
9 Godard, H. 'Le souffle, le lien' in *Marsyas*, No.32, op.cit.
10 Shurr, G. in Horosko, M. (ed.). *Martha Graham: the Evolution of her Dance Theory*, 1982, p.22.
11 José Limón cited in Lewis, D. *The Illustrated Technique of José Limón*, 1989, p.18.
12 Merce Cunningham. 'The Function of a Technique for Dance', 1952, p. 252.
13 Dupuy, D., 1994.
14 Deleuze, G. & Guattari, F. *Anti-Oedipus: Capitalism and Schizophrenia*. London: Athlone, 1984.
15 Dupuy, D. 1994.
16 Ibid.
17 Ibid.
18 Monk, Meredith. 'Notes on the Voice' in Banes, S. *Terpsichore in Sneakers*. 1980, re-ed. 1987.
19 See Steinman, L., 1986, for a description of Monk's teaching.
20 See Pomarès, J. 'De la formation à la création' in *Parcours*, notes published by the Direction
Régionale des Affaires Culturelles, Provence Alpes Côte d'Azur, 1995.

The Four Factors – Weight

The body is not thought if it is not thought of as weighted.
J-L Nancy[1]

Laban's genius, in the first instance, lay in considering the body 'in move-ment' and not as a fantasmatically originary, immobile body upon which movement would come to make its mark. The copula linking the term 'body' to 'movement' (and to 'dance') must always be an 'in' not an 'and'. It was in consideration of this that, initially, Laban was able to identify the four constitutive factors of movement; and, in a second phase, the idea of 'effort' which is so useful for perceiving what is in play poetically in movement. For Laban and his followers, the body as a 'geography of relations', is elaborated out of an 'inner impulse' in order to exteriorise and then to symbolise a relation.[2] But we should be careful not to assume a relation between inside and outside that is reducible to the exteriorisation of the enclosed contents of a 'me'. The 'me' in dance circulates. It is, in fact, at once the object and the actor of this relational circulation. The four factors which Laban identified are 'the keys,' in the musical sense, of this circulation.

The four factors: weight, flow (i.e. the degree of intensity of muscle tone), space and time are the 'able-to-be-sensed' vectors of this elaboration. Amongst the four factors, the most important – weight – has a special place. It is at once the agent of movement and what is acted upon. All movement is defined by a transfer of weight. Laban's cinetography of the '20s makes weight transfer the open unit founding any motor act. Weight is not only displaced: it displaces, constructs, symbolises from out of its own sensation. The other factors serve to define the sensation of weight qualitatively, and to distribute it according to different corporeal 'colours'. In fact, the four factors do not exist in themselves: they are not apprehended from the perspective of their own substance but only in the relationship that we maintain with them. This tenet of Laban's thought was to be affirmed more explicitly with the elaboration of his 'effort' theory. Space, time and even weight do not exist if I fail to weave into them my own intentionalities. These are life itself: they are the vectors both of energy and of the aesthesias or drives.

Nothing is more revealing than the body language (*gestuelle*) of the people with depressive or schizophrenic illness who were documented in Laban's cinetography and who manifest an atrophy of the factors: segmented movements without the postural ground that in the case of schizophrenics cannot even be constructed, and an absence of any relation to space. Such were, in general, Bartenieff's observations when she notated patients' movements before they undertook dance therapy with her as a way of opening to the relational (i.e to the field where the subject is constituted). It goes without saying that 'healthy' subjects are not always in touch with the four factors. A similar atrophy can impoverish our relations with space, time and body weight and the variations of energetic intensity. Here we find the diminution of kinaesthetic sensibility and the kind of corporeal 'deafness' that makes people impermeable to musicality and spatial aesthetics; and causes a greater insensitivity to dance which plays on this 'geography of relations'.

Amongst the four factors, weight is thus the most important. It is, however, mostly perceived very little by the public for it is not one of the standard principles for judging works of genius or of art. If our higher senses (hearing and, in particular, vision) are considered the conduits of an idealising thought, touch, which is ranked among the lower senses, is hardly credited with such potential. But it is essentially to the sense of touch that changes in the treatment of weight address themselves – both in the other and in oneself. Laban's audacity and power were to make the treatment of weight not only the site of a symbolic construction as important as that of sound, words, line, colour. But in the last years of his life to make of weight the root (hitherto unthought) of all cultural processes on all levels, from the individual to the group.[3]

The importance of weight is one of the great discoveries of contemporary dance – not only as a factor of movement bio-mechanically speaking, but as a primordial poetic investment. Firstly, through the acceptance of weight: *One of the best discoveries the modern dance has made use of*, recalls Cunningham, *is the gravity of the body in weight, that is, as opposite from denying (and thus affirming) gravity by ascent into the air, the weight of the body in going with gravity, down.*[4] To accept weight and to work with it as one might work with a living and productive material has been a founding principle of dance modernity. In the teaching as well as the art of the German school this has been particularly well developed. Karin Waehner, a student of Wigman, for example, makes weight not only an artistic inspiration but a theme, justifying in itself a compositional investigation (as a workshop of Nikolais' might treat 'motion' thematically).

The treatment of weight when a subject takes control of it or gives in to the attraction of gravity are the two poles across which a poetics of weight is primarily articulated. The 'vertical death' evoked by Doris Humphrey derives its stasis from the body's whole weight being fixed by the tensors which, as they 'continually adjust', hold the whole corporal tissue in position.[5] To escape from this, to liberate one's weight, two forms of movement are required: swing and fall. Contrary to the purely mimetic interpretation of falling made by observers outside dance, particularly the post-Bachelardians who classify it within the 'nocturnal' order of the imagination, falling in the body's own imagination, has nothing to do with death.[6] On the contrary the body is liberated from vertical death through surrendering to its own inclination. It is always close to a swing (and thus to a rhythm) but without swing's return. All movement is a deferred fall and it is from the manner in which this fall (elsewhere fully embraced) is deferred that movement aesthetics are born. Numerous texts, beginning with Humphrey's, have been written on the poetics of falling. They form part of a very beautiful corpus connecting the fall and its different recoveries to the poetics of instability so important in contemporary dance: a play of movement around the gravitational axis, suggests Hubert Godard, asserting the idea of *a value which can only be one of wavering.*[7]

The fall as a recurring figure in contemporary dance finds its final conclusion in the use of the floor – another element on which Karin Waehner bases studio explorations and important propositions: floor support, amorous partner, the floor to push against. One can give oneself up totally to the floor, releasing all the tensors in absolute weight, allowing the supporting surface to take charge of the whole weighty mass that one gives up to it qualitatively as well as quantitatively. Sometimes the supports fall away and this is a source of drama. Thus, in a famous duet in Pina Bausch's *Café Muller,* a woman throws herself into the arms of a man who doesn't catch her. She falls as if the earth itself opened up beneath her. But the floor in itself is not only a place to lie down. As Odile Rouquet says it is our best ally against gravity.[8] It is the surface of rebound but also the surface that carries us and reinscribes in us the experience of being held, when our gravitational architecture did not yet exist and when our supple and fluid spine flowed with the maternal support.[9] Bodies abandoned to the ground but not prostrate. This floor work where the body thinks and loses itself, lets itself go into a ground that in turn gives itself up to the body, provokes exceptional movement qualities because the tensors can be at rest. Numerous practices but also numerous aesthetics use this. There are entire dances such as Trisha Brown's *Accumulations* (from 1970) that take place on the floor; and floor sequences are almost obligatory in any dance practice. These sequences can be rolling ones where the body peels itself from the ground, gathering itself together, then lets itself go and rolls again. Such 'passages' are to be understood in the 'initiatory' sense (rites of passage) because the return to the ground to re-organise verticality is as indispensable to the dancer as it was for the giant Antaeus – but without his fusional and regenerative quest. These returns, according to Doris Humphrey's poetics again, allow a rebound where the body's objective verticality in relation to ascending-descending is only justified as a kind of 'soaring' to use the title of one of her pieces (*Soaring,* 1924). The (essential) ascending-descending dynamics are closely connected to the treatment of weight.

They guarantee its elasticity and the possibility of moving between the two opposing poles or of maintaining the ambivalence of fall and rebound. Humphrey and Brown have this tonality and, in France, Hervé Robbe, and Odile Duboc: an aesthetics of flexibility where elastic space is created in an arc of suspensions.

But there is no factor – of weight or any other – that can be considered outside of a relationship amongst them all. The other most significant factor working specifically on the poetics of weight is flow. Indeed, if weight constitutes movement's basic matter and is its object, its stake and inner 'charge', flow is linked even more with the 'mode' of its treatment. In conceiving the idea of 'motion' Nikolais is certainly thinking of Laban's flow as the agent which colours, activates and enlivens the way a movement is undertaken. According to flow preferences, the transfer of weight will have different resonances. In bound flow weight takes on a pouring quality. In the gamut of effort-shape actions Laban characterises it by the action of 'gliding'. In Odile Duboc's piece, *Project de la Matière* (1994), undoubtedly one of the most important in the recent French corpus, weight is in bound flow. Weightedness is then intensified by a sustained gliding: the body never stops falling. Its relationship to the sculptures of Marie-Jose Pillet, discussed below, involves this combination of factors, shaping from without the character of the gliding. This was a completely new use of weight in Duboc's work in which previously weight transfer had usually been in free flow. Drawn slowly towards the ground or supported against a vertical wall which displaces the relationship to the ground, the movement follows the weight of the body until, impressively it 'holds its own'. But in Duboc's style, as elsewhere, the weight-flow combination automatically brings with it specific treatments of the other factors. Giving priority to this combination tends firstly to weave a relation of slow, sustained time with the movement of weight held back by an increase of muscle tone. And, in the same way that time can be sensed in the shift of weight, resistance carves a thick space where the body can read its own marks, a receptive space with different tactile properties. In this configuration, movement can create elastic or rigid, soft-edged or liquid spaces according to the qualities at work in the specific distribution of tone and resistance to which its intensification is leading.

The factors appear very different in their reciprocal relations as soon as weight is catapulted into free flow, as is usually the case in Brownian release and also, as we noted above, in most of Duboc's work. There, we can see the gravitational element propelled without restraint into indirect space. Time becomes if not 'sudden' at least (and this is aesthetically stronger) seeming to promise an inevitable acceleration which can be slowed, deferred or otherwise accentuated, phrased in miraculous ways with suspensions and irregular accents. But this acceleration is not of a physical or mechanical order: the laws of falling bodies and their determining impact on the vectors of time and space must be forgotten at the threshold of the body's thought. Trisha Brown's early work with the famous *Equipment Pieces* shows this.[10] As the body works on the very terrain of the law which founds it in order all the better to transform it, it reinvents an existential fall that immediately summons a poetics. That is why one can intervene in (and not on) falling in different ways and according to different objectives. Doris Humphrey, in playing with the flow and time factors, 'declines' a whole series of bound or free falls and contrasting recoveries.

In the very pure work on weight in Contact Improvisation, Steve Paxton allows 'chance' (in the etymological sense of what falls unpredictably) to intervene:[11] which sometimes means allowing the flow to be free, sometimes instead augmenting one's muscle tone a little in order to sharpen one's tactile perception. Contact involves two partners: the idea is to move continually supporting one another, always keeping a point or a plane of contact. The movement is invented, proposed, given and received out of broad waves of mutual support in an improvisation where the subject gives over all initiative to her/his own weight shifts in a gravitational touching of the other's body. Concerning the paths of communication between the two bodies, then, Paxton notes that, *the pathways are better perceived when the muscle tone is a little taut, in order to extend the limbs but not to the point of obscuring the sensations of momentum or inertia.*[12] This light augmentation of tone allows the movement to develop in a soft and continuous rhythm, even if spasms and sudden jumps sometimes disturb this. The relation with time is not alone in being modified: space which seems to be contained between the joined bodies expands on both sides. The dancer's peripheral vision expands. The space dilates around her/him like an undifferentiated milieu where, as Kent de Spain remarks, objects are no longer 'territorialised'.[13] Because the spectator's kinaesthesia is strongly solicited, right down to its gravitational core, s/he very quickly joins this expansion of the visual horizon.

Another exemplary treatment of the four factors is at work in Trisha Brown's *Set and Reset*. There, the release of weight into free flow, a relationship to space of multidimensional simultaneity produces a sudden 'time'. But it is not only time that is in play here, and perhaps not at all. Time is really completely given in changes in the release of weight. The quality of speed that seems to emanate from this piece comes in large part from the presence of impetuses/impulses which release the body into space. The un-controlled catapulting of weight through the body provokes a suddenness which automatically links to the 'sudden' of Laban's effort categories.

Thus the four factors exchange their reciprocal influences and are col-oured in turn as one of them changes. But a factor can also be eliminated. One might ask how. Isn't the dancer always in space and time? Doesn't s/he always have weight and tone? Certainly. But as we have said, the factors are not to be taken as entities or categories as such: Laban and his followers have insisted on the purely relational character of their becoming in our experience. So what is the poetic impact of such elements when our relation to them is cut? The practice of effort-shape allows one of the factors to 'sleep' when we cut off a relation to it, mostly thanks to a certain organisa-tion of the three others. Thus the constellation: sustained time – bound flow – strong weight, as is the case in *Project de la Matière* or in the *Accumulations* of Trisha Brown, abolishes the relation with space. The body dialogues with its own matter/material, its time and its inner fibre. Of course, within a composition or even a phrase, the relations can be exchanged and evolve across an infinite palette of gradations – to which 'effort-shape' gives the lovely name of 'shades'. [14] Clearly, this is the heart of dance poetics where subtle changes of body state invoke the inner lights that, in order to bring forth their innumerable reflections, movement will find in the body's depths.

However fine, however seductive in its applications and poetic ramifica-tions, the theory of the four factors and its exploitation in 'effort-shape' (which, let us not forget, proposes more than a theory of movement, namely, a poetics) might be, it cannot represent for us a moment of absolute finality. It represents an essential step but only a step in the search for 'cho-reographic materials' that are more global and also more disseminated so as to escape fixed frames of adjudication. These 'choreographic materials' fig-ure in our theoretical horizon without our for the moment being able to establish an approach. They may be found less in movements and body states themselves as in the play between them where the 'grain' of a lan-guage is elaborated. (This 'between' of bodies of course cannot be reduced to a topos.) But the four factors themselves have already taught us how much a language is elaborated in the relational network which weaves it-self, ties and unties the elusive textuality which circulates, not only between bodies, but between the whole qualitative array of its mechanisms. Only a considerable corporeal and philosophical labour to renew theoretical tools will allow us to advance towards the unknown along a path that contempo-rary dance has been down so many times before: to set free the always luminous modes of practice (more than of representation) and without ever pre-determining what the end point of a research might be, without ever allowing a limit to be set. Once again, far from simply providing a scaffolding, the theory of contemporary dance is called upon to redraw/withdraw, sometimes to move the frontiers of its fields of exploration. As if the dancing body were already working the sensitive territories where awareness can gradually be awakened and can recognise the anticipated traces of it own discoveries.

1 Nancy, J-L. *Le poids du corps*, 1995.

2 A formulation of Irmgard Bartenieff and Dori Lewis in *Body Movement: coping with the environment*, 1980.

3 Laban, R. *Effort* (with F.C. Lawrence), 1947. Theory developed in *The Mastery of Movement*, 1971.

4 Cunningham, Merce 'Space, Time, Dance' in *Merce Cunningham: Dancing in Space and Time*, 1992, p.38.

5 Humphrey, Doris *The Art of Making Dances*, 1959.

6 Durand, Gilbert *Structure anthropologique de l'imaginaire*, 1969, pp. 127-146.

7 Godard, H. 'Singular moving geographies', 1996, p. 19.

8 Rouquet, Odile *La tête aux pieds*, 1991, p. 79.

9 Bainbridge-Cohen, Bonnie. *Sensing Feeling and Action*, 1993.

10 For a description of Brown's *Equipment Pieces*, including the famous *A Man Walking Down the Side of a Building* (1968), see the photographic commentaries of Sally Sommer in Kirby, Michael. 'The New Theatre, Performance Documentation', in *The Drama Review*, in T. 55, Sept. 1972, pp. 135-141.

11 In French *chanceler* means to totter or stagger. (Transl.)

12 Paxton, Steve. 'Contact Improvisation' in *Dance as a Theatre Art*, 1974.

13 De Spain, K. 'More Thoughts on Science and the Improvising Mind' in *Contact Quarterly*, Winter-Spring, 1994.

14 Bartenieff, I. & Lewis, D., *Body Movement*, 1980.

The Poetics of Movement

It is in a sense another way of 'thinking', but one that produces ideas that are impossible to conceive in stillness.
Kent de Spain[1]

First, a question of terminology: in the case of dance ought we to speak of 'movement' or 'gesture'? Isabelle Launay has already posed this question but it is one worth returning to in order to develop further its problematics.[2] Dancer, Sylvie Giron, brings the essential function of both terms together under the theme of 'engagement': *It is unsettling to realise that a gesture, a movement engages everything.*[3] What is most important in movement (*le geste*), to use an idea dear to Bartenieff, is its capacity to 'mobilise'. Indeed, for her, the smallest shift of weight made by a disabled person, requiring as it does the mobilisation of the whole being, is as intense, rich and moving as a dance. This reminds us that the 'charge' of a movement depends neither on the nature of the movement, nor its amplitude but upon what it engages. That is where we find its poetic depth. Even if, as is often the case in the best French dance, we are dealing with movements that are very soft (Stéphanie Aubin for example), consciously unaccentuated and light. Poetic engagement is present, even if it is treated in a negative mode as in the unaccented movements of the Judson Church period (Steve Paxton's *Transit* and Rainer's *Trio A*, for example, used 'marked' movements). Outside of the whole self's engagement in a movement other considerations are peripheral. Janet Adshead toyed with a morphological approach in terms of a series of forms that she regards as fundamental: curves, twists, etc.[4] But in the end she renounces these in favour of Laban's system for describing 'action' in the famous inventory he made to catalogue the exemplary 'effort' combinations.

The reader will pardon this terminological digression. It is just that the different uses of the terms 'gesture' and 'movement' have brought together some preoccupations (or even aesthetic perceptions) which are of some importance in dance thought. In common usage, the word gesture has an intention, and a life, while movement could just as well be the result of a human 'automatism' or come from an animated object or non-human mechanism. It could also be said that 'movement' concerns the whole body, and that 'gesture' is more fragmentary, visibly at least, making movement more global, closer to posture and thus to an unconscious charge which is more interesting poetically than a segmentary gesture which is 'decided' and clearly 'emitted'. It is true that gesture in the sense of movement involving only a part of the body has more to do with the extremities, and does not affect the proximal zones considered as non-signifying and which, as we have already noted, in fact produce the profound sensibility of contemporary dance. But the extremities can also be made non-signifying: hands, legs can become a means whereby movement arising elsewhere in the body is propagated or expunged. *The hand is divested of a past, of the sensory experiences that would have affected it. There it is, still there and then suddenly it isn't any more. It never becomes. As though it were possible to believe in a virgin expressive act, an act without memory*, writes Elizabeth Schwartz about Merce Cunningham's hands.[5]

But as we have seen, this 'bleaching' of the areas traditionally reserved for a more or less 'extra' expressivity or ornamentation (the face and hands) was at work from the beginning of modernity. *The hand, the wrists are not ornaments, but the completion of the breathed central movement, they complete a movement integrated into a whole form. They participate in articulating the movement language* (langage gestuel).[6] This retreat from the specialisation of the hands and the arms can be found in the strange closed arm movements of Doris Humphrey. The arm and hand movements which are so present in the work of Dominique Bagouet have a very different genealogy: the whole body ends in them, as in the 'body parts' which, for Alwin Nikolais, receive the 'travelling centre,' the journey of the centre as Carolyn Carlson also teaches it. One of the most opaque elements of Bagouet's language has been his moving the centre around, making it an enigma that touches us lightly, a movement containing its own questioning and enclosing its own mystery. No less fine and enigmatic are Dana Reitz's dancing fingers – a whole weighted play inspired by t'ai chi with, as Deborah Jowitt writes, *many quiet looping hand gestures close to the body ...*[7]

In fact, this description is of whole body movements but applied only to a tiny organisational unit. One could therefore say that 'gesture,' expresses 'posture' on an extremely clear enunciatory level – the two concepts being nevertheless opposed in the movement analysis of numerous theoreticians.[8] 'Gesture' is above all the visible emanation of an invisible corporal genesis, but it carries the full intensity of the whole body.

Remember Martha Graham's beautiful expression in her *Notebooks*: *Movement is the seed of gesture*. To finish with definitions: Laban and Nikolais, in turn, found a possible solution in a third term. In the '30s, Laban began to prefer the idea of 'action' to that of movement – and even sometimes 'act'. In the framework of *Tanztheater*, the dancer-agent thus inhabits the realm of human acts and thus of history. 'Gesture' here, in some respects like the Brechtian 'gestus', indicates not only gesture as an accomplished act but also the 'geste' or 'la geste' – the Medieval verse chronicle – an utterance (*énoncé*) situating the event in the evolution of the human community (for Brecht in the dialectic of history). Nikolais on the other hand brings together in the concept of 'motion' conscious movement and an awareness *of* the movement. *The art of dance is the art of 'motion' not of 'movement'...*[9] Motion is conscious movement but first and foremost a consciousness of the movement: consciousness of the path, of all the paths whether through the whole body or just the ends of the fingers, whether visible or invisible. Movement is 'motion' in terms of undergoing one's own experience. There is 'dance' when this experience of a being-in-movement, the qualities and modes of its surrendering to motion holds sway over all other parameters, be they action or artistic creation. *If I take two hours to lift my hand to my head'*, the master wrote in jest, *'it may be terribly boring but it will be dance.*[10] This humorous remark is also profound: dance as the poetics of movement is so not by its originality, nor by its spatio-temporal configuration but by the intensity of the experience which carries it (and which it can transmit). In this regard, the example cited by Nikolais reveals a judicious choice: the slow elevation of the hand towards the top of the head is not only devoid of a functional end point and is thus by definition expressive, but by its slowness and unfolding it is perfectly metaphorical of what a pathway is that can engage a whole corporeal awareness: a sense of weight and attentive awareness to what is happening. Murray Louis has a convincing sequence in his film *Motion*: we see a trivial gesture (lifting the hand to scratch the head) literally transfigured into an artistic act simply by his attentiveness to the experience as it occurs.[11]

As Jacqueline Robinson rightly points out, for the first time in history modern dance allowed the individual to find her/his own movement. *A profoundly original movement,* according to Hubert Godard.[12] This has led not only to existing vocabularies being discarded but has meant that it is obligatory to do so. In this regard, dance belongs to a whole modern project involving each creator in reinventing an entirely personal language (even if, today, this horizon of a personal language can seem like an illusion dependent upon a modernist utopia). With Maurice Blanchot, we understand it more as an 'exigency' (a hope) than as an actual fact.[13] In dance, inventing a language no longer only means manipulating pre-existing material, but giving birth to this material while justifying it artistically, if not theoretically. It is clear that for dance, the art of movement, the genesis of material particular to the artist, poses different, deeper problems which are riskier to raise and confront in the sense that movement, tied to the history of the subject, to her/his very identity, claims freedom and independence by tearing itself from the social institution of the body. The social weighs much more upon the inhibition and regulation of human conduct than it does on the pure invention of forms and substances in the world of the representational arts. In this regard, it is not surprising that the inventors of dance modernity, like Isadora Duncan, needed to be personally rebellious, or to look for support from aesthetic currents grounded in violent individual resistance, as was the case with the German dancers who joined and were encouraged by expressionism, the Die Brücke movement in Dresden, and the Dadaism of the cabaret Voltaire and the gallery Dada in 1915-16.

One of the main provocative strategies of the Laban school was to de-sacralise the so-called 'beauty' of sanctioned movements by trivialising them in an exaggerated way. Thus, they joined forces with artists involved in the gallery Dada who denounced western culture and its traditions seen to be obsolete and ridiculous. We can understand Arp's and Hugo Ball's admiration for the sudden new developments of a nameless body which were much more transgressive than the nihilistic deconstruction of art objects (whether poems or paintings), because the transgression was by and on the subject her/himself. If Sophie Tauber's choreography at the gallery Dada (*The Song of the Sea-Horses and flying fish* around 1917) was *inventive, capricious, bizarre*, if *each movement was decomposed into one hundred sharp cuts*, its admirer Hugo Ball was himself moved to participate in a Labanian dance deliberately debased by *symmetrical movements, a rigid rhythm, and bad mimicry that were ugly on purpose* (Hugo Ball writing about the gallery Dada exhibition organised by the journal *Der Sturm*, and about a performance with Marcel Janco, Kandinsky, and Laban's dancers based on an idea of Kokoschka).

Without the solidarity of dancers coming together around a common thought, without their alliance to the political and artistic avant-gardes, the artists of dance modernity would have been condemned to an isolation like that of Nijinsky who lost the support of his milieu once he sought to free his body from all canonical regulation – a move which in every society constitutes a serious act of alienation from the collective codes in which the congruity or the meaning/sense of a movement summons the recognition of the group. Laban and Mauss remind us that treason in respect of the movement community is the worst sign of non-conformism (even more than linguistic dissidence). The fact that the body represents or symbolises the social body only aggravates the situation. Because, here, the subject is not content to distance only her/his own movement from the common law: the spectator's body is also compromised and threatened with an analogous journey. This is the reason for the 'modernity of the body' having been condemned even recently, and, as it was even more violently, in the first half of the century.[14] One German audience was disgusted by Wigman's solos in 1919-1920: *a sickly frenetics...an imbecilic dislocation of her movements* (the horrified reaction even of certain intellectuals).[15] The Parisian intelligentsia were also revolted by Valeska Gert when she appeared at the Théâtre des Champs-Elysées in 1931.[16] Gert, who came from the Berlin cabarets and occasionally performed with political artists like Huelsenbeck, was particularly significant in contributing to the radical decomposition of the socially constituted body. The celebrated brawl between André-Breton and Yvan Goll shows how a body's unintelligibility can perturb even those apparently inclined towards 'disquieting reality'.

Invention and, of course, courage: modernity in dance is an adventure. It is also an opening – to all possible movements where none are forbidden: an enlargement at least as revolutionary in relation to the human past as the first emancipatory moves discussed above. In fact, traditionally, dance is an art which has consisted in selecting from the mass of motor possibilities a certain number of authorised forms. Contrary to a common perception of dance as an art involving a greater range of movement than that of everyday life, according to the laws of tradition it is, on the contrary, an art of subtraction which offers, said Laban, *a restricted gamut of authorised motifs.*[17] It involves a process of restriction whose end is, of course, to distribute and order systems of representation. Dance as a 'technique of the body' to use Mauss's expression, but also as an art, according to the anthropologist Judith Lynne Hanna, consists of a *system of classifying movement, a cumulative set of rules, or a gamut of allowed motor motifs.*[18] Obviously, the immediate question for interested anthropologists or dance ethnographers is to find the criteria which have brought about this selection and hence the restriction. This is a succinct approach, and the one taken by anthropologists like Hanna or Alan Lomax. Without wanting to disqualify their serious and revealing work it is important to recognise that they do not have the acuity of Laban's analyses and those of his disciples for whom the relation between movement and the social context involves a deeper dynamic and cannot be described simply in terms of mimetic forms. Without wishing to pre-empt this kind of analysis of movement's constituents, it is possible to identify a significant invariance amongst those, especially in the United States, who have been interested in the relations between dance and anthropology: they have privileged locomotion as the individual body language by means of which, within a social group, symbolic force is brought into relation with a productivity or value that the group recognises: for example, the turning and advancing rows of some Amazonian dances are related to sowing seeds in the temporary rainforest gardens.[19] These are the orderly line dances which pivot on an axis. They are sublime in their refined simplicity. For in these spatio-motor selections there is always extreme beauty, whichever ones a group chooses. What is so moving in traditional dances, from the triplets of the bourrée to the pelvic undulation of the Solomon Islanders? It is their obvious power to attain an essential goal in poignant and mysterious ways, to touch a pertinent and 'just' objective as a reply to the question of a human group. Traditional so-called 'learned' (*savantes*) dances (which are not always more so than certain popular ones) sharpen the broader selections theoretically, canonically, educationally redistributing them more systematically, rationalising the structures within which they are judged (what they gain in visibility and guarantee of technical permanence, they often lose in force and emotional quality...). In full awareness of this heritage and above all of the human charge attached to it, the moderns were nonetheless moved in a very different direction. We have seen that individual invention, often as a break from the values of the group (and at the expense of being rejected by it) was their fate, more than their vocation. This awareness meant that *all* possible movements could be part of this individual creative universe: individual creativity would treat them according to its own poetics. But how to find the immense fund of unknown movements? *How to extract from dance its movements?* Christine Bastin asks the question today in relation to poetry as the rising up of words within language.[20] But the dancer knows only too well that her/his dance as language (as a coherent ensemble and referential code) does not exist, that no secondary system of articulation can stand for or hold back the movement that must be torn from what s/he does not know in her body.

For us, two steps at the inception of contemporary dance are important: that of Etienne Dalcroze and then of Rudolf Laban. Dalcroze, in searching in the body for the basis of rhythm, wanted to free the body from mastery, to return to it an uncontrolled vitality through the will of unbounded movement. It is enough that my centre of energy be touched in a 'rhythmic' situation (i.e. involving accent or contrast) for desire in me to loosen and for the cohort of motor reactions to rise up tumultuously. They have no form. They have no name. Dalcroze quickly understood that he had touched something fundamental; like a vast hidden reserve of all possible corporealities. But he didn't want to make an aesthetic. His 'rhythmic' vision was not dance, because he refrained from elaborating a symbolic system of representation out of the material he had identified. Even if, today, this undifferentiated corporeal ground appears, clearly, to be the most radical constituent of modernity in dance.

Then Laban opened up and multiplied movement possibilities from the infinite ways of organising the transfer of weight. As soon as weight, the least objectifiable and least figurable element, enters the domain of art it becomes possible to escape all the Apollonian structures of mimesis governing established forms and their representation-reproduction. We witness equally the death of all limitations in dance. Danced movement knows no bounds, neither in its form, organisation or scale. The concept of a kinesphere containing all possible movements, the space that the body carries with it, or better, where it constructs and constitutes itself, is the coming together of all possible motor events in which all modes of weight transfer, all qualities or tensional orientations are distinguished. Laban, of course, was to classify them through his 'scales' but he never sought their closure or codification. On the contrary, the icosahedron, the twenty-sided polygon which crystallises the multiple dynamics into possible directions, is the volumetric form of an infinity of possible movements which, if they could each be analysed in their different qualities, would never be bounded by a specific organisation, or formal mould from which their very degree of potentiality wrests them.[21]

Within the immense corpus which, as Isadora Duncan has said, has always existed, there are of course erratic movements which we carry in ourselves and which often inhabit other movements without being completely revealed through them. They are, amongst others, the 'phantom movements' about which Laban spoke so wonderfully. We will return to these enigmatic horizons of gesture and to movement's reading of its own unknown. But how precisely to make their existence visible? As we have said, contemporary dance does not exclude any movements. And life is already inhabited by movements as an immense storehouse of possible forms. In daily life we use two types of movements: fundamental movements, which are universal acts necessary to any animate and animal conduct in the world – getting up or down, walking, jumping, hopping and skipping, stretching out, falling, stamping – forms that the pioneers of modern dance, like Duncan, hastened to integrate into their choreographic language, giving them a status equal to that of any 'artistic' movement. The simple walk, going down to the ground, the jump, the hop were part of a vocabulary which she mixed with other movements regarded as less 'natural' (accented steps, curves and arches of the body). Later dancers would add other fundamental forms more related to social and material life: crouching, sitting etc. as Cunningham often does with a chair. It is important to note that in this use of fundamental movements there is rarely a 'miming' of common utilitarian gestures. The latter, as we will see, constitute a second group of everyday movements that stay attached to their utility or to 'reproduction'. The fundamental movements, specifically, are the object of a deep research since they connect to what is most ancient in the phylogenesis of our behaviours. Very early in the history of contemporary dance they were, firstly, questioned in order that their real dynamics might be grasped. For modernity in dance often consists in questioning what seems given or inscribed in the body. Thus, in Duncan's teaching, walking was studied practically and aesthetically for several months at the beginning of the dancer's training. In France, Elizabeth Schwartz's performance of a long walk forward to the chorus of *Iphigenia in Aulis* by Gluck is a very clear example. In this apparently elementary 'walk' (*marche*), a Dalcrozian rhythmic approach has allowed the primary forms of mobility to be perceived. Françoise Dupuy recalls its elements: *Doesn't the dance begin at the moment when this walk is mastered in time, space and energy so that it can say something else than the simple daily identity of the one who walks it or whom it walks?... Anyone who dances must control the support of the foot on the ground, the way the foot is left behind and the way it suspends the body which it supports and which supports it.*[22] Support, elevation, suspension: aren't these essential elements in dance's fund of poetic tools? This way of revisiting the oldest and most basic of our movements contains, of course, an important theoretical dimension.

Sometimes it is the actual use of fundamental movement which constitutes the field of investigation – but in order to identify this movement and disengage it from the symbolic forms in which it was found. Thus, keeping the example of the walk, Michèle Rust claims the *camminar* of tango as a fundamental element of dance, and therefore regards this historically and choreographically important dance as one of the most pertinent treatments of the major basic movements. But another area of research consists in tracing back, beyond its contemporary 'mechanics', a primitive form that has been lost or transformed. Thus, in a well-know text, Laban has our movements originating in two archetypes from which all the articulations of human movements have flowed: the 'gathering' or concentric movement of bringing an object towards the self; and the 'scattering' which puts distance between the subject and its object.[23] According to Laban, these two movements have existed since the beginning of human experience in order to assure the satisfaction of both need and defence: these movements remain inscribed in us, they inhabit all other movements which are only variations adapted to other circumstances. These two archetypal movements reveal the first framework of tensional axes on which the body constructs itself in space (extension, nucleation, *Spannung* and *Ballung*), building and producing what he calls the 'kinesphere'.

All the movements of daily life not only flow as so many variations from these two antithetical forms but the different dances of the world are examples of their different treatment. Their symbolic and artistic interest is measured in terms of the degree of pertinence of this treatment. Subsequently, other approaches to fundamental movements have been proposed in other theoretical frameworks: in France, for example, there is the work of Pierre Philippon, who classifies movements according to a range of principle actions: throwing, pushing, cutting etc. and who has undertaken a practical investigation into the structure and function of this body language (*gestuelle*). It seems, in fact, that every action to come out of these motor channels derives from an ensemble of foundational behaviours. What is the difference between a fundamental and an everyday movement? For many dancers and in many currents of dance, none. What the English speakers call 'pedestrian movement' includes movements taken from life outside of any defined choreographic context. All these movements have in common a 'natural' amplitude and an absence of accentuation which gives them the discrete, atonal character that in our culture characterises everyday movements. It is also this quality that they were keen to show in dance. Often movements created choreographically and thus not 'everyday' i.e. not functional movements, are meant to have the qualities that avoid the emphasis of danced movement. This can be seen in the small hand movements common with French dancers – a way of toning down the musicalised and amplified dimension of danced movement. Often this retreat from the dancerly can been seen as a refusal in dance itself to take hold of space and to 'take off' (*l'envol*).

Personally, I define everyday movement according to the use made of it, which as a result can change its quality and reach. On stage, Merce Cunningham walks, sits down, runs and even gets undressed (in *Walkaround Time*, 1968). But these movements (apart from the walking to get to a place in the dance) are without objective, they are intransitive as much as elementary. Alwin Nikolais's remarks about 'motion' are useful here especially in distinguishing between theatre and dance. 'Mimesis' requires that codes of recognition are in place without concern for the qualities that are undergone. Dance is the study of the distribution of transfer of weight, accenting etc., and consequently it also uncovers the fundamental qualities of an action, and escapes naturalism: for the dancer cutting, striking, throwing are essential schemas whose tenor should be analysed in relation to a knowledge of the action's roots. The difference in approach between theatre and dance is not so much a question of definition as of practice, as we will see. From this it is possible to appreciate the 'work of dance' which interrogates the tenor of an action from its foundations.

A interesting problem posed by Foster for dance semiology generally and its relation to theatre is the mode of performing movements of 'reflection' and 'imitation', what I call 'acted' (*joué*) movements which are more theatrical, involve heightened accents, greater muscle tone and larger gestures and contain nothing of the 'pedestrian'.[24] The 'pedestrian' is what interests us by its atonal quality, its raw, material aspect, its 'found' quality as the partisans of 'junk art' would say, like the rubbish Rauschenberg used in his works in the way that Cunningham mixed commonplace movements with dance: visibility's waste, movements whose theatrical intensity has been evacuated; 'flat' movements whose original function has been abolished, devitalised, relegated to a symbolic limbo. Another interesting perspective comes from some of Karin Waehner's improvisations which involve de-naturalising everyday movements by slowing them down, giving them a spatial resistance, creating a different, non-mimetic experience of gesture. This transformation of movement can be effected with the help of objects, themselves lifted from the practical environment of which they are a part; or otherwise becoming part of a body process that makes the context un-readable. One of the most beautiful everyday movements, flattened and faded, without accentuation and amplification with its particularly com-monplace, intimate and non-spectacular contents, a non-gesture in its very triviality, is that of Susanne Linke's sitting on the toilet seat in *Im Bade wannen*. She does it naturalistically, but how carefully non-mimetic (and ambiguous) it is in a solo where all the other bathroom objects, the bathtub, the sliding screen and her self-inspection are used non-naturalistically. But the everyday *'geste'* figures less in the chosen *vocabularies*, or lexicons of contemporary dance than in the degree and perspective in which it is treated. Besides, introducing everyday and fundamental movements purely as lexical elements is part of neoclassical processes. Amongst such liberated and obviously inventive artists we can cite the mechanical or frankly pedes-trian movements of Massine's *Parade* – at least as far as we can tell from the Joffrey Ballet's reconstruction made with the help of the choreographer's own memory. We could also cite Nijinsky's *Jeux,* and his sister Bronislava's audacious *Train Bleu* which integrates flirting gestures, daily life and sport. There is also Balanchine's mysterious *Ivesiana* to Charles Ives's wonderful score, *Central Park in the dark*, with its final sequence where the dancers come forward on their knees as though on a pilgrimage to the obscure gods of an urban night. The pedestrian quality of non-qualified, disconnected movements is absolute here. In spite of the artistic reverence we give to these inspired geniuses, we owe it to ourselves out of pure respect for the identity of their project not to integrate them after the event into the project of contemporary dance. Such was neither their choice nor orientation. Eve-ryday movements included in a contemporary work entail, as we have said, certain ongoing purposes, not in terms of a motif or recognisable form but in terms of the theoretical and practical function that can be made of them in the broader economy of a poetics and a process. And, above all, the role given them must exceed their simple exploitation for spectacular or short-term gains.

Everyday movements are used in contemporary dance according to the different characteristics determining the double orientation discussed by Foster: 'imitated' or 'invented' movement. When a Pina Bausch dancer sits or crosses her/his legs s/he 'imitates' a 'real' movement and is thus 'acting' (*jouer*). Furthermore, the flow of the movement is intense and this usually indicates the presence of acting (*jeu*). We are, as Jean-Louis Schefer notes, in the realm/regime of representation which is by definition that of the excessive.[25] Bausch's movement is thus not at all used in the same way as Anne Teresa de Keersmaeker's in *Rosas danst Rosas* or still less Merce Cunningham's in *Antic Meet*. With Bausch, even if the movement is imitative in the first instance, as Michèle Febvre has remarked, it is always de-naturalised, interrupted or transformed (Jo-Anne Endicott spitting out each piece of apple that she nevertheless seems to want to eat in *Walzer*).[26] And again in *Walzer*, the famous arm movement procession of the two lines of men and women. Each sex performs caressing movements that were initially made in couples and which now, without the object of their embrace, become pure movement constructions, and because they are deprived of their object (and executed rhythmically and thus accented differently) they are completely non-figurative.

From this we can see that the use of everyday movement is worth studying as long as it can be discussed within a precise treatment or aesthetic. Under these conditions its qualities in terms of composition or symbolic complexity hardly differentiate it from any other 'dancerly' or invented, non-functional movement. Even its mimetic quality can at each instant be redoubled and overcoded or otherwise emptied, interrupted and transformed. Further, it can be coloured by all the expressive 'range of gears' and, for today's dancer, does not have an artistic value superior or inferior to a movement that might be purely poetic. Everyday movement has been used, for example, in the experimental, aesthetically minimalist dances of the Judson Church to create a non-intensified, unaccented, flat and neutral movement consonant with the theory – relevant also to the sculpture of Judd or Bob Morris – of a neutral enunciation from which all tension, all desire for intentional or categorical brandishing are banished. Taking off one's clothes to go to bed, sweeping, making coffee, opening and closing doors are interesting from a double point of view: they come close to non-dance, a dance of pure action without an objective, still less seeking any choreographic 'effect', close to performance art where movement is not accomplished for its 'tenor' but is simply utilitarian in the sense of accomplishing a precise action: crossing the room to join a partner (Klaus Rinke), to gauge the terrible slenderness of the vital space (Acconci), to affirm a journey taken (Joan Jonas), or undertake a compulsive repetition (Bruce Naumann); as Alwin Nikolais describes so well, these are movements accomplished uniquely in view of their terminal phase. They are only important in being done, their conclusion conferring on them the desired finality and banality. We are at the opposite of his vision of motion – movement produced and sensed in the totality of its unfolding and where each succeeding phase is of equal importance in a full and whole awareness of one's own qualitative experience (a possible definition of 'motion'). De-intentionalised, quotidian movement is akin to a danced movement that is also emptied of all 'tension'. Thus, in his already cited composition, *Transit*, Steve Paxton (at the age of twenty) simply 'marked' his choreography. By 'marking' – a rehearsal activity of going over the material but not 'full-out' – dancers mean doing the form without expending the energy. This shows how this current of contemporary dance put all of the givens of dance into question, including those that seem most fundamental such as, for example, the presence and intensity of being that it requires. Yvonne Rainer denounced the excessive, contorted aspect of dance action ('Why must we be so intense?' she asks ironically). *Transit* which used non-figurative movement was a 'non-dance' as much as the dances of pedestrian movements. For what counts in the definition of a dance movement in the absence of any dynamic quality is above all an awareness of its qualitative components. Fundamentally, movement in itself is nothing. Non-dance was in fact a hyperdance, for it renounced the superficial character of forms in order to make visible, even if negatively and by its absence, the (non-) intensity through which, alone, our movement exists.

By contrast (perhaps) French dance of the eighties developed what has been called 'graphic' movement: a small fragmented motif without real functionality, mainly in the extremities. Much could be said about this fragmentation which has now been abandoned. Was it a refusal to compose a whole body, influenced perhaps by the risk of an overexposure from which this movement became an elusive, fleeting and, above all, detached strategy of retreat? Was it a way of regulating emotion, blocking it in a smooth seamless aesthetic from which any attempt to breach the integrity of the whole body could be deflected? Was it the fear of excess common at a period whose ideology is still to be discussed? Often, too, the inability amongst classically trained dancers to work off-centre, and for whom a fragmented gesture was the only resource for distorting or disarticulating a too homogenous body? A way (illusory perhaps) of creating a spiral where there was only a pillar. We can only hazard a few interpretations about such a recent period as tentative approaches to a blind spot (if only because it still concerns deeply the history of our own body, and the discourse which is still at work on it and its schema, and probably its unconscious image.)

But first, we must consider the 'little movement' in the work of those (Daniel Larrieu, Dominique Bagouet) who introduced it and who gave it its *raison d'être*. There is a big difference between their poignant vision of a universe limited to the flowering of a discreet, contracting space where interiority and inner emotion are constantly questioned, and the purely formal mimetics of their followers who were most often involved with the edges of the body, as though at the edge of intention. The 'little movement' provided an opening through displacements of scale. Firstly, its visible size is not necessarily what determines its real trajectory: an even apparently restricted movement involves the whole body. From Feldenkrais to Bartenieff, movement theories teach us that the smallest modulation rises up from the deepest heart of a whole. For Bartenieff, the dispositions of the scapulae give all their colouring to the slightest movements of the fingers. To return to Bagouet's hand movement, it often functions to draw our attention to space: at the beginning of *Assaï* the 'two acrobats' turn their palms to one another as though to open a space between them, to give it continuity and mobility. As intense sites where the elements of touch are gathered, the extremities can be charged with a greater tactile value, creating poetic and sensuous links with direction and duration: like so many touches or caresses. Or it is their power to feel the skin of things; and this can spread out over the whole body in a 'dance of the skin'.[27] The dancer's body becomes a tactile organ, where every fold or crease possesses the sensitivity of the most perceptive of the phalanges or the most attentive lips. Small or large movements then fold and refold sensations according to multiple prisms across all sections, all sides of the kinesphere. Since, in dance, the question is principally one of organising movement in different qualitative modalities and analysing it as such, it has been necessary to elaborate perspectives of reception or interpretation which, in turn, can become reasoned and analytic springboards for creation.

According to Laban's theory of the four factors, movement in fact engages in concert both time and space. But using elements that are movement's alone: the body's weight, the intensity of tonic function. With weight being the essential element identified by Laban and contemporary dance more generally, a hierarchy of aesthetic evaluation was immediately instituted: anything that allowed weight itself to have the greatest initiative was closest to the poetic project of dance modernity. In their quality of 'letting go,' of dropping or mobilising uncontrolled weight with its own energy, the dances of Duncan, Palucca, Hoyer, Humphrey, Limón, Hawkins, Andrews, Brown, Paxton will always be the strongest poetically because they are dominated by weightedness. Weight, then, as primary, then flow (or tonic variation), space and time are not givens in themselves: once again, they are not originary. Nothing exists unless it is engaged relationally. Hence, at the end of Laban's life, the work of movement, or movement as work, becomes the mechanism of weight displacement and what he calls 'effort'. If the first period of Laban's work during which he elaborated his first system of notation – cinetography – insisted on the relations between the Four Factors, the second theoretical and notional approach elaborated in England after his exile from Nazi Germany departs from this. At this time, he recognised the 'work' of movement as the motor of all symbolising – in dance, but also in the movements of artisanal or industrial production (would dance again be the most effective mode of escaping from 'representation'?). Hence an astonishing new interpretation of movement, not as development of a dynamic but as the mechanism of its emergence. 'Effort' referred not to the movement but to the 'attitude towards the movement' (according to Bartenieff, the transposition of the German '*Antreib*'). In a sense, 'effort shape' theory gives us modes of instrumentation that are well 'upstream' of the instrumentation itself. It is also not irrelevant that Julia Kristeva conceives a (rhythmic or poetic) pre-signifying action predisposing the subject to engage in language.[28] In dance, this 'palette of gears' is as important to the perception as it is to the production of movement. Hubert Godard particularly insists on this. He confers a poetic importance, more charged than ever in the context of current dance, on this space of preparation. He develops the idea of the 'anacrusis' as the spring of movement, an inverted spring (an inhibition of tonus without which no movement can occur) which 'colours' the movement's whole projection. Furthermore, Godard sees there a privileged structure for linking movement to the semantic, an interstice where the essence of a movement can, in contrast to many of its other forms, name itself.[29] This very important aspect of the 'pre-movement' is not unconnected to the visualisation processes found in the corporeal thinking of modernity. For Feldenkrais, the most active movements, those that are connected most closely to the metamorphosis of the individual, are the interior or minimal movements commanded by the imaginary.[30] The visualisation that anticipates a movement to come already designs bodily paths and intensities.[31] Movement, then, enriches itself in the inner journey which brings it forth for an instant into the visible. Can one speak of a 'before of movement'? No, because at this extreme point of a poetic apprehension there is no longer a question of anteriority or posteriority in a linear understanding that might dry up the sensuous wealth of the experience. But rather of being displaced with the dancer in the meanders of these gearings. This is how Bartenieff perceived not only dancers but human life in general, catching in passing, in the ceaseless adjustment of gears connecting us to the world, the inner music in each of us. Her reading of 'the inner impulse to move' makes her attentive to these movements all around us. *Even before any visible manifestation one could see the inner impulses working on the preparations,* she said of an infant running in the street: *First, an inner impulse towards the space and whatever was in it around him. Then, towards the sense of his own weight and force, an intention towards a goal. Third, of time as the urgency of deciding. All these preparations interacted with the flow of movement whose fluctuations varied between freedom and control. Such internal investments offer a combination of kinesthetics and analysis which appeared simultaneously along several registers of awareness.*[32] This text not only calls attention to the adjustment of the impulses to the 'Four Factors' but it makes clear the finely woven complexity of the phases of preparation where movement emerges at the crossroads between desire and knowledge of the context. It is in this multiple qualitative opening that one can then follow the transfer of the body's weight as the operator of a cognitive and sensuous space of play which is its own. One can see that perception, or better still, the poetic apprehension of danced movement, pertains to the interpretation of all movement. As the mobilisation of being. As the expression of a desire to be at work in the world which, even if it passes unnoticed, has nevertheless made its mark upon the great palimpsestic book of human intention. Dance is nothing but the site which gives visibility to this inestimable and immemorial deposit.

    But the contemporary move does not only receive an already there. It must, primordially, clear a path for all the as yet unknown movements. So-called 'authentic movement' practised today in the United States seeks to enable this movement unknown to the dancer and to us and which does not yet have a model or real criteria of existence to emerge from the dancer's body. It is a technique recalling Alwin Nikolais's theory of the 'unique movement', a movement as untoward as it is completely necessary, which no pre-given form can define and which sleeps in the body's imaginary until the power of the work of dance reveals its sudden emergence.

1 In 'A Moving Decision: Notes on the improvising mind' in *Contact Quarterly*, Vol.20, No.1, 1995.

2 Launay, Isabelle. 'La danse entre geste et mouvement' in *La danse, art du XXe siècle*. (Actes du colloque), 1990

3 Giron, Sylvie. in *L'oeil dansant*, edited by Laurent Barré. Centre National Chorégraphique de Tours, 1995.

4 Adshead, Janet 'Discerning the form of a dance' in *Dance Analysis: Practice and Theory*. 1988.

5 Schwarz, Elizabeth. *L'expressivité de la main en danse contemporaine*. Mémoire for the Diplôme d'Etat in Kinésiologie, IFEDEM, 1994 (unpublished).

6 Ibid.

7 Jowitt, Deborah. 'Calligrapher in Dance' in *The Dance in Mind: Profiles and Reviews 1976-83*, 1985, pp.182-183.

8 Parallel with the work of psychologists like Henri Wallon on postural tone, the Laban tradition observed and opposed 'posture' and 'gesture': work which links anthropologists like Warren Lamb (*Posture and Gesture: an Introduction to the Study of Human Behaviour*, 1965) to Laban Movement Analysis. Today, Hubert Godard continues this reflection on postural tone in the emergence of danced movement. (Cf. Bibliography)

9 Nikolais, A. *Dance Perspective*. No. 48, 1970.

10 Ibid.

11 *Motion* is one of a series of four films called *The Art of Dance*, made in 1980 by Murray Louis. See also Louis, M. *Inside Dance*, 1981.

12 Godard, Hubert 'Singular Moving Geographies', 1996.

13 Blanchot, Maurice *The Book to Come*, 2003.

14 In 1988 you could still hear contemporary dancers described with complete impunity as *scrapings who dance bare-foot in makeshift theatres* on a national radio station (France-Musique). Recall that the word 'scraping' (*raclure*) was part of the anti-semitic vocabulary of the extreme right in France before 1940 (cited in the catalogue to Sophie Tauber's exhibition, MNAM of the city of Paris, Nov.-Dec. 1990).

15 Comments in the Berlin press during Wigman's tour in 1919-20 and cited by Maggie Odom in 'Mary Wigman: the early years, 1915-25'. *The Drama Review*, 24-IV, December 1980.

16 Fossen, M. (ed.) 'Valeska Gert' in *Empreintes* No. 5, March 1983.

17 Laban, R. *Choreutics*. Posthumous publication by Lisa Ullman, 1966.

18 Hanna, Judith Lynne. *To Dance is Human: A Theory of Non-Verbal Communication*, 1979.

19 Bartenieff, I. with Paulay, F. 'Cross-cultural description of dance' in *Four adaptations of effort theory*, op.cit. Cf also Lange, R. *The Nature of Dance*, 1975.

20 Bastin, Christine. *Mon Oeil*, no. 11, publication of the Compagnie Christine Bastin, 1996.

21 Laban, R. *Mastery of Movement*, 1971.

22 Dupuy, Françoise. 'Pas de danse' in *Marsyas*, No. 18, Paris, IPMC, June 1991.

23 Laban. R. *The Mastery of Movement*, 1971.

24 Foster, S. *Reading Dancing*, 1986.

25 Schefer, Jean-Louis. 'Figures de mutants' in *Traffic*, No.1, 1989.

26 Febvre, Michéle *Danse Contemporaine et Théâtralité*, 1995.

27 Dupuy, D. 'Danser outre' in *Etats de corps, Io: international revue of psychoanalysis*, No.5, Levallois, 1994.

28 Kristeva, Julia *Revolution in Poetic Language*, translated by Margaret Waller, 1984.

29 Godard, H. 'Singular Moving Geographies', 1996.

30 The experience of/with minimal movements is important in the teaching of Feldenkrais: in particular in France with Claude Espinassier. See also Feldenkrais, M. *Awareness through movement*, 1972.

31 Dowd, Irene 'Ideokinesis: the nine lines of movement' in *Contact Quarterly*, Vol. 8, No. 2, 1983.

32 Bartenieff, I. & Lewis, D. *Body Movement: coping with the environment*, 1980.

Styles

The most precious nuances of style can only be understood after a complete study of the rhythmic contents of the attitudes in which combinations of effort are used in specific series.
Laban[1]

Every one of us, says Laban, has a style in the way we relate to the environment or to others. Our daily movements and our treatment of proximal space allow qualitative preferences to appear which not only constitute our relation to the world but, more importantly perhaps, give it an aura. Around every being there is a shimmering that rises from its body and its movements – and which 'composes'. As the halo of an invisible luminosity would. Dancers notice, physically, this variegated bundle of existential registers, which they make use of both in themselves and in others, and which extends them outward enabling them to reach others.

Style in dance seems, a priori, to be something vague and elusive. In fact it is what is most immediately perceived by the spectator, what works most quickly on his or her sensibility. Style is situated well this side of any formal elaboration: it is neither in the vocabulary nor in any of the lexical parameters of choreographic *écriture*, but is at the heart of the functioning of this *écriture*. It is simply the determinant of the paths through which we will capture the 'grain' of movement. The Noh master Zeami speaks of the 'mode' of movement, in the musical sense. But he also speaks of 'style' (with all the necessary reservations in regard to a borrowed term originating in a distant context), of an 'absolute style' without movement: *To make a comparison, it would be the appearance of a bird caught on an updraft. This is what one calls the mode of dance.* [2] This mode or 'absolute style' is thus the very soul of dance. It is aerial, held in suspended latency, at the limits of the mobile and immobile, before and after movement, and thus probably at the heart of movement.

Susan Foster gives several interesting and suggestive definitions of style: the first consists in distinguishing the material in terms of its treatment. Using the example of Martha Graham's language, she observes how Erick Hawkins or Paul Taylor has been able to take elements from it while giving them quite a different coloration. [3] The same could be said of Anna Sokolow, who was perhaps the first to take an already elaborated vocabulary and to use it to convey her own message, without going so far as to re-construct a singular body relevant to this message. In this sense Sokolow is, to our mind, the forerunner of French choreographers who followed in the wake of the '70s and who, in turn, were to make use of ready-to-hand tools for their own projects and dreams. It goes without saying that Sokolow gave the Graham language a more engaged, tragic, more irrational definition than did the original stylistic nuance. Here we find Foster's distinction between language and style: *The style washes over the entire vocabulary of a dance giving it a cultural and individual identity, whereas the vocabulary sets limits on the number and kinds of movements in a given dance and determines their discreteness.* [4] Style here is thus open and expansive, while the idea of vocabulary, even in contemporary dance, remains restrictive. Choreo-

graphic material is still presented as a process of selection – from an infinite
set of possible movements. Foster formulates style on several occasions as
'choice' and thus as the elimination of foreign elements which would
'other' its identity. *Any stylistic choice in dance implies a background of alterna-*
tives rejected in favour of some feature of movement which lends distinctiveness
to, by signifying an identity for, its bearer.[5] Here, style is thus, like vocabulary,
approached in terms of 'preferences'. But preference goes much deeper. It
concerns – in the history of the subject (or of a group) – more secret strata
and also more essential ones: not with what the movement is but what it
inclines towards. Into what sensuous landscapes does it lead us?

For us, Laban's approach to the notion of style in the context of effort-
shape practice and theory constitutes one of the heights of aesthetic
reflection in dance. It requires a total empathy with the other's body and
the sharing of subtle experiences which bind me to all the shades of the
dancer's choices in their slightest manifestations – sometimes in a fleeting
burst on the threshold of a movement, sometimes in the pure being-there of
a movement in its being present to me and to itself. For Laban, as we have
noted, artistic choice does not pass by way of the factual identity of an
element (a constituent of movement or of the movement itself), but in the
relation it establishes. If we examine the four factors (weight, flow, space
and time) we can see that none of them relates to the more usual essential-
ist and substantivist concepts of space and time, etc. 'Effort' (*Antrieb*) theory
is one in which the changing qualities of weight transfer equally inform my
perceptions and my actions. This informing is not a determinism as long as I
do not think of my body in terms of a biological fatalism but rather as the
agent of my symbolic universe whose operations combine to elaborate and
enrich my imaginary and cognitive possibilities. Thus, I situate my identity
through the relations that my mobile weight has to the parameters of experience. This identity is affirmed by my inclinations towards the world and
the character of these relations. Preferences show themselves in the inner
attitudes well before any movement is undertaken: in an inner movement
which carries all the marks of my being and which can emerge (or not)
depending upon what Bartenieff was to theorise as the *inner impulse to move*
where, even before the slightest movement is begun, an incredible quantity
of information and affective dispositions already palpitate.[6] In a way that
can seem a little didactic, Laban has outlined the schemas within which
these possible relational mechanisms are articulated: my relation to space
will be direct or indirect; to time, sudden or sustained; my relation to flow,
free or bound; and weight as a quality (not, obviously, as a quantitative
measurement) will be categorised as light or heavy. Within these param-

eters there exist an unbelievable quantity of overlappings, nuances and possible combinations. No movement is *described* by means of this grid. It is simply 'qualified'. This manner of describing what Laban calls 'style'– that is, our main relational options (through the combination of drives) – seemed to him as time went on much more important than the recording of movement as visible action in space and time. The configuration or outward form of a gesture is unimportant in comparison to the deepest preferences that find their accomplishment in it – to such an extent that Laban's second notation, elaborated in England after his flight from Germany and which was specifically concerned with 'effort,' only deals with the qualitative mechanisms connected to inner attitudes. At the end of his life, when exile and the visionary quest for the meaning of movement had distanced him totally from dance, Laban was no longer interested in what the dancer does or 'just the movement', (*le mouvant*) but in what the dancer is in his movement, and even 'on this side of' the movement, in its pure initiatory phase, when its qualitative shadings are first established.[7]

Indeed, it is especially through the stylistic (qualitative) aspect of these relational mechanisms that a movement, danced or otherwise, carries what Laban calls moral or philosophical 'values' which animate us in the strongest sense of the word. Our thought in movement (and the movement of our thought) does not depend upon any stated intention nor even vocabulary or aesthetic, visually speaking. The 'values' that are borne by our intentions are situated in the margins of the visible, and often appear indirectly in the timing or spatial orientation of our movement. In fact style is the subtext, that is the true text, which murmurs under the choreographic language. Movement analysis and more specifically Laban's vision of 'style' can be applied to the apprehension of a choreographic work, the dancing of a single dancer, to a choreographic 'school' or to a whole society, not only through its symbolic motor activities but to all of its acts, its modes of production, etc. But let us remain for the moment with the 'reading' of dance. We will leave it to others – dancers, researchers, anthropologists, to observe how this reading enables interpretation of human corporal acts in general, whether or not they are concerned with processes of symbolisation.

A relation to the most important constituents of movement – weight and flow – presides over the formation of a style. We could say that these two factors travel beyond the relational aspect and into the act produced. They are its very material, its motive and 'seasoning'. As we have seen, tonic choices are linked to the dancer's deepest 'engagements' to the point where, in contemporary dance, the freeing up of tonus was the rallying point for a whole family of bodies (Duncan, Humphrey, Hawkins, Brown...). For these

artists 'letting go' was an absolute condition of dance: that is, of all movement refusing, on one hand, to conform to a formalised idea and, on the
other, not produced by a simple 'dumping' of weight. As Nicole Walsh has
noted, Erick Hawkins explained in his numerous texts that, *only relaxed
muscles are sensitive ones.*[8] Observing the work of Hawkins and Brown,
Hubert Godard goes further in analysing tonic choices and in particular
'free flow' as the refusal to collude with an ideology of hardening that constrains bodies by obstructing the free circulation of weight. Hawkins's and
Brown's (and, in France, Stephanie Aubin's) opting for flow is an integral
part of their style. Style then contributes to situating the body in relation to
ideology and to history. Here, we are talking about a corporeal humanism
of non-violence, a refusal to take part in authoritarian processes or, even
more, in seductions linked to the vision of a body auto-affirming itself in its
tension.[9]

But there are still other stylistic positions that are just as important for
the interpreter of dance: style in terms of the treatment of space for example. Laban has given us the first key to reading this relation: the
convergence of the body around a single direction is direct; and when space
is approached through several simultaneous orientations it is indirect. This
relational quality is for us a fundamental of style whether in daily behaviour, in the art of the dancer, or of choreographic composition. Merce
Cunningham, for example, is direct; Trisha Brown indirect. Odile Duboc
occupies an extremely interesting intermediary place between a directness
of the body, coming undoubtedly from her original formation in classical
ballet, and an indirect one where, in her locomotion, there are many shimmering facets of space. In certain dance companies the choice has never
been resolved and this has contributed not a little to what one might call a
heteroclism. But it might also be considered as the wealth of a multiple
aesthetic in dance of the '80s where bodies were never unified, still less
ordered: where the dancer-performer was often the master of the style more
than the choreographer. It is specifically through the style, that is, the
gamut of its colours as relational preferences towards the world that the
dancer assures a transmission between the choreographic statement and
the sensibility of the spectator. The dancer becomes the 'interpreter' in a
(textual) hermeneutic sense, of the one who translates with her/his body.
But also, as Emmanuelle Huynh remarks, of the one who travels 'between'.
The performer is the one who is situated between the choreographer and
her/his text, between her/himself and what s/he shows. I particularly like
this idea that the dancer-performer is this 'between,' this channel through
which the sense of the text circulates.[10] Thus the choreographic 'sense' in

the deepest meaning of the word, that which bears the values of the text (and not just its forms), is what provokes the spectator's responses, the inner attitudes, to return to Laban's terminology, by which the thought of the body is touched.

Certainly other parameters of difference can be imagined. It could even be said that at the same time as it proposes a language and a style, artistic work involves a system for appreciating these expressive categories. Remember that well before he conceived of style in terms of 'effort', Laban tracked the mysteries of style in the treatment of transitions between the key attitudes. Gradually, with the notion of 'tension' replacing that of 'movement' he came to the idea, which is foundational in contemporary dance, that the transitional phases are the most important. At the end of his life, in *The Mastery of Movement* he reiterated that it is these which bear the marks of the style and of 'sense'.[11] In giving information about her/his corporeal choices the choreographer or the dancer establishes an important relationship with the spectator. The 'values' carried in the movement, says Laban, awaken mechanisms of empathy or resistance in the spectator which provoke in her or him a 'critical' work (perhaps the only critical work that should be undertaken on dance) by means of an active and lucid corporal 'response'. It was upon this belief in a possible awakening of the spectator's consciousness to what he was later to name the 'deeper values' that, in the years 1924-27, Laban was to found his theory of *Tanztheater* as the site of an historical consciousness of human action. In fact, with the staging of a dramaturgy of motor choices we are led to *a new perception of life which speaks to us of the inner options taken up by the characters*.[12] According to Vera Maletic, the 'character', so important in the aesthetics of dance theatre, then becomes *the incarnation of values and attitudes*.[13] 'Character' in dance can only be created through a consciously integrated style or, in a more informed way according to Laban's processes, through my body's integration of fundamental options not my own. This involves an incredibly fine work to apprehend stylistically what a 'character' is in order to arrive at a 'physical fiction'. Only in this way can 'I' become an other. The character which is so important in the works which lie between dance and theatre (Gerard Gourdot, Joseph Nadj, Nicole Mossoux – Patrick Bonté, etc.) can no longer be considered as the result of 'acting' but of a qualitative transmutation which destabilises the very definition of the subject. The main thing is to know how much critical (stylistic) activity there is to explore the intimate choices of a being, as opposed to purely representational effects and simple manipulations of the imagination. Amongst some of these artists it is this catastrophe of the imagination that is sought, almost beyond the conservation of an imploding subjective identity. This is what makes the power and radicality of work, like that of Mossoux-Bonté, which is always taken to the point where being is ruptured through forms of dramatic invention.

From the way Trisha Brown has treated certain figures in her recent works it has been possible to grasp several very different ideas – ones which are much closer to Laban's vision: for example, the 'little man' incarnated diffusely in *One story as in falling* for the Company Bagouet in 1992. On the other hand, in the same company, the 'character' who was so important in *Saut de l'Ange* did not displace, but rather assumed, the stylistic qualities of each dancer. Here, the character was created from an extraordinary coming together of the self with its role – 'we play ourselves' – and as an accentuation of the individual styles of the dancers, which was basically what the work staged. This aesthetics of 'playing ourselves' which was widespread in French choreography of the '80s produced some very beautiful pieces such as *Chacun appelle* by Jacques Patarozzi (1984). The 'presence' of the performer is treated as the absolute texture of a poetics of being. These situations are exceptional and depend entirely on the quality, authenticity and engagement of the dancer. For the decision to work with 'personalities' is dangerous. It can lead to processes of 'casting' and feeds into an aesthetics of the image more than into the refinements of 'presence'.[14] Nevertheless, the state of grace achieved by Maïté Fossen or Dominique Mercy has made the spontaneous equivalence of being and style shine as the direct and inexplicable expression of a unique personality living a poetics of the body on stage.

I have mentioned work (*travail*). Work on style takes a long time: it proceeds by the slow impregnation of one corporeal system by another. Dominique Noël has said that his former partner, Dominique Bagouet, loved 'sponge-dancers' – those who absorbed a body poetics by capillarity.[15] But the sponge needs time to become engorged, to change in contour and consistency. A dancer as fine as Vivianne Serry has said during a Bagouet repertoire workshop that she was able to transmit the movement but not the 'style', not having spent long enough in the company.[16] This is a profound remark: it recognises the time necessary to penetrate and be penetrated by a body state. We will see below that it is precisely in the choreographic community that the style is elaborated, not only as the emanation of the choreographer's kinesphere but as the web of relations that is woven gradually within the group. That is why, what is most important in the choreographic *écriture*, what Bartenieff calls bodily 'signature' and what we are trying to suggest by the 'grain', can only be transmitted or at least shared by a sharing of the experience itself. Work with a choreographer evokes for me that of kinesiologist-enthnographers and dancers who, in order to penetrate a movement system, stay for a long time in a society reproducing the movements of the people alongside them until they have integrated the rhythms and understood the dynamics as well as all the nuances of 'effort'; and who can then draw important conclusions regarding the way a culture elaborates its imaginary or its social relations out of bodily experience, and in the sharing of this experience. But what does the time a dancer might take to integrate a 'style' represent in relation to whole societies which, through combinations of 'effort,' have taken centuries to recognise themselves in a meaningful body state and to impose it on all members of the community as the behaviours of belonging?[17] Another time-frame, another law governs them. Remaining within dance, that is, within the symbolic transposition of such relations in an artistic process, we could cite the remarkable analysis by a dancer of one of her Javanese colleagues who had come to study in New York. Here is Judy van Zile's analysis, summarised by Bartenieff: *The dancer mastered the forms and structures but always retained a Javanese look* and thus remained completely outside what modern dance is in the United States.[18] An 'effort' analysis was then able to approach the Javanese 'style' as a specific treatment of variations in flow. It involved small variations where flow became levelled out and only evolved by slow changes from 'bound' to 'free' or vice versa, while in modern dance in the United States the style often implies abrupt changes from 'free' to 'bound'. Thus the Javanese dancer's underlying style of flow affected the form and the structure of the movement, which he had nevertheless mastered, to the extent that its expressive sense was completely transformed.

From this I would like to make two points. The first touches on the power of style which we believe to be evanescent or less directly imposing on 'sense' than the composition itself: in fact, style, as the ensemble of relational dispositions of the dancing body, is probably what carries the whole message of the dance, in an infra-text which any 'reading' must take into account. The second consideration, which is perhaps more serious, concerns the experiences of cultural mixing such as can be observed today in a current of opinion favouring ideas both of identity and of alterity, ethnicity and mixing (*métissage*). We can see what is at stake as soon as there is juxtaposing or even mixing within the one body factors which have not been analysed. Knowledge or staging of world bodies cannot do without the fine work described by Bartenieff and through which she defines the place where a system of representation is at work. In self-imposed exile from Nazi Germany she doubtless knew that, in the history of bodies, it is the only way to avoid the double risk of blindness or conformity. At the same time, within an artistic culture or given artistic current, a dance company perhaps, it is impossible to regard stylistic matters as absolute and self-evident, and not to make them the object of a process of wide illumination enabling the dancer to adhere consciously to their corporal solicitations.

1 In Laban, R. *The Mastery of Movement*, 1971.

2 Zeami. *La tradition secrète du No*. French translation by R. Siffert, 1970. The passage on 'mode' is reproduced in *Bulletin du CNDC*, No. 5, 1989.

3 Susan Foster, *Reading Dancing*, 1986, p. 91.

4 Ibid., p.76.

5 Ibid., p.76.

6 Bartenieff, 1980, and Maletic, Vera *On the aesthetic dimensions of the Dance, a Methodology for researching Dance style*, 1980.

7 Louppe has already noted that a linear anteriority-posteriority is not involved here. The author uses *en deça de* which means 'on this side of'. (Transl.)

8 Walsh, Nicole. 'Eric Hawkins, signification du geste dansé' in *Danse, le corps en jeu*, 1992.

9 Godard, H. 'Singular Moving Geographies', 1996.

10 Huynh, Emmanuelle 'Réflexions sur l'interprète' in *Ecriture du Corps*, 1992.

11 Laban, R. *Mastery of Movement*, 1971, ch.4

12 Laban, R. *A Life for Dance*, 1975.

13 Maletic, V. 1980, pp. 140-141.

14 The expression 'casting', inspired by Jean Pomarès (oral source), is reproduced in Louppe, L. 'Piège pour un espoir', *Art Press*, No.163, April 1992.

15 Dominique Noël from the colloquium, 'Mémoire de la danse, mémoire des oeuvres, mémoire des corps'. Alès, March 1993 (oral source).

16 Vivianne Serry: studio presentation by the Carnets Bagouet, Théâtre Contemporaine de la Danse, 1994 (oral source).

17 Cf more particularly Lomax, Bartenieff, Paulay, 'Dance, Style, and Culture' in *Folk Song Style and Culture*, 1968.

18 Van Zile, J. cited in Bartenieff, 1972.

Reading Time

Wherever there is movement between things and persons there is a variation or a change in time, that is, in a great opening which takes hold of them and into which they plunge.
Gilles Deleuze[1]

I remember. I remember having felt that mad desire to stay... and, struggling against the wave of movements, words, energies, and heightened senses, I decided, in that very moment, to play with time.
Odile Duboc[2]

During a choreographic experience/experiment the dancer and, likewise, the spectator become actors in and witnesses to time. Sound, according to

John Cage, in distinction to sculpture, rises out of and disappears in time (a factor which for him is equally illustrated by the mushroom). This disappearance bears witness to the existence of time as the thread or vector of execution and completion. Of an act.

The relationship to time is one of the most delicate amongst the Four Factors: the one that has given rise to the most differences, sometimes the most discord. The problematic of time is one of the great questions of contemporary dance. Sometimes it has been an almost exclusive source of inspiration, sometimes the object of the greatest suspicion. Laban did not like time. In his last writings, at the point when his thought takes on a visionary breadth, he dramatically opposes space and time: space, the site of simultaneity, welcomes the accidental and the contingent. Time, the locus of succession will always lead to chains of causality. Worse: in giving time an excessive degree of attention, culture (due to industrial modes of production?) has atrophied in us knowledge of space. *In our primordial memories still slumbers knowledge about the nature of space (instinctive knowledge) but we have lost or at least weakened it by an exaggerated cultivation of time (causal knowledge).*[3]

Wigman is similarly suspicious: time is a schema given from the outside: unlike space it is not generated by the dancing body. *Time, strength, and space, these are the elements that give the dance its life. Of this trinity of elemental powers, it is space which is the realm of the dancer's real activity, which belongs to him because he himself creates it.*[4] In contrast to space, time is not a poetic resource in the strongest sense because it does not support a '*poiein*' (forming) in which movement has to confront a matter/material: *The same way as music, dance too is called an 'art of time'. This holds true as long as one refers to the measurable, countable rhythmic passages which can be controlled in time. But that is not all! It would be little else but stale theory were we to determine the rhythm of the dance solely from the element of time... In the same manner as time, if not even more compellingly, the element of strength plays its part in the dance – the dynamic force, moving and being moved which is the pulsebeat of the life of dance.*[5] In fact, for Wigman, the musicality of movement has nothing to do with time. Faithful to her first mentor Dalcroze (as she often is without admitting it), she regards the poetic rhythm of movement as the body's integration of spatial depths and densities, as a series of frictions, slow collisions, and tensions whereby movement is aroused and shaped by the presence of souls and bodies along its trajectory. The accidents/accents of this inhabited place – slowly penetrating a mass, momentarily brushing the air, in tensions that are either bound or free – are what give the evanescence of time a spatio-organic anchor. And thus a rhythmic one: through working with resistances, intense decelerations, suspensions and letting go of weight, and breath-supported dynamics. The body invents its own restraints (or breaks free of them), generating many obstacles which articulate its impulse (thus modulating its duration). An accent or release between a tension and a counter-tension within the body, however, is never a break but rather always a transition. Dalcroze: *Rhythm is the product of a struggle against a resistance and the effort made to avoid rupturing an equilibrium. It is a compromise between two opposing forces.*[6] In this compromise which includes all the elements of movement, how does the rhythm organise these transactions: through a created space, and a 'score' of corporeal durations. In the way he develops the idea in one of his first works, *Gymnastik und Tanz*, in 1926, Laban was to ask exactly the same question about rhythm as the opposition between contrasting materials of the body, between tension and release, and closer to the notion of flow (*Anspannung-Abspannung*).[7] There is, thus, in dance and in the phrasing of movement no 'time' as such: only contractions and convulsions of matter at poles of opposing intensities. Thus it is perhaps that the Wigman dancer *weaves with time dumbly*.

In complete contrast, Cunningham's vision of time is as the supreme matter/material, the very purpose or objective. Cunningham's dance is an epiphany of time. Witness him in his composition classes setting up a large stopwatch to indicate that a dancer's action will be pure duration. After a ('disastrous') rehearsal, Viola Farber and Carolyn Brown heard his only qualitative remark, *It's two and a half minute's fast*, without any mention of the dancing. *Merce was totally* there *and his character was totally in the movement.*[8] For Cunningham, in fact, time is not tacked on to movement, it proceeds from its very essence. *Change the time and the space, and the movement changes*, writes Carolyn Brown, citing the following workshop exercise: *Make three phrases and do them in one minute. Do the same three phrases in two minutes. Do the same three phrases in thirty seconds. Observe the differences in the movement.*[9] To this end, it is important to free time (and movement) from an externally imposed rhythm, from the presence in it of anecdotal material (which would potentially make it narrative, allusive, even emotive and thus parasitic). Carolyn Brown: *Merce worked with the stop watch from the belief that rhythm comes out of the nature of the movement itself and the movement nature of the individual dancer* (a wonderful phrase: through the movement which arises in it, time is the inspired emanation of an individual awareness).[10] The structure, the 'counts' can be perceived in the ongoing movement as a time 'frame' that distributes the accents, but they are not always marked by a change of weight and even less by tonic

changes in the body – which remains neutral. This is Cunningham's ongoing project (unfinished even today) to eliminate affects and their
corresponding tensions, not so much perhaps because of their referential
character but because their spasmodics tend to make time itself unread-
able: Cunningham's heraclitean materialism, like that of his poet friend
Charles Olson, sees time-matter as ongoingness, the dance as a fluid, where
the dancer never bathes twice in the same pool. Time escapes its power to
retain, whence the importance of 'durations' as phases, as neutral structures. *Time is useful when one considers longer phrases rather than the smaller
particularities of rhythm and accent.* [11] Already in one of his first pieces *Root
of an unfocus* (1944) he had worked with this exchange between an affective
reference and structures that had no other contents than their temporal
frame. *The dance had to do with fear. It was to do with the awareness of a presence
that was foreign to the character, and after its development in time it finished with
him crawling out of the light.* [12] Cunningham freed himself simultaneously
from psychology and the modern dance compositional norms of the period
through the expedient of temporal structures: *the piece was divided into three
large sections, each section in relation to its tempo was structured in 8-10-6
beats. The temporal structure was a square matrix such that the first section was
8 by 8, the second 10 by 10, the third 6 by 6. The dance lasted five minutes
(1.5mn-2.5mn-1mn).* When he began to use aleatory compositional methods, the manipulation of time as the primary poetic material became more
and more evident. One day Cunningham organised a workshop on aleatory
methods with John Cage. The only element chosen (and thus engaged) was
time: four minutes, to be augmented each day by another minute to reach a
final duration of 15 minutes. This work tends to give time an expansive
quality, overflowing all the other creative components.

Strangely, time, which was considered by Laban to be deterministic because of its sequentiality, was, on the contrary, to be the vector of freedom
from causality for Cunningham. Vera Maletic relates their inverted positions on the question of sequencing, necessity and contingency to their
respective encounters with the Dada movement: in Laban's case that of the
Cabaret Voltaire, then the galerie Dada between 1915-17; and, in
Cunningham's, with the ideas of Duchamp, displaced and enriched by the
influence of Cage and the I-Ching. At home amongst the Swiss and German
Dadaists, from Richter to Schwitters, modern dance very quickly caught on
to 'collage' techniques and different uses of chance. Remy Charlip recalls
that Cunningham's use of chance process places him in an 'historical'
(even political) current of 'disconnection'. [13] Laban's encounter with Dada
may have given his spatial explorations with the movement 'scales' its play-

ful aspect. For Cunningham, the same idea of 'play' and of an infinity beyond any human psychology is almost entirely borne by the chance
process. Maletic writes: *Beside the potential personal benefits from using chance*
methods as a mode of freeing one's imagination from its own clichés, dancer-
choreographer Cunningham also espouses a universal vision of chance
procedures. These are for him a means of access to get in touch with natural
resources which rise out of common pools of motor impulses, and is far greater
than his own personal inventiveness, much more universally human than the
particular habits of his own practice. Laban has similar concerns arguing that in
contrast to mechanical and old-fashioned movement commands which makes the
dancer into a marionette-like puppet, the puzzle-game can awaken movement
forms which emerge out of our natural movement flow. Laban envisaged a sort
of chess game with all possible moves in all the directions of the
icosahedron as the ensemble of all possible movements in the kinesphere.[14]
Maletic notes that this was certainly closer to improvisation and thus to
subjective choices than the actions dictated 'objectively' to Cunningham by
the throwing of dice. In each case, the notion of time was affected. Laban
was still within a movement seeking to destroy the schemas imposed on the
individual by industrial civilisation: he struggled amidst the efficient cogs of
both the oppressed worker's body and the positivist thinking out of which
he sought to extract another consciousness. In a later period, Cunningham
was already well beyond the horizon of our culture. To the space-time of
thickness and obstacles worked by the Wigman body, he opposed the temporal mechanics of fluids, of water as a continuous milieu, as change and
impermanence, to use a concept from the I-Ching.[15] Wasn't this in dance,
as elsewhere, what distinguished the moderns from the post-moderns? The
latter escape history: they abandon its linear and vectorial character. After
Cage and Cunningham came repetition and the 'repetitionists' for whom
time no longer exists or can no longer be constituted: repetition destroying
even the possibility of its own ongoingness. Through the influence of Cage
and Master Suzuki, non-Western time was an important discovery with its
'disposition' of events, to use the concept François Jullien develops in his
comparison of the Chinese vision of history and Hegel's finalism.[16] This
'disposition' with Cunningham does not lead to a necessary sequencing. On
the contrary: the juxtaposition of elements under aleatory influence in a
purely dispositional score naturally creates a time-frame of homogenous
blocks. For chance modifies perception not only of the movement event but
also of time, thus destroying any idea of sequencing. *A causal law proceeds*
with certainty in so far as it is protected against perturbation, remarks
Bachelard, a propos of the constitution of duration.[17] Cunningham's gen-

ius was to have introduced durations that were totally exposed to the unpredictable and to indetermination. But from one to the other of these
moments of time and the body, from Laban to Wigman and to
Cunningham, the work of dance was to connect or oppose corporeal approaches to time as so many planes of immanence, to use Deleuze's
expression.[18] As in the other arts, as Deleuze discusses beginning with the
cinema, these planes of immanence are not only factors of creation, they
are time laid bare, exposed by the body's very matter/material. This exposed, raw time is no longer a categorial element: it exists in itself, as a
sensible fabric; it appeals to our perception.

   The question of time in art does not strictly pertain to works traditionally
classified as 'art(work)s of time'. We know that the so-called visual arts
have integrated time as an agent in 'evolutive' works ever since Man Ray's
Elevages de Poussières where drying powders accumulated on Duchamp's
Large Glass, and since Jean-Pierre Bertrand's changing colours or since
Joseph Beuys used organic matter such as honey or fat. But this is a physical
or biological time which works according to its own laws: not a created
time, compressed, dilated, produced by the deliberate choices of a subject
who invents. For, in order to invent time, one must oneself secrete its matter. One must create forms of time (durations or instants, temporal
dynamics or pure undynamic layers) and through them make time emerge
as a poetic force. We come, inevitably, to that fatal conjunction which in all
traditions has united dance and music, often as two facets of the same dy-
namo-temporal phenomenon. We will not discuss this immense
problematic here as it merits a separate treatment but will simply note several forms of their double relationship to time and of the isomorphic
crafting that has resulted from it. This fatal liaison was anathema to some
dancers at the beginning of the century. The arbitrariness of the traditional
order coupled with the impoverished relationship between the two arts
pushed the pioneers of the 1910s and '20s to radically refuse music which
imposes a timing not created by the movement (even if, as Dalcroze recalls,
at the origin of every rhythm in sound there is an original muscular experience). Cunningham, on the contrary, did not fear the encounter between
dance and music. In an art of juxtaposition inherited from the Dada practice of collage or in tune with the 'happenings' like the 1951 *Untitled Event*
at Black Mountain College, music without a direct tie to the dance can,
according to the choreographer, *add something interesting.*[19] There is no risk
here and no guarantee either. Any relation between the two elements happens by coincidence or from the mood of the spectator–listener. The only
link is time. Furthermore, this *aesthetics of simultaneity* as Daniel Charles

calls it, is precisely what can elicit a pure perception of time.[20] *It is difficult for many people to admit that dance has nothing in common with music except time and the division of time,* says Cunningham.[21] But shouldn't time be allowed to appear in its very chronicity? On the contrary, as soon as there are too obvious dynamic connections or anecdotally illustrative and redundant relations between music and dance, time disappears. One enters a thick and forced stasis with petrified and inert images.

In respect of time, French dancers have had a very different approach, even if once again they have used theoretical and practical tools provided by the great Germano-Americans. One of the elements that most touches us in the organisation of time is certainly the notion of phrasing. It is certainly one of the essential constituents of a movement aesthetic, but is not especially subservient to the factor of time. Phrasing involves weight distribution and the energy of dynamic forces as much as time itself. But for us, phrasing has so much to do with a syntagmatic idea of ongoingness and duration that the time dimension prevails over all the others, especially in francophone culture which is more impermeable to (and because of that more concerned, to the point of irritation, with) the fluctuating modulations of an *énoncé*.[22] Not that phrasing is a privileged characteristic of this or that national corporeal heritage: its character is universal. It grows from the breath, from the movements of the diaphragm which colour or are the source of all movement. Doris Humphrey's *Water Study*, which we have cited often (because this work is so revelatory of contemporary dance thought), uses great waves of breath to sustain the general phrasing of body and world. Child psychologist and Labanist, Judith Kestenberg, relates phrasing to our earliest experiences of regular or sudden and conflicting tension flow rhythms (the sucking of the breast-feeding baby, for example or the sudden contractions of emotion).[23] But, in France, could it be the fact that our unaccented language gives us an experience of time that is more metaphysical than empirical, more fluid than accented, so that a need to re-establish accent was in place from the beginnings of French dance? There is also the great dancer, Françoise Michaud, later Dupuy, who was introduced to phrasing in the 1930s by the Lyonnais rythmicians.[24] Something could well have shaken the ground of French dance, its 'mulch' (*terreau*) as Dominique Dupuy calls it, through a founding use of diaphragmatic impulses. Much more than any isomorphism between dance and music, phrasing consists in the sensori-motor organisation of durations, in breathing into life from within a singular temporality. In her dancing and teaching, Françoise Dupuy practices an art of phrasing that prevails over all the other poetic dimensions of her dance, allowing impulses to touch a body free to respond to ongoing syncopations. It is a breathed art where the whole body spasms. This indulgent, impulsive, interstitial body reappears for us in filigree in other forms: there is the withheld falling of Odile Duboc who spatialises time in multi-directional paths of multiple speeds and orientations. While in her contrasting *Projet de la Matière* (1993), time distends in the weighted flow of bodies shaped by the space, the supporting surfaces, through their contact and falling. Stephanie Aubin who is another musician of released, fluidly swinging weight, works with a continuum between time, weight, and tonic release, creating punctuated phrasing with little syncopations that keep re-activating a fluidity in the continuous movement. As with Trisha Brown, whose disciple she is, freedom of the pelvis enables the propagation of this ongoingness. But the most important aspect for Brown is the weight and its journey through successive propulsions. For Aubin, weight shifts serve in the first place to make the phrasing sing. It is like an utterance furling and unfurling upon itself. Her body is transported on the crest of these rhythmic waves. Phrasing in dance is thus given in the confluence in time of three other factors: weight, space, and tonus. The phrasing distributes changes in matter: the tensions, releases, and suspensions which will define the accents, pauses, ruptures, accelerations or decelerations. Maintaining continuous muscle tension – increasing or not – slows time down (as it thickens space). Time becomes a malleable, elastic, flexible material. In its poetic state, time is no longer subject to physical laws. Thus a body's fall, still sometimes defined in terms of the distance fallen and the weight and shape of the object, can in dance be transformed into a dreamy or slow flowing down as in *One story as in falling* (1992) for the Company Bagouet, where the movement retains the vertigo of falling (as the body gives in to its speed but not to an acceleration). And as time is 'truly' a movement element, it is this phrasing as much as the shaping of the movement which gives it its quality and essence. Two movements that are dissimilar from the point of view of morpho-kinesis can be twinned in terms of phrasing (or vice versa). We can perhaps understand, then, what is at stake in phrasing – and where the intense interest in working without music (an external phrasing), comes from. The dancer who does not use music enters more deeply into her phrasing. Without music, the body becomes entirely responsible for the way the movement unfolds and we can immediately see how the dancer is invested in it. Dancers of the *grande modernité* (Duncan, Laban, Humphrey, dance in the '60s and '70s) initially wanted to renounce music in order, no doubt, to go against traditional schemas. But also because they had heard in their own bodies the rhythmic resources of silence. Thus Duncan: *These dances were not accompa-*

nied by music, but seemed to come forth from the rhythm of an inaudible music.[25]
This radical attitude appeared again at the end of the '70s with Dana Reitz
who, looking for pure movement phrasing, worked with small temporal
cells like so many poetic utterances carried by the movement and the breath
which in her work gives birth to the movement, as it might give birth to her
voice. Today, in the wake of the dance of the '80s, passages of silence still
exist in practically all contemporary choreography even and especially
those which are closely connected to music – not as an accompaniment but
as an aesthetic partner, mirror or model – for example, in Anne Teresa de
Keersmaeker. Or dance and music can resonate from an immense symbolic
fund held in common. This is the case for Dominique Bagouet's use of Pascal Dusapin's *Assaï*: in his piece of the same name the music only starts at
the third 'tableau' with the arrival of the most enigmatic figures, redoubling its ambiguities through the power of sound. For this reason it could
also be said that between silence and noise the choreographer invents another score, another musical composition, with diverse phrasings and
diverse relations to sound. He becomes himself 'the author' of silent sequences, breathings, intervals of time as bands of frequencies where music
is absent. In the bodies, then, everything can stop or intensify. And it is here
that the general phrasing of the work or of the choreographic language
appears: it is at the same time both fluid (through the musical line of the
movement) and suspended (through rarefying the movement). There is a
subtle art of two track phrasing in Daniel Larrieu's work. Phrasing is elastic
and swinging for Hervé Robbe, bouncing and discontinuous with Bernado
Montet. Nevertheless in these examples, phrasing only represents one poetic element amongst the range of materials that are in play in the
constitution of the choreographic style and the movement poetics. Others,
however, make phrasing the primary choreographic resource. Odile Duboc
works from an 'inner music', an originating pulse from which movements
gradually spread out multi-directionally in a whole play of corporal and
spatial instabilities. George Appaix who danced with Duboc works from a
textual phrasing, as if in the resources of language there were also a temporal matrix where the body can decode an utterance common to prosody,
punctuation and movement. The text, the rhythmically spoken verses of
Homer, for example, with which Appaix has been for some years weaving
an immense 'work in progress,' serves as both an impulse and a rhythmic
framework which is propagated and developed from one piece to the next,
moving further and further from the metre through time lags or complex
syncopations. From this brief approach to phrasing in dance the wealth of
its different possibilities should be evident. But we may perceive, too, how

dangerous it is for dance to be on too friendly terms with sound that is regulated according to mechanical and regular pulses – as has unfortunately been the case in some contemporary dance performances that have aimed at cheap effects rather than an authentic experience of time.

Nevertheless, because of its very 'meaningfulness' (*pregnance*) and especially because of its lyricism, phrasing was subject to radical condemnation by the avant-garde artists, as were all the elements that in their lyricism exceed a simple movement declaration. Phrasing was not spared in the great destructive and critical project of the dancers of the Judson Church. In the parallel tables of negative values in minimalist dance and sculpture Yvonne Rainer classified phrasing amongst the categories to *eliminate or diminish* in regard to the role of the *hand of the artist*.[26] That is, at the foundations of what would 'depersonalise' movement most profoundly, make of it a 'specific movement' along the lines that a 'specific object' is as far a possible, freed from artistic intervention, are elementary forms or materials, free from any projection or story that would link them to something antecedent in memory or in the history of an individual. To support this vision, in *Trio A* Rainer proposed a sequence of discrete movements each of which could be understood as a fundamental or everyday movement: fall, get up, stand, etc., and where the sequence was to be accomplished, at least in the beginning, in an even flow of energy without time being either perturbed or 'treated' by the slightest dynamic accent. This was the means by which the choreographer could withdraw her artistic '*facture*,' freeing a time-movement to its impenetrable existence. Furthermore, isn't a phrase as the unit of phrasing the emblematic cell of any narrative, distributing dynamics to create so many vicissitudes that shape the choreographic text into a syntagm, making every duration an articulated fiction? *Most of the Western dance familiar to us can be characterised by a certain distribution of energy: maximal deployment of attack at the beginning and end of a phrase, with a moment of suspension in the middle.*[27] We will see below that the dynamic curve of the phrase carries in itself the whole compositional impulse (*élan*) which, according to the different aesthetic periods of contemporary dance, has been accented, enforced or conversely denied and questioned; but, historically, these stages are not linear ones. What *Trio A* refuses by stringing together events containing an even quality of duration and intensity, contemporary French dance has reinvested hundredfold. The shuddering, irregular, impetuous phrasing of Catherine Diverrès, the alternating suspension and sudden catastrophes of Anne Teresa de Keersmaeker, take up this treatment of phrasing in a new aesthetic where paroxysm, far from piling up information in durations saturated by contrasts, touches on something like a void, or a new feeling of futility, destroying action. As if the encounter between weight and time, which for Laban defined rhythm, ended more in the undoing of a discourse constructing itself in duration than in the mastery of a time into which the dancer plunges. A sacrifice made willingly to Chronos in expending movement and in the dynamic of the phrase, rather than in its duration.

Phrasing works with ongoingness, even if there is contrast. But the sensation of discontinuity in time relates much more to the interval, the moment of suspension or instantaneousness creating a rupture, an exception, sometimes shock or vertigo. Time itself can become empty in the pure expectation of an invisible movement. This is not simply a useless disconnection. It can correspond to the Chinese idea of the 'empty median' discussed by Maldiney. *The empty median is not a lacuna. It doesn't result from a lack. It is at the heart of fullness, a first great emptiness and a final opening.*[28] It is what makes the whole poetic charge of the anacrusis, the moment which precedes the emergence of the movement but where, what Bartenieff calls *the inner impulse to move*, is suddenly revealed with its whole mechanics, its whole palette of gears prepared. The notion of anacrusis which was present in Dalcroze has been revisited and very much enriched by Hubert Godard. Concerning the 'gestural anacrusis,' this brief calm which is an absolutely foundational moment, he affirms: *The pre-movement is an empty zone, with no displacement no segmentary activity. And yet, everything is already played out there, the entire poetic charge, the tonal colouring of the action.*[29] If the anacrusis and the 'visualisation' which it produces set the inner movements in train, the 'momentum' of Alwin Nikolais as the *élan* or thrust but also the interval that precipitates the movement is no less interesting. Let us remember that the term 'momentum' in spite of its resemblance to 'moment' does not refer to anything temporal: it belongs in the lexicon of dynamics. But its actualisation requires a particular time, an interval, a gear. For Steve Paxton 'momentum' is also the *interval between two opposing tensions* – less a question of rupture than a pause which in Contact Improvisation lets the deciding mind empty out in order to allow the body, led by its own and the other's weight, to pursue its own dis-orientation (to lean, to slide, to tip over etc.).[30] Dance poetics particularly involves these dynamic 'joints'. Whether it is the infinitely small suspensions between fall and recovery (dear to Doris Humphrey), or Paxton's letting go of his axis completely by pouring his own weight into the weight of another. It is at this moment, says Paxton, that a new time *which is nonmetric and of no particular duration* reveals itself.[31] Time, he says is manifest through endocrine reactions to loss of equilibrium and brings about *a g r e a t s t r e t c h*

in g o f t i m e... This is the sort of thing meant by 'sensing time'. Of course this
new perception of time coincides with a new perception of the body, of
weight in relation to space and of objects: when the head is always disoriented in relation to the centre of the body all the dimensions of movement
are apprehended outside of the habitual field of awareness. All these intervals of time when an impulse is revealed or when a gear is engaged make
both the dancer and the spectator sense the importance of the
'moment'(*l'instant*), produced and provoked by these processes. The moment as the only possible frame in which the unknown can make its
appearance, as the fracturing of experience. The only temporal dimension,
says Bachelard (cited by Odile Duboc) which occurs as such in memory.[32]
The dancer works on the moment but also in it. Complete presence in the
moment without any congealing delay or anticipation is what constitutes
the quality of a dance act. It is an element that is equally essential to the
dancer's 'presence'. Presence can be read as a quality of 'being-there'
(which could follow from a topological understanding of being), how a
person extends relationally through the communicative force of the self,
and the tensional and spatial aura that a body exudes and organises. But for
the dancer it also has to do with the urgency of being present in the present
(a time concept). Without 'presence' nothing happens in the instantaneousness of an act, nothing of the deep correspondence between the
movement and the nature of the moment that it creates (and which creates
it). Being present to the moment can be defined, as Odile Duboc suggests, by
the *moment of awareness.*[33] With her and her dancers the awareness of
being-in-time engenders an exceptional state of presence: the fully engaged
body holds time in suspension. *In the pieces that Duboc has choreographed in
the street, the dancers who are on this occasion called Fernands (in order to
confuse them more with the everyday), share with non-dancers the everyday
urban spaces and journeys. They are dressed like them, animated like them. They
are different however. Why? Because they are in another time. They are themselves this other time... They are what the others are so rarely: present in their
action, even in the action of walking along the opposite footpath.*[34] The absolute
co-substance of the movement with the moment or the duration of its unfolding (in the Nikolaisian sense of 'motion' as the undergoing of a
sensori-motor experience) is one of the foundations of contemporary
dance. It would be useless to try to impose an added meaning upon these
corporal sensings of time. They rise up simultaneously as a bursting forth
(*éclat*) of time and sensation. This 'present' quality proper to dance but also
to other *practices of the moment* according to psychoanalyst Claude Rabant,
lives in the energy of a present that is always precisely new.[35] It is perhaps this

union of the danced act with the moment of its 'actuality' or presentness which makes us believe in the ephemerality of dance, as if the movement was forever – irretrievably – incrusted in the present. *What will return? Everything but the present. The possibility of a present*, writes Maurice Blanchot in *Le Pas au-delà*. For in the moment of movement it is not so much the movement itself that is ephemeral, but the flash of the encounter, the ungraspable shimmer of several perceptions crossing between bodies and gazes. The idea of dance movement as ephemeral is born in the experience of the subject who dances and looks in surprise. Movement itself knows nothing of the dimensional categories of time and the linear representations we make with it. It unfolds itself in the time that it creates or rather in the 'all,' according to the Deleuzian concept of a multidimensional milieu which he applies to the cinema. *He dives in to lose himself there.* Yes, but also in order to survive. For, liberated in time, movement reinvents all its poetic factors there: spatialisation, tensility, modes of weight transfer, paradigmatic and diffracted relations with the world. All are used to make an experience of duration as matter/material, and of the moment as the epiphany of an ever-renewed spark. The 'work of dance' on time tears from Chronos his power to devour bodies. In 'losing' her/himself in time, the dancer elaborates counter-destinies tied to movement's letting go of its own conclusion.

1 Deleuze, Gilles in *The Time Image*, 1989.
2 Duboc, Odile 'L'épreuve du temps'. *L'art en scène première*, 1994.
3 Laban, Rudolf *A Vision of Dynamic Space*, 1963.
4 Wigman, Mary *The Language of Dance*, 1966, pp. 11-12.
5 Ibid., pp.10-11.
6 Jaques-Dalcroze, Emile *Le rythme, la musique et l'éducation*, 1924.
7 Maletic says that these are *words which better express the process of increasing and decreasing tension* and goes on to say that *for relaxation, Graham's term 'release' is more appropriate than 'relaxation' which may imply passive limpness*. Op.cit. p.165.
8 Brown, Farber, Vaughan et al. 'Cunningham and his dancers' in Kostelanetz (ed.) *Merce Cunningham: Dancing in Space and Time*, 1989, p.103
9 Brown, Carolyn 'Carolyn Brown' in Klosty (ed.) *Merce Cunningham*, 1975, p.24
10 Brown, ibid., p.24.
11 Cunningham, Merce. 'A Collaborative Process between Music and Dance (1982)' in *Merce Cunningham: Dancing in Space and Time*, 1989.
12 Ibid.
13 Remy Charlip in ibid., pp. 40-43.
14 Maletic, Vera. *Body Space Expression*, 1987, p.142
15 Merce Cunningham, 'An Impermanent Art' in *Esthetics Contemporary*, edited by Richard Kostelanetz, 1978.
16 Jullien, François *La propension des choses*, 1992, chap. 6, pp. 210-211.
17 Bachelard, Gaston *La dialectique de la durée*, 1993, p. 57.
18 Deleuze, Gilles *The Time Image*, 1989.
19 Leschaeve, J. *The dancer and the dance*, 1985.

20 Charles, Daniel in *Revue d'esthétique*. Special issue on John Cage. 1988, pp.123-138.

21 Cunningham, Merce *Changes: notes on Choreography*, 1969.

22 In linguistics we call 'syntagm' the unfolding of an *énoncé* in time, in opposition to the 'paradigm' which is the bundle of connotations evoked by the *énoncé*. We could say that the syntagm is the vector of succession which plays with rhythm. Whereas the paradigm, the vector of simultaneity, plays on the meaning (*sens*).

23 Kestenberg, Judith 'The Rule of Movement Patterns in Development. Part One: Rhythms of Movement', *New York Psychoanalytical Quarterly*, No. 34, 1964, pp. 1-36.

24 Poudrou, F. Article on A. Wiskeman and H. Carlut in Jacqueline Robinson, *L'aventure de la danse moderne en France, 1930-1970*, 1990, pp. 137-142.

25 Duncan, Isadora *The Art of the Dance*, 1928, p. 102.

26 Rainer, Yvonne 'A Quasi Survey of Some Minimalist Tendencies in the Quantitatively Minimal Dance Activity Midst the Plethora or an Analysis of Trio A' in *Work 1961-1973*, 1973, p. 63.

27 Ibid.

28 Maldiney, H. 1993, p. 157.

29 Godard, Hubert 'Singular Moving Geographies', 1996, p.17.

30 Paxton, Steve 'Contact Improvisation' in *Dance as a Theatre Art*, 1974, p. 224.

31 Ibid., p. 224

32 Gaston Bachelard, *L'intuition de l'instant*, cited in Odile Duboc, 'L'épreuve du temps'. *Les Cahiers du renard*, No. 15, Autumn, 1993.

33 Ibid.

34 Louppe, Laurence. 'Le danseur et le temps' in *L'art en scène Première*, 1994, p. 7.

35 Rabant, Claude. *Inventer le réel, le déni entre perversion et psychose*. Collection *L'espace analytique*. 1992, p. 34.

The Poetics of Flow

What makes one kind of movement different from another is not so much varia-
tions in arrangements of parts of the body as differences in energy investment.
Yvonne Rainer[1]

The poetics of tensions

We have seen that to speak of the time factor in movement involves, through time and energy coming together in phrasing, making an immediate link with the qualities that Laban associates with his marvellous concept of flow.

After his first experiments in body 'eu-rhythmics' in 1905, Dalcroze was the first to note the importance of changes in muscle tone. His genius was to understand that changes in the tone of muscle tissue are our first relation to the symbolic, and that these changes construct space and time as much as any of the other expressive tools. Further, Dalcroze's art proposed to *establish immediate relations between external music and the music which sings within each of us and which is simply the echo of our individual rhythms, our chagrins, joys, desires, powers.*[2] Here, we are alerted not only to the way in which the rhythm of our inner life is immediately transposed into corporal discharges but also to the body as the vector of Nietzsche's 'bottomless desire' in *The Birth of Tragedy*. Any product of the imagination is only the material emanation of an 'inner song'. This song, as Adolphe Appia, Dalcroze's friend, student and collaborator well understood is, more than a 'representation' of the world, the quality of our orientation towards it. This new vision of movement, *tolerates nothing that does not emanate from an incorporated rhythm.*[3] Space, objects, and light are the reflections of rhythmic body states and functions directed into space: breathing, change of support, etc. Rhythm is a kind of 'transformer' between signals given off by the sonorous and symbolic plastic environment and the body which integrates them, returns them and transfigures them through the gamut of its organic reactions. *A sudden or well prepared attack, continuous or sudden intensifications or softenings, accented or calm, light or harsh rhythms find echoes in all our limbs...*[4] And these echoes are channelled in the first instance through changes in muscle texture, that drapery of fibrous intensity which makes our body into a resonating chamber and the instrument and bow of an inner song.

For let us not forget that rhythm is not, as it is so often defined, the regular (or irregular) return of a periodic 'beat'. In other words, rhythm is not the measure nor even the metre. It is in many respects the opposite. Rhythm involves a deep transformation of matter/material, a dynamic unsettling of substances and energies. Dalcroze reminds us not to confuse, *the rhythm which is the body's animator with the measure that is only its regulator.*[5] Tonic work is the first way of re-arranging and animating the body. When not taught in a watered-down version, the Dalcroze 'method', consists primarily in confronting the subject with perturbations of space and time – using obstacles and other challenges where changes of weight and support, stumblings and recoveries can make the strongly accented flow of the rhythmic tissue be felt. Rhythmic experience is thus brought into relation with the variations of emotional experience and emotive life in general, which Pierre Kaufman regards as a *perturbation in the adaptive functions* through which, in exercises and improvisations, the subject will re-invent his own recoveries and integrate into a corporeal poetics his own imaginary precipices. But it is in the body itself that changes in the world's stability are felt. One of the most important elements of rhythm is its shading or nuance. Dalcroze discovered the roots (more than the analogy) of changes in the intensity of sound – *sforzando, crescendo, decrescendo* – in the major experiences of change in muscle tone: its intensifying or lessening in different modes and durations. Through his treatment of rhythmic shading he gave instrumental music back the body it had escaped in order to take up residence in different organological substitutes. Dalcroze's overall undertaking is worthy of our attention today more than ever, not only because of its discoveries but also for its method of investigation: its way of going back to the body to identify the original state of musical phenomena, as if the body concealed the whole ensemble of artistic expressions and the secret of their engendering. For, contrary to what is usually thought, Dalcroze did not found a 'mimesis' or a system integrating sound phenomena with the body. It was, instead, in the carnal that he discovered the world's song. He did not incorporate, but rather ex-corporated. From bodily reaction he drew out another music – sonorous fibres with their stretching, their cracking, their rupture and their beat.

En route towards rhythm as the pulse of life, Dalcroze discovered dance in the colliding or brushing of bodies stumbling between and amongst things and places (adaptation to the environment?) – a dance that one could call 'original,' before or beyond any anatomical localisation or any gestural 'emission' identifiable by its shape. Dalcroze understood, then, that shading is in us: it is the augmentation or diminution of muscular and nervous texture which the smallest contraction, the least passing emotion works with, makes vibrate or subside. And it all makes sense. It composes. There is thus an inner tonic song. This major artistic revelation, taken up again by Laban (who did not always bother to cite his sources) is central, currently, to Hubert Godard's deeper reflection – one that is more relevant to the needs of today's dance. This important practitioner and theoretician parallels the role of tonus in dance with the theories of Henri Wallon on the 'tonic dialogue' as the first expression and weaving of affective relations between the infant and its 'object of love'.[6] For Dalcroze, change in tonus was already the first poetic language of the body, and the first language for what he sought beyond the body: music as first art (according to conceptions available in 1905-10). Not only because Dalcroze was originally a musician and asked questions of the body from his musical perspective but because he was in the wake of Nietzsche, at a historic moment when music was a model for escaping the arts of mimesis. It also had this role for Kandinsky who was writing *The Spiritual in Art* at the time.

Today the problematic is somewhat displaced. The dancer does not look for music beyond her/his movements, but within them; and the 'song' of tonus, its variations and colours, from the atonic to the hypertonic, are what compose the first elements of her/his inner music. This tonic musicality, which is one of the strongest and most intimate elements of choreographic 'grain', has been elaborated in very different theoretical and practical treatments, each carrying a singular poetics which, despite bodily differences, can sometimes in large measure define an aesthetic. This is what Laban understood in making 'flow' one of the four important elements of his movement thought. The notion of flux/flow is important in Laban's thought since for him everything in the universe is flowing: flow is the quality with which weight is 'declined'. And thus amongst the forms and forces which surround us, it is the very condition of existence. Let us recall the etymology of the word 'rhythm' which Benveniste links to its first meaning in pre-4th century Greek where '*ruthmos*' refers to 'form', that is, to the way a body has of 'flowing' in the world.[7]

Laban distinguishes two states of flow: 'free' and 'bound'.[8] The whole quality of flow is not however in the *state* of a tonic yielding or intensity, but in the passage from one to the other, as an interval of change. Contemporary dance has worked on these intervals a great deal either by elongating them like waves emptying and refilling (which one sees in the swing exercises of the Humphrey technique) or, by contrast, in shortening them by a movement of ellipsis in which the body changes instantaneously from one tonic state to another. Rupture between two states is seen frequently on the contemporary dance stage and is generally destined to translate or provoke strong sensations, but also breaks in linearity. For example, in the work of Bagouet, a tonic ellipse which is used frequently from his *Crawl de Lucien* (1985) onward, counteracts the psychologising and descriptive tendencies of a slowly unfolding state. A movement initiated in a certain tonicity continues in a different one and the spectator feels a break in the continuity of the phrase. Often the intensification is slow and held while its release is rapid – like the opening of a valve letting off surplus pressure, the 'accursed share' whose tonic intensification is often the corporal metaphor of something that is being expelled, with a slow subsidence or ecstatic increase of tone.[9] Once again we must invoke Doris Humphrey and her philosophical view of life where a slow growth is opposed to a rapid decline – a structure visible in the rising and breaking of waves, in the length of life and quickness of death, the increase of sexual tension and the depressive suddenness of orgasm – the last two constituting without doubt the central motor of all her pieces. The idea of the 'accursed share' here is used to indicate the act of suddenly expending all accumulated intensity.

The anacrusis, as an invisible transformation that nevertheless has presence, an empty moment in which the whole symbolic is born, is what music and dance can most deeply reveal to the other arts. It is in the breath, perhaps, or in this light systole of absence, that imagination is born. Thus, the way flow is organised in a dance has many important philosophical and poetic consequences. Through tonic lyricism more than through other movement elements the dancer's body touches the body of the spectator and works with it to change its consistency and stability. If displacement of weight speaks to the other's body symbolically (and speaks 'it'), almost as (non-figurative) representation, tonic change on the other hand represents nothing: it sings. It converses musically with our kinaesthesia and, playing on our own deep or light vibrations, carries us along into the most lyrical regions of our corporal awareness. The choreographer, then, has to choose a poetic orientation in relation to this lyricism: whether s/he draws from it the half-tint of an atonal body or by contrast the paroxysm of a body carried to the maximum intensity of flow. Let us consider two very pertinent examples: that of Trisha Brown (discussed further below) who moves freely between tonic states allowing a wonderful circulation of flow; and that of Odile Duboc, with her fluent quality where the movement is only just contained by imperceptible articulations. Between these two tonic styles there is the musicality of Stephanie Aubin with her light and continuous changes of flow. The theatre theorist Jean-Marie Pradier rightly notes that paroxysmal tonic states are easier for an actor to hold because s/he will always prefer to 'represent' the strong emotions which require this tonic augmentation – the violent passions, anger, surprise, etc., that are 'acted' in the theatre. Pradier compares these intense tonic states (accompanied by shallow breathing) with low tonic states linked to deep breathing which are, for example, the tender or amorous states that actors much more rarely frequent.[10] There may be a technical difficulty in entering into this state or a reluctance to be seen on stage disarmed and exposed, without one's tonic shield. The same problem exists on the dance stage: there is a tendency to adopt bound flow to support an impassioned existential tension taken to an extreme, or the opposite, to ward off the too literal exploitation of an emotion; and choreographers often work only with body states in which the flow remains bound throughout the whole phrase or even maintains the same intensity for the whole piece. Such was also the case in the renowned 'extreme' theatre of the '70s where actors portrayed the most moderate, even anodyne, feelings with extreme corporal and vocal tension – a process that quickly became conventional and monotonous but which was also evidence of a lack of work on bodily resources in favour of external appearances. In fact, the choice and quality of flow are not stable. The regime of tensions, the way they are changed through the movement, makes the alternating qualities of flow sing. In some pieces, the body's flow dominates the other choreographic elements. In such cases, tonic preferences become operators of space, time and also thought. Let us not forget the primordial importance in contemporary dance of work on the tensions. Tensions are not directly visible in a form; but they drive the lines of force which make the movement. They are at the heart of a movement's whole expressivity: in their degree of intensity, in their spatio-temporal regime, in their work on its dynamics. Extreme tension to the point of tetanising the body was one of the tools of *Ausdruckstanz* to express impatience, inner revolt and explosion of repressed instincts. But tension does not work on its own: on one hand it forms many magnetic contacts with space, making the space-body spark and vibrate in the electrified dynamosphere. Tension is not homogenous. For Laban, each tension is counter-balanced by a more or less visible opposing tension, in the way that a movement is inhabited by its shadow. At each moment the body is multiple, including in its intentions and intensities, and in the tangled play of tensions and counter-tensions which continually tear apart the inner plan. Hence, Laban's famous 'scales' are an exercise almost in solfège. They allow opposite states of tension to be 'declined' in different directions, planes, and levels and with their whole qualitative palette of gravitational engagements. It is wrong to consider Laban's scale exercises in a reductive and simply technical way: they contain on the contrary a (practical) vision of the body's complex heterogeneity, one which cannot be resolved from any single perspective. Generally, systematic work on tensions, 'upstream' of the shaping or construction of movement, constitutes a way to observe the body as producing 'forces' which gradually integrate the rhythm of space-time. This rhythm can only be elaborated if the tensional pathways have been fully explored – not forgetting the philosophy of 'release' in which they are rejected. But 'release' itself belongs to the realm of tension: it is one of its registers, in the negative. And it is the excess of tension and ultimate contraction that, as it subsides, leads the body to let go. Just as 'release' has been conceived as refusal of tension, in the same way, historically, there had to be an intensifying of tensions in modern dance of the first half of the twentieth century (linked to aesthetic currents like expressionism where aggravated tension is required) in order to arrive at the 'clear', relaxed and objectal body of Hawkins, and his many epigones during the '60s. Passage from the one to the other of these tensional states is more necessary than is a mode of 'ease' imposed as the only register, without its inverse and its source, namely tension, having been explored – not as a rigid holding in the body but as the variation of textures and the shifting of tensilities. These are the manifestation, finally, of the 'unnamed forces', to use Novalis's term, which have been revealed by contemporary dance. But the 'revelation' of forces (for us of historical, not to mention essential 'political', importance) is automatically doubled by another task: the conscious treatment of these forces to make sense of them, and to enable them to create readable forms. Dalcroze's work, for example, on 'dissociations' where, within a single body, different tensional states are distributed making it a kind of polyphonic instrument, a material with multiple shadings, a vibrant canvas of contrasting colours. There are also Limón's 'oppositions' of tensions and counter-tensions which disorganise the body through contradictory spatio-temporal choices. In both cases, as with Laban whose scales we have mentioned, a single body or a single preference no longer suffices to reconcile the play of tensions but on the contrary becomes the field where forces confront and disturb each other. As if each of our bodies were in itself a page in the history of these forces: with their ending in contraction or release, imperceptible signs of the 'motility' of the living being which suddenly take on the fullness of a hitherto illegible textuality.

Dance thinking is not added like a metaphor or narrative supplement to the thought of these first corporal preferences and essential supports of 'sense'. Hubert Godard reads in the elaboration of muscular or postural tonus a dance's whole ideological or political engendering. Trisha Brown's *Primary Accumulation* (1971) comes from the legendary period of American radicalism in the '60s and '70s where her *Accumulations* were part of a 'cycle' (as she likes to call the different stages of her oeuvre) completely concomitant with the most outstanding minimalist sculptures of Carl André or Donald Judd – an art where what is important is the levelling of affective or formal extremes, and where there is minimal intervention in material and meaning, an evacuation of tensions that might hierarchically distribute categories and values. Processes are put in place to protect the work from an excessive overcoding by attributes generally identified as artistic: unity, '*éclat*' etc. Such processes include repetition which makes the object 'banal', neutral, simple, poor in materials, modest in scale and soothing to the perceptions.

It is striking to see how dance anticipated this aesthetic by its power to play on the tonic texture, to cause it to implode, and to make the body a place where points of tension are eliminated and equalised in a neutral distribution free of all local accentuation. It helps us especially to understand that form is not given from the outside by a structure but by an inner tensional organisation that distributes matter. Thus, Brown's quietly relaxed, prone body escaping any law and undisturbed by any centring of weight at the beginning of the *Accumulations*, evokes the large felts by Robert Morris that are suspended or laid out on the ground – inert matter without any point of centred cohesion (the works revealing what the artist himself calls 'anti-form'). As in Brown's body, there is only matter dropping downward, resting evenly on the ground, a place without architecture where the weight is distributed so that nothing is assembled or erected. In fact, there can be no form without the intervention of a tension to organise the gravitational flows. On a symbolic level there is Simone Forti's 'return' to an archaic body, like that of a newborn not yet organised around a gravitational axis and simply flowing towards the support of the maternal enclosure, the interface with what is not yet its body schema. Crawling, rolling, experiencing surfaces of support like animals or human young, *the relations internal to mass*, were some of the principle activities of an art staying clear of verticality.[11] Another influence at the origin of Brown's atonal body in the *Accumulations* was Elaine Summers and her work on eliminating points of tension (what was later to be called 'release technique'), her double exploration of the body (in the spirit of Elsa Gindler who was her mentor) as both made up of separate elements and as a totality.[12] It is worth remembering this while watching Brown's solo: its depth, its mysterious thickness, its soft quality arise from an immense fund of knowledge and the quasi-historic memory which is produced there, not just the search for an 'effect'. In the same way that the 'political' meaning given to this renunciatory dance at a time of anti-imperialism amongst North American intellectuals and artists could not occur without an infinite awareness of and labour upon corporeality. Renunciation of all self-construction as if retreating from history – the only possible strategy for bodies that no longer recognise themselves in any system. This dance on the ground is composed, as we have seen, of 'fractions' of accumulated movements, each apparently separate from the other but which in fact connect the whole body. Most striking is the calm softness of each *énoncé*, the movement occurring without any intensification of tone as if emanating from an a-corporeal obscurity. Each movement can be either tiny in its habitus (a simple turn of the head) or ample in its development (lift one leg diagonally over the other lifting the hip diagonally) but never with any temptation to 'centre' it either through timing or accentuation. This equality of tonus speaks to a non-hierarchised body where each element exists at once isolated and supported by infinite connections. The non-verticality, as the choreographer herself explains, allows the legs to be freed and to be treated not as *supports but like the rest of the body*.[13] In the solo, these freed legs have a flat tone reflecting the purest 'dropping', and a body content to 'flow' into the world without occupying or dominating it. A utopian world where the body restfully gives up its own weight, falling from where it was raised onto the earth. Today, a long way from minimalist debates on the necessity for series and cyclical repetition, we are particularly taken by its peaceful silence, and by the quality of each movement, sharing the sweet hypnotics of this body devoid of all conflict.

The choreographic 'readings' made possible by 'Effort Shape' remind us that the absence of tension and of any mechanism structuring change of weight ruptures the relation to space and puts it 'to sleep'. Here, there is properly speaking no space. The *Accumulations* lead us on inner journeys. It is the dialogue between tonic sensation and duration as the slow unfolding of successive movements which takes the place of space. Once again politics emerges in this absence of the territorial. As the ultimate memorial of a world where everything has been let go, the body only expresses itself through its last resources, which are this flat and silent tonicity.

During the 1980s an important sector of French dance cultivated bound flow. This involved, amongst other things, a rigid back untouched by a sequencing that might have freed the torso. Doubtless, this was a way of reinforcing the back as a protective shell for the palpitating and vulnerable interface represented by the front of the body as the carrier of the organs of communication and, in principle, of meaning (you had to be Trisha Brown to dare to expose yourself in a dance of the back, with all the capacity for articulation that make this area not an enclosure but a poetic geography of letting go). Perhaps French dancers needed an auto-defence: to be enveloped in a protective corset which, once acknowledged, appears as enigmatic as it is shocking. Controlling the tensional regime as though from within, directing tensions towards areas at once meditative and held back has often led to the fragmented aesthetics of a gesture suspended this side of its impact. This can delicately rarefy the dance event, but it leads nevertheless to a lack of abandon, to a sort of permanent withholding both of the act and the use of space.

This is why there is relief, almost, in the increasingly visible freeing up of the tensional system in body states of the '90s (the consciously acknowledged use of the deeply poetic tools of the contemporary body) – this very return belonging to another history or rather to what is not yet history, but just the transitory moment when works blossom forth to themselves in a time which is not identified as such. They can already think themselves in an 'historical' difference which has more to do with changes in body state than directly interpretable changes, and without having to pass via a concept of the body or of social, political, cultural or geographic contexts. Many choreographers today, through a much less congealed or hardened tensional variation, are bringing to the fore again the aliveness of fleeting colours. There is nothing more beautiful, for example, than a simple arm gesture which can sometimes powerfully lift a mass of air, or float on a light inner breeze. It would seem, in view of such dances, that the history of tensions has finally made a detour to reveal the urgency of thinking of them as such. And to treat them as an essential material of the contemporary poetic field.

Accent

Accent was thought for a long time to be a purely musical concept until Dalcroze and Laban showed that it belonged in the first instance to body experience – to the inner fall of weight or the tensional mechanism that intervenes in a movement. As usual, human imagination has projected many elements from its deep organic experience into sound, poetry, and prose. Some singers maintain that an accent used to inflect a movement, word or musical phrase strongly affects their body's axis along the central canal (the digestive tube), with the accent exerting pressure on the diaphragm as though to connect with the anus in a movement of expulsion. This biological theory regarding the value of the 'beat' – with its likely genito-anal symbolic character – and its use in music, dance, poetry and all of the dynamic arts (not forgetting that there are accents in painting, cinema, and even more in sculpture) is interesting. But no corporeal process in dance can be assimilated to a physiological one, even mimetically or metaphorically, without passing through an extremely complex series of representations (only available through a kinesiological approach). The subject is vast, and we will have to limit ourselves to observing the practice and role of accent in the field of dance.

The whole body can make an accent when, within a movement, its weight falls creating a dynamic perturbation. An accent can be provoked by putting obstacles or unevenness along someone's path as Dalcroze did:

bumping into a piece of furniture, going down a step, provoke an accent in our bodies. These training methods are no longer used and they have practically disappeared from knowledge and memory. But employed in a basic way on stage, they are still good for producing the dramatic 'effects' of collisions (between a dancer and a table, a dancer and another dancer etc.). Accent can also affect the axis, and the body's interior, as noted above, and it produces fleeting softenings which pass along a thousand possible itineraries according to the aesthetics of body state. With Trisha Brown, accent passes lightly scattered through the tonic network and is immediately gathered up again. In Dominique Dupuy's diaphragmatic thinking the diaphragm, or rather diaphragms, are so many filters between deep movements: absorption and expulsion, or breathing in or out join and intermingle, creating a spasmic symphony: the body as a channel much more than a body amassed. A body which circles around its cavities, like a painter around an inner space that gradually becomes a landscape.

Accent has had a singular significance in the theory and practice of German dance. In Laban's thought, accent is more structuring than the particular way that the movement unfolds.[14] Accent not only gives movement its quality but its meaning and symbolic reach. If we consider movement according to its three phases of beginning, middle and end the place of accent, according to these phases, leads to different qualities. In the initial phase accent gives the 'impulse'. The movement is dominated by affect and maintains an emotional relation with space. This is the '*Auschwung*', one of the first qualitative elements by means of which Laban tried to 'read' the new path – infinite and invented – of movement's modernity. By contrast, when accent is placed on the terminal phase, its 'impact' gives the movement a more demonstrative value, and it is the meaning or intentionality (according to the current use of the word) which is valued. Kurt Jooss and his collaborator Sigurd Leeder, students of Laban, both accorded the dynamics of accent an essential role, not only in their aesthetic but in their training technique where accentuation engenders and draws out the engagement of the whole body.[15] In Jooss's choreography the place of the accent guides the spectator toward the intention of the story. It is one of the pillars of *Tanztheater* where movement not only carries a dramatic story but has a role in awakening a critical awareness in the spectator.[16] Accent is an important element because it is what most plays on our kinesthesia. More than from any other corporeal manifestation, the spectator feels this 'pressure' on the consistency and stability of the material as it punctuates the unfolding of any 'utterance' in the time arts. Thus, in the first tableau of *The Green Table* the emphatic movement is often accented twice. First on the *Auschwung* which gives it elasticity and amplitude, and then at the end as if to underpin ironically the futile and demonstrative rhetoric of the puppet figures gathered around the negotiating table. The accent, emphasised by the clownish visibility of the white-gloved hands, is carried to an extreme and gives ridiculous emphasis to their silent discourse. In *Tanztheater* it is the movement itself which engenders its own critique – with the accent playing the role both of movement's impulse, and its commentary on itself.

Without always understanding (that is, in a physical sense) what its stakes were, French dance of the 1980s was very destabilised by the disaccentuation in Merce Cunningham's work. For Cunningham, as for Jooss (two great masters who have articulated their movement around a philosophical choice), the role of accent has major importance in their treatment of time and movement poetics. But with Cunningham accent has a negative value. Accent gives a higher value to certain privileged moments and thus re-establishes a hierarchy between different elements of the artifact, a hierarchy that Cunningham never ceased struggling against, whether in the relations between the forms of expression at play in a performance or in the distribution of information in space and the body. Even more than seeking a democratic equality between the factors at work on the choreographic stage, Cunningham sought a 'flat' time without punctuation, a time of impermanence where the accidental occurs without being determined by a fall of weight. If accent occurs it happens in the attack at the moment of a change of direction: then it becomes a factor of space, much more than of dynamics. It is simply a variation on contingency as articulated by the hexagrams in the *Book of Changes*, the I-Ching – and which in fact uncovers only that change which is the *internal process of things*.[17] Already at work in the music and thought of John Cage, this new vision of a time without accent, a time only functioning in and through the curve of its own ongoingness was to find itself prolonged in the whole post-Cageian artistic current. Repetition in movement, as in sound, allowed dynamics to be annulled in favour of the periodic return of a cellular unit in an immobile, inalterable, unaltered time untroubled by any intervention. Thus in the post-modern years, music and dance were to realise the oriental ideal imparted to Cage by the master Suzuki to *allow things to have a life of their own, separate from oneself and to project neither desire nor values on to them*.[18] Here in obverse is the real value of accent: the projection of a desire that marks the intervention of the subject in the treatment of duration. Accent is eminently a subjectivisation of time and conveys the phases of affective investment with an untold force, as diaphragmatic contraction does for the voice, as we suggested above. French dancers for whom a subjective 'branding' of dance is essential have been de-railed (literally) by Cunningham. Hence the opaque ambivalence which once again inhabited the bodies of French dance in the 1980s where a multiplicity of influences and the difficulty of reading them, of situating oneself historically in relation to them, produced uncertain poetics, and where this inner rupture gave them both their fragility and their value. It is as if the body, far from mastering or possessing a theory of its own, was wandering indiscriminately through the history of bodies. Bagouet knew how to make this a true aesthetics of movement's own self-questioning – not without relation of course to what Isabelle Ginot calls the 'cracks' (*fissures*).[19] That is why accent in his dance shifts the beginning of his movements in the direction of an unfinished tentativeness. The accent, placed at unexpected moments, suspends the impulse or makes it detour in a softened curve. We see this process especially in the arms which take on an increased importance after *Déserts d'Amour*. These arm or hand movements often occur in a tonicity and according to accentuations that are opposed to those in the rest of the body. Bagouet's body is almost never homogenous. It 'declines' all the cleavages of its inner changes. It is a 'disconcerted' body in the double sense of a break in connection and a feeling of astonished uncertainty. But this astonishment is rich. It leads the spectator and, I imagine, the dancer to question more, to reach perceptual limits beyond those already coherently defined. In all cases it integrates, as dance knows how to do, an empty space within the movement which shows it.

It is not surprising to find in the work of a former Bagouet dancer, Christian Bourigault, a particularly effective distribution of accent, even if in an apparently very different aesthetic. But we have already noted that the quest for artistic kin in dance is almost never based on what Laban calls the 'apparent aspect' of dance. Movement, in fact, always leads us beyond what in psychoanalysis is called the 'manifest content'. We need to locate the deeper springs which percolate under the forms and which bring them forth. Even if, in this case, an almost opposite aesthetic is involved. Nor is it by chance that Bourigault began his journey with the painter Egon Schiele: Viennese and German expressionist painting gives a primordial importance to tension and to the accent that it creates in space. Watching a performance of Bourigault's the spectator's perception is carried away in the dynamics of the accent. In a piece called *Matériau désir* even more than in his first solo, *Autoportrait of 1917*, the polarities of space and time are traversed by four characters, restaging in a less directly identifiable way the four characters of Heiner Muller's *Quartett* – in turn inspired by *Les Liaisons*

Dangereuses. It thus involves a set of exchanges between men and women. What is effaced in relation to the Laclos and Muller texts is the power rela-tion between the protagonists. Rather, each is confronted with her/his personal struggles and the encounters between these conflicted fields re-animate the tensions within the movement of each, but also in the shared space. The accents are like the splash of these tensions. They allow us to perceive the crossing or confrontation of lines of force. They illuminate like so many magnetic points the relational tissue of space. Thus in *Point and Line to Plane* Kandinsky saw the point as an incommensurable place with-out surface or dimension, a pure impact that the ten fingers and the feet of the dancer Gret Palucca drilled into space in a leap piercing space and time the better to mark there the conflicts at the sharp intersection of tensions. Like accent, the point or inflection of the line, the knot at the intersection of planes, and the voluminousness of volumes organise our pathic vision of the world. This is why the way that we accent (or disaccent) our relation to the world, like phrasing, contains fundamental symbolic decisions to which the even slightest of our movements bear witness.

1 In *Work: 1961-72*, 1973, p.64

2 Jaques-Dalcroze, Emile *La musique et nous*, 1981

3 Appia, Adolphe *Ecrits dalcroziens.* Complete Works, vol. III, presented by Marie-Louise Bablet, 1988.

4 Jaques-Dalcroze, Emile *Le rythme, la musique et l'éducation*, 1984.

5 Ibid.

6 Godard, H. 'Singular, moving geographies' 1996.

7 Benveniste, E. 'The Notion of "Rhythm" in its Linguistic Expression'. *Problems in General Linguis-tics*, 1971, pp.281-288.

8 Which Louppe, likes to translate as *noué* (knotted). [Transl.]

9 See Bataille, G. *The Accursed Share: an essay on general economy*, 1988.

10 Pradier, Jean-Marie 'Le théâtre des émotions' in *Evolutions Psychanalytiques*, No.7, 1990.

11 Forti, S. *Handbook in Motion.* Halifax: Nova Scotia Press, 1966. See also Banes, S. *Terpsichore in Sneakers*, 1980.

12 Sergeant-Wooster, A. 'Elaine Summers: Moving to Dance' in *The Drama Review*, No. 24, Dec. 1980. According to the author one of the objectives of 'release' was 'to move lightly with a minimum of tension.'

13 See the commentary by Trisha Brown on the *Accumulations* in Banes, 1980.

14 Laban's texts make little reference to accent. However, the tradition of his teaching, whether through Wigman's *Ausdruckstanz* or in the teaching of Jooss and Leeder, reveal its importance.

15 Winearls, Jane *Modern Dance, the Jooss-Leeder Method*, 1978.

16 Laban, R. *The Mastery of Movement*, 1971.

17 Jullien, François *La Propension des Choses: pour une historie de l'efficacité en Chine*, 1992.

18 Ibid.

19 Ginot, Isabelle 'Fissures, petites fissures' in *La Danse, naissance d'un mouvement de pensée*, 1989.

Space

In other words, space opens and hollows out. It ceases to be the milieu where things are located. It is their continuous pulsation and in their springing forth a gaze is precipated.
Pierre Kaufman[1]

Every movement changes the space.
Jacqueline Robinson[2]

Reading space

When Irmgard Bartenieff, a dancer, notator, therapist and student of Laban exiled to the United States in the '30s, was treating a disabled child at the William Parker Hospital, rather than focusing on the affected area, she tried to restore a 'spatial intent'.[3] The transfer of weight, then, does not obtain its identity from an inner substance but from that spatial summons through which the body is constructed, and from the movement which elaborates it. Thus, movement does not have its origin within the subject (even if the notion of 'inner' is validated in the 'inner impulse to move') but, on the contrary, comes from an essential otherness. Hence the importance of Bartenieff's vision of the body as a *'geography of relations.'* It is through this geography that our relation to the world is built – on the affective as well as poetic planes. It is why we need continually to explore, maintain, or open relational pathways or sometimes repair them when they have been too deeply scarred. Here again, those who are thought to suffer a body deficit, a break, an incompleteness can reveal the body's great knowledge. A map of this knowledge can be read in the traces left by the wounding. The dancer only aspires to this knowledge in order to redouble and activate her imaginary cartographies. With his theory of the Four Factors, Laban had already understood that space is not simply a parameter of movement in general, and even less a frame for its propagation. It is a constitutive force. The dancer lives from space and from what space constructs within her/him. This is why the 'spatial intent' of the choreographer and dancer must be the object of a particularly attentive approach and perception. Spatial choices carry the essential marks of a dance's philosophy.

Of course, the dancer does not 'treat' space as an objective, manipulable element. We have seen that space is co-substantial with the moving body described by Laban. It has nothing to do with 'objective' space or its abstract representation or the idea, criticised by Merleau-Ponty, of *a milieu in which things bathe*.[4] Nor still is space an accumulation of perceptions of its 'forms' or its categories. Certainly, in her/his working process or when clarifying spatial givens, the dancer must come to grips with ideas of levels (high, intermediate, low), orientation (lateral, perpendicular, oblique etc.), planes (vertical, horizontal, lateral, sagittal – which in fact Laban made into experiential terms in order to relativise their abstract character: the horizontal table, the vertical doorway, the sagittal wheel), and distance, etc. Sometimes these elements taken in isolation are explored or are the object of abstract creations in improvisation or in composition, as in the case of Oskar Schlemmer, Alwin Nikolais, Merce Cunningham and particularly Gerhard Bohner whose *Exercises for a Choreographer* (1986) are so many 'studies' or sketches on the categories listed above. Except that Bohner adds to this the sensibility and the density of a body that is the measure and surface these givens confront and by which they can become artistic matter. But, once explored, these categories are revealed as relatively impoverished compared to a wholly poetic approach to space – that of Mary Wigman's 'absolute space': both a metaphysical space no longer based on categorical or descriptive definitions – a space beyond space – and a space-matter. This is the space that the body encounters as another body: space as a partner where the body, if it knows how to play with its tensional states, can invent consistencies and 'sculpt' them (Laban's 'carving space' which begins with shaping the proximal space).[5]

Those involved in dance can always sense when a dancer activates her/his relationship to space. The dancer is often said to be 'taking hold of' (*prendre*) space but in most cases it is space which takes hold of the dancer, and ourselves along with her/him. Alwin Nikolais says that, *the dancer is bewitched by space.*[6] In his vision of 'dynamic' space, Laban had already described an active exchange between space and the subject. *Alongside the movement of bodies in space, there is the movement of space in bodies.*[7] Certainly 'displacement' ('travelling' or changing place) is not the only form of this relationship: in immobility, even on the ground, the body maintains a vibrant dialogue with space. But in dance, throwing oneself at, not to mention losing oneself in, space has something extravagant and exultant about it because, when space is not inscribed in it, space, more than the movement, loses its functionality. As Nikolais says, body and space no longer serve as the means to travel from 'a' to 'b'. They become themselves this journey: 'being-in-trajectory' according to Virilio's expression.[8] Changes of speed, breadth of space covered, simultaneous opening to all possible orientations, these free being from the closed itineraries of everyday life. Space becomes an affective partner, almost able to change our states of consciousness. Space moves through us, but also in us, following internal directions, mobile or immobile, and with the help of the 'inner voyages' which are perhaps our most important experiences of being taken hold of by space.[9] Anyone who has not felt that space can be propelled, sculpted, and made to vibrate musically by the body's presence, has not known a fundamental or, more correctly, foundational experience. In our culture, dance performance is without doubt charged with providing this experience through the intercession of another body. Not only so that we can feel space within us but also to make it perceived and understood. I have already cited Dominique Dupuy's phrase: *To dance is to render space visible.*[10] This is why a combined kinaesthetic and semiotic interpretation of space in choreographic works is one of the most important propositions of contemporary dance, and probably responds to a demand as pressing as it is hidden in the body of the spectator. In dance theory, in fact, a relation with space does not exist in itself: it is we who institute it. And the characteristics of these relations contain practically the whole gamut of our symbolic investments in the world and in others. Space is never given: we work with it at every moment, as it works in us. More than a construction or structuration, space is a 'production' of our awareness. The qualities of this space vary with each person. And vary more still with each choreographer who constructs a singular, explicit space: a space that lives, moves, thinks and is thought.

One of the most important tasks incumbent on the dancer as well as the theorist is to distinguish 'space' from 'the place' (*lieu*): place in the concrete objective sense of being in a place. But also place as the representational frame of objects in the world in the sense that it was conceived in classical painting, for example. Certainly dance is familiar with a topological poetics: in dance, as in all twentieth century arts, there have been numerous 'in situ' works. Pieces using a local site like Deborah Hay's famous *Hill* (1972), with an actual hill that the dancers ran down, have been very important.[11] Trisha Brown's famous *A man walking down the side of a building* (1969) or *Roof* (1970) can be considered 'in situ' works, even if the question of the site was not foremost: *A man...*was intended rather to deconstruct the urban location by changing the perspective and distribution of weight in the body (which can be linked to the dancer's friendship with Gordon Matta Clark, a specialist of demolition and unused sites). *Roof* already belongs to the series of *Accumulations*. It is a negative accumulation since it involves losing movements in their transmission from one hazy downtown Manhattan roof to another. Similarly with the art of disappearances and invisible appearances in Odile Duboc's street dances, including amongst others the famous and inspired *Entr'acte* at Aix en Provence (1985). At the conference 'Autres Pas' (1995), Joanna Haygood showed her interesting work on 'place' as the surface of exploration and corporeal sensations. When a place is lacking, nothing prevents a provisional one from being constructed: *Factory*, by Hervé Robbe and Richard Deacon (1993) was a non-theatre space whose form and boundaries were determined by objects and lights – a huge lighting batten supporting a modular sculpture. This served both as a mast and a column, an incandescent scaffolding which was the pivot point of a space shared by both the public and the dancers.[12] Elsewhere, this work on site might also be a way of subverting the authoritarian givens of a topological space. In the western tradition, space is constructed, pre-determined and even pre-compartmentalised according to quantifiable subdivisions, all more or less analogous to the planes of accommodation between the horizon and the eye of the spectator defined by perspective, the *'costruzione legitima'* inherited from the Renaissance. This is a measurable and measured space, surveyed and geometric as Baxandall and Damisch have shown: a representation of space which orders things homogeneously, where each thing, each body takes its place according to the rules of a common scale, as chess pieces take their place on the chess board.[13] This image of the chess board, particularly useful as the measurable grid of represented space such as we find in the pavements of Quattrocento paintings, an idealised *'vista'* which the parallel and perpendicular lines and their different relationship to the perspectival vanishing point makes more readable, was the frame of one of the first ballets evoked in literature.[14] The *danse savante* thus showed its allegiance to humanist philosophy with its vision of a celestial and rational architecture of the world. Out of this vision 'theatres' in the broader sense of the word were to develop: all the spaces where an imaginary was to reorganise and regulate projections of the world within a constructed spatial enclosure. In classical western culture the dance stage reproduced images already inscribed in intellectual thought and its symbolic forms: circles, diagonals, trajectories reproduced by bodies as one makes forms on the ground of already given geometries. From the *'sacra rappresentazione'* of the Middle Ages to the *ballet de cour*, in simple travelling patterns, dancers traversed the archetypal forms of the firmament or the mystery of cryptic signs. This was undoubtedly a sublime moment in dance's history from which, later, the ballet was to conserve the spatial forms while, alas, losing the greater part of their mystery. At the beginning of the seventeenth century and the development of the first baroque ballets, lines of travel were essentially inscribed on the ground. Even if, subsequently, the line of movement was to occupy at least two spatial dimensions, the dancer traced her/his journey on a single plane. Then, the body became a potential element of elevation as in an architectural drawing. This theatre of vision would become the theatre as such – inspired by Vitruvius, revisited by Palladio, and remaining practically unchanged right up to the present: not only does the stage conform to an architecture and an institution anchored in indestructible systems of spatial representation, but we have interiorised this architecture in our own mental and imaginative spaces. Following Frances Yates, the philosopher Jean-Louis Schefer and others have evoked the strange 'theatres of memory' which were elaborated by Quintilian in the wake of Aristotle where, from a single, centralised point of view a fictive spectator contemplates the world's objects ordered and stacked in a neat geometric space.[15] *Thought and imagination, then, are constituted theatrically as the subject's fantasmatic production onto a ground of figurative resistance.* Not only have the representational structures of the theatrical black box, in parallel with those of the mental and mnesic visual box within each of us, totally invested our perceptual co-ordinates but, likewise, Western civilisation through its cultural habits. Just returned from a world tour, Susan Buirge showed us in her enlightening workshops that the European viewer perceives a moving body – this was the case amongst all the workshop participants – in absolutely simultaneous stages as if the appearance of a body was immediately set in a collective, homogenous, undifferentiated (and, perhaps in many respects indifferent, in its extreme convergence) captation.

How did the body of contemporary dance free itself? And was it able to inaugurate a space of its own? As Isabelle Launay has shown, drawing on the early work of Laban, for a long time in the beginning of its modernity, at the moment of the *Freie Tanz* and the comings and goings of dancers foreshadowing 'absolute space' on the lawns of Monte Verità contemporary dance rebelled against this space.[16] But the economy of spectacle still keeps the dancer chained to specialised places of performance. How to work with a theatre space that squeezes you as though into the frame of a picture, with its edges, its centre, its foreground, etc? How to occupy or re-occupy the institutionalised stage while consciously avoiding its traps? There are several paths: staging a theatre of suspicion (Humphrey, Brown); converting the space into a utopian bi-dimensional, non-illusory space, or working 'in the plane' as Jasper Johns said of Cunningham.[17] Or even by abdicating, pure and simple, as did a large number of French dancers during the '80s who, like those in the theatre, resigned themselves to treating space as a purely scenographic (that is, mimetic) category.

With a critical and extremely lucid eye, Doris Humphrey studied the 'strong' and 'weak' places, and the way visibility fades along the trajectory of the diagonal. She rummaged in the recesses of a space that was hostile enough for any immanent strategy to be constantly undermined.[18] It was a difficult undertaking but she was able, not so much in her texts but in her pieces, to implode the restrictive scenic lines of force. *Passacaglia* and *Water Study* are whirlwinds of space where the instability of the bodies propagates clouds of falling particles. Here it is the vortex, the helicoidal ecstasy of space in the freely moving bodies, which prevents the 'staging' of the dance from converging around a single point. Merce Cunningham's radical solution was to make of the theatre stage a 'non-place', or in other words, etymologically, a 'utopia', which, in one fell swoop, was to efface the whole centralising structure. He transferred to the stage the pictorial space of the 'all over' painters of his generation, where all points have equal value (or an equal absence of value): a peaceful space-time around what he calls the 'quiet centre,' a centre discharged of energy, where there are no privileged points of intensity, and where bodies take the initiative. *A prevalent feeling among many painters that lets them make a space in which anything can happen is a feeling dancers may have too.*[19] By allowing our eye, without any 'stage directive' to follow the moving bodies, Cunningham grants us an essentially liberating experience. All the more for the fact that the agent of this liberation, as always in contemporary dance, is the dancer her/himself. It is the dancer who 'spatialises' by opening up the plane of a perceptual field which is transformed by changing directional choices. There is no space but the one that my eyes open upon and which at each moment reinvents both the world, and the circulation of the real. *To claim that a man standing on a hill could do other than be there is to cut oneself off from life* – life as a sequence of unpredictable events, but also as a succession of multiple directions which are precisely so many acts of appearing before this unpredictability. This spatial language always privileges the 'plane' not only as the face to face of body and perceived field but also as 'plane-ness' (*planéité*), the bi-dimensionality dear to the painter and the one that steals the dancer away from an illusory depth where her/his movements and space are in danger of being de-realised. Here is a space where the continual exchange of 'polarities' (a notion inspired by the I-Ching) creates a happy anarchy but where, today, on the horizon of contemporary dance, there is still (too often) an attempt to re-assemble the fantasmatic and allegorical sites (*lieux*) of figurative space. For it cannot be said that the Cunningham revolution has really taken place, or that theatrical space has really been freed from its archaic bonds. In its material and institutional mechanisms it remains a representational space where successive generations have hastened to re-establish the old totem of the figurative vanishing point and as Bernard Remy has noted, *what they most want to conjure: the phantom space.*[20]

One can understand the more distrustful attitude of Trisha Brown who feels constrained by this space and who denounces the historical and ideological system from which this constraint arises. She still feels that her return to the theatre after the experiments of the Judson Church and the Grand Union was a forced submission to the market of the spectacle. With *Set and Reset* (1983) after warily examining the 'theatrical furniture', she decided to denounce its constraints: in particular the pressures on the body, caught as a target of the theatrical look, to excessively 'appear'.[21] With Robert Rauschenberg as designer, she replaced the flats with black tulle as a way of undressing (not without allusions to indecency) the areas that are normally hidden and thus of making more uncertain the line between appearance and disappearance. As in other works, she created 'occupied zones': here, the centre being deserted in favour of the sides, which always attract and sometimes swallow the dancers. In other works, by contrast, (*Foray/Forêt* 1990, for example) the centre of the stage is occupied by centrifugal eddies while the edges (which she described to me as 'slime') make leaving the stage a struggle, the body extricating itself with difficulty from the site of its overexposure, as if the scopic captation of the body created an excessive viscosity from which the dancers could not free themselves.

To what values do these processes for avoiding the traps of an impoverished and obsolete theatrical wizardry uninhabitable and unusable unless it can be subverted (or overcoded as in Decouflé and Nikolais), transformed, revoked, or avoided, correspond? It is that contemporary dance, unlike the classical arts of representation, does not reproduce spatialities. It produces them. Bodies do not organise themselves in the form of a circle or triangle: they are the circle; they are the very angle which cuts a diagonal. *There is more to a round than just making a circle. You will have to run in circles for many days before you will know what a circle is. Then all of a sudden you will realise that you are not yourself any more, that your space is dynamic and powerful and that you have to master that force*, writes Hanya Holm.[22] The contemporary body is the agent of its own space: it is as always in a reciprocal relation with and engages all the movement parameters. Let us recall that for Laban there is no isolated entity. What he calls space is nothing other than our relation to space, with all the colours and qualitative modes which characterise this relation. As Forestine Paulay says, *the choreographer is the one who knows how to give meaning to this relation* – and not only to give meaning.[23] Space must still *be*. And it is through the proximal sphere that our symbolic space is elaborated in the first instance. As we have seen, everyone constructs and manages her or his own kinesphere, which is all the movements that connect us with the world. In the same way that each of us possesses a whole symbolic gamut of movements which express us, so too each of us is linked to a specific space whose imaginary charge, whether or not we think of ourselves as dancers, has an extreme signifying force. But we are talking about an individual space, limited to the immediate region of our body and whose web of significations we cannot convey in daily life except in moments of affective sharing: in love relations, or in relationships between a parent and child – and we will return to this latter kind of sharing which for each one of us founds our relation to the movement sphere. Not only do dance and choreography teach us to share this space but also to know it and accept it – the space of the other and our own with all of its symbolic fault lines to which only dance can give meaning. They teach us to dilate this space, to make it tangible and readable. Kinespheric space is shared in workshops, and in the studio. It is shared with the spectator when her/his own spatial sensation is encountered, however distant, mysterious and possibly atrophied or scarred it might be. When a spectator looks at a work they make the space of movement and the space of perception communicate with one another.

One of the most important thresholds across which bodily and spatial experiences slide into one another (Roland Barthes and more recently Gerard Genette and Rosalind Kraus, speak of 'shifters' or what we might call 'gears') can be found in the relation of the body to its own dimensions (front, behind, side). In principle, in Laban's theory, these planes of the body do not have an identity in themselves. Ideas like front and back are determined not by anatomical location but by a directional impulse. It is the direction which decides the real plane of action between verticality, horizontality, sagittality. However, for a long time in dance a very great poetic value has been attributed to these sites of the body as keys to space. This can be found in the opposition between front and back in the Noh master, Zeami.[24] For him, these planar values are linked to the fact that if the front space and contours of the body are mastered by the gaze, the back can only depend on skin perceptions – very rich ones, in other words. This back plane which is neglected in practical life, since it does not correspond to any productive or communicative function, is so important, as we have seen, in the contemporary dance body. It releases a space that enlarges as we advance to become a fund of resonance for the movement, a space that holds us and at the same time lets us go. The 'behind' is the space of the back, the most unknown, perhaps most charged of our own surfaces, as we have noted. For the dancer the frontal space is a space of projection which is always dangerously subject to overuse. But contemporary dance has found ways to limit the formidable effects of overemphasis common in the representation (and presentation) of the self. This 'emitting' of the body's form or outline towards the front, in the autoproclamation of a bodily façade, marks uninspired and conventional practices which have developed in all kinds of artistic and non-artistic expression (cinema, publicity, the staging of bourgeois social relations, etc.). It is important to recognise that numerous contemporary French choreographers have stayed true, aesthetically, to the philosophical postulates of their art. Spatially, they have worked on themselves and even worked 'in retreat' so as not to ostentatiously 'take' space. In this sense, the discreetly projected space of Odile Duboc, Stephanie

Aubin, George Appaix and Dominique Bagouet is completely faithful to the spirit of Wigman, Humphrey, Cunningham. This opting for a relation to the self over 'the space in front' works on the proximal auras. The choice is poetic but also political and concerns the dancer's choices in relation to her/his power over the other's gaze.

On the other hand, an interesting use of frontal space consists in risking, not the spectator's gaze, but that of the dancer her/himself as the operator of space, as an opening to the directional impulse: for example, in Duboc's way of looking towards the front as an unknown space to explore, or Cunningham's look towards the space in front as a multiple and always changing presence: a look that guides the dancer as the light of his eyes guides the man's march in Plato's *Timeus* – which Cunningham cites in one of his texts.[25] With Duboc as with Cunningham, the look to the front does not seek to control still less to conquer this space: it is rather surprised, disarmed by it and continually re-oriented, as though led towards the moving truth of the world. The look can also be transported by the movement. In *Locale* (1981), Cunningham's and Charles Atlas's video-dance, space moves and turns like a body. Frontal space becomes the giddy space of instability whose axes and planes vary with the paths taken.

Jacqueline Robinson makes a useful distinction between the space immediately around the body and 'change of place', the journey through space which involves another kind of relation.[26] But Robinson would agree that, in principle, choreographic art consists in establishing relations that are coherent and, in particular, resonant between these spatial moments. A weight transfer can be carried into space, or rather, one can be carried by it: movement contains the impulse proper to its trajectory. What has been worked at the proximal level in respect of important elements like direction is transposed to the level of 'travelling'. In contemporary dance there is no fundamental difference between the micro- and the macro-organisation. However small a movement might be, as in the works of Dominique Bagouet for example, it resounds throughout the entire space like the reverberations of a flash. Individual movement does not lodge in space: it builds the distant space alongside the 'gestosphere' to use Hubert Godard's useful neologism. For example, the 'going line' found in Merce Cunningham's work circulates across the entire space whatever its dimension or from whatever location it begins. Without wanting to establish criteria (which would be ill-judged in relation to an art whose extreme freedom we have affirmed), I admit to being partial to the art of choreographers for whom the extended space prolongs without rupturing the 'body language' (*gestuelle*): where the kinesphere is the poetic hearth of a development into space without the need for an added construction, where the body travels in its own movement as well as in space. This is proof that a coherent imaginary has been found and that known vocabularies are not used to 'furnish' a space which ought to elaborate itself as a 'generative field', to use an expression of René Thom. It is a palpable generative field, a conjunctive tissue which weaves itself into the very experience of the subject.[27]

Nothing of this space is 'given'. Far from it. In the same way that each creator invents her/his movement, each choreographic language creates a singular space. This 'spatial language' as Laban calls it, has to be deciphered differently according to each artist, sometimes according to each work.[28] The choreographic space lives, as the dancer's body lives and dances. Often, it even emanates from it: made visible by the movement, space sometimes appears as the exteriorisation of the 'inner landscape', a purely poetic space whose articulation with objective space is only transitory, analogous to an imaginary spatial resonance and unable at any moment to actualise itself completely. This individual, interior space lives through its own texture and dynamic. Its life depends on the work of the body that gives birth to it. There is the 'full space', for example, with which Wigman works in the way one might work with another body, a body-space whose energies she feels converging towards her, a body-space which leans and presses on her body, as if her body weight were also part of the space-body. In *Hexentanz* (1913) or *Totenmal* (1929) she stretches and kneads it, drawing it towards or away from her like a thickened mass. She works on the resistance of this medium, her body stirring it with its own tonic changes. Beginning with Cunningham, the new American dancers of the '50s, were not mistaken: Wigman brought with her on her American tours the 'absolute space' evoked above, a space which lived its own life, not dependent on the scenographic 'place', or on any objective frame.[29] It was a space that she re-invented with each movement because it was the very matter/material of her being. But she re-invented it with the complicity of the spectator. She did not present her/him with a closed spatial system: through her very gesture she allowed the other's perception to perceive and inhabit this space. This is the famous 'feeling through' which according to John Martin, *establishes the rhythm with the greatest clarity and consequently only designates the intense points of its design leaving it up to you to fill the space and complete the form.*[30] How can we not evoke Matisse's famous phrase, *I provide a detail and through rhythm I lead from this detail to the totality,* made not in reference to space, but to creative tools like rhythm that lead the eye itself to construct the space of the painting (he was reflecting on his painting *The Dance* created in 1933 for the Barnes Foundation).[31] It is the space created out of body experience that Laban identifies as the object of a work of 'sculpting' space, when we build the invisible volume which, like the points of a crystal, contains the final discharge of our energies, and of which Laban's icosahedron is the concrete image. Furthermore, this Wigmanian space is one of the prophetic vehicles of a new relation to space no longer functioning as a classical space or empty frame where the object in its plenitude is inscribed. The dancer, on the contrary, makes the vault of her/his inner space reverberate in a thick texture. The inside-outside relation which allows multiple landscapes to resonate with each other gives rise to one of the most important problematics not only of dance but of all 20th century art: what mode of representation will realise the artistic act? The inner-outer movement proper to expressionism in dance, in painting and even in abstract expressionism reveals spaces that have been forced open, almost shattered (as in Pina Bausch's *Café Muller*) as if their precipitation into objective space, *fallen from an obscure disaster,* still carried the stigma of an impossible reconstitution. [32]

Another important element of contemporary dance space is that it is not made from a single moving body, nor even from several. It is found, as John Martin again notes, in the interference of personal spheres, what he calls *fields of action.* [33] It is actually the 'feeling through' of these multiple auras that dances between the bodies. Ehrenzweig describes it marvellously in relation to Cunningham and the 'interaction' amongst his dancers' kinespheres: *Each of them threaded and wove an invisible cocoon, constructed a protective (uterine) space around herself, somewhat as an animal takes exclusive possession of a territory. In order to allow each dancer to freely complete her/his sequences, the others had to change place, skirting and following the lines of invisible frontiers. These frontiers were continually changing: they contracted, spread out, prepared themselves for harmless or dangerous encounters until finally at a certain moment the individual spaces opened themselves to each other and fused in a sudden union.* [34] Hence the choreographer's delicate work to make these personal spheres overlap, to make them play and resonate with each other without at the same time restricting or rupturing them. This space continuously modifies itself: it swells, hollows out, frays. The sculptor-dancer Oskar Schlemmer also saw this when he talked of the *plastic inscription of movement in space.* [35] In contemporary dance, even in impromptu settings one can see the space emerge, move, sculpt itself from one body to another. It does not matter if the focus is on the movements converging or parting, there is always a conjunctive relation which makes space itself exist and dance between the bodies.

Abandoning a linear vision is not just a matter of the three usual dimensions: the width, length and depth within which visible movement takes place. It entails the total revision of an idea that is not often broached outside dance: that of the ground. In other fields of expression, the question of space is only raised in terms of problematics in the visual (scopic) arts: painting, sculpture and today, cinema which with few exceptions (Jacques Tati, for example) closely follows the tridimensionality of representation. Since these representational arts do not deal with weight, the question of the support is, generally at least, foreign to them. With several artists who are very often influenced by dance or performance (Robert Morris, Richard Serra) the angles of support, their importance or fragility, their presence or absence are essential and can even be the subject of the work. By contrast, in dance, the apprehension of space begins with our first relations, those that are most elementary, the most tactile and thus one could say the least favourable to projection: in other words our supports. In the evolution of one's biography supports are essential. The child, who is not in charge of its gravitational alignment, feels itself in the first instance through contact with the parental body. But we do not have this body at our disposal throughout life. Freedom gained through conquering verticality, walking, etc., does not prevent the dancer from spending a lifetime revisiting these supports, interrogating them, changing them.[36] The supporting body, the substitute body is the ground. The world allows us all our lives the security and plenitude of this single surface-for-letting-go. As we have pointed out certain choreographies do not leave the ground: they invent the whole danced space there. This is the case with the first part of Wigman's *Hexentanz*, and of some of Rosalia Chladek's 'underworld' solos. Hideyuki Yano had a particular way of inhabiting the ground which was both a place of listening and waiting. From this apparently full and ordered space where he rested with his legs and arms in the air he made an empty cocoon (especially in *MA Ecarlate*, 1980). In *Salome* (1987) we could see him supported on a tiny tripod, but in the air as if the ground was beginning to withdraw from under bodies' disquiet. Joëlle Bouvier and Régis Obadia's first compositions had a surprising relation with the ground as if, like something mineral or mysteriously fermenting, their two bodies were a scarcely human emanation of it (*Tête close*, 1982). The ground is not only the functional surface for getting from 'a' to 'b'. In modern dance and in contemporary dance it has an organic and philosophical role: it has an affective role. As Irene Hultmann says *it is our best ally against weight*. But it also has a cognitive role including as the interface between the force of gravity and the experience of the body. As Kajo Tsubi says in his workshops, it is that by which we can *dance: that is, dialogue with the centre of the earth.* [37] Contemporary dance does not dance on the ground it dances with it.

With Adolphe Appia, Dalcroze conceived the first multi-levelled spaces of ascending and descending surfaces to make spatial structure enter into the very body of the dancer, and create a dialogue between body and space in which space is a transmitter between the body and its environment. At Hellerau, in the building which from 1910 housed the Dalcroze school, the stage built by Appia with its platforms and stairways undulates and flows with the movement of bodies. [38] It is rhythmic and irregular like the phases of human experience. After such experience/experiments dance could not but continue to include spaces for 'giving way': firstly, by body practices which resonate the body cavities, the 'basement' as Daniel Dobbels has called them, and give voice to its hollow-chambered qualities. [39] But it is also possible, by means of external architectural or scenic contraptions, to recreate the experience of the ground giving away: for example, in Trisha Brown whose 'Equipment pieces' took away the dancers' own supports, replacing them elsewhere or nowhere in the body; or in Pina Bausch with her floors covered in chairs, flowers, sand...Bernard Remy writes that: *The ground full of holes seems to offer a series of unreliable supports. The surface is unpredictably uneven. Pina Bausch composes a rhythm from this changing ground. Sometimes the dancers move with their eyes closed, compelled, stopped, knocked, drawn on again by the tactile rhythms of the ground's broken syntax.* [40]

More recently, choreographers have reconnected with the ground in a more metaphorical way in order to retrace lost lines of a distant archaeology where the body might re-connect with some of its meanders. There was Jean Gaudin's very beautiful piece, *Summum Tempus*, filmed on video and danced in a plaster factory where the powdery ground rises up to envelope the dancers. The piece represented the choreographer's first important reflection on verticality. He pursued this in *l'Ascète de San Clemente et de la Vièrge Marie* where his body, confined in all directions, escapes the logic of self-representation. Dominique Bagouet's *Necessito* can be read as an imaginary voyage taking place upon an emblematic ground: the mirror of a double place, the Alhambra of Grenada. The garden was traced on the ground like the deposits of faded memories, a space with a false bottom catching the disoriented bodies in its own traps. Sometimes the ground serves as décor and becomes the background upon which the dance finds its own references (Régine Chopinot's *St Georges*). Finally, in an unusual experiment with the sculptor Amish Kapoor, Catherine Diverrès (*L'Ombre du Ciel*) used a mobile floor. The dance aimed at the kind of trembling that occurs in earthquakes.

But on the hither side of these experiments linked to passing fashions in the poetics of spectacle, there are the great choreographers for whom any treatment of space reflects a permanent philosophy where each work is inscribed in a continuous movement of thought. For Trisha Brown the absence or the displacement of the ground proceeds from a refusal to 'territorialise': on the one hand the dancer refuses to be complicit with imperialist territorialising in a 1970's America living through the last intercontinental wars of economic colonialism. On the other, these same culturally invested territories are refused the dancer once s/he no longer functions on a stage dominated and ordered by the ideology of representation. The only spaces left to use: deserted roofs, walls, stretches of water are the unoccupied, useless, discarded places which for the society and the system have no plus-value. Not only does the body escape the law there, but it inverts the givens of the law by walking on walls and redistributing both gravitational organisation and the general relation of the body to the horizon. According to Bernard Remy, Pina Bausch's treatment of the ground re-opens a history which ideology had thought to fix inalterably: *Pina Bausch begins from what remains under the ruins of German villages.*[41] But this ruined ground is not at all a symbol of death or disappearance as Remy has been the first to point out: on the contrary, its holes re-establish lost rhythms: *the lightness, too, is implacable*, he says. Hence this intermediary world of a space where stumbling amongst the gravitational debris of the ground can act as a vital spring.

Closely linked to our ground-support is the ascending-descending axis which locates us between earth and sky through the experience of verticality. Verticality is fundamental to our construction and affects all our perceptions. Odile Rouquet recalls how the earth-sky relation is at the origin of our whole corporeal or imaginary phylogenesis and how dance continually formulates the question: *What path have I taken in my desire to go towards or away from the ground?* [42] But this double orientation which is our essential relation to space cannot be measured in terms of an objective locality. Certainly, from experience, there is a high and a low, but as intentionality, as direction, much more than as separated zones. In a contradictory way, we often get our relation to the sky from the ground. We have already seen how for Doris Humphrey there is no rise without a fall; that the rebound is our only chance of briefly regaining an orientation to the sky. One of the commonly used forms of elevation, for example, is the jump. In certain schools of contemporary dance, the jump, a moment of escape from earthly gravitation (but with its complicity since it is the chthonic that propels us towards the sky) is made possible through practising a deep relationship with the ground: hence, in Graham's teaching you begin with a lengthy floor work, exploring the sensation of the ground in stretching, flexing, rolling etc., before taking off not as it happens from the legs, but from sensations of the back, and in relation to the whole contact of the body with the ground. This is what gives the deerlike (quasi 'fauve') power of the Graham jump which is executed with contraction of the torso. In relation to this path from earth to sky all the other dimensions of space are possibly illusory. Walking which seems to take place on a horizontal plane will only ever be, as we have seen, *a displacement towards the centre of the earth.*[43]

The poetry of verticality permanently inhabits our bodies, even when we are lying on the ground. In fact, verticality has, fundamentally, nothing to do with the erect stance. Look at a temple column lying on the ground at an archaeological site in Greece and listen in the marbled silence to the song of the earth-sky direction sung by its vibrant cannelations. It is the same with the human body which is constructed, thought, and moves towards the sky in that alignment: it has 'taken root to fly' to use the title of Irene Dowd's important work. The choreographer Kitsou Dubois has propelled dancers, enclosed in a capsule simulating interplanetary flight beyond the earth's gravitational attraction. *To imagine living weightlessly,* she remarks, *is to give birth to a different physical 'man' with as yet unknown rhythms and movements.*[44] But even if, *in the near future, this idea might include the existence of inhabited stations on the planets or the moon,* the dancer will always be able to refer in a bodily way to what dancer-researchers rightly call 'subjective verticality'. This reminds us that our spatial perceptions will always be tributary to our own activity and reflection as subjects. That is why the 'cliff-hanging' dance (*danse escalade*) of the Cie de la Roc in Lichen is so convincing: attached horizontally to a wall dancers move around in that position. It is not just acrobatics or spectacle. From their first piece, *Le Creux Poplite* subsequently named *La Salle de Bain* (1987) they succeeded in making us share a different sensation of space. Not simply through the idea of turning the décor on its head but through an empathy with new experiences of support. Thus, the dancing body becomes the medium between the perceptive life of the spectator and a spatial world which is firstly decomposed and then reorganised through falling-suspension, well beyond scopic givens.

It is understandable that in these ascending-descending spaces an image forms in the contemporary choreographic imaginary which is that of flight. Not through a literal mimesis, but through a conscious corporeal thinking which divests itself of the dominant and powerful idea of a body that struggles against weight. Flight, in contrast, can transport us far away as we willingly let our supports disperse (which one feels so strongly in dreams of flight). *Anyone who has at some time fallen unexpectedly in a hole,* says Dominique Dupuy, *knows that there is flight in this fall.*[45] The flight is that of Dupuy in his 1983 piece *En vols* (recently partly restaged by the Cie Isosaèdre). The choreographer also writes: *I seek flight, flight as translation, displacement (transhumance) in space. The transmigration of being in space –* which does not mean that it is necessary to magically or superficially deny the forces which tie us carnally to the ground.[46] Being drunk with space for the dancer is not as it is for Mallarmé's *Cygne* destined to conjure a *horror of the ground. The dance of flight is not a dance without supports, far from it. It is a dance of spatial 'transport', of weight which is not detained but moved high and low.* For the dancer in both cases it is a question of suspension: that which connects us as weighted bodies to a sky into which we never stop falling, sucked or plucked up by height, and at the same time being born of and pushed away by the earth. Another form of flight and which remains for me one of the most beautiful memories of contemporary dance is Duboc's *Les Vols d'oiseaux* (1982) performed in a square at Aix-en-Provence. Divided into several groups, cohorts of dancers performed a simple travelling dance like a flock of birds magnetised around a single signal. Here, again, it was the supports, the bent legs of a grounded run which had the windy force of a take-off. This 'ventilation', which is so miraculous in Duboc's work was intensified by the changes of direction especially when the group of dancers, like a single organism with multiple antennae, listened to the secret rhythmic message which not only changed their path in an astonishing about-face but, like so many shattered particles, even dispersed space itself. *Oiseau au vol inversé* (bird in inverted flight): isn't this the definition of the dancer whom the earth holds while giving her/him the force of elevation? But this expression of Henri Michaux's could characterise Bernard Glandier's dance in *Azur* (1995). As in *Sentiers*, his earlier work, Glandier is inspired by a line of verse which for him stands for a 'poetic moment' in suspension – here not at all metaphoric – between what passes into the corporeal from the verbal, what is 'seized' in language by the poet, and what captures a body in dance. From Paul Eluard's, *It is not far by bird from cloud to man*, Glandier creates a number of areas by a series of crossings: these areas are empty and the centre-stage is mostly deserted in favour of other regions of intensity. This creates, like an inner turbulence in the movement of the dancers, a cyclone's eye that the bodies skirt around or just touch. The bodies themselves are part of the ambiguous dynamics! Sometimes earthly, with galops and bounds. In fact the sky-like dimension suggested in the title occurs on two planes: the broad open plane of the space crossed and recrossed, and most often embodied. And, at another level, through the instability of the bodies themselves, drawn into these great trajectories as if born by the wind but keeping the intimate quality of their instability. The relation rising-falling is precisely what makes the dancer escape the perspectivist space attached to a horizon line, so that territories no longer dominated by representational strategies open up, unknown, unmarked, without signposts to indicate limits. Here, perhaps, the true dream of flight begins: one that involves exploring all the dimensions where something still exists that has never been named. This 'unknown territory' to use the title of a piece by Christine Gerard, is not necessarily out of reach or virgin because of a pure distance. It can be the immediacy of 'between-two', the uncertain place of the impalpable: thus, and to finish with the bird (if it is desirable or possible to do so), Cunningham's *Beachbirds* (1992) evokes an imperceptible edge, this spatial universe opening up only at the limit of a threshold we touch continually without localising, still less without defining. The dance evokes this space. We cannot say whether it traverses it or, still less, treads in it: a floating, indefinite space, never invaded, simply open.

Spirals, curves, spheres

The moment has come to evoke the spiral in which each circle recedes further and further from being able to 'control' any level territory.

In the spring of 1892, Miss Genevieve Stebbins did something that was decisive for the future of dance. At a school festival in the institution for young women where she was teaching, this student of Steele Mackaye's (himself a disciple of Delsarte) decided to make a presentation on the spiral: in other words, on the continuous relation between the centre and the periphery, the front and back, the high and low. This was the solo *Dance of Day*, and it constitutes possibly the first contemporary dance proposition. Firstly, let us pay homage to Miss Stebbins who is usually represented as having a rather affected, effete style consonant with the '*tableaux vivants*' and statuesque poses that were propagated in the new performance becoming prevalent in the vision of Delsartist America.[47] Beyond images, however, our aim is to tap into the real body work and the body states that this work awakens as so many states of awareness – not as a text that underlies the dance but as the text itself in which the 'spectacular' elements are frequently only metaphorical resonances. With a movement continuously linking the spatial exterior to the interior of her body, Stebbins, who started on the floor, slowly rose from it in a spiralling movement before returning to the ground by the same process. She did not move anywhere:

space circulated between her centre and periphery, and in such cases it is the body which opens (with)in itself its own spatiality. This solo is interesting in several ways: firstly, it curiously prefigures the two solos which compose Doris Humphrey's *Ecstatic Themes* (1930), the rise in *Ascented Point* and its contrasting movement in *Circular Descent*. Furthermore, it had more or less the same thematic motive. (Which proves that we are touching one of the essential focal points to which contemporary dance has always returned). The important point is that, from its beginning, contemporary dance has affirmed that there are no spatial forms except those which are elaborated in body experience. If an archetypal spiral exists it is because the coming and going, the movement towards the centre and movement towards the outside is not only a practical possibility but animates our whole corporeal activity. The 'sense' (*sens*) of the spiral is not to be found in the form produced but, once again, in the spiralling journey in which contrasting tensions oppose each other, especially in the 'torso' (one of the most important forms, precisely, of 'opposition'). This spiral appears again and again in contemporary dance like the flame of a torch which is always there to be re-lit. From Harald Kreutzberg whose solos are simply a spiral continually reiterated along the rising-falling axis, to the rolling movements used by Pina Bausch at the beginning of *Café Muller* (movements which are amplified and multiplied in her *Sacre du Printemps*), to Ingeborg Liptay's very beautiful *Ciel de Terre* in which she creates a veritable bodily corkscrew where all the spatial resources are caught up in the same turning impulse. Spirals traverse all this questioning and experimenting, all the ruptures, and deliriums, and the moments of faltering consciousness, always managing to 'pulverise' univocal or homogenous responses to the enigmatic. From Mary Wigman to José Limón to Trisha Brown the spiral speaks the body's refusal to be constituted as one block, to inhabit a single plane, to be an arrested body in an fixed space. In France, in *Les Tournesols* (1993), Dominique Petit made whirlwinds spiral between bodies as if the whole space, or space itself was winding and unwinding. Exactly one hundred years after Miss Stebbins's solo, in Bagouet's *Necessito*, in 1992, Olivia Grandville danced a new version of circular movement which, by a simple shifting of weight, allowed her centre to pass continually outward without any form being imitated, nor especially any form being 'demonstrated'. These are moments and transformations of the spiral chosen at random from the history of contemporary dance.

Spiralling or rather 'the spiral body,' to use the title of a dancer's writing, entails innumerable consequences for all of the axes of body work.[48] This supports the conviction held by many dancers (a family which includes

Duncan, Humphrey, Hawkins, Brown) that the body must almost always be in a relaxed tonus in order to allow the flow of a directional impulse to pass to another muscle. Relaxation of muscle tone allows the transfer of weight to occur freely without the impulse being controlled. For some time in France it has been possible to observe this release in dancers influenced by such body thinking, and particularly in the body language (*gestuelle*) of Stephanie Aubin. Her work on spiralling, where the movement sequences through a released body, is based in a deeply integrated practice leading to a true musicality which is hers alone. Aubin's movement, weighted and fluidly curving, travels sequentially in her body from one place to another. It is this which gives her dance the billowing, self-generating quality, and its fluid, swinging, quasi-nonchalant aspect. The furling and unfurling is not impeded by a will to shape it. As in the *Necessito* solo mentioned above, the impact of the flow of weight produces slight syncopations set in train by vast anacruses. Oceanic music of a broad, indolent, billowing body.

Spheres, circles and curves are related to the spiral. What they have in common is that they cannot be described as forms external to change in muscle tone, to 'letting go', to use Aubin's term. Anyone who curves tensely will remain in the same shape without really achieving any sphericity and they will never become the kind of moving wave that the circularity of space can absorb. It is not by chance that the spherical is predominant in the art of Doris Humphrey and José Limón. In their work, a free torso, an unstable vertiginous body authorises a circular relationship to space. In many of their choreographies circles are formed at different moments of the piece: Humphrey's *New Dance* (1937) and *Passacaglia* (1938), Limón's *Musical Offering* or *Missa Brevis* (1958) etc., and especially Limón's *There is a Time* (1956). There, the circle takes us back to the archaic community described in the somewhat fatalistic verses of Ecclesiastes – *There is a time for everything under the sky* – which oppose indifferently life and death, love and hate, war and peace as the two outcomes of a single vector. From this resigned duality, Limón has made a powerfully energetic work. It is a circle dance, as are the first 'dances' of Matisse, and they respond to a timeless, primitive vision of the dancing human group. Here, dance is representing itself. But in other works, the use of the circle on stage is an excellent way of escaping a frontal perspectivism. Another space is created which is not only a representational space: the inner space of the closed circle is experienced as a reciprocal relation of spatial linking. It might be argued that the spectator has no access to this space enclosed by a chain. But the power of these pieces is precisely in making us enter into the spherical enclosure and in catching us up in its turbulence. But this power only exists because the dancers are themselves in a state of 'sphericity': in *There is a time* there are precisely two circular levels, that of the bodies which themselves encompass an interior volume; and that of the macro-organisation which reflects back this interior volume on a more ample plane. It is not therefore a question of 'making' a circle as in the remark above from Hanya Holm, still less of 'shaping' or even more of showing a circle but of making it exist out of the experience of the body, of 'being' the circle suspended between sacrum and shoulders, continually unfurled and recaptured on the rebound.

That dance functions in this way leads us to reflect upon the spatial representations that are attributed to it. But the way that Bachelard and especially his disciples draw from human imagination a universally recognisable image is perhaps neither the point nor the aim of contemporary dance. Taking spatial localisation such as high and low, for example, it is striking that someone like Gilbert Durand makes them directly into fixed affective images, even creating an opposition a little like in the classical vision of space where each image has its place and its allegory.[49] Do movement and space, in order to be understood, really need to be related to a referential ground – however rich and suggestive – always acting externally to the experience that engenders it? Doesn't movement create imagination in the way that, for Deleuze, time is what draws the cinematographic image towards its own epiphany, to its signification? Isn't it also necessary to see that movement itself creates imagination? Besides, Deleuze, by taking up while somewhat displacing Brecht's notion of *gestus*, imagines in the time-image an efficacious corporeal 'gesture' of the figural contents of the cinematic sequence. Especially in an engaged cinema like Godard's where the ideological discourse is not delivered 'as an extra', still less through a referential filter, it is in the very bodies of the characters: in *Prénom Carmen*, for example, the attitudes of the bodies ceaselessly return to a musical *gestus* which co-ordinates them independently of the 'plot'.[50]

In his *Poetics of Space*, Bachelard provides an inspired description of *images that, we believe, illustrate in elementary forms perhaps too distantly imagined, the function of inhabiting*. Perhaps these imagined structures of spatial representations serve to revise its claim to be a study of 'pure imagination', and eliminate from the Bachelardian quest what he considers to be the 'positivist' or even 'biological' universe. Dancers have often been attracted by the images that emerge in Bachelard's thought – images which have an non-deterministic, existential beauty. The image only obtains its identity from itself; *in its newness, in its activity, the poetic image has its own dynamism.*[51] The image, thus freed from a causal reference, inhabits its true realm which is that of the virtual; and thus, too, the dancing body does not remain exterior to the imaginary. It is revealing that Bachelard's thought is invoked by numerous choreographers (Odile Duboc, Dominique Dupuy, Bernard Glandier). Work on the elements and on reverie is used and appropriated in workshops and rehearsals, as if through body work one could refind the missing links that might reconnect poetic discourse to dance. As if what was missing from ideal and pre-existent forms in a pure imagination could find another mode of existence and even make the image otherwise through body experience. In fact, concerning space we can, with Laban, consider there to be no pre-established forms even if the human imagination has given birth to their shadows. For forms exist and co-exist in the rapidity of the discourse or the dreaming that, unresisted, stirs them up. The space-time of the dancer must be found through body work and can only exist in dance through an economy of weight transfer which alone is capable of transforming and inciting a form or place. In fact universal imagination can serve, as do tropes, as a foundation where compositional themes can be sourced – the chiasms, inversions, metonymies that are the generative structures found in all the compositional arts (writing, literature, music, choreography, cinema). But the pioneers did not do this: they had to reinvent everything in order to legitimate, by force of the body, the eventual birth of a form. Even Martha Graham with her work on the Jungian archetypes, in her way of evoking the primary forms connected with universal fantasies, anxieties and the undercurrents of affective life, did not seek to conform to structures that were already in place. She evokes them but reinvents them through a body experience. This is the case with the immemorial figure of the labyrinth. Even in its own legend this construction does not draw for its existence on a given architecture but from the experience of a pathway: we know from Homer that it was from an unpredictably meandering line-dance that Daedalus imagined the undulating path of an architecture continually unravelling upon itself. In *Errand into the Maze* the labyrinth is inscribed or rather, in the convolutions of Noguchi's plaited cord, already placed on the ground. We do not know if it is a pathway inviting a journey or the traces of this same journey between desire and the horror of the monstrous and bestial object of this desire: at once both loss and flight towards the central construction, a kind of open hut where Graham's body shelters between retreat, protection and refusal.

Motifs that reveal the traditional symbolic frames: shells, corners, ladders and wells certainly offer objects for exploring certain problems concerning the more or less anecdotal relation of the body to its environment, during an improvisation workshop, for example. But in this warehouse of spatialities the dancer will not find a place. As a nomad even in imagination, s/he must construct out of her/his body the local forms that s/he plans to inhabit – a way of reminding us that spatial relations will always be tributary to our own activity and reflection as body-subjects. Which is what is expressed in a particularly sensitive way by the undertakings of the Cie Roc in Lichen, mentioned above. These artists' work in the vertical plane, the ascending-descending relation does not only come from its literal application to the cliff-face. It overtakes the very thought of this relation. But a choreography of elevation (in the figural but not figurative sense), such as that of Bernard Glandier in *Azur*, is no less relevant: high and low for dance do not exist as localisations. What is important is to see how the body, as the ascending-descending vector, links sky and earth in a double and concomitant experience of high and low. In these ascending-descending spaces, verticality is not truly strong unless it allows what might cause us to lose it to oscillate. Here again it is the helicoidal action of movements that brings all dimensions into relationship. Knowing of course, after Doris Humphrey, that there is no rise without fall (*verticality as the precarious and vulnerable moment of creation* writes Dominique Dupuy).[52] And that an intense stratification, an objective verticality, leads to a hardening that is closer to death than the letting go which prostrates us, releasing us around the gravitational axis to all the possibilities of the spiral – which is at once both the birth and dispersal of imagination in the space-body.

1 Kaufmann, P. *L'expérience émotionnelle de l'espace*, 1967.
2 Robinson, J. *Eléments du langage chorégraphique*, 1981.
3 Bartenieff, I. 1980, p. 6.
4 Merleau-Ponty, M. *Phenomenology of Perception*, 1962, p. 281.
5 Bartenieff, 1980, p. 25; and Laban *Choreutics*, 1980, p. 25.
6 Nikolais, A. *Dance Perspectives*, Special edition, 1970.
7 Laban, R. *A Vision of Dynamic Space*, 1963, p. 23.
8 Virilio, P. *L'inertie polaire*, 1992.
9 Godard, H. 'Le geste inouï', 1993.
10 Dupuy, Dominique 'La danse du dedans' in *La danse, naissance d'un mouvement de pensée*, 1989. This citation was used at the beginning of 'Matisse et la danse du futur', our text for the catalogue, *La Danse de Matisse*, Musée d'Art Moderne de la Ville de Paris, 1994.
11 Banes, Sally. *Terpsichore in Sneakers*, 1980. See also Goldberg, Rose Lee. *Performance, Live Art: 1909 to the Present*, 1979.
12 Louppe, Laurence *Hervé Robbe – Richard Deacon, voyage dans l'usine des corps*, 1993.
13 Baxandall, Michael (*L'oeil du Quattrocento*, 1973) and Hubert Damisch (*Origine de la Perspective*. Flammarion, 1989) argue that the layout and measuring pieces of the abacus are at the origin of classical space.
14 In the *Songe de Poliphile* of Francesco Colonna, Venise, 1510.
15 Schefer, Jean-Louis *Sur un Fil de la Mémoire*, 1991. Theatres of memory have been discussed by Frances Yates in *The Art of Memory*, 1974.

16 Launay, Isabelle 'Laban et l'expérience de danse' in *Revue d'Esthétique: 'Et la danse'*, Autumn 1992.

17 Jasper Johns in *Cage, Cunningham, Johns, dancers in the Plane*, 1990.

18 Humphrey, Doris. *The Art of Making Dances*, 1959.

19 Cunningham, Merce 'Space, Time and Dance', 1992, p. 38.

20 Remy, B. In 'Adage'. *Biennale Nationale de Val-de-Marne*, No.1, 1985.

21 Goldberg, Marianne 'Interview with Trisha Brown' in *The Drama Review*, Vol. 30, issue 1, 1986.

22 Holm, Hanya in J. Morrison Brown, *The Vision of Modern Dance*, 1980, p. 80.

23 Paulay, Forestine, in Bartenieff et al. *Four Adaptations of the Effort Theory in Research and Teaching*, 1972, p. 64.

24 Zeami. *La tradition secrète du No*, 1970, pp. 119-120.

25 This citation of Plato's *Timeus* by Cunningham is in the first edition of *The Dance Has Many Faces* by Walter Sorell, 1951. It was taken out in subsequent editions.

26 Robinson, J. *Eléments du langage chorégraphique*, 1981, pp.49-50.

27 Thom, Rene 'La danse comme semiurgie' in *Apologie du Logos*, 1990, p.123.

28 'Spatial language' is an idea developed by Laban in his early works, then taken up and developed by Bartenieff et al. in *Four Adaptations of the Effort Theory*, 1972.

29 Cunningham, M. 'Space, Time and Dance', 1992, p. 37.

30 Martin, John *The Modern Dance*, 1933.

31 Matisse, H. *Ecrits et propos sur l'art*, 1972, p. 154.

32 I have broached the question of the relation between the different states of subjectivity or non-subjectivity in 20th century art in 'Dada danse' in *La voix et la geste*, plaquette de la Biennale de Charleroi, 1990. The question has subsequently been developed by Roger Copeland in 'Beyond Expressionism, Merce Cunningham's Critique of the Natural' in Adshead, 1988.

33 Martin, John 1933, p. 71.

34 Ehrenzweig, A. *The Hidden Order of Art: a study in the psychology of artistic imagination*, 1967.

35 Schlemmer, O. 'La scène de la danse' in *Théâtre et Abstraction*, edited and translated by Eric Michaud, 1978, pp. 53-59.

36 Pilates technique is one the one which most deeply constructs the body-space from supports. This method was created in the early 1930s and has become extremely popular today on both sides of the Atlantic. Cf. Dominque Dupuy. 'Le corps émerveillé' in *Marsyas*, No. 16, Decembre 1990.

37 Oral Sources: the citations from Irene Hultman and Kajo Tsuboi were obtained at the conference, 'Autres Pas 92', organised by the IPMC and the festival of 'Danse à Aix'.

38 See texts and photographic documentation in Appia, Aldolphe. *Oeuvres Complètes*, Vol.III ('Les écrits dalcroziens'), 1990.

39 Dobbels, Daniel 'Le sous-sol' in *Le corps en jeu*, 1991, pp. 205-207.

40 Remy, B. 'Visions de danse' in *Nouvelles de Danse*, No. 26, Winter, 1996, pp. 18-25.

41 Ibid, 1996.

42 Rouquet, O. 'La tête aux pieds', 1991, p. 33.

43 Paul Virilio, 'Gravitational Space' in *Traces of Dance*, 1994.

44 Dubois, Kitsou. 'Pédagogie de la danse appliquée au personnel soignant, aux malades mentaux, aux astronautes' in *Marsyas* No. 18, June 1991, p. 51.

45 Dupuy, D. 'Danser outre, hypothèses sur le vol', 1994, p. 52

46 Ibid. p. 47.

47 Ruyter, Nancy Lee Chalfa 'American Longings: Genevieve Stebbins and Delsartean Performance' in *Corporealities* edited by Susan Leigh Foster, 1996. Stebbins had previously been discussed by Ruyter in her celebrated *Reformers and Visionaries: the Americanization of the Art of Dance*, 1978.

48 Atlani, Catherine *Corps spirale, corps sonore*, 1991.

49 Durand, Gilbert *Structures Anthropologiques de l'Imaginaire*, 1982.

50 Deleuze, G. *The Time-Image*, 1989.

51 Bachelard, G. *The Poetics of Space*, 1964.

52 Dupuy, D. *Danser outre*, 1994.

Composition

Art frames a piece of chaos in order to make a composed chaos which can then be sensed.
Gilles Deleuze and Felix Guattari.[1]

Composing transforms tensions into signs.
Christian Bourigault.[2]

Tensions, in their organisation or their 'contradictions' (there is no tension, says Laban, without a counter-tension to oppose it) work the body as a space which becomes the very field of a hitherto formless '*Spannung*' (energy). Tensions are productive not only through their own 'becoming-sign', but also through the latent meanings harboured by the body in history's margins. Composition in dance, Christian Bourigault might also have said, involves the infinite treatment of a long forbidden imaginary.

In France, an extremely interesting terminological distinction doubles the concept of 'composition' with that of *écriture*. It is very difficult, in the absence of widely shared reflections and a genuine debate, to grasp where the distinction between the two terms is to be made. The word *écriture* also applies to musical and cinema composition.[3] And it is certainly linked to our culture's 'textual model'. The etymology of the word 'text' which relates it to weaving, gives preference to the notion of a 'weft' and of the close and subtle imbrication of diverse threads, of paradigmatic and syntagmatic fluctuations at the origins of that which remains the model: the *énoncé* (utterance or 'wording'). The act of composing (*componere*: to put together), meanwhile, spatialises what orders art on a more architectural and logical plane. Pending further investigations to clarify this distinction which is perhaps more linguistic than theoretical, conversations that I have had with Stephanie Aubin, Christian Bourigault, Odile Duboc, and the ideas and writings of Susan Buirge lead me to conclusions which are often divergent and in which opposing shades of meaning allow a very rich field of 'percepts' to appear. Bourigault, as we have seen with the idea of an *écriture* in terms of 'signs,' translates composition semiotically as a dynamic assemblage. It can thus be likened to composition in modern painting as a distribution of lines of force: *a work is nothing but an organisation of tensions,* writes Kandinsky in his *Course at the Bauhaus.* Similar definitions can be found in cubism where it is the 'agitation' of pictorial matter itself that organises the tableau. *Let our forms be ruled by our actions,* wrote Gleizes and Metzinger. But we are concerned with visibilities without any semiotic elaboration.[4] Composition in dance, of course, is elaborated primarily through what Deleuze calls (à propos of Bacon) 'pathetic logic,' the sensuous and emotive contamination of one zone by another.[5] But as Bourigault points out, in the very particular art of dance there is a singular transaction between one's being moved or 'touched' corporeally and what 'semiotises' out of this or what trace of the self gets woven into the *écriture*.

For others, the idea (and the word) 'composition' apply more to processes of elaboration or apprenticeship. The *écriture* is the result of this work. Susan Buirge says that, *in composition there is only the movement, only the body of a dancer carrying the whole intention (propos). In choreography, all sorts of other elements can intervene giving sense to or contradicting this proposition.*[6]

In any case, *écriture* concerns perception of the work: when the choreographic composition makes itself felt as an epiphany. The *écriture* is for us
what founds the choreographic act, however it might be conceived or defined. For it contains the whole 'work' of the dance. In the course of the
'80s a too great importance accorded the scenic 'flavouring' of the *écriture*
often shifted the interest in dance to the spectacle, to its 'packaging' to the
detriment of the *écriture*. Not that the elements which are added to it such
as lighting, costumes, and the whole frame of the performance are merely
accessory: on the contrary, they are the revelatory agents of the *écriture*.
The choreographic work is in fact a complete, imaginary universe where
every choice has its raison d'être. But they must never substitute for the
écriture itself as the organising agent of all these choices. Even though it
might be contradicted or denied in certain experimental situations, the
écriture is the heart of dance. And the drying up of many currents during
the course of the '80s has proceeded from the sacrifice of *écriture* to a concern with 'image' – or with effect, which often amounts to the same thing.
In a communication about the relations between dance and cinema,
Marilen Iglesias Breuker has remarked that, in competing with cinema's
power of make-believe, dance has been led to inflate its own images; and
this has not occurred without loss of the *écriture* as a register of the sensible, and as the fabric of the invisible (and in her own dance she is able to
work the sensible and the secret).[7] Most of the choreographers discussed
here have been particularly involved in the search for an *écriture*, from Odile
Duboc or Stephanie Aubin to Dominique Bagouet and the dancers who
were close to him.

Knowledge of 'composition' which is a kind of laboratory for the *écriture*
can provide means for reading the intention and the construction of a
work. As the matrix of invention and organisation of the movement out of
which the work will be born, and even more as a philosophy of action,
composing is a fundamental element of contemporary dance. Its definition
and role in the contemporary school belong only to it and are linked to its
whole history. Composing, in fact, is an exercise which begins from the
personal invention of a movement or personal cultivation of a gesture or
motif and ends with an entire choreographic unity, work or fragment of a
work. The composition such as we understand it in this context cannot be
elaborated from an already fixed vocabulary, which is why it cannot be
practised in a *'tradition savante'* where the dance is created within a given
lexical palette.[8] In fact, not only does it imply a development from original
movements created out of individual inspiration, but its poetics require that
this very invention make room for all the constitutive work that confers on

it its singular 'grain' and even the whole arc of its trajectory. *The slightest movement*, remarks Michèle Rust, *can jeopardise everything.*[9] This is why in contemporary dance it is impossible to dissociate the emergence of the movement and the sensuous conditions of this emergence from the whole of the composition – except in precise and explicit cases where one is deliberately cut off from the other, as in certain minimalist projects. And more recently in France, choreographers recruit dancers with very different sensibilities or origins and they allow the expression of disparate corporeities and ways of moving (*gestuelles*) – 'singular morphologies' whose 'infra-theatricality' is allowed to play out, as Michèle Febvre has observed.[10] The choreographer's role here, as Nathalie Shulmann has observed of Joseph Nadj, is limited to organising encounters and groupings between people who are working in different movement modes.[11] This is what certain choreographers, currently, prefer to call 'dramaturgy'. Dramaturgy entails distributing states, lines of force or tension from given homogenous or heterogenous corporealities, recognised as such or not, but *given*, not reworked into an organic totality. In fact, the term is justified whenever there is a *mise en scène* or the simple distribution of 'roles', even if they are simply spatial and temporal ones; or in a true work of choreography where it is necessary to establish lines of interdependence between all the levels of the dance work. Even a 'theatricalised' work, if it does not take into account the grains of personal signature that lie 'upstream' of a characterisation, is condemned to convey an enormous 'unthought' and to deliver a sub-text that is much more marked and more significant than the narrative itself. These innumerable hinges or oscillations of meaning/direction (*sens*) are extremely difficult to identify and treat. As Susan Buirge rightly says, the whole is not only the sum of its parts: it lies in that which, at each moment, in each articulation, works on and disturbs the whole. In other words, composition begins with the 'invention' of the movement, the qualitative particulars of its relation to space and time; and continues until a complete construction has been elaborated out of these same characteristics.

It is possible to go even further back towards the factors out of which a composition is elaborated and from which its first choices are made: Sylvie Giron has said that, *composition begins with the choice of performers.*[12] It is in fact out of each performer's palette of 'gears' that the atmosphere and even the intention of the work find their qualitative roots. At its most powerfully poetic, a composition must involve an expanding, or at least a questioning of the kinesphere: with the choreographer knowing how to engage the dancer's body state in her/his own kinespheric sensibility, how to create this quality of resonance (or why not resistance) upon which the real identity of the choreographic text will be woven. Christine Gerard, a choreographer with a very refined *écriture* has also extolled the delicate attention to the birth of material in a dancer's being: *Everything depends on the matter/material of each person. How does one choreograph this personal, unique, irreplaceable matter?*[13]

Thus any group of people – even one that comes together by chance – is already a 'composition' in the etymological sense, where the play of affinities, contradictions, contrasts and, especially, tensions begins composing even before the slightest organisation has been sketched out. In such a delicate and complex 'weft' it is useless to try to distinguish what is primary from what is secondary, what is incorporated from what incorporates. What is important in composing is to bring into being a non-existent matter/material, to find one's way towards the unknown and to what has never been created before. In a fine study called *The choreographic studio*, which seeks to define the fragile circumstances of poetic becoming of what has not yet existed (*l'incréé*), Jackie Taffanel notes the cognitive but also perceptual complexity of the stages of compositional process. *The choreographer's gaze works according to a multitude of modalities that are superimposed and interrelated in relation to each moment of the creative process, multiply imprinting it.*[14] Even if we agree with this author-choreographer in keeping at arms length a 'hypothetico-analytic' approach to dance knowledge of which she is rightly suspicious, it would seem that in these very stages, movement like language (*la langue*) reciprocally implicates the enunciation in the whole of the *énoncé*, as '*parole*' (speech) is implicated in '*langue*' (language). And it is not without good reason that René Thom relates choreographic organisation to a 'double articulation' like the one Saussure noted in language (articulation at two levels of complexity between the word unit and the whole of the utterance). Nevertheless, in dance and to some extent in literature (with which there are rich comparisons to be made) we ought not to impose an orthodoxy. It is up to each individual to organise the internal syntactical laws whose only limit should be legibility, but not of course a legibility defined by pre-established norms. As we will see, it is the work, or at least the great work, which establishes the terms of its own legibility. This will not be the same for Graham or Cunningham, Linke or Childs: any more than it was for Rimbaud, Mallarmé or Céline. The work of compositional legibility in dance is directed essentially towards arousing the intimate adherence of the 'partners' in the work (the performers and the spectators who are also '*interprètes*'), to participate in the interpretation firstly of a coherent artistic object (what Alwin Nikolais calls the Gestalt), but above all in the choices and distribution of the sensuous elements which lead body states toward the wholeness of the *écriture*. The work of the spectator is to accept, to enter into the paths of this legibility beyond the spectre of ready-made perceptions. The surprising success of mediocre or mannered works (in the sense of following a 'method' and not an original mode of production appropriate to the intention), come from re-using systems of legibility that are already in place and, apparently making the spectators' perceptions easier, but without enriching them. Original and powerful creators have thus often had less favourable critical and media attention than their imitators. Here again, we need to reflect on how choreographic works might genuinely be judged.

Composition intervenes at two moments in the life of choreography. In the making of the work, obviously. But also at the level of opened-ended 'practice' in the formation of the dancer. Experience of composition is indispensable to this formation. We say 'dancer', not choreographer, only to the extent that these two functions can be disassociated in contemporary dance: for any contemporary dancer is primarily a producer, even if s/he is involved in another's work. Without this apprenticeship in being a producer-body contemporary dance does not exist, or else it loses a major part of its poetics. And the relative neglect of teaching composition today in favour of so-called technique classes destined to reinforce a competitive and fantasmatic ideal dictated by the laws of a market that is itself responsible for that ideal, is regrettable. The result is visible everywhere: at the end of the '80s an aesthetic watering down of contemporary dance occurred, due amongst other things to an increase in teaching a 'cost-effective' or exploitable technique and, in a devitalised choreographic milieu, to the facile success of the latest fashion. Happily, since the '90s, we are beginning to experience a revitalisation not only in teaching but in a more acute awareness amongst dancers that they must return to the deep sources of the art. Most of the choreographers and dancers whom we have mentioned here are part of this movement and are instigating a new call to return to the composition workshop. For the dancer, this alone, as Susan Buirge has said, can truly push back the limits of the known, lead to new potentialities, renew and enlarge the field which s/he is able to command.[15] A dancer-producer is, again, one who can truly propose rare and refined perceptions to an audience, leading it towards the hidden place where, often, s/he too discovers more of herself.

If knowledge of composition is indispensable to the dancer, so is it also, as we have seen, for anyone concerned with a hermeneutics of choreographic *écriture* – where the reading is not of a fixed form but where the reader is, instead, dynamised by the composition's own tonal changes. This is why, within the framework of a poetic approach, it seems important to evoke the *écriture*'s poetic sources and motives. Of course the approach I am proposing will remain as much as possible outside artists' strategies. My point of view is that of a reader/spectator – even if the latter ought to be as aware as any connoisseur of contemporary art of the processes which generate the work and shape its tonalities. To begin to gain some literacy in the processes of choreographic composition in France, we can recommend the enlightening works of Jacqueline Robinson and Karin Waehner – albeit that composing in dance opens unlimited fields which no written work can saturate. In order to understand the perspectives and infinite resources from which choreographic composition draws its possibilities nothing can replace watching, or better still participating in, what is aptly called a 'workshop' (*atelier*). But the work occurs along intimate paths, even if the intimacy is shared amongst several people. The ritual of the composition workshop involves a 'private' relation between dancers using a particular terminology (to designate the different moments of the emerging material, for example); and a host of metaphors, to which the outsider will never have access, circulates within the group. Sometimes choreographers keep their intention or imaginative mechanisms to themselves so much must the space of creation, visible or invisible, interiorised or objective, be protected. Let us remain for a moment at the threshold of the studio and observe, through the frame of a 'tableau' (perhaps even through a light and deliberately maintained veiling), the outlines of an extraordinary working process. This consists in making a complete artistic object out of nothing, out of a simple coming together of bodies and sensibilities: an object that has its ambience, its visibility, its meaning and the codes internal to its functioning. Knowing that on the day of its presentation to an audience we will be able to find again in its workmanship the constitutive layers of its creation. Only a vision that is aware of the problematics internal to the act of composition can lead us to comprehend these layers.

In his *L'esprit des formes*, a text with a rather strange title, for the concept of form is largely exceeded in it, Elie Faure describes a scene which revealed to him the essence of composition in the arts: a surgical operation, in which the function and attentiveness of each participant and each movement are interconnected in an intensely attuned way. *The group formed by the patient, the surgeon and the assistants seemed to me like a unique organism in action...An inner functional logic rigorously determined a visible structural logic where nothing could be changed without that functional logic suddenly ceasing to carry out its aim.*[16] Thus, composition in any art form, and especially in dance, comes out of a mysterious, visible or invisible, network of necessary relations and intensities. In fact, composition in contemporary dance is accomplished through the dynamics that emerge in matter. It is not moulded from the outside. Terminology is always interesting in terms of what it reveals of the underside of words and acts, for example, of a ballet master who says that he 'set' (*règler*) a dance. The contemporary choreographer 'composes' which is different. S/he does not 'set'. On the contrary: s/he agitates and disturbs things and bodies in order to discover an unknown visibility. Or rather, as did the cubist painters, s/he allows densities to undergo their own fermentation. In all cases, s/he creates material, assembles it and, above all, 'dynamises' it, handles a provisional chaos in the secret network of lines of force. This network can be found in the diffuse and moving reality that surrounds us. Karin Waehner writes, *See how the people walk...some quickly...others slowly...still others hesitate between right and left... they stop and go again...You see? You already have rhythm, direction, dynamic and different expressions. Now you can imagine.*[17] It can also be found in oneself, in what Kandinsky calls the 'inner necessity', a term that Karin Waehner also cites in her teaching (and which was perhaps emblematic of the whole *Ausdruckstanz* (expressionist) school, in its continuity with the romantic theories of the Blue Rider Group). It was, hence, not by chance that in the German school, at least that part which came out of *Ausdruckstanz* and from Wigman, that work on the tensions that are constitutive of movement and of our 'emotional heritage' – to cite Wigman (in turn alluding to Laban) – has remained the most pure. There we find, prior to any formalism, the exploration of a state or movement, of its qualities and intrinsic sensuous elements without recourse to any authority external to experience: even if this exploration leads to corollary narrative or dramatic constructions or symbolic applications or 'transpositions'. In her courses and in her book *Outillage Chorégraphique* (*Choreographic craft*)   Karin Waehner proposes a whole range of explorations which, beginning simply with sensation and its analysis, leads to a 'situation' or even a story set in train by the situation. Alwin Nikolais retained elements of this compositional philosophy inheriting them through Hanya Holm not only from Wigman but from her teachers, Dalcroze and Laban. It can be seen resurfacing without specific reference to this lineage in numerous choreographers for whom the 'very matter/material of action', to quote Jerome Andrews, summoned from different points of view (and above all by dynamics) is what nourishes the whole creative process.[18] Here is evidence of Laban's influence revitalised in the USA during the '50s. The major first generation choreographers had been more autocratic: at the risk of making a broad opposition between the German and American schools, one could say that the latter were more autocratic in relation to form and the former to matter (at least in the initial phases of their modernity). In *The Art of Making Dances* Doris Humphrey prescribes in very detailed way the canons of her composition which, in order that she might share the extreme modernity of her departure, are not the less formalist.

Inheritor, in fact, of this German school and one of the masters of contemporary composition, Alwin Nikolais has proposed principles of a compositional aesthetics grounded in the internal givens of choreographic matter/material, what he calls 'abstraction', which is the extremely concrete manipulation of material (*materiau*) for itself and not in the service of a story or subjective expression. Hence the prominence and force of the sensations that are provoked by his dance, and that of dancers in his lineage whose presence is very important in France. The *sensations of round, pointed, flat, tilted space, of (fast, slow, suspended) time and of (percussive, vibrational, linear) energy become tangible*, writes Marc Lawton, an articulate dancer and writer of this thought.[19] We note in passing what Nikolais has retained of Laban's constitutive elements of movement: out of four he makes three (the famous idea of 'motion' combines weight and flow but in a more qualitative manner). These elements are not external to the body. It is the body which through its own investigations produces the qualities of its existence. The Nikolais body, however, and it is here that we find one of the most admirable aspects of his aesthetic, is not *limited to a collection of bones and muscles which move in space*: it is itself the site of interrogation by means of which space 'becomes'. The human body is not the centre of the universe. Firstly, because Nikolais was profoundly opposed to the anthropocentrism which under the guise of humanism or subjectivism had marked modern dance until the '50s: *I began to elaborate a philosophy of man as a traveller through the machinery of the universe rather than the god from whom everything flows.*[20] The dancer as a space 'wanderer' is linked to the 'travelling centre,' a centre which can travel everywhere in our bodies but which can also wander off elsewhere. It is thus a decentralised choreographic world, but out of a decentralised body. Marc Lawton again: *With Nikolais the dancer sculpts space and time. He is versatile like a fish in water, always there where you least expect him.* In fact, by allowing the body to explore and invent the dance's subject (*matière*), any recentring around an introduced concept becomes impossible and the composition grows out of internal givens, organically, catching the perception of the spectator up in its own vortex. This is what gives the compositions of Carolyn Carlson their force and makes those of Susan Buirge unsettling. Both of them have been influenced by Nikolais – even if for their generation other elements come to enrich (or perturb?), in any case to create a certain hybridisation of thought. Carlson, for example, re-introduces autobiographical elements that the master refused. Susan Buirge, often inspired by minimalist or aleatory compositional methods, allows her compositional knowledge to remain open-ended – like a fault in the homogenous fabric of the Gestalt. Even in this they are faithful to the spirit (but not the letter) of the master who never tried to impose a model and for whom the art of composition is only ever a means to find one's own way.

Christian Bourigault studied at the Centre National de la Danse Contemporaine, Angers, with Nikolais. He is one of numerous French choreographers to have come out of this teaching. And if we owe the epi-graph above to him it is because he was deeply touched both by this philosophy in which the dance's theme composes itself through the body of the dancer; and by this important influence through which he could feel what is at stake in composition. It is not surprising therefore that in the history of imagination, it was the expressionist period, especially in paint-ing, that brought him back as though to the cradle of his own body, to an essentially tensional world. But to return to Nikolais' philosophy: in it the dancer must structure, out of her/his 'organicity,' a readable and pertinent wholeness appropriate to the suggested starting point and dependent only upon itself for its existence. This search within the body's experience, work-ing solo or in a group can be found in quite different contexts and philosophies with very radical artists like Steve Paxton for whom, according to Cynthia Novack, *the composition is not created by a choreographer but arises between the dancers.*[21] The becoming/event in its pure emergence providing itself, the matter/material, and those who know how to read it, with the keys necessary to approaching and understanding it.

It is at this point that an essential element of composition intervenes: the producing of materials (*matériau*) through improvisation – insofar as in choreographic thinking compositional components only find their legiti-macy in the qualitative resources of the dancing subject or subjects (as individuals or in the framework in which they come together), to the exclu-sion of external givens. For an essential characteristic of choreographic creation is the working together, an element which artists and theoreticians in other disciplines have difficulty accepting and even conceptualising. For the musical composer, as for the writer, composition is a deeply solitary act. Having another person join in would at one stroke jeopardise the originality of the adventure and the acuity of a compositional logic that brooks not even a limited consensus. It would lead to a compromised sharing of the unshareable. It is difficult to accept that, in dance, solitary creation is practically impossible. Even for a solo, with oneself as partner-performer; and if we add Wigman's 'invisible partner,' that already makes three... I had the opportunity during an experiment, exceptional both as an idea and in terms of its process, in which Stephanie Aubin gave us insight into her art publicly and corporeally, (which happens rarely in France), to confirm with the choreographer the difficulty of having it accepted that an '*oeuvre*' exists as such when it includes the work of its own performers (*interprètes*). It is especially difficult for musicians to accept this, as in the Western musical tradition the moment of writing and the moment of 'interpretation'/performance are very separate. But the contemporary choreography is a work made 'in vivo'. It cannot be otherwise because it deals with the matter/material of beings, and specifically with being-in-movement as the privileged site of awareness (*prise de conscience*); because it works firstly with the relational networks amongst bodies and between bodies and imagination, and because the choreographer him/herself is implicated in this relation or, otherwise, does not choreograph legitimately. It is important, in fact, that the choreographer's self is put into play and is 'affected' by the movement, by the lines of intensity of the becoming event. It is regrettable to see people today calling themselves choreographers without their having been or no longer being dancers. However fine or sensitive their approach, they will always be closer to directors. The ruffling of the subjective texture which is only achieved by a personal investment of the creator's body will be missing. This is why, for example, the presence of Merce Cunningham amongst his dancers, younger than him by two generations, constitutes an important testimony: the pieces themselves tell the story of a risk taken in body and thought. Even if processes such as aleatory ones or, more recently, composing using computers – which could indicate a certain distancing – seem to be distant or 'cold' activities whatever the compositional approach, as soon as the body is implicated, they are not.

It is true that Cunningham and others do not work directly on the transsubjective texture that I have evoked but compose and sometimes notate alone ahead of time – as was the case with Dominique Bagouet and is always with Lucinda Childs. But there is no question of its being a soliloquy, since no movement in contemporary dance is foreseeable either in its nature or in its quality. Merce Cunningham works with chance in order to eliminate the associative stereotypes that burden and set limits to our imagination. Composition for Cunningham, as for the majority of great choreographers, is in fact not only a working method; it is a path towards the infinite. Regarding Cunningham's chance process, we might evoke the thought of one of his great admirers, the art critic and psychoanalyst

Ehrenzweig cited above. His theory of 'disruption' envisages surface constructions fragmenting to allow deep structures usually inaccessible to our consciousness to appear.[22] Thus Cunningham's composition links two dimensions: that of the unknown which lies secreted in the world, and that of the experience of the dancing body. He suggests an even and neutral unity. Two processes, then, work with this element: the chance process which will distribute numbers or sexes of dancers, the duration, and the spatial or corporal location, etc; but especially, and this is what gives the movement its real existence, what the dancer does with it – even if he/she does not succeed in doing anything with it or does otherwise. *Sometimes this is more interesting*, says the choreographer with his wisdom and habitual good humour. To 'give' movement, then, as Dominique Bagouet did, means that the other 'invents' it, in all senses of the word. *As you feel it* is an expression heard in dance studios. This 'felt' is the yeast which 'raises' the unexpected truth of a motif whose source only the body of the dancer knows. The whole labour of the work's construction will be to bring this emergence to the perception of the audience, while keeping it unpredictable.

We can see then that improvisation is, like composition, an indispensable element of contemporary dance. And like it, is simultaneously a matrix of the work, a training technique and also a means of investigating the material and oneself, the productive potential of each person and the field of potential in the dance workshop and the community which gives it life. We must also distinguish between improvisation in contemporary dance and what the word designates in other periods and disciplines. Traditional oral poetry, traditional or baroque music and jazz (excepting 'free' experiments) rely on improvisation for the invention of new or unanticipated arrangements executed in the moment. But they do not, as in contemporary dance, 'produce' unknown material that no standard of evaluation or definition can criticise. Improvisation in traditional disciplines is a making up on the spot, of course, but from an already established lexicon which has been consciously selected and even, in the case of group creations, coded according to certain rituals of pre-established relationships, exchanges, agreements, duplications, etc. These restrictions subtract nothing from the value and attraction of such processes: nor from their prestige, and thus has Trisha Brown dreamed to Bach's improvisations on the theme of the *Musical Offering* which as we know was proposed by the King of Prussia. On the understanding that for us, of course, they are more like 'variations' and manipulations, because as improvisations, their beauty, their spontaneous architecture belong to another history and share nothing with the manifestations of improvisation (or composition) in contemporary dance.

It was the German school from its very beginning which, through Dalcroze and then Laban, prescribed the processes of improvisation as fundamental in an art without referential foundations. For Alwin Nikolais improvisation is essential: it is the place of 'theory', that is, of the exploration of movement and choreographic material in and of itself that alone can reach deeply into artistic resources. Overall, choreographers make a very clear distinction between improvisation on the one hand and composition and *écriture* on the other as the two moments in the making of dance. Composing as the treatment of material discovered in improvisation involves an identification, selection, and a re-orientation of the discovered elements. Improvisation doesn't only have to be the production of choreographic material using a dancer-supplier, who delivers merchandise for creation like a raw product that the choreographer is only too happy to refine. Improvisation is a dialectic between the deep resources of the dancer – the becoming that is stirred up by experience/experiment – and a gaze which reflects and gives new perspectives or displaces and pushes back the boundaries of the possible with a new summons. Jackie Taffanel: '*Each field of experience nourishes and sediments the knowledges of the dancers and the gaze, at the same time as it helps them to forget so that they can attempt a new adventure.*'[23] That is why, as Jean Pomarès has remarked, improvisation requires a practice as strong and rigorous as it must be inventive.[24] Rigour here does not mean 'sanctioning inhibition' but attending and listening to the material produced. Again, our intention here is not to discuss the mysteries of the studio. But it is important that a composed or 'written' work appears to the spectator charged with this work of choices having been made or of having been 'scraped' or worked over as Jackie Taffanel puts it. The substance of choreographic work is born out of fragments, things rejected, deliberate losses, that have disengaged artistic mystery from its invisible matrix – even if at the moment of its presentation to a public, its simple beauty, its transparency or its mellowness do not (or no longer) bear these stigmata. Improvisation gives a particular direction to the piece when it is based on the self-material of each dancer and the group. It can produce works with strong emotional or autobiographical connotations like those of Bernardo Montet and Christian Bourigault where the dancers, even though they are not narrating, function in a mode of confiding, either on behalf of the group or of the choreographer. By contrast, the improvisation that is Pina Bausch's main creative tool uses broadly biographical material provided by the dancers who plumb their own memories. But this material is de-personalised and poured (i.e. rather than 'set') for the benefit of the piece, transfigured into an image of universal humanity. It becomes a metaphor but one marked by the strangeness and mystery proper to singular experience. Even if this singularity must include the banality (not to mention the cast-off meanings) of daily life. The piece can unfold in a way unlike that of any pre-established narrative structure, but can also show, as in *Nelken*, the *modest, ordinary little dream that the Wuppertal dancers take absolutely seriously.*[25] It can bring out this 'little dream' of the everyman and the fantasies of his conformist desires. Pina Bausch wants to find this through the precise experience of the dancer in her/his own life.

Improvisation can be a tool of construction, but it can also on its own constitute the work. A figure who is not always agreed with, the severe Louis Horst, who will be discussed at more length below, takes literally Susan Langer's assertion that, *No dance can be called a work of art if it has not been deliberately composed and can be repeated* – a definition which is continually contradicted either in total or in part by work in dance.[26] Improvised moments can be part of the *écriture* of a piece and even give it its structure, its plan, its temporality. This does not at all prevent the work existing as a complete artistic entity: not in terms of a definitive 'form' but in what is much more important, namely, the depth of an understanding around a common project, the qualities of phrasing and of mutual attention. In the history of improvisation, the current of 'contact improvisation' made famous by Steve Paxton, took the work of improvisation to its most radical extreme (even while integrating the theoretical tools developed since the turn of the century). With the help of a partner-body the dancer improvises (with) all of her/his possibilities of support: *There are lifts and falls, evolving organically out of a continuous process of finding and losing balance*, writes Sally Banes. *There is a give and take of weight, but also of social roles: passivity and activity, demand and response.*[27] The concern of 'contact' is firstly to re-find the essence of dance which Laban identified as the primacy of weight. Here, the gravitational 'option' sweeps away all voluntarist weight decisions. Movement unfolds through the modes of exchange of weight in and with the other. The qualitative consequences for the formation of the dancer are immeasurable: familiarity with instability, freedom from an objective verticality, a multi-dimensional relation with space, attention to the other's body and to the unknown which, because rational and spatial co-ordinates are lost, cannot be anticipated and still less legislated. Paxton writes: *Getting lost is proceeding into the unknown...when lost we will have to relate appropriately to unknown and changing conditions.*[28] But however rich contact improvisation is as a practice it is no less rich as a mode of creation. For Paxton and the many contactors of the '70s, this experience/experiment came to represent a body *écriture*. In front of an audience, dancers in couples embrace, rise, fall and slide on one another sometimes for several hours. We could talk of moments that create works, that is, of an *écriture* which does not need to fix or repeat itself in order to exist. Mark Tompkins is a choreographer working in France who has come out of this current. For a long time his flowing, anti-conformist work moved away from Paxton's (without ever denying, even in another poetics, the force of rupture) but he has recently returned to improvisation as 'instantaneous composition' after an idea of Paxton's. As if the choreography might be born, authentic, strong and identifiable in one burst.

Improvisation as performance, but firstly as experience/experiment is one of the essential elements of contemporary dance and of its commitment to exploring limits. This is why those who, like Jacqueline Robinson, witnessed dance modernity, maintain and prefer this indispensable practice. It is also the just or at least 'justified' site of an act dependent only on its own immediacy and the givens of the moment. This is why, as Deborah Jowitt explains, the Japanese dancer Min Tanaka refuses to dance otherwise than improvising.[29] Absolute presence to the immediacy of an act caught in the moment of its emergence: is this not the kernel of poetics in contemporary dance? At the same time, improvisation touches other not less enigmatic and essential limits of the contemporary project: the tenuous border between form and non-form, between foreseen and unforeseen organisation, between the structure and chaos of spontaneous rhythms. *Improvisation offers a* representation *of chaos* (our emphasis) says Kent de Spain, who immediately clarifies: the unforeseen is not indeterminate, *there are (personal, historical, morphological functional) factors that establish limits to the infinity of possible movements.*[30] Cage had already said that between improvisation and the indeterminate we must find middle terms which authorise the one without allowing the ego and all the other determinisms to block the other. (He cites Master Suzuki: *Reduce the activities of the self.*) *Improvisation often comes out of memory and taste, thus from the self. In my current work I try to find ways of improvising that are independent of me, which is where my interest in the contingent comes from.*[31] Even less in dance than in the universe of sound, 'the accidental' as supreme artistic event, in fact, cannot arise from a direct intervention of the artist as subject; and, here, we need to rid ourselves of various misleading traps and images. Nothing is less accidental than movement. In dance, its predictability is, as we have seen, curtailed in numerous approaches – or, as Jean Pomarès has remarked, is pushed radically outside dance's constitutive problematics by calling an 'other' subject of action to bear witness (my weight as pure awareness of movement in contact improvisation, for example, but there could be other approaches like those which proceed from tasks and which displace the site of decision-making). In fact, one could say that in contemporary dance chaos is hoped for and always implicated in the sensuous weft of awareness and body knowledges. Deleuze and Guattari remind us that chaos becomes an indispensable limit of compositional complexity without which the world's opacity could never be torn to reveal the unknown.[32] But familiarity with the factors that generate or initiate movement, whether these are ordinary deterministic ones (personal or socio-cultural history of the dancer, biographical memory which is sometimes deliberately exploited as we have seen) or deep knowledges of the body (stylistics, for example, or postural reading) can simply make this appearance of the unknown into an outward 'form' of chaos. Partisans of the accidental, like Cunningham, know it well and have little trust in improvisation, preferring to let an inhuman chance remain the master of disorder. It is this extreme contingency adapted to dance which not only authorises a liberation from the 'me' and the emergence of the 'indeterminate' but broadens the field of artistic possibilities. Regarding Cunningham's aleatory techniques, Remy Charlip writes; *not only do they liberate the choreographer from his habits and the pressure of personal preferences or dislike but they offer infinite possibilities for movement in space-time which, as much for the performers as for the public, lead towards a world beyond imagination.*[33] It is in this attempt to go beyond the limits of the imagined world (a very different choice from that of Cage) that Cunningham dreams of expanding the universe into its chaotic dimensions. The dancer, with her/his movement infused by an infinite possibility, might sometimes dance, *what man believed he saw.*

We have insisted that the compositional project of contemporary dance is deeply original. But in its compositional resources there is also a remarkable trans-disciplinarity, like a spectre that hovers between languages. This is not specific to dance but concerns all the arts where, from the beginning of the 20th century, the stakes have become universal ones or where interdisciplinarity has been a means to enrich or renew specific tools by borrowing structures that have long been emblematic or canonical in other practices. This migration can be willed, planned, and deliberately provoked: like Kundera's (or Jean-Luc Godard's) use of the structure of the string quartet, a process of displacement that has been analysed by Guy Scarpetta.[34] In fact, in this way, the processes of creation proper to an art have not only been renewed, but their limits have also been tested or displaced as has occurred in the visual arts: for example, when Broodthaers uses writing as a system of pictorial representation. Counter-definitions have been found, borders crossed. In the accumulation or displacement of forms, a vertigo, a depravation, an elsewhere, much more than a construction, has been effected. There are many choreographers who integrate elements of cinematographic composition in their work and, reciprocally, without knowing it, the cinema arranges spatial or body states according to essentially choreographic processes. But this problematic would require a book in itself. Let us simply examine the process of Anne Teresa De Keersmaeker, who integrates elements borrowed from music into her choreographic composition: which, in view of the traditional conjunction between music and dance, obscures somewhat what is really at stake in her borrowing. Her intention obviously does not lie within this conjunction. If we read in musical structures, as she does, universal units of construction which have served just as well for mannerist or baroque rhetoric as for minimalism – a reading that brings her close to Kundera – we can understand how, for her, music represents an exemplary art, a science, from which any syntax can draw. Also, Keersmaeker's art is based in a repetitive movement language (*gestuelle*) that values syntactical articulations such as repetition, superposition, suspension, phasing. And often in her work the complexity of the architectonic idea contrasts with a relative paring down of the movement material, without preventing this material from being qualitatively rich: passing quickly from a great fluidity often in the upper body, to an extreme intensity – a tendency found in all Flemish dance to have come out of the same creative milieu. Her movements are often repeated homophonically by all the dancers, intensifying the movement and the forces or tensions inhabiting it and increasing its expressive heat. By contrast, with its excess of motor information, a dense piece like *Ottone, Ottone*, a commentary on Monteverdi's the *Crowning of Poppea*, has perception teetering on the brink of a void. Underlying her approach there has been a long meditation, leading her from the study of minimalism to a fascination with the interleaving and superimposition, the rounds and retrogrades that are found at all moments of musical history from the baroque to serial music. This has undoubtedly brought her close to Peter Greenaway and to a complex aesthetic of discourse and cross-referencing. The success of the artistic collaboration between these two personalities is well recognised. In the film *Rosas* (1992) they were both attracted by the complexity of tropes (chiasmas, palindromes, metonymy of forms) where the two universes are not grafted on to one another but seem to slot into identical permutations. Similarly with *Amor constante* (1995) where three elements are treated in parallel: a sonnet of Quevedo, all paradox and inverted spirals of meaning; the famous Fibonacci series infinitely contracting to nothing; and Thierry de Mey's composition which follows parallel structures.

This is a recent example illustrating a general tendency in our era towards what one might call the 'effacement of genres' which is found in
many manifestations of 'mixed' rather than 'accumulated' media – and
where the confusion is just as bewildering or fascinating as it is construc-
tive. But choreographic composition's relationship to the other arts also has
another meaning in the history of contemporary dance and is part of its
tradition, not to mention of its adventure. Louis Horst instigated this trans-
disciplinarity in the '20s. A musician who taught composition to dancers
for half a century, Horst judged the material produced 'lawlessly' (meaning
without laws that are universally generalisable) by the body, in the way that
Duncan's did, to be too evanescent. Except for some belated allusions in his
course, Horst systematically ignored the already advanced work of the German dancers. He wanted to confer on dance, if not models, at least a basis in
structures drawn from other arts, whose exploration by analogy with
movement would allow him to isolate analytic and synthetic tools proper to
dance. Amongst these inspirational arts, the first was music which shares
with dance the treatment of time and dynamics. The musical tradition,
with its most orderly period as far as syntactical articulations were concerned, namely, 'the baroque' (and which in the period was known as
'pre-classic'), offers a fertile field of legible forms (canons, fugues,
symmetries, counterpoint etc.) whose exploration was to initiate the young
dance composer. Next, the future choreographer moves on to more adventurous forms inspired by modern art and its stylistic colorations:
primitivism, neo-symbolism, expressionism, abstraction, etc., leading on to
dissymmetry, distortion, discontinuity, dissonance, contradictory or unexpected structures of space-time, etc. Much has been said of Horst's
objectives as he strove for an easy formalism. This in part explains the great
break away from 'modern dance' of the '40s and '50s – such as that of
Alwin Nikolais and Merce Cunningham and the departure, for us henceforth legendary, of Jerome Andrews who came to Europe in search of new
risks. But we must do justice to Horst on another level: in proposing the
cubists or pictorial primitivists as examples of expressivity or of construction, in making Brancusi or Picasso (who were essential to Martha
Graham) known to the dancers, he established a first link of resonance and
correspondence between avant garde practices and dance. This process of
looking elsewhere for structures capable of providing openings to choreographic composition (thanks to Horst?) was to remain an important trait of
American dance and its continuous relations with other modernities
through a sharing of the same questions – when it wasn't the other arts
that were being inspired by dance's methods. One could say that Horst

founded a kind of tradition which was to prevail even amongst his most vociferous detractors. We can, paradoxically, see examples of it in Cunningham's use of all-over space or his aleatory post-Duchampian and Cageian processes. We find it in the composition course of Robert Dunn, himself a musician who taught composition according to aleatory structural methods, more deconstructive still than those of Cage. Then, the exchange was to become reciprocal with musicians and minimalist sculptors who, like Robert Morris, profited from dance teaching with its solipsistic and organic treatment of body information.

But Horst's dogmatic teaching, his manipulations of the body's physical material, following other articulatory models, however exciting and useful they may seem today, like Doris Humphrey's admirable course in composition, very quickly frustrated generations for whom the organisational force, the coherence extolled in the imitation of forms, particularly musical ones, became intolerable. One principle in particular was spurned as being excessively structuring: *A composition consists in showing a theme and manipulating it.*[35] This phrase was intensely opposed by those who revolted against the formalisation (and institutionalisation) of 'modern dance'. Even if a 'theme' (a gesture, a move, a thematic seed, a phrase) can still today serve as the basis of a series of transformations in dance, as in dance pedagogy, it has long become out of the question to develop it in the manner of classical music. (Even though the work of Anne Teresa de Keersmaeker or Trisha Brown has recently transformed or displaced this problem). Another element comes into play here, namely, the distribution of units of maximum intensity which centralise or orient the flow of sequences towards a climax. Merce Cunningham's condemnation of traditional structures of theme and variation applied to dance is well known, but so also is his condemnation of the centralising dramaturgy of crisis *towards which one advances and then retreats* – a linear form centred on an acme that would end by erasing every conquest of modernity.[36] Curiously, this same condemnation is found in Raul Ruiz's denunciation of the temptations of reactionary cinema with its aesthetic of 'central conflict' where, according to the most traditional paths of classical dramaturgy, any story (or for us any choreographic text) should lead towards a 'knot' and then its untying. Ruiz provides a persuasive analysis of central conflict which he links to the 'American way of life' prevalent in the inspiration of American cinema and perhaps in a very diffuse and more discrete way in modern dance: namely, that in American culture a decision, whether verbal or practical, is immediately followed by a conflict which underscores its precisely 'decisive' or emphatic character. The consequences Ruiz draws from this are more interesting when he writes: *other societies which maintain their value systems in secret have adopted the rhetoric of Hollywood externally.* Ruiz concludes that, sadly, art like politics has adopted the modes of representation of the dominant economic culture.[37] We must be careful not to generalise or seek to decipher in the *chefs-d'oeuvre* of modern dance the use of a process of construction as archaic as 'central conflict'. We would search in vain for a focal element in the work of Doris Humphrey who championed asymmetry and a centrifugal structure out of an unstable body. Nonetheless, we know that Cunningham's whole work was to undo the central conflict (to borrow from cinema and from Ruiz this useful concept) and that this refusal in all art of our time went hand in hand with the refusal of perspective and linear logic.

But contemporary dance was to take its solutions for getting out of these compositional straightjackets still further. Beyond the alternative proposed by Cunningham's use of the aleatory, the movement associated with the Judson Dance Theatre went furthest in questioning systematic ordering as the means by which a work must be put together. Historically, everything began with Robert E. Dunn's famous course. Dunn had been invited to give a workshop at the Cunningham studio on the advice of John Cage. For Dunn, recourse not only to aleatory methods but also to techniques already proven in the literary or visual arts such as 'cut-ups' or collage, were to free dance from the burden of sequencing movements according to voluntarist processes. Dunn's course provided the first context for the experiments with constraints or rule-games determined by scores.[38] According to Mami Malaffay's account, reported by Banes, these scores, *could just as well have been the phases of the moon as the cooking of an egg.* You had to integrate and follow structures that imposed limits but not organisation, such as the famous Judson 'tasks'. One of the instructions used by Dunn as an escape from voluntarist composition and organisation was to use 'a single thing'. For, by definition, any system of organisation implies that several elements be linked to each other with a whole train of possible baggage: like the hierarchy between them. The 'one thing dances' were simple and factual and in particular, as is often the case with 'performance art,' they dealt with only an isolated proposition (and remember that this was also the approach of Schlemmer at the Bauhaus). They responded on an abstract level to Simone Forti's 'constructions' of the same period which were more related to 'performance' (not surprisingly since their 'stage' was the Reuben Gallery), partly because of their concrete, material element where an object plays a determining role in the production of a trajectory, a movement mode, a body state. In pieces like *Rollers* or *Seesaw* all corporeal initiative proceeds from a series of accessories which affect whatever actions are undertaken. An unstable plank, boxes on rollers which erratically transport the performers hanging on to ropes, and which keep getting jammed up, remove the risk of known co-ordinates and stereotypes just as the numerical or abstract constraints of Dunn took away from the dancers the possibility of conscious decisions.[39] At the same time, the action, completely divested of any directly expressive aesthetic elaboration, does not call for an evaluation: everything that happens is interesting since it is what is happening. And the simplicity of the gesture or the move is to be taken for what it is: a neutral act, without reference or arbitration. The Judson Church followed these transformations of the act of composition with 'tasks' inspired by Anna Halprin's work: in the tasks, the constraint of an instruction apparently forbade any direct personal initiative, but also made the choreographic organisation a non-premeditated journey, whose structures depended entirely on accomplishing the 'task', in an arbitrariness that, according to Sally Banes, *substituted for that of the 'chance-process'*.[40] The task's power of 'inhibition' (to take up a concept already at work in the Alexander technique) barred the way. All sorts of processes were then put into play: scores, prescriptions, physical constraints, rule games or the use of objects rupturing and dislocating the compositional project itself, at the same time as they opened up the explosion of an anarchic dance no longer recognising its own law (even if it endowed itself with 'rules') to infinite possibilities.

During the '60s in the United States, an aesthetics of repetition was a way of overcoming the centralising 'crisis' or climax. Repetition, the immediate reprise of a motif similar to the preceding one, in fact constitutes an obstacle to the temptation to control a logical and linear structure. Here, it is important to see the difference between repetition as destructive of organisation and the reprises or re-occurrences of a motif which is an integral part of what is most traditional in composition whether in choreographic, musical, literary and visual art contexts, etc. There, where these processes assemble, repetition disassembles. The continual return to a cellular unit which is often interrupted undoes organisation and construction. This was the theme of post-Cageian music and minimalist art in general: not only is the 'crisis' levelled away but everything which could lead to it crumbles away in repetitions neutralised by their own redoubling. It was the same with Lucinda Childs in pieces such as *Radial Courses* (1976) from the '70s where only one spatial form is distributed to all four corners, only a single dimension of space – direction – is developed, and only a single series of motifs is used to travel along each trajectory. As for the basic unit, it did not depend on *well constructed phrases with beginning middle and end. There were only modules without inflexion of time, without climax and little accent.*[41] In the *Accumulations* series that dates from the same period, Trisha Brown serialises rather than repeats a certain number of movements which must be done in order before they are started again from the beginning, with a new motif added each time. Phrasing abdicates in favour of pure series. Still in this aesthetics of the series, each movement proposition must return to its starting point before the next is commenced. It was, she says, the only possible solution to making a dance after choreography was annulled in the '60s. By removing the risk of the 'climax', repetition leads to a questioning of the whole choreographic act. It can be related to the death drive discussed by Deleuze in relation to the return of the same.[42] But what affects the choreographic object in its structure, in its very existence as an existence to be legitimated, is the inverse of what is produced in the spectator's awareness. Seriality and the relativity of a present always renewed through minuscule processes of differentiation (like Childs' repeated pathways) change the subject's perception. In relation to this Deleuze cites Hume's empiricist thesis: *repetition changes nothing in the object which is repeated, but it does change something for the mind which contemplates* and, one could add, in the body which produces it. Clearly serial or repeated movements in minimalist dance bear witness to such an equalisation of tensions that their repetition only confirms the perfect similarity of the movements. But this permanence is hypnotic. Perception lets go of its evaluative prerogatives: we are lead to a quasi-ecstatic acceptance of a threshold opening onto the void of an absent construction. And the action-movement is offered to us in its pure and peaceful materiality where any contraction or febrile intensification is no longer necessary to assure its logical jurisdiction.

It is clear that finding a way out of her total questioning of the whole act of choreography was difficult for Trisha Brown. For a long time she gave herself extremely structured rule-games in order to accomplish the journey that would bring her back to a legitimate exploitation of compositional material. One of the pieces in which this journey is most evident – almost an abdication after the radicalities of the Judson Church – could well be *Set and Reset* with its singular genesis: Brown and the dancers set a phrase from improvisation, the one at the beginning of the work which, even today, is danced at one side of the stage where exchanges of energy, relations between centre and periphery, and collisions (not always by direct contact but often through energy transmitted from a distance) occur. This phrase is 'the delivery phrase'. It can then be exited according to two types of instruction: the first, to explore space in all directions, and especially all sides, with the stage becoming a sort of spatial score with places of 'over-investment' that have to be avoided or confronted in turn. Then, another series of instructions are given as permanent principles: 'stay simple, and when you don't know what to do stand in a line' etc. Thanks to these principles of construction a series of cells develops with variable geometry: duo, trio, etc., made from the almost unlimited conjunction of the dancers' spontaneous decisions. Gradually, Brown explains, the material grew and was set. Created in 1983, *Set and Reset* has no reason to remain the evolving work that the dancers of the period made it. Let us simply note the restrictive and constraining character of its elaboration. Once perceived this mechanism contrasts astoundingly with the freedom of the movement. The supreme dance expression of the period, dubbed 'unstable molecular structure', Brownian movement of that era is today the one for which the choreographer is most known: the emanation of a continuous movement circulating unhindered through all of the shifts of the body and through the whole space. It entails a permanent letting go of the centre of gravity, a limitless dispersal of the body's matter/material. And it is, of course, precisely the rigour of the compositional framework (and at the same time its availability for all possibilities) which gives birth to Trisha Brown's wonderful chaos as it propagates through the whole piece the 'molecular instability' of a body without an axis; and which is only the inverse of an order composed in order to create its own disorder – what Sally Banes calls 'exquisite disorder'.

In France, putting aside the endless reproduction of minimalist processes which have been fashionable in many mediocre pieces, we find some very singular treatments of 'climax'. As we have seen, young French dancers have a tendency to use a formal device without concerning or informing themselves regarding the philosophy that inspired it or without going through the often risky and transgressive process which might enable them genuinely to own it. In addition, imitation of minimalist processes (seriality, juxtaposition, repetition) has often served to mask weaknesses in or absences of the art of composition, as if one could destroy before even having experienced what construction is. What a Lucinda Childs or Trisha Brown can deconstruct in full consciousness having, both of them, undertaken a long and searching study with the great masters of 'modern dance' as Merce Cunningham did before them, cannot occur without an equally long and reflective journey having been taken. Except by simply using effects as empty gadgets slavishly and conformistically copied. Nevertheless, even this side of fashionable effects, it is true that the destruction wreaked by Cunningham and the minimalists on traditional dramaturgy with its story and denouement, either taken as a whole or in its details is really no longer possible. The irreversible force of 'disconnecting' (*désenchaînement*) seems to have marked the whole modern choreographic milieu. Bagouet recalls of *Saut de l'Ange* that *the sequences follow one another without any principle of construction having been pre-set.*[43] The 'little stories,' to use one of his expressions, of French dance are often thus, like the episodes of an unknown mythology, picked off like so many disconnected motifs, 'little myths' of which *Saut de l'Ange* is an admirable example. But the problem of the 'climax' is always there. It inhabits the recesses of the dance, as a ghost against which all disappearing acts fail. In Bagouet's work measures to keep indefinitely at bay the menace of an always possible climax seem to be taken moment by moment. In *Le Saut de l'Ange* as previously in *Le Crawl de Lucien* there are not climaxes but moments of intensification or bursting out. In the solos (Catherine Legrand in *Le Crawl de Lucien*, Sonia Onckelinck in *Le Saut de l'Ange*) it is a sort of ineffective existential rebellion that is immediately re-absorbed. Perhaps the whole mystery of Bagouet's work rests in this conflict whose imminent breaking out (in violence perhaps) is possible but always avoided.

We have Catherine Diverrès to thank for raising the question of climax – in her art as in her writing. In her work, it is always present but always diverted from one moment to another, even and especially in moments that are, energetically speaking, apparently atonal and disarmed – perhaps an even better way to keep it from catching fire. Choreography in pieces like *Tauride* (1991) and more recently *L'Ombre du Ciel* (1994) introduces delays or rather caesuras which modulate these implosive moments. In some of Bernardo Montet's solos the climax is in the sketch of an action that remains incomplete, at the threshold of its impulse, simultaneously exhausting and turning back on itself. We should mention the influence of Georges Bataille on these two artists and of art as the treatment of an 'excess' in the subject – '*La part maudite*' ('accursed portion' or 'share'), a function as much of the Law as of a destiny in which *the exuberance of life is dedicated to revolt.*[44] There is no climax in Daniel Larrieu's work but a sort of empty stretching out which could almost take its place. Here the evacuation of climax has carved out a poetics of absence, a sort of lost moment of nothingness whose trace is found in the depletion of movement, a void becoming a compositional element. (It is the same sometimes with Jean Gaudin, Daniel Dobbels, Paco Decina). We also find it in certain treatments of space, where the centre of the stage is often emptied as though to indicate a place where meaning/direction (*sens*) has fallen away. What might have created a tension between magnetic poles or differently charged presences (in *Anima*, 1990 or where the densities in the movements multiply; *Jungle sur la Planète Venus* for the Frankfurt Ballet restaged in 1995 by the CCN de Tours) is re-absorbed and pacified and begins to play as children or small animals play, as if the dancers had lost the world's memory. Repressed in the choreographic language, as in contemporary aesthetics, climax leaves its trace and often its wound. It cannot but conjure up the '*vanitas*': the image of death in certain famous classical paintings such as the tomb in Poussin's *Bergers d'Arcadie*, and the macabre anamorphosis in Holbein's *The Ambassadors*. In the same way that painting has been able to mask its effacement of the vanishing point by the very symbols of its disappearance, the deliberate abdication of any centralising tension in French dance of the '80s has led dancers to mourn their own dislocation. Today, nevertheless, a reaction amongst the very artists I have cited is evident. The aesthetics of disconnection seems to have reached its term in an exhaustion of resources too quickly transformed into method. A desire to create and construct, to find the articulated threads of an organic globality between body and intention, is emerging. A reappropriation of compositional tools in teaching as in creation is visible everywhere. Very young choreographers demonstrate an extreme rigour in their choices and also in the logical and corporeal development of these choices; many others, too, and all those already mentioned, accustomed to the complexities of their art, who have come out of the Company Bagouet. In France it is to this school that young artists are referring. Odile Seltz sees in it a resource *for facing chaos*.[45] Not the Cunningham chaos which breaks up rational surface articulations but, on the contrary, the chaotic proliferation of mimeticisms and the jumble of parasitic formalisms. For rediscovering the art of composing, here, does not correspond to new certainties. On the contrary, compositional knowledges and their transformation into an *écriture* do not seek to institute established, normative or reproducible forms: it is in the growing complexity of their processes, in the attentive manipulation of their delicate materials that dance must continue to advance towards the elusive.

1 Deleuze, Gilles & Guattari, Felix *What is philosophy?* 1994.
2 Bourigault, Christian, Programme note for a professional dance composition workshop.
3 Readers may also be familiar with the term '*écriture féminine*' from Hélène Cixous's *The Laugh of the Medusa* and others. See also my note on *écriture* in the Introduction. (Transl.)
4 Gleizes & Metzinger, *Du Cubisme*, 1913.
5 Deleuze, Gilles *Francis Bacon: The Logic of Sensation*, 2003.
6 Buirge, Susan 'La composition: long voyage vers l'inconnu' in *Marsyas*, No. 26, June 1993.
7 Marilen Iglesias Breuker (oral source): Cinemathèque of Toulouse, February 1991, an evening devoted to Alain Resnais.

8 '*Danse savante*' refers to the courtly dance tradition which had associated with it a body of written, theoretical texts. (Transl.)

9 Rust, Michèle, Oral source: conversation with the author, 24th September 1995.

10 Febvre, M. *Danse Contemporaine et Théâtralité*, 1995.

11 Schulmann, N. 'A propos des Echelles d'Orphée de Joseph Nadj' (unpublished), 1994.

12 Giron, Sylvie, in Barre, L. *L'oeil dansant*, 1995.

13 Gerard, Christine 'Enseigner l'improvisation et la composition', Interview with Particia Kuypers in *Nouvelles de Danse*, No. 22, Winter 1995.

14 Taffanel, Jackie *L'atelier du Chorégraphe*. Unpublished Doctoral Thesis. Université de Paris XIII, 1994.

15 Buirge, Susan, 1993.

16 Faure, Elie *L'esprit des formes*, 1922, republished by Folio, 1991.

17 Waehner, Karin *Outillage Chorégraphique*, 1995.

18 Andrews, Jerome 'Le rayonnement de l'instant' in *Marsyas*, No. 26, June 1993.

19 Lawton, Marc 'Inventer la danse tout le temps' in *Marsyas*, No.26, June 1993.

20 Nikolais, A. 'No Man from Mars' in Selma Jeanne Cohen: *Modern Dance: Seven Statements of Belief*, 1965.

21 Novack, Cynthia J. *Sharing the Dance*, 1990.

22 Ehrenzweig, A. *The Hidden Order of Art: a study in the psychology of artistic imagination*, 1967.

23 Taffanel, J. *L'atelier du Chorégraphe*, 1994.

24 Pomarès, Jean 'De la formation à la creation' in *Positions*, notes of the DRAC PACA, January 1995.

25 Servos, N. 'Pina Bausch: Carnations' in Cohen, *Dance as a Theatre Art*, 1974.

26 Langer, S. *Feeling and Form* cited in Louis Horst, *Modern Dance Forms*. Princeton: Dance Horizons, 1961.

27 Banes, S. *Terpsichore in Sneakers*, op.cit.

28 Paxton, Steve 'Improvisation is a word for something that can't keep a name', 1987.

29 Jowitt, D. 1985.

30 de Spain, D. 'Creating Chaos: Chaos Theory and Improvisational Dance' in *Contact Quarterly*, Winter-Spring, Vol. XVIII, No. 1, 1993, pp. 21-27.

31 Cage, John *Silence*. 1966.

32 Deleuze & Guattari, 1994.

33 Charlip, Remy 'Composing by chance' in Kostelanetz, *Dancing in Space and Time*, 1989.

34 Scarpetta, Guy *L'impureté*, 1985.

35 Horst, L. & Russell, C. *Modern Dance Forms*, 1987.

36 Cunningham, M. in Charles, *Revue d'esthétique*, special issue on Cage, op.cit.

37 Ruiz, R. *Poétique du Cinéma*, 1994.

38 Banes, S. 'Choreographic Methods of the Judson Church Theater' in *Writing Dancing in the Age of Post-modernism*, 1994.

39 Forti, S. *Handbook in Motion*, 1966.

40 Banes, S. in *Writing Dancing in the Age of Post-modernism*, 1994.

41 Goldberg, M. 'Interview with Trisha Brown', 1986.

42 Deleuze & Guattari, 1994.

43 Bagouet, D. Introduction to *Saut de l'Ange*, text published in the Programme for the Atlantic Ballet of Régine Chopinot, for the re-staging of the work in 1993.

44 Jean Baudrillard writes that the 'accursed portion' in Bataille's theory 'refers to whatever remains outside of society's rationalized economy of exchanges'. See Bataille's *The Accursed Share: an essay in general economy*, 1988.

45 Seltz, Odile, in *Programme du Théâtre Le Cratère d'Alès*, 1st December, 1995.

The Works

Beginnings

(seed, theme, intention, reference)

No matter what the subject, the first test to apply is in one word – action.
Doris Humphrey[1]

What is there at the beginning of a choreographic work? Nothing: no specific support already in place. The dancer does not dispose of an already given medium as the other arts do: no sound, colour, or machine and light as in the cinema; no supporting text such as is traditionally the case in the theatre (the dancer can use a text, as we will see, but differently); certainly not a synopsis, as in classical ballet or in the way that, as Michèle Febvre says, a narrative organises from the outside the internal components of a danced movement.[2] Today, when there is a narrative in the choreographic work it is the work, as I discuss below, which produces it out of its own economy, or it takes an already elaborated narrative but 'works' on it. Dance is an art whose practice is based on so very little: the matter/material of the self, the organisation of a certain relation to the world. Such are the slender threads the dancer possesses for weaving a universe, an imaginary, a thought, a 'demiurgy' which, says René Thom, is a 'semiurgy'.[3] A choreographer must find everything in her/himself and in the specific rela-tion to the other. Establishing this relation is also already part of the work of composition. This is the miracle and the challenge of choreographic crea-tion: to draw out threads from the invisible, to give body to that which does not exist: as Wigman said, to make 'invisible images exist'.[4]

It is said that movement is the medium and the body is the instrument. But what movement? What body? We have seen that neither movement nor body exist a priori, before the sensory activity (*kinésies*) that founds them. The choreographer's work is to invent a body (or at least to elicit from al-ready worked and conscious bodies a corporeity that is consonant with her/his project). The movement which at the beginning of a choreographic process is absolutely unknown and always to be rediscovered, is, in contem-porary dance, presaged by nothing if not by its own emergence (*surgissement*) – the pre-movement discussed by Hubert Godard (after Cunningham). This pre-movement is captured in the furtive interstice be-tween non-moving and moving (the famous transition from 'Stillness' into 'stir' from which Laban created a whole poem.)[5] Composing in dance al-ways depends on a momentary revelation and on it alone. It is what gives access to the great 'already there', this already present but veiled depth which Jackie Taffanel discusses, citing Deleuze: *a language that speaks before words, gestures elaborated before bodies have been organised...*[6] Fortunately, in the face of this desert of references, and in addition to what s/he can al-ready decipher from that which has not already been represented, the dancer is not unarmed: s/he has at her disposal a formidable inheritance of knowledges and processes. Upon entering the universe of contemporary dance one is struck by the wealth of resources that in scarcely a century have been put in place by the creator-theorists who first worked on this evanescent matter. More importantly, they very quickly provided the keys that have allowed it to be brought out of non-existence, putting it to work and giving it a profile and an identity.

In principal, as we will see below, choreography bears the 'signature' of an author, an isolated individual or sometimes a couple. It is from this author, even if s/he is 'two-headed' like Joëlle Bouvier and Régis Obadia (whose aesthetic is extraordinarily coherent, a twinned corporal identity), that the dynamic of an original intention emerges. In contemporary dance there are few collective creations in spite of the essential role played by the dancer-performer with whom and in whom a work is born, and who sometimes engenders it through her/his presence alone. Very few moments in the history of contemporary dance have questioned the status and function of the unique choreographer.

In France, several examples of collectives (Lolita founded in 1981, dissolved three years later; the Company de la Ronde which defined itself as a company of dancers, with the avowed intention of renouncing the obligation to have a choreographer) are the very interesting exceptions. In the USA, there was the legendary period of the Grand Union, a group founded by Yvonne Rainer whose goal was the democratisation of the hierarchical dance company structure inherited from modern dance: no choreographer, and equality of status in the creative act. *With its aspirations towards a spirit of collectivity, equality and spontaneity, the Grand Union seemed non-conventional in relation to the mainstream modern dance companies*, and its members, adds Sally Banes, *had worked for years to find alternative solutions to the established structures of power in the dance world.*[7] The Grand Union model, however, seems poorly adapted to our situation today. Firstly, it belongs to a world which came out of the history of co-operatives and other communal associations of the '70s. Second, paradoxically, there was nothing more aristocratic than a 'democracy' that brought together personalities of the highest rank in dance and who appear to us today as so many sacred monsters: Trisha Brown, Yvonne Rainer, Deborah Hay, Simone Forti, Steve Paxton, David Gordon. It is so easy to feel equal amongst princes... among artists possessing an unheard of mastery of their practical and theoretical orientations. In addition, artistic initiative in the Grand Union always came down to an individual choice: Rainer's famous *Continuous Project Altered Daily* (inspired by the work of Robert Morris), undoubtedly one of the major productions of the Grand Union, was, for better or worse, led by her as 'boss', as she has explained.[8] In fact the equality of tasks, or of titles, ought not obscure the need to preserve the initiative of a creator: to renounce choreographic signature, as we will see, is to maintain an archaic situation which was dance's for centuries: a practice without works (*oeuvres*) where

the performer, overexposed and magnified, is all there is to see. In the traditional courtly dances (*danses savantes*), no matter how beautiful and
intelligent they are, the dancer 'contains' the whole dance. There is no
écriture to make of her something other than simply a faithful and sublime
executor, a sort of 'presenter': whereas the contemporary performer is the
'producer' of the movement that inscribes her in its own history, a body at
work in a thought where it recognises itself. For the dancer as for the dance,
these archaic structures are still too close and too threatening for it to be
possible with impunity to annihilate the role of choreographic creator, a
role which belongs to modernity and where all the partner/collaborators
are engaged around a singular artistic philosophy. And even when this
choreographer has gone, the dancers gather in her/his name because her/
his vision (*projet*), as much as her/his work, still constitutes the 'scene'
where their self-understanding is elaborated and chosen. In France, this is
what is happening at the Carnets Bagouet, an association of dancer-
choreographers of different backgrounds united by a common vision
which is the stronger for having been constrained to identify itself in
mourning. *Others bear the names that he no longer can*: thus does the writer
and poet François Dominique evoke Yano who has disappeared from a
world in which signatures persist as shadows.[9]

Generally, the point of departure of any work relates to a fundamental
trait of the contemporary dancer: the necessity, the urgency, even, of saying, sometimes of shouting to the world her/his overflowing sensation and
desire (*attente*). It is rare to see an artist going through a guide-book seeking
a subject matter, even in subsidised situations where regular productions
are demanded. Of course, Doris Humphrey does suggest some guidelines –
with a pedagogical rather than creative purpose – and these correspond
rather poorly to her own wealth of inspiration. Still less do they correspond
to Merce Cunningham's sketch of the choreographer obliged *in order to
create a dance...to bite his nails, beat his head against the wall or rummage
through old notes looking for an idea*.[10] Generally, the choreographer's fault is
in having an excess of multiple ideas. As in all the arts, proceeding by subtraction and isolating an essential element, the deep thread of 'desire,'
constitutes the first step in the choreographic work (*travail*).

For some artists, the first thematic work depends on a plan that is well
defined in advance. It can be dictated by an external inspiration as in the
case of Karine Saporta, for example, for whom each choreography treats a
precise and definite problematic upon which her imagination will set to
work. It can be from a novel or personal 'fiction' as is the case with Jean-
Claude Gallotta who recounts to himself and to the audience a thousand

little stories even before the work is begun (and often the work in question will speak of something else entirely). In these two cases, there is an intention known in advance and the whole work flows from that intention even if it does not seem to develop in a linear or rational way.

This type of choreographic creation is closer in its weft (even if the aesthetic contents are oriented otherwise) to the compositions based on external prescriptions evoked at different levels by modern dance masters (Humphrey, Horst, Nikolais) who were partial to, if not objectifying, at least clearly and decisively formulating the intention. In other cases, closer to the 'internalist' current of Wigman, the intention is discovered within the work where, initially, the objective of the dance is to draw out, more than a specific 'motif', and not a precise thematic, but the 'inner sonority' or the 'inner necessity' to use Kandinsky's terms. Even if it can subsequently develop in terms of an image (everything is possible) and even, and why not, into a narrative. The choreographer is one who knows how to read in her/himself these silent resonances, and who knows how to make them sing in the movement and to share them with others. Thus, the process described by Lebenzstejn as the very essence of expressionism: interiorisation and maturation of a received impression, then its later restitution.[11]

Jacqueline Robinson has a beautiful way of describing the first work of necessary 'abstraction' on a diffuse, as yet unstructured terrain: *The image or interior sensation perceived by the artist before it is incarnated is not an image in the sense of an illustration, but the crystallisation of a lived or imagined experience.*[12] The choreographic, then, becomes a vast machine for deciphering (and interpreting) this image which is often without contour, often unknown to itself or the artist – this 'vague desire' as Susan Buirge's puts it, whose object is hard to pin down. The specificity of the choreographer's work itself will be to project this 'crystallisation' – not to objectify it, but to transsubjectify it. Hence, the patient work with the group, admirably described by Taffanel, where through 'reactions' in the chemical sense of the word, from body to body, from consciousness to consciousness, questions and responses will be sent as so many furtive shimmerings from which a choreographer will draw in order, out of them, to distil the essence of the actions. Whether the theme is exterior to experience or whether, on the contrary, it comes out of an internal experience that comes close to the mystical state discussed by Bataille (not at the level of registering an excess or of an alteration of consciousness but simply of a questioning where the object is provisionally held in suspension), the relation of the choreographer to her/his 'intention' is, to an external eye, very strange and unlike the forms of 'inspiration' such as one finds them in the other arts. In fact, in the long run the choreographer will share her/his 'idea' with the dancers who will become the very flesh of her/his desire.

This act of transsubjectivation, even in the relatively consensual milieu that a dance company can sometimes be, is not easy. Some choreographers keep their intention a mystery as long as possible in the secret of their reverie. This was the case, for example, with Martha Graham who nurtured an idea (*projet*) sometimes for as long as two years before revealing it to others in order to begin rehearsals. Her famous *Notebooks* reveal this subterranean work. It is a mosaic of citations brought together around a theme, images gleaned haphazardly from her reading or from exhibitions. Graham's notes retrace the path of the theme: it seems that she did not choose, but it 'came' to her out of an obscure and distant imaginative horizon. Whether it was 'ancient', and inspired by the fundamental figures of Greek mythology, or 'modern' (literary, historical, political), the theme deposited itself through a thousand textual fragments and artistic and philosophical references, from Aeschylus, Freud, Calder or Brancusi. There was a long secret path by means of which, for her, a history, a myth took bodily form. Then the dance arose from the depths of time and the unconscious like a long buried '*objet d'art*' (according to an archaeological image dear to psychoanalysis) and was gradually disengaged from the debris of the imaginary where the essence of the absolute movement she knew how to find was being held prisoner. Limón also used to acknowledge: *There is always a period of two years during which I live with an idea.* And he sketches an amusing self-portrait of a choreographer seized by irrepressible movements 'coming' to him while waiting for the lift or on public transport.[13]

Testimony from dancers who worked with Bagouet reveal that he, too, brought them the mysterious body of an already constructed plan. The dancers received no explicit information about it, but the movement he taught them allowed them to go further into themselves, into the interior of the '*écriture*-labyrinth'. Besides, the dance interpreter (*lecteur*) does not need all this information to apprehend the wealth of accumulated materials of certain choreographers (Larrieu, Diverrès, Bastin, Gaudin, etc.), or in order to perceive the web that forms the underlying text of choreography, the underlying movements, the mental spaces traversed, before the choreographic space precipitated into objective space is illuminated in the relations between kinespheres. In choreographic work the author passes very quickly from the 'primary' stage of creation to the secondary stage of sharing, where the other comes into play – as active partner in creation, not only as confidant or interlocutor. It is a situation peculiar to this difficult art where, on one side or the other, there is the risk of feeling exploited – dispossessed of one's creative and ontological project: in other words, fundamentally dispossessed of one's desire (much more than of the object of one's desire). Although, to my knowledge, they are not consulted regarding this kind of situation, psychoanalysts have much to say concerning art and its thought. For Ehrenzweig, there is an irreparable loss between the intimate plan or idea of the artist and its actualisation in an objective manifestation, to the point where the spectator does well to be suspicious of a work's poetics, because of the many rationalising or structuring approaches to it that, little by little, impoverish the imaginative and sensuous material: *Art is a dream, the artist's dream which we, the awakened spectators can never see in its true structure. Our alert faculties can only give a too precise image, produced by secondary elaboration,*[14] and if it is true that access to the work must go back through the mystery of the artist's desire, then we have to agree with this aesthete-analyst that *the work of art remains the unknowable: Ding am sich.* A work and especially a choreographic work is always in conflict with what is unknown within it: it, itself, creates the limits beyond which another field of experience might open out. This is why some (valuable) performances which show this wounding of/in desire are more convincing than a total 'success', and are sometimes, more than others, able to show the impossible frontier in relation to which, as Emmanuelle Huynh rightly says, the constraints of processes of realisation can *oblige a falling back on more facile or more familiar territories.*[15] These, as we know, hasten the work and gain the adhesion of an initiated public which easily recognises the 'brands'; and seals by its approval the secret terms of a defeat.

Working in a very different analytic current to that of Ehrenzweig, Michel de M'Uzan focuses on literature and particularly, with regard to the starting points (*premices*) of artworks, on the *remarkable psychic state which, commonly given the title 'inspiration', appears to preside over their birth.* But to this term he prefers the notion of '*saisissement*' (a thrill or seizure) – so important for us in dance – which finishes with *an act that is not only descriptive, but generates and organises a new order and constitutes an acquisition.* A strong vision indeed if we link it to choreography's 'generative field' and the invention of a new 'order' which might perhaps precede an intention itself or become inseparable from it... Similarly, the suggestive idea that we must abandon, albeit regretfully, the 'dream' of the primary process in order to confront, in the secondary, an intention towards real objects or bodies. *I consider that, in fact as far as primary narcissism alone is concerned, there is nothing to stage because everything happens before conflict.*[16] Thus, it is not in the dream, but in the birth of tensions between it and the world that the choreographic project is born and carves out its field. The dance company is this scene of tensional development par excellence. The 'work of dance' is to organise this scene. And what is more, to render it still active and readable as such at the moment of performance. An unparalleled artistic experiment, but also a human experiment, hitherto unknown as the foundation of a new poetics. Certainly, it is a utopian experiment in the sense that it invents a hitherto inexistent 'site' – but one which is neither fusional (in spite of the affection that binds certain companies) nor paradisiacal: at every instant, as in any moment of creation, anxieties of dispossession threaten action's elaboration. Because these anxieties are stronger (and closer to death) as soon as it is the body itself which is invested, confidence in the choreographer and her/his project, the attachment of the ensemble of dancers (whether formal or informal) to a common reference must open a clear, life-giving passage through the dark, perilous regions of the different stages.

In other countries, particularly in Germany where the tradition comes out of modern theatre, the role of 'dramaturg' has been created in order to provide the choreographer with a palette of references taken from different bodies of knowledge which, depending on the circumstances, can be used as inspiration or ideological justification or even aesthetic renewal at certain stages of creation. This is a function that Marianne Van Kerkhove fulfils in relation to Anne Teresa de Keersmaeker. The contribution of her theatre experience is not without influence on the work of the choreographer. In France, it is most often the choreographer who is her/his own dramaturg even if, in certain pieces, assistants can be involved in iconographic or literary research. Alain Neddam first filled this function for Dominique Bagouet when he was making *Mes Amis* (1985), a piece for solo actor from a text of Emmanuel Bove. When one throws oneself into these unsignposted experiments I suspect that it is better to be several – at least so as to be able to name things. Outside of economic considerations, there is a very intelligent conviction in French dance, namely, that dance does not have to thematise itself in terms of knowledges that are already in place – but must integrate these along with the appearing and evolving creative dynamic, through its reactive stages with and in the performer and the spectator. All the marvellous texts of dancers and choreographers describing these beginnings of the creative process show how a theme is proposed, how the creative team works on it with improvised and directed approaches, and how the choreographer's look perceives what is happening, and what is revealed and produced out of this. For it is through a sequence of 'reactions', reversible operations producing transmutations and displacements within the group that the dance gradually first takes flight, then finds its *raison d'être* and legitimacy. In this sense all true creation (except when using existing schemas) is a step forward and hence a research. Whoever has witnessed the rehearsals of a work in process knows with what demanding rigour the dancers discuss the material amongst themselves and the pertinence of this or that way of approaching it. And with what radicality. Beginning with descriptive and analytical texts, very serious study is starting to be undertaken today of these '*séances*', in all the senses of this word, that lead to an original creative act. I have often cited Jackie Taffanel's, *The choreographer's workshop*. It is clear that the witness (or the agent) of a work's beginnings is the only person able to bring together both a perception of events and the aesthetic mode of their emergence.

If the choreographic act, including the formulation of its intention (*propos*) is a shared act with multiple resonances, there is often an undesirable partner, a clandestine passenger accompanying many artistic enterprises: 'the inner spectator' which, while the work is being made, judges in the name of (ever changing) public opinion, inscribing the work according to consensual criteria. Michel de M'Uzan, again, best defines this 'look' which is often internalised despite ourselves and is capable of bending the creator and her/his group to the law of compliance: a depository that is at once dangerous and indispensable (so as not to remain in the narcissistic circle of an unproductive regression), what the analyst would call 'the inner public' reproducing the parental gaze that the infant desires to seduce in order to be loved.[17] It is a dangerous situation in dance: dangerous for the dancer and for the spectator in so far as it is the body which is produced, shown (in the dancer's case), and solicited by kinaesthesia (in the spectator's). This idea is further enriched by Michel Bernard who relates it to the experience of the body more generally and by remembering, after Merleau-Ponty, the 'chiasm' between the perception of others' bodies and the other's look upon the body-subject, which in turn nourishes sensory experience.[18] The relation between the other's look upon the body and what is elaborated in choreographic work is precisely what opens the choreographic field. Hence the fragility, on a narcissistic level, of such a complex network of mirrored looks. However, there is no better milieu for eliminating this interiorised public than a dance company – which is not to say that the encounter with a 'real' pubic might not be envisaged, including an encounter that could validate from a buried and very archaic place, a 'judgement' upon both the artistic propositions and the presence of the bodies. We will see that criteria of legibility and the projection of an empathy are constitutive of the choreographic act. At the beginning, however, there is a formidable need in contemporary dance to keep its intention private: to

formulate or shape it within the company (*en compagnie*), according to
Larrieu's beautiful expression. Thus the 'social neurotics', a term of
Schilder's cited by Michel Bernard, acting on bodily presence is avoided, in
that relations within the company allow the elaboration of an alternative
'reference' through which the dancer frees her/himself from the oedipal
relation.[19] We are discussing Godard's 'third term' which is essential for
establishing a choreographic dialogue from out of a reciprocally agreed
body state in those communities of dancers that I would call philosophical
communities – from the fact that two activities are at work there: an understanding of common ideas, and their practice. This understanding goes
further than in other creative communities. Amongst other things, it depends on a field of shared experience in the daily class or different types of
workshops. Hence the importance of the study undertaken in the company
to create between the dancers this common area of corporal cognition from
which they can understand each other. This understanding can be based on
different things. For example, with Trisha Brown there are no 'courses'
strictly speaking but the creation of a common body state according to
different paths chosen by the dancers themselves through different preferred 'release' or other still more sophisticated techniques, such as the
fundamentals taught by Susan Klein or ideokinesis. But these dancers all
master deeply a wide array of body knowledges and they can immediately
perceive the context from which their partners are broaching their work
in common. Here, the terrain of understanding is established unproblematically. It is precisely this corporeal understanding that will permit a true
dialectic overseeing not a mechanism of seduction but one of pertinence.

Where does the power of this mechanism (*dispositif*) come from? From
several sources: firstly from a training in composition that allows an
appropriate and rigorous understanding of starting points and their development; from the choreographer-dancer relation which mediates several of
the gaze's points of reference and where an archaic affectivity can dissolve
in favour of a desire directed elsewhere. This economy by no means elimi-
nates the risks or narcissistic wounds. But it is powerfully salutary on an
aesthetic plane. It is in large part thanks to these completely original
mechanisms that contemporary dance has the power and diversity that we
recognise in it today. The dance company is a vehicle that is well equipped to
go beyond consensual schemas to work towards the unknown. It is not for
all that a therapeutic cell: the lived experience of the body in relation to the
look of others remains perilous. Anticipation of a darker side, including in
the movement itself, can at each instant bring the dancer (and perhaps the
spectator) to the brink of unsuspected abysses. Some have willingly gone

into this place: Anita Berber, Valeska Gert, Dore Hoyer – dancers for whom the dance only began at a moment of rupture, when any look became untenable.

At the beginning of any piece there are two things or at least one: the intention (*propos*) and the theme. The theme is what is given first, and is the basis upon which an understanding can be shared. The '*propos*' is more an objective or intentionality (even though this last term, which has a very specific usage in contemporary dance, cannot be used lightly). The intention only reveals itself during the workshopping process. But it may also be inscribed before this process: if only to be eliminated. In certain practices the intention is not to have one. One wants to begin naked, as we will see, and to wait for a diffuse and unanticipated poetic matter to be elaborated between the dancers.

The intention of a work can remain sealed within its matter or structure. Sometimes at this point it is drawn into the turbulence of what is being constructed, so that it escapes what it might have been at the start. Thus, in the portrait of Kahnweiler by Picasso, Michael Baxandall sees the figurative intention losing itself in the tumult of the planes.[20] For in painting, for example, some very powerful works take their intention along with them. It is not clear that such re-routings are ordinarily possible in dance: the strength of the intention, its treatment in the composition where it must be both free and coherent, are absolute necessities of artistic awareness in contemporary dance. It is around the relevance of upholding this necessity that the choreographic community works and makes its allegiances. Of course, this is not a question of a straight-jacket: on the contrary, whatever comes out of improvisation, for example, must be the object of particular attentiveness in that the intention is often discovered there in a more advanced form, having come through apparently irrational pathways, but ones that allow other layers of intentionality to appear. The problem for the reader of dance will be to identify this very intention (*propos*). It is not strictly narrative. And we must note an important distinction between 'reference' and 'intention' here. In French, Flemish or Quebecois dance, for example, where the (literary or cinematographic) culture is dominant, there is frequently a reference, including in the title of the work, for example. This does not mean that the reference determines the poetic contents of the work, nor does it completely cover the terms of the intention. And when a narrative intervenes it does not always go to the heart of the project. In pieces by Christine Bastin, for example, where the thematic charge and narrative seem considerable and where a figurative situation is clearly indicated, the referential frame is only there as a springboard to precipitate a corporeal and emotional catastrophe that has no illustrative goal. Bastin's pieces, often inspired by literary sources (as in her 1995 *Siloë*) play on the ambiguity of these contradictory sources. The vocal presence of a text spoken on stage only further dislocates what could otherwise become centralised and homogenous. In fact, Bastin's theme is nearly always different from the textual contents to which she refers even when they are works as powerful as Lowry's *Under the Volcano*. The gap which can exist between the reference and the intention is one of the most beautiful conquests of contemporary dance. One can use many kinds of works, say, by Marguerite Duras (Susan Buirge's '*Des sites*', after *Savannah Bay*, 1983) or by Heiner Muller (Christian Bourigault's *Matériau désir* in 1994) without being obliged, as cinema makers are, to follow the linear unfolding of the text. What contemporary dance has most deftly destroyed is narrative in the traditional sense. Even if, like Deleuze, we believe that the cinematic machine has created an unfolding where the 'time-image' engenders its own dynamic, the story still remains to orient its vector. By way of an extreme contrary example in contemporary dance, let us take Santiago Sempere's remarkable work, *Don Quichotte: petites et grandes morts* (1990). There is nothing at all in it that relates directly to Cervantes's novel. The latter remains latent in an imaginary reference. The real reference is the myth of a writer and of a famous book that have both lost their identity and perhaps, as it was to be in Borges, their very existence. Such is the theme and Sempere explains as much in an excellent declaration of his intention. It is up to the spectator to perceive the way in which the theme is treated as a figure of dispossession (typical of Sempere) in a mindful chaos of actions executed in the pseudo-realist décor of a contemporary apartment, in all its incoherence and dilapidation.

First, the theme: every dance has a theme, whether or not this is in the order of a narrative. Except perhaps Doris Humphrey's 1934 *Drama in Motion* which she insisted was free of any elements external to the dance itself: neither music, nor décor, nor literature (no story). But there remains nonetheless an 'intention' to make a dance that is completely autonomous of any source of inspiration exterior to the movement: whence the title *Drama in Motion*. Obviously the theme does not have to be narrative. When Jackie Taffanel talks about her themes she talks, as Karin Waehner might, about her treatment of an oblique, of a support, of a succession of falls.[21] Sometimes a choreography is based around a single movement which is repeated, amplified, submitted to variation and distortion, etc. Even if the 'subject' (in the sense of 'theme') of the piece is oriented entirely towards something else, this initial movement will possibly remain the founding, secret thematics until the end. Duncan, as Jacqueline Robinson has noted, was the first to identify a 'key movement' which becomes the permanent element of a dance; and at the same time its 'seme' in the sense both of sowing or engendering but also of a semantic node. This was an idea taken up by Wigman both in teaching and in her dance-making: to find what Nikolais was to call the unique, unexpected, unknown, totally founding and perhaps forever invisible movement. By contrast Hubert Godard gives us to understand that a whole work and perhaps a choreographic language arranges itself around a 'missing gesture' where the body's discourse is used to saturate an irreducible absence.[22]

There can be a movement 'mechanism' underlying the work's structure: thus in *The Moor's Pavane*, José Limón chose as a surface story the Shakespearean drama of Othello. But in fact, as elsewhere, the title allows those who are attentive enough to understand that what is important is the *pavane* with its circular quartet grouping (even when it seems to disperse spatially) with the two couples facing each other as Caroso or Negri described it at the beginning of the 17th century. This circle authors the whole poetic material of the piece: as the dancers throw back their torsos, corollas open out from the centre of the circle, and the characters cross the circle, or Desdemona's body lies alone on the ground – death being nothing other than an exit from the circle of the living... This circle, as we have seen, is the motor of numerous Limón works and probably has to do with his thematic choices which are often centred on human communities (*There is a time*, *The Unsung*, etc.) as the circularity of relationships. Passing from Limónian sphericity to the directional plane of Merce Cunningham we find *Summerspace* (1963): here, Cunningham's thematic is the rapid crossing of space just as in *Torse* he starts with movements of that part of the body creating, in view of its primordial importance for the moderns, a veritable manifesto of contemporary dance. As we can see from these examples the choreographer almost always gives her/himself as a theme a functional proposition in relation to movement or space and time (like Cage's pieces which treat time to the exclusion of all other musical parameters).

It is important not to confuse theme and narrative/narration. The theme is in the initial inspiration or the proposition: the narrative/narration is a development. By narration we often mean in dance something theatrical. Specialists in the arts of representational action from Christian Metz to Patrick Pavis (essentially, theatre and cinema) have made it a category within regimes of 'telling-showing' more generally.[23] These categories restage the ancient duality of mimesis (imitation) and diegesis (story) formulated by Plato before Aristotle. Through the 'demonstrative' or mimetic character of movement as we have seen, dance was always tempted by story, and its proximity to theatre favours this tendency. But there is another theatricality in the poetics of dance: the institution of a 'scene' where bodies but also the compositional resources, through the play of dynamics and contrasts, organise a 'dramatisation' without story, a conflictual or progressive structure of energies or colours – what the Anglo-Saxons call 'dramatic' without intending to suggest any notion of a theatrical intrigue. 'Dramatic' is quite often used to describe all the so-called abstract works from Doris Humphrey to Merce Cunningham. It is precisely their having within them neither story, mimesis nor discourse which links them to the roots of a pure drama no longer needing contents to found the frame of its actualisation. Narration, as in its ancient forms, can be constituted upstream of the work. This was the case in *Tanztheater*, in the 'dance dramaturgy' promoted by Laban and after him, the *Notebooks* of Jooss: the explicit 'fable' that dance transposes into action inscribing it historically in a (critical) representation of the real. We have already noted the connections that should be made between this process and the Brechtian use of 'fable' in the '*Gestus*'.[24] In fact the *Tanztheater* gave rise to a theatre of virtual language out of which human action, crafted and charged with all its social determinants, was able to be shifted to the site where it was put into movement: and this was so in the treatment of movements that were appropriate less in terms of mimetic 'expressivity' than through work on the deep symbolics of movement and its relational constellations – directions, tensions, accents, rhythms etc. This makes *Tanztheater* a non-naturalistic art providing the spectator with information on the energetic economy of individual or collective human actions much more than on the formal appearance of those acts. Putting aside these henceforth historical forms of narration, the 'story' that appears in contemporary dance today is elaborated organically in the body of the work. The narrative material, as for example the 'character,' is found in the initial improvisations. Sometimes the character is the thematic element at the origin of a solo or group composition. Read, for example, Wigman's marvellous text about her discovery of the character of the Sorcerer, the theme of *Hexentanz* when, with a cheap fabric draped around her, she saw emerge the frightening, unspeakable brute being that she harboured within her.[25] This work on the 'unknown other within' was one of the resources of *Ausdruckstanz*, likening the dancer to someone possessed, someone with a dark and double identity: a shadowy being that the dancer nurtures in her/himself and which s/he discovers in the folds of improvisation. Improvisation for Pina Bausch is very much within this tradition (even though she does not explicitly acknowledge it).

Her approach brings to light the unnameable (or absurd) forms of aborted desires and regressive fantasies. This 'other' who is to be invented (that is, in the etymological sense, to be found or recognised) is still there at the beginning if not of 'pieces' at least of many studio investigations linking dance practices to those of certain theatre practitioners – from Barba to Langhoff – where the search for the character takes place within the performer.

A thematic whose itinerary the piece will develop can originate in a character or characters. This is often the case with Gallotta or Nadj. With Nadj, especially they are mythical characters who are (re)found rather than invented from collective or personal memory. They have been re-discovered rather than 'invented'. On the whole, however, characters in contemporary choreography are not part of a sequential narrative. Contrary to the theatre, the 'character' and the 'role' are not always superimposed or they are so ambiguously because most of the time the dancer dances the role as her/himself (Bagouet's *Le Saut de l'Ange* is exemplary here) or s/he changes role during the piece, a single character being able to float between different performers and vice versa. Here, the narration proceeds by jumps and bursts, and remakes a 'story' of 'states'. These states are not continuous, and produce as many formal particles as a single dancer might traverse without her body state being touched by them: they work by association and the projection of a linear narrative has little hold on them. Michèle Febvre has analysed these characteristics and meanders: *All dance today escapes dramatic continuity and establishes itself as a succession or a juxtaposition of sequences between which vague links which have nothing to do with any narrative wholeness are maintained.*[26] She also mentions what she calls 'processes of bifurcation' where, from the moment a possible narration is proposed, the very notion of the story atrophies and is lost or disfigured. Here, there is certainly a contamination of dance by modern literary forms from Joyce to the *Nouveau Roman*. But this fragmentation can be understood, too, through the 'intention' and the process of creation which flows from it.

The narration is not given in advance but is elaborated in and with the body. *Each movement is there because it must be there, because, often, at a given moment in the creative process evidence appears for which it would be pointless to look for a reason (one could find a thousand!) – even if that reason were only that it works.*[27] This judgment is blunt, and certain choreographic undertakings have shown themselves more exacting with regard to criteria of relevance, which are discussed and explored with a greater legibility in mind. The theme or 'situation' at the beginning (the idea on which a readable Gestalt, to recall Nikolais's term, is to be elaborated) will thus be worked on according to the immediate corporeal and sensory engagement of the community of dancers who will give it its real profile, one that to start with is unknown. It is these modes of narrativity, between the corporeal necessity of movement's emergence and the 'literary' referent, which make narrative dance one of the new completely contemporary forms of story. In her study of 'choreographic story' Febvre examines the coexistence within the one work of diegetic processes (where the discourse passes by way of the intermediary of a narrator) and clearly mimetic figures who present an act directly. Even beyond this 'showing' there is the famous dance dramaturgy already spoken about by Laban, a dramaturgy which is unavoidable as soon as an incarnation of meaning is effected through the presence and the action of a subject 'in movement'. We have seen that all movement, even if it does not have a directly mimetic function, (more than rare in contemporary dance) nevertheless functions as an act in the very unfolding of its material. By virtue of this, the 'choreographic story' whose ambiguities (even regarding its status *as* story) Febvre evokes, most certainly founds a new narrativity, one of the new modes of fiction, of which cinema, video and the visual arts have given us similar examples: *not what it recounts but how it realises a perspective.*[28] To follow up Febvre's investigation into these choreographic territories of telling-showing (*narration-monstration*) it will be necessary one day, going beyond dance, to interrogate these fictional mechanisms all of which in some way invest the body as the expressive and existential medium of a not always uttered speech. Or, when there is speech, it tells less the story than the *mis en scène* of its own utterance (like Jean-Luc Godard's video *Puissance de la Parole*). But, here, we are simply discussing a 'thematic' which summons a mode of narrating but not the narrative means that might develop it.

Some thematic frameworks are much more difficult to detect. And this is the case if the choreographer hides them, or only reveals them later when the work has already evolved. Sometimes the choreographer does not reveal them at all. This process of hiding/obscuring (*dissimulation*) involves part of the intention and the created materials. It can be directed to the audience or even the dancers; and sometimes, although more rarely in such a demanding and rigorous art, to the analytical consciousness of the creator him/herself. Clear or obscure, stated or latent, these sources permeate the work sometimes in an intermittent way like so many vibrational signals. If present in contemporary dance these flickerings of meaning would be called 'references' to distinguish their indexical, and often veiled or distanced character from the nuclear evidence of the 'theme'. In fact, the less the thematic is apparent or stated, the more an infinite network of refer-

ences whose latent presence gives a resonance to the work is woven; and all
the more for not being anchored in an intention conveyed at a single stroke.
Stephanie Aubin speaks aptly of a *hidden text*.[29] This under-text is neither
linear nor even constituted. It can be made of allusive shreds, small textual
flashes which are framed or dispersed without revealing their origins. They
are half-sketched citations which, when they reach the stage seem already
half erased.

Contributing to these in the overall construction, as in the detail of its
constituent elements, are the structural and functional analogies that numerous dances maintain with the literary. Firstly, the continuous thread of
an action, even if it is not directly narrative, can be likened to the syntax of
story: one that is formed from events (and 'becomings' [*avènements*], as
Dominique Dupuy would say) that are by nature corporeal or sensuous and
not necessarily ending up as actions that are identifiable to a spectator.
Within this development, processes which have a striking isomorphism
with literary forms such as apostrophes, metonymic displacements, shortening by collision, ellipsis or condensation, dilatation by periphrasis, can
intervene. These of course are the elements of phrasing. But they arc also
the emergent peaks of the 'hidden text' which only becomes visible through
these occasional punctuations. In a study entitled 'Visible Secrets' (which
evokes the hypothesis of Lacan's *The Purloined Letter* after a story by Poe:
that of an object whose visibility is 'stolen' by an overexposure), Marcia
Siegel evokes the literary text underlying the work of Paul Taylor whom she
calls *the most literary choreographer of our time'*.[30] In fact, as Siegel notes,
Taylor cultivates under his *faux-naif* disguise a recognised literary talent
(hiding autobiographies behind pseudonyms – as Gallotta has done); and
he shows this literary foundation by using 'literary tools' in his choreography. Hence, *the visual sous-entendus, the analogies, double meanings,
metaphors or actions which play on themes or characters like the leit-motiv in
music*, which can better develop within the choreography a veiled narrative
material whose discrete allegory the danced action focuses.[31] Heterogenous elements can be overlaid in ways (completely specific to
contemporary dance) that oppose coherent and unique compositional
choices. In Merce Cunningham's work complex thematic grids interlace;
Sixteen dances for soloists and Company of Three is apparently a prime example since it deals with the 'emotions' expressed in *abinaya*, the narrative part
of classical Indian dance, with clear distinctions between the eight positive
'white' emotions and the eight negative 'black' ones: material that is se-
mantically charged. However, it is also the first of this master's pieces to
make use of aleatory compositional processes and thus where the turn to

'unsequencing' (*désenchaînement*) is most evident. This aleatory aspect also puts into question the piece's very theme: namely, the emotional, even if coded or mimetic, whose source is the human subject. These complex imbrications of subterranean referential frameworks are frequent in Cunningham's work; and Carolyn Brown once remarked on the anguished expression on Merce's face at a certain moment in *Second Hand,* which was inspired by Satie's score, *The death of Socrates,* in the piano rendition by Cage (a 'second hand' version which explains the title). *It's because at that moment,* he explained, *Socrates dies.* Brown concludes from this that in Cunningham's work there are crypto-stories carrying a latent reference: *What I mean by this is that like most of Merce's dances* Second Hand *is for him meaningful.* Perhaps Merce feels that his dances only need to have meaning for himself and not for others. Certainly, he has arranged things so that very little is decipherable for an outside person. Or, in this particular case, for someone on the inside. But he leaves signposts.[32] By means of these simple 'indices', traces of meaning which emerge from a buried narration, we can perhaps get close to dance's thematics – that 'crystallisation' of an inner utterance (*énoncé intérieur*) that Jacqueline Robinson has spoken about. In fact, this agony of Socrates, and shadow of a lost thematic emerging in the choreographic discourse (and which does not for nothing refer to death), reveals to us that other element (which is neither the theme nor the intention): the reference. The reference – like a secret visible or invisible spark – is an underlying theme which can manifest itself in a continuous way or in bursts, almost by a spark of meaning. It can advertise itself or remain invisible, its existence sometimes only known by those involved in the dance's creation. This is the case with many pieces in which, stories, allusions, citations which have been put into play in the work of conception or creation, remain 'floating' like undeciphered dreams. It is what gives certain pieces their thickness: pieces with events superimposed in layers in which the most important often remain latent, in the margins of what is danced. Again, regarding the reference or references at the origin of works, a problem confronts the choreographer, the dancer, and even sometimes the commentator in terms of what he ought or ought not say. Should one disclose the keys to which one has had access through chance circumstances or experiences when one of the mechanisms of the piece itself is its founding enigmatics? This is the case in France with numerous works that have a complicated line of development and whose sources and subject are only weakly illuminated by their 'signposts'. It is the case with numerous pieces by Daniel Larrieu or Dominique Bagouet that have been elaborated out of an immense corpus of references which will never be acknowledged, or at least only partially, because the greater part of the choreographic work aims, on the contrary, to keep them at the edge of the visible, like so many fragile and unsettling suspensions of meaning. These thematic sparks play on the perception of the spectator at many levels. But to give her/him its keys directly would perhaps be fatal, like the light of Psyche's lamp on the face of the sleeping Eros – as though breaking in too quickly on the choreographic signifying field. Wouldn't it be better instead to allow the piece itself to reveal its own constituents – even if it might take years for its secret birth to be revealed in the very terms of the *écriture?* Why not evoke with Ann Hutchinson-Guest the seventy years necessary to read and understand Nijinsky's *Faune* and the secrets locked up in its movements?[33]

An overt thematics in Bagouet's work started to break down after *F et Stein* and was finished with *Deserts d'Amour*. He then embarked on an apparently non-narrative but intensely referenced creative path. The great literary and artistic erudition of the choreographer meant that before, or in the margins of the work's unfolding, there were a great many referential signs weaving a texture of resonances: nothing was explicit, everything was felt intuitively within a contextual coloration. Thus, the costumes with their bell-shaped white satin sleeves situated the dancers in another time as if they were not living their own history but something from the eighteenth century – which Bagouet adored. Thus, by the play of a single reference he set up a sliding between two temporal layers: one relating to the personal experience of the dancer in the present moment where, in the new movements at that time, the body flowed into new depths. And at the same time this very depth opened onto another dimension, the vague memory of another time where a defunct affectivity lay forever asleep – the beyond of feeling which so often appears in Bagouet's work and which the present movement hardly touches. Or risks destroying if the separation (between the layers of time, of spaces and bodies) that allows these intervals to breath is not observed. These double givens of the work accord with his choice of music: two types of sound and numerous silences, Mozart's divertimento and a composition by Tristan Murail. And it is difficult to say which of these two composers better distils the ambience of an incurable nostalgia. Whatever the case, these referential elements are simultaneously taken into account and 'deported' by the movement material which places over them a web of intimate experiences: movements of uncertain provenance and very 'contained' (*cernés*) as Michèle Rust says, which encourage the dancer to travel within what contains and seals her/him in its contours.[34] If the referential play of *Déserts d'Amour* is complex, impalpable and almost illegible, pieces like *Assaï* or *Necessito*, as commissions, are explicitly informed by the circumstances in which they were created. *Assaï* was created for the Lyon International Biennial of Dance in 1986: the theme was modern German dance which in France is usually reduced to its expressionist current alone. Bagouet chose to treat expressionist cinema and this displacement was largely justified: German dance and numerous dancers such as Harald Kreutzberg or Valeska Gert worked with film-makers of the period and influenced them in the same way as their own movements approximated the intense and contracted movements of actors of the silent era. Also, one of the main events of this Biennial was the night of expressionist films curated by Daniel Dobbels from some very rare examples. Nevertheless, Bagouet's choice here perfectly emblematised an intellectual attitude within French dance of the eighties: a refusal to take its references from the history of dance and a determination to choose from other artistic fields their theme, imaginary sources and ambience. These dancers who always made their 'family story' out of a borrowed genealogy totally rejected the history of dance and especially of modern dance. Bagouet did not lack this desire to re-invent his sources, his 'mother-images'. And they were striking ones (connecting with expressionist dance, in fact, at more than one point). The work is constructed in stages according to successive figures from a dream worthy of Hoffman as much as of Murnau or Pabst: dolls who move up and down, arranged according to the beat of an inexplicable mechanics. The acrobats, the 'creatures' come from an unknown species or realm, if not from the obscure material of an incubus. Couples dressed in 1830s costume pass along the back. There are other characters – doctors, fragile white young girls whom a screen divides into parallel diagonal rows. Then this horde of 'figures' disappears to be replaced by an invasion of performers in worn out leotards. Finally, entering from the side through parallel doorways, all these figures join and are snuffed out, cut down in silhouette by a sharp and mortal collapse. This description is not in itself important. We must go further into the structuring of this very rich piece: to see, as Rust invites us to do in a very fine commentary, the numerical division of the characters by means of a game (four, two, three, one) which, like an encrypted mathematics, founds a fatal order. Or the standard unit of a symphonic organisation. It is especially important to see how each series of characters is given a particular movement language (*gestuelle*) which the number of dancers amplifies according, says Rust, to their relations of reflection, mirroring, or doubling.[35] Shadows for fictive characters who have often lost their own. The theme of the Shadow dominates the entire work: not only does the lighting project the bodies and the movements as gigantic moving apparitions on the backcloth, thus transformed into a cinema screen for outsized phantom dancers, but the piece's ending in silhouette leaves the menacing outline of a 'creature' victorious and implacable while all the dancers are felled by the mysterious fatality of a mortal blow. All that is left in a corner is the agitated silhouette of a little, light, fragile dancer obstinately continuing her dance – the only form of resistance to the advance of these deathly forces. Here, pictorial, cinematic and literary references abound (Füssli to Kirchner, from Kleist to Kafka by way of *Leider* poetry) but they are totally effaced in the exceptionally clear and poetic compositional structure. To someone who knows contemporary choreography, however, a relation perhaps unknown to the choreographer is evident: the resemblance between the little dancer at the end of *Assaï* (who will perhaps be dancing at the end of the world) and Mary Wigman, facing the monster of destruction alone at the end of *Totenmal*. In 1927 this was the prophetic vision of a period that would pulverise even the conscience of the dancer herself. At two moments in history these parallel figures emerge from bodies. They evoke an essential reference, pivot, inexorable destination conjured and never completely masked by any danced movement: death. It ought to be remembered that Dominique Bagouet had at the time just learned that for him it would be premature. Commenting on biographical elements is a delicate matter especially when the work itself does not proclaim them. And Bagouet, like Brown later in her piece, *One Story as in Falling*, composed with his company, knew, as do all great artists, how to transform the meaning of a personal event and transfigure it into a poem of existence by means of the body's imagination. It is better to follow and admire the elaboration of the symbolic material: how the multiplicity of references, expressionist art in particular, are treated here in contracted, distorted forms (the acrobats). Or through tensions in the bodies that are at once abandoned and reticent (the young girls led by their partners in the 1830s couples); the floating stillness animated by small, inexorable movements of the creatures, sub-human beings who do not belong to any natural kingdom unless to the fermentations of a tortured imagination; the young women dropping to the ground, martyrs to unassuaged dream or desire of which they never asked to be the object. Finally we must cite Pascal Dusapin's composition which gives its title to the work and which, according to the choreographer, stirred up within him the images of expressionist cinema. It is deep music, exceptional in the contemporary field to which it belongs, a veritable orchestral tide heard by chance one day on the radio. Music is often an imaginary seed – not producing images but leading to them. If many moments of *Assaï* are danced in silence, the musical dust rising over certain *tableaux* creates a resonating space, like a vault opening within the bodies to allow the world's soul to enter.

The problem of reference explains why it is so difficult in this art to oppose the narrative to the non-narrative without falling into naïve or
arbitrary classifications. Delicate distinctions are misunderstood in the
name of related concepts but wrongly applied to this field of the 'inner
narrative', and narrative being mistaken for the idea of theatre while what
is not narrative for the idea of abstraction. The concept of 'abstract art' is
applied in a general way to all that is not figurative and this can obviously
go against the extremely 'concrete' character of many 'visual' (*art plastique*)
and choreographic works where it is the material that is foregrounded before any process of representation. The pinnacles of modern dance and
contemporary dance such as Doris Humphrey's 1928 *Water Study* are not
narrative, but they speak of the breath, the *élan*, the organic loss of the self
in falling, and are evocative of the crashing of the wave and its rising again
(we are aware of the importance for Humphrey of the opposition between
the slow rise and the rapid fall as the Nietzschean symbol of the world's
energies), but by association not by mimetics. Nothing is more anchored in
bodily experience. It is the same with the non-figurative work of Trisha
Brown and with many others of her generation who took their immediate
inspiration from a corporeal impulse rather any symbolic projection. In
dance, the use of the word 'abstract' in relation to the body is even more
questionable. Furthermore, a linear vision of dance modernity has a tendency to valorise choreography's 'abstract' orientation as though it
represented 'progress' – hence the 'return' to narration in dance of the
'80s. I have already suggested the dangers in this approach denounced in
20th century art criticism. Today's analyses no longer address the formal
modes of expression and nor do they make an opposition between the figurative and the non-figurative. The important issue is 'what question is being
posed?' Braque's *Maison à l'Estaque*, which is figurative, poses questions in
its treatment of ruptured, tensional and organic space which are as essential as those of any of Kandinsky's non-figurative works from the same
period, or very nearly. It is precisely here that the identity of the 'intention'
must be carefully circumscribed and with the greatest aesthetic attention.

And all the more for the fact that, in dance, it is the dancer's body which
carries the greater part of the intention and that it is to this body speaking
in its singular language to which the sole crucible and semic charge of the
work belongs. The aesthetic danger of figuration in dance – and it is an
enormous one – consists in the temptation to layer a narrative burden over
the bodily acts, and over the *écriture* as the process by which these acts are
organised and relate to one another. It is the danger of directing the spectator's perception to a 'story' articulated externally to the *écriture* in the

virtual frame of a verbal 'theatre' lying outside the deep call of movement and the body. We are aware that the temptation of the public to 'milk' an immediate meaning greatly affects the economy of work in dance and of its reception (Michèle Febvre talks of the spectator's appetite for semiotising). It is precisely this appetite that the resources of 'abstraction' tend to ameliorate by eliminating the threat of story. In fact, in dance, 'abstraction' is a term that should be used with caution because it relates to a specific use in the theory and practice of certain artists (Schlemmer, Nikolais, etc.) 'Abstraction' is not of the order of a 'category' – but more of the order of 'work', and of this famous 'dance work' through which dance is different from all other arts. Abstraction in dance is a process, not the term for a fixed aesthetic typology. Abstraction is still yet another 'tool' in the immense studio (in all sense of the word) of the dancer. The question would be as for any tool: what is it used for? Alwin Nikolais, a champion of abstraction explains: firstly, recounts Marc Lawton, get rid of anecdote,... *mannerisms, tics, overly symbolic movements, too egocentric, dramatic or 'mystical' interpretation, and pantomime.* Then he recalls the master's motto: *Motion (that is, the quality of being in the movement), no emotion (that is, compensating for the absence of a lived movement by simply indicating emotion using non-dance means.* [36] The work of 'motion' is, following the great pioneers of contemporary dance, a new form, revisited and taken further, of the turn from mimesis. Nikolais adds that the work of abstraction on the concrete qualities of the matter/material (high and low, heavy and light, excessive or moderate...), a long and meticulous work that must be undertaken by every dancer, and must lead to greater freedom: *The artist no longer has to direct her/his theme in view of a defined scene. Nor does he have to distort, enlarge, reduce or eliminate elements with the aim of freeing their contents.* This is why, adds Nikolais, the approach that he defends *is more meaningful by its sensibility and its instrumental capacity to speak directly in terms of 'motion', time, shape and space.* From this point of view, the absence of a story that must be negotiated or followed enables the artist to go directly to what is essential, and to work on the very flesh of dance's signification, beyond any necessary 'representation'. For Merce Cunningham, freedom from story is one of the ways that the autonomy of movement and of the dancer can be attained. It has always been Cunningham's pre-occupation to grant the dancing body its own resources, so that it is not dependent on a source of energy outside itself. A story with its already given emotional or factual baggage is at risk of weighing as heavily on the dancer as the unacceptable tyranny of musical dynamics, which Cunningham mistrusts so much. The so-called 'post-modern' dancers, most of whom were disciples or dancers of

Cunningham's fought for a movement or rather an act that was pure and which would not even be encumbered with pre-occupations of aesthetic form. For them action is intransitive and to put it into an artistic grammar, even a non-narrative one, was inadmissible in the context of 'non-dance' or 'non-literal' dance (which must be translated practically by its opposite, that is, by 'non-literary', thus 'literal...'). Here, we have gone well beyond a debate about the thematics of a work: all movement having no other objective than to saturate its own completion (*fin*).

Other, still more radical methods were put in place to ward off any subordination to a theme: for example, the 'rulegames' or the 'equipment' which, through the '60s in the United States, replaced choreography with a simple 'situation' in which the dancer had to improvise solutions. This process started with Anna Halprin and was taken up particularly by Simone Forti. Following them, Trisha Brown and Steve Paxton responded to the call of this aesthetics of the task. Halprin seems to have started applying constraints towards the end of the '50s. The 'equipment' was firstly a technique, as we have seen, for overcoming the anticipation of, and analytic control over, the emergence of the movement. But it soon became the sole springboard of a work. Replying to Yvonne Rainer who remarked in an interview: *I thought that the constraints were designed to make you aware of your body. It wasn't necessary to keep the idea of the constraint but to accomplish the movement or the kinaesthetic behaviour that was called for by the constraint,* Halprin said, *Afterwards we became more attentive to the constraint itself. We emphasised constraints whose challenging character would bring about the very idea of movement.* [37] Simone Forti's choreographies, for example, are nothing more than situations and thus much closer to the structure of 'performance' than to 'choreography' understood as the development in time and space of an intention and its matter/material. Forti's pieces like *Over, under and around* required each participant to undertake a precise trajectory over, under and around a partner. [38] The entire work is engendered by the rules of the game. Here the 'idea' is not in the formulation of the intention but in the possibilities of the space opened up by it. The starting point of the work then implodes in the work itself, in the same way that the *écriture* no longer exists. This supports a pure aesthetics of the score where the movement ingredients are only one possible version of the project. This means that, in this purely historical series of works, the intention, as in performance, is over-exposed to the detriment of its accomplishment in order to render the latter a purer experience of being which no shadow of reference external to its own frame will disturb.

1 Humphrey, Doris *The Art of Making Dances*, 1959, p. 34.

2 Febvre, M. 'Les paradoxes de la Danse Théâtre' in *La Danse au Défi*, 1987.

3 In Greek the demiourgos is the craftsman: demiurgy is thus the crafting or making of a world which Thom suggests is also the making/sowing of its meaning (semiurgy). (Transl.)

4 Wigman, M. 'Hexentanz' in *The Language of Dance*, 1966.

5 Laban, R. *A vision of dynamic space*, 1963.

6 Taffanel, J. *L'Atelier du chorégraphe*, 1994.

7 Banes, S. *Terpsichore in Sneakers*, 1980.

8 Rainer, Y. *Work*, 1973.

9 Dominique, François *Aseroë, figures de l'oubli*, 1994.

10 Cunningham, M. *An Impermanent Art*, 1978.

11 Lebensztejn, J-C. 'Douane/Zoll' in *La Peinture Expressionniste en Allemagne*. Exhibition Catalogue MAM de la Ville de Paris, 1992-93.

12 Robinson, Jacqueline *Eléments du langage chorégraphique*, 1981.

13 Limón cited in Lewis, D. *The Illustrated Technique of José Limón*, 1989.

14 Ehrenzweig, Anton *The Hidden Order of Art: a study in the psychology of artistic imagination*, 1967.

15 Huynh, E. *Anatomie d'Insurrection*. Mémoire for DEA in Philosophy, Univ. Paris I, 1991.

16 de M'Uzan, Michel *De l'art à la mort*, 1972.

17 Ibid.

18 Bernard, Michel 'A propos de trois chiasmes sensoriels' in *Nouvelles de Danse*, No.18, 1993.

19 Bernard, Michel *Le corps*, 1978.

20 Baxandall, M. *Patterns of Intention: On the Historical Explanation of Pictures*, 1985.

21 Waehner, K. *Outillage Chorégraphique*, 1995.

22 Godard, H. 'The Missing Gesture' in *Writings on Dance*, volume 15, 'The French Issue', 1996.

23 See Metz, Christian. *Le signifiant imaginaire*, 1984, and Pavis, P. *Voix et images de la scène*, 1985.

24 Cf. Louppe, L. 'Kurt Jooss et le Tanztheater' in *Programme Jooss*, Opera du Rhin, October 1994; and Laban. *A Life for Dance*, 1975.

25 Wigman, M. 'Hexentanz' in *The Language of Dance*, 1966.

26 Febvre, M. 1987.

27 Ibid.

28 cf. Genette, G. *Nouveau discours du récit*, 1983.

29 Stephanie Aubin in *Dossier des débats sur la relation entre la musique et les autres arts*, 1996.

30 Siegel, Marcia 'Visible Secrets' in *Moving Words* edited by Gay Morris, 1996.

31 We employ this word deliberately, for allegorical processes have been much used in American modern dance: action in Limón and Graham, for example, is not directly 'descriptive' or 'demonstrative'. Emblematic structures or representations are invented to generalise the evoked situations. According to Siegel's description of Taylor's *Speaking in Tongues* (1995), Taylor seems to continue this kind of approach. In this sense, Taylor's story is related to literary models that predate the nouveau roman or the new cinema, for example.

32 Brown, C. in Klosty, *Merce Cunningham*, 1975.

33 Hutchinson-Guest, Ann 'Nijinsky's Faune' in *Choreography and Dance*, Vol.1, part 3, 1991.

34 Rust, M. and Picq, C. *Planète Bagouet*. Video.

35 Rust in conversation with the author.

36 Lawton, Marc 'Inventer la danse tout le temps' in *Marsyas*, No.30, June, 1994.

37 Rainer, Yvonne 'Yvonne Rainer interviews Anna Halprin' in *Tulane Drama Review*, 10-2, Winter, 1965.

38 Forti, Simone *Handbook in Motion*, 1994.

Choreographic works: forms of appearance

Man on stage has become an event.
Oskar Schlemmer[1]

Every component of dance activity discussed here can be found in an object visible to and interpretable by a public. Such an object is at once a site of poetic fruition and an ending. Here, the dancer's thought and work cease to be creation activities and become (powerful) tools of actualisation and precipitation into a state of performance. We cannot hope to survey all the aspects of that state, but will simply discuss as 'fragments' a small number of the forms it has taken. This discussion will remain discursive rather than descriptive (imagining, if you like, that this re-examination could stir up a debate in the works' own processes). Description requires a completely different study involving aesthetic (or semiological) analysis of performed entities.

Several givens intersect in the identity of a choreographic work. The first is the traditional definition of the choreographic work as an original creation worthy of being 'signed' by an author. Let us recall that this definition goes back to the Quattrocento and that it began with the compositions duly attributed to the Italian dancing masters. Let us also recall that a stable, traditional notion of the choreographic work only exists within Western civilisation. Whether s/he likes it or not the contemporary choreographer is inscribed within this heritage as it defines her/his practice and status. The second given of the contemporary dance choreographic work is that it belongs as much to contemporary art as to its own discipline. Thus, it is free to choose its form and its contents. We know that this freedom in the modes and forms of the work constitute not only a conquest, but also a 'canon' of modernity. *Every piece must be an exception*, writes Simone Forti.[2] Consequently, against the traditional heritage it is essential to propose counter-definitions, and more or less radical departures. It is within the frame of these operations that contemporary works will invent their own kind of 'exception'.

The contemporary choreographic work must be polymorphous. It flows from an original intention (*propos*) which founds its own codes, its contents and at the same time its modes of actualisation. This is why it is difficult to propose uniform frameworks of interpretation. Let us note that the only systematic frameworks provided by dance criticism – the analyses of Susan Foster and Marcia Siegel – have always dealt with works that were, relatively speaking, not similar but analogous: mainly, a corpus of choreographic work (*travaux*) from the '40s and '60s arising out of both the language of a 'master', that is, a coherent ensemble of givens linking in all cases the corporal language itself and the dramaturgical preferences, and the characteristics of the American 'dance concert' where, across the different languages of Graham, Balanchine, Cunningham, Tharp, modes of actualisation and aesthetic references witness a certain permanence from one language to another.[3]

Let us return to that part of its heritage that defines the choreographic work, and in particular, beyond aesthetic choices, the unconsciously reproduced modes of representation. The Western choreographic work (the reader will excuse the pleonasm) has been perpetuated for three centuries principally under the title of 'ballet', a form which had many avatars before it stabilised in the 19th century (the period in which most major genres in all the arts from the novel to the symphony orchestra became fixed).[4] During this period, ballet showed several defining characteristics: it unfolded according to a continuous logic (which was for a long time a narrative one, but this is of little importance); it was served by an important theatrical apparatus (*appareil spectaculaire*) including décor and costumes; and it was composed of silent movements danced to music. Not only the ballet but its name is inscribed in our culture. The name 'ballet' remains linked to the definition of the choreographic act. For the Western classical dance in which the word 'ballet' was born, its use is unproblematically justified. For contemporary dance things are more ambiguous. Attitudes to 'ballet' as a term or practice are varied: from a desire for recognition within the world of dance which has pushed the moderns (in France and Germany) to use the word in the title of their companies, to the intentional archaism of a stylistic exercise such as in Schlemmer's *Triadic Ballet* (1924) where the first phrase of his preface announced as a clarion call: *Ballet? Ballet!*[5] In fact the word remains in current usage and is even applied to contemporary dance performances – alongside more modern terms which relate the danced work to any one of the other contemporary visual or musical art productions (Bausch's *Stuck* or the 'piece,' inspired by Anglo-Saxon art terminology). For while it lives in the wake of ballet and ballet's constitutive elements, the contemporary choreographic work never stops combating and transgressing ballet's normalising characteristics: by casting them off, by introducing heterogeneous elements, by disturbing or contradicting their proscriptive terms.

Forms and Formats

In the twentieth century the most visible transformation in the choreographic work has been in the multiplication of its modes of actualisation: changes in 'size' (*format*), displacement of its representational frames, quantitative and qualitative diversification of forms. Each great modern dance founder practically invented her/his own kind of performance. In Germany there was the little 'Kammertanz' – Laban's experimental propositions taken up by Jooss and Leeder and opposed to the large choric dances, the solos in which Wigman expressed the poetry of her 'condensed message', 'absolute dance,' right down to the dance theatre which was itself divided into group and choric dances: small forms, large ones, free forms, invented and inventive; not forgetting 'non-forms' which broke moulds and created the paths towards this freedom. Like the famous *Sonnentanz* organised by Laban for the 21st June, 1917 at Monte Verita which lasted the whole of that short night, and prescribed only a space (to stay within the limits of the famous domain), a time – from nightfall to dawn – and an assembling around the fire in a clearing for the central tableau of the 'night demons'.[6] What is striking in this first third of the century is not only the inventiveness of the dance forms but the variety of its 'size': a Graham or Wigman solo might last only five or eight minutes. Harald Kreutzberg and Yvonne Georgi's tour to the United States involved a programme of twelve pieces in the same evening. Humphrey's seminal piece *Water Study* lasts from twelve to twenty minutes (with no musical accompaniment its length varies but solely in relation to the state of body and breath of the dancers) and delivers a powerful discourse on breathing, rhythm and instability. This kind of temporality also prevails but in a more regular way in the American style 'dance concert' where several pieces make up a recital or retrospective – perhaps more pretentiously than before, at least in the ritual of the large 'concert halls'. In Europe today, with its programming ruled by the clock where the choreographer, far from sharing a sensed, symbolic time and a singular duration, must fill the social time of an evening, we might well long for these forms of a happy freedom. Today, a great uniformity is imposed on the modes of actualisation of the choreographic work despite a wealth of contents and a certain autonomy: fifty minute works have become the royal standard alongside of which the 'little form' figures as a minor work. (This is to forget that Nijinsky's *Faune* only lasted ten minutes...) A curiously quantitative appreciation. But the loss is greater than one might think: in becoming assimilated to the dimensions of the theatre (*format spectaculaire*), dance has returned to impoverishing frames within which the very status of the work (*l'oeuvre*) dissolves. The choreographic 'object' far from being apprehended through its main elements – its intention and *écriture* and their interpretation/performance – is encountered through its 'spectacular' external appearance and the theatrical criteria organising its actualisation.

   The solo was one of the great innovations of contemporary dance in a civilisation where it had practically been lost since the solo entrances (*entrées seules*) of the *danse noble* (either in the theatre or the ballroom) in the 17th and 18th centuries. Soloists certainly existed but they always appeared at a specific moment during the ballet. The solo in academic dance of the 19th century could not be a whole or a proposition by itself. By contrast, contemporary dance made the solo one of its pinnacles, as a form best corresponding to its original project: to affirm the presence of a subject in the immediacy and wholeness both of her/his being and movement. There was no other law. This is why the solo could reach unparalleled degrees of intensity while remaining impalpable, on the edge of form. *A small lyrical poem, a breath.*[7] Thus did Wigman describe her marvellous solo *Abschied und dank* (1943). But even aside from its intrinsic poetic qualities, for the contemporary choreographer the solo is an inevitable rite of passage. In modern dance history when the great masters felt the need to go back to the beginning in order to re-invent their own language, the solo was the means to test their own discoveries, and to test themselves through these. The solo was a laboratory for movement and being beyond the limits of body knowledge. Obviously you could not invite others to join you before you had tested all possibilities (and limits). At this stage in creating a new body the creator looks, for better or for worse, for her/his own language. There is nothing to share. What happens has neither name nor image. Any relationship with another dancer is dangerous and mystifying as long as there does not yet exist a gamut of practical references out of which the body might construct its identity. This is what struck Cunningham so strongly on the threshold of his *Untitled Solo* composed at Black Mountain in 1950 and in which he first worked with discontinuity in the organic tissue of movements. But before him, there were the solos of Isadora Duncan, the first expression of an individual feeling, an individual dance according to her belief that each dancer is unique in her/his relation to the world. Then Humphrey's superb *Hoop* of 1924 where she explored the curve of a circle using the curves of her own body, naked and in silence – before the two famous sections of *Ecstatic Themes* of 1929: 'Circular Descent' and 'Pointed Ascent' investigating instability, the permanent journey between two deaths which her theory and art never stopped exploring. Graham's solos of 1926 were no less solitary and singular. These are all solos which have been seminal in contemporary dance, which have given rise not only to body states but to choices, currents and schools. Even though today the solo does not have the same historical reach, it still serves the dancer as a path of self discovery, as a threshold to her/his own visibility. It manifests being. Not from a pre-existing ontological given but from a tension which makes presence emerge in the movement that gives it birth. The solo can be more or less literally autobiographical, it can be the story of a life, an inner journey or an affective one as in Carolyn Carlson's *Blue Lady* in which several 'characters' appear as so many 'moments' of the dancer's existence or simultaneous aspects of her personality. Bourigault's *Autoportrait de 1917*, a self-portrait that revisits and doubles a self-portrait of the same name by Egon Schiele, is a means for Bourigault to be involved in a personal work to find his tensional-torsional body, a body limited by its own skin. But the solo as self-portrait can also trace less a journey already made than a moment of change, a way of bifurcating or questioning choices. This was the case in Bagouet's solo in *F et Stein* (1984). Although it was part of a larger work, this solo has the force of a theoretical manifesto. In its unsettling, even denigratory elements in which the body is blocked or contorted as though by the arrival in the choreographer's body of some unknown form, the character's and the work's 'monstrous' side, as Charles Picq has noted, it emblematises the emergence of something still to be born to the visible. In fact, this solo prefigures a change in Bagouet's language which was to be put to work in his more 'secret' dances where the form of the movement opens on to another world that it does not enclose but hollows within itself. *La Tentation de la Transparence* (1991), a solo by the Quebecois choreographer Paul-André Fortier, revised the terms of his work at the moment when, after a number of group pieces he became more involved in interiority, even if something of a 'character' was still evoked.

It is most certainly through the solo that contemporary dance comes closest to 'performance art'. Its subject matter, like that of 'performance', is primarily the engagement of the subject in the work at the moment that the work manifests itself. In the solo as in performance, the subject-creator subjects her/himself to rules. We know that in performance as in various choreographic projects 'constraints' are very important: these can be postural or situational constraints subjecting the body to different challenges: in dance as we have seen a constraint is often used to find untoward solutions and to avoid falling back onto known schemas. Such constraints were seen to be necessary in the thought of Feldenkrais whose disciples like Ann Halprin were involved in the dance renewal of the '60s and '70s in the United States. At the heart of the constraint a new path to freedom could be found. In 'performance' the notion of an obstacle or difficulty is used for its power to directly affect an action, or to change the body through taking a risk, or to make an impact on the performer's behaviour. But there are many intermediate kinds of situations: thus in Reinhild Hoffman's sublime solo *Solo mit Sofa* (1982) the choreographer is attached by the fabric of his costume to a divan. With each movement of the cloth he is pulled towards or away from the divan so that his movements are ruled and determined by his relation to the furniture. Another solo from the same period, *Solo Abend*, has him burdened with very heavy rocks attached by rods or knotted fabric.

Each movement, therefore, is torn painfully from the weight of this implacable load. In both cases the performance has a second, sculptural dimension due to the qualities of the material from which the obstacle is made – which makes these solos (visual) 'art' works on several levels (in their visual arrangement and their process). We could say as much of many other examples from Tauber's already mentioned 1915 solo (where the mask by Jean Arp is more like an art object attached to the body than an innocent and undifferentiated costume accessory) to the '80s solos of Dominique Dupuy in which he works with an object of the same substance as the body – an object (a human bone, some powders) whose material, sculptural, violent or rare qualities affirm it as such. Another element relating the contemporary dance solo to performance is that not only is the subject-creator contained within the art object, but s/he has an almost pure presence without any form being permitted to dominate the identity of this presence. This is what occurs particularly in the German school from the '20s where the project of a subjective presence, whatever the degrees of formal elaboration it gave rise to, prevailed over all other parameters, as in Wigman's solos in the cycle *Shifting Landscapes* (1931). The same could be said of Valeska Gert's solos such as they appear in the film *Faces* and probably of all the other dancers who came out of the *Ausdruckstanz* and the subversive spectacles of the Berlin cabarets in the '20s and '30s.[8] The proximity of dada artists (Huelsenbeck, Hausmann) was no small encouragement to work on the matter/material of the self as the material of art. With such precedents, the young dancer today has inherited an invaluable tool for working on what is called 'presence' – namely, the laboratory par excellence that is the solo. Presence as an act of commitment to the identity of the present moment and to the matter of the self in relation to the world is a specific practice of contemporary dance that is much envied.[9] Presence is equally strong in performance but, like all of the qualitative or active elements of performance, it is not the object of an apprenticeship or investigation as it is in dance. In this regard, dancers have often reproached visual artists with depending more on their identity, and the notoriety and proclaiming of this identity, than on their knowledge and the depth of their engagement in experience. The visual artist is clothed in the prestige of a 'signature' which s/he shows off while acting, whereas the dancer who maintains the charge of her/his presence, and is engaged there as subject and author, is only considered a movement artisan. *If Bob raised his thumb, it was something very special because he was doing it; if I raised my thumb, it was dancing.*[10]

It is perhaps in the history of the solo, the most experimental of forms as we have seen, that avant garde experiments in 'displacements' most contravening the traditional contents of a choreographic work have been most at work – especially in the radical dance currents in the United States in the '60s and '70s, but not only then. Rosalind Kraus gives an example in her famous 'Notes on the Index'.[11] There was a performance that Deborah Hay gave in the autumn of '76, writes the art critic, during which she explained to the audience that *instead of dancing she wished to talk*. For more than an hour, Hay addressed the spectators with a quiet but insistent discourse whose substance was that she was there, that she was talking to them but not this time through a movement routine because, for such a routine, she could no longer find a justification. In this 'choreographic work' Kraus perceives several elements of avant garde departure from the traditional medium: first *a refusal to dance, or what might be more generally characterised as a flight from aesthetic convention*. In the third instance, *a verbal discourse through which the subject repeats the simple fact that she is present*. As far as the second element is concerned, Kraus refers to a part of Hay's discourse not yet cited where she refers to a particular domain of dance knowledge and thought of the '70s which Kraus describes thus: *The aspiration for dance to which she had come she said was to be in touch with every cell in her body*. Any informed dance commentator would recognise, here, the ideas of Bonnie Bainbridge-Cohen on the role not only of the viscera but also of the cells in the ontogenesis of the subject's expression – such as was popular then and is still taught today in Body-Mind Centring. Although not party to this work, Kraus astutely concludes in terms of 'total self-presence' which is, more than she may have known, one of the fundamental codes of contemporary dance. Then follows her very fine analysis which leads us towards the sign's partial erasure by the 'index', the trace of a lost or 'abolished' event like the physical manifestation of a cause, of which traces and imprints are examples. But this 'index' of dance of which an act of pure presence could be the ultimate palpitation, can become in the framework of a contemporary dance project wholly in itself a dance act giving much more qualitative information than the index. An example: in the same artistic and historical current as Hay, Trisha Brown in *Skymap* invites spectators to lie on the ground in the dark and listen to movements that have been replaced by words.[12] There is also in the work of both artists, beyond the modernist foregrounding of the signifier pertinent to an art that questions its own supports, a reduction of elements proper to the minimalist current to which these choreographers belong.

In fact the processes discussed here formed part of the negatory attitudes which were a way of exploring those undefined regions where a medium could be questioned in the mirror of its non-reflection. This was one of Robert Morris's practices in his 'non-sculpture' and 'non-architecture', also described by Kraus as being so close to what was then happening in 'non-dance'.[13] Of course the dancer today cannot deny this heritage of extreme experiments/experience. But when s/he wants to explore unidentified choreographic objects, dance works outside habitual choreographic definitions, it seems that 'non-dance' is no longer called upon: on the contrary s/he looks for a surplus to inscribe in a defining frame. Sometimes new spaces are the means to de-reference the dance, but the work remains totally identifiable as a choreography. This was the case with Larrieu's *Waterproof* (1986), danced in a swimming pool. To understand this surplus of choreographic indexation we can compare *Waterproof* with an avant garde event, Oldenburg's 1962 *Whales*, which also took place in a swimming pool. In *Whales*, a hydraulic apocalypse of diving, plunging bodies, etc., Oldenburg created a frenetic performance where the situation existed in and for itself. Larrieu had a multiple but precise intention. The dancers, in, out of and between the waters, experience and allow the audience to share deep sensations of weight and apnoea, leading the spectator into their own floating or their own breath-holding. The sharing of corporal, gravitational and breath experience is so strong that it is a more-than-dance at the limits of bodily action. We could say the same thing about Odile Duboc's pieces which are just as de-localised spatially and where form is redoubled in the sense of commitment to the form of the medium. In *Entractes* danced throughout Aix en Provence, or more recently in the streets near Belfort, the location of a Centre Chorégraphique National, Duboc's dancers who were called 'Fernands' mixed with the crowds, sometimes imperceptibly or out of range. These processes of integrating or disappearing can be likened to certain works of the '60s (Hay's *Museum*) where dancers mix with guests at an exhibition opening, stopping like them in front of paintings, chatting, etc. But far from questioning whether dance is a separate 'genre', Duboc activates a 'hyperdance' (she even spoke of 'over-dance' for one of her solos) as the immense dance of the whole world. In fact the disappearance of the dancer over the horizon or amongst the crowd does not aim at a strategy of 'negation' dissolving the identity of dance in the banality of urban life but, on the contrary, it valorises the latter as absolute dance, the human trajectories become a legitimate dance with which the dancers movement can be associated. We can see the immense change in point of view between the de-localisation of danced action in relation to traditional venues in radical American art of the '60s and that of questioning by changing the place, path, perception, and poetic essence of a dance sought after and celebrated in the later work of the '80s and '90s in many French choreographers.

One of the pieces that most opposed the definitions of a work in France, not by its alternative frame or mode of representation but because the inner contours of the work itself were subverted, was without doubt Bagouet's and Boltanski's *Le Saut de l'Ange*, and it is not irrelevant that a major (visual) artist collaborated on this deep experiment. Apparently inoffensive from the fact that it seemed to occupy the traditional stage and to subscribe to other accepted choreographic rituals, this work, as Boltanski has said, was deeply 'aberrant'.[14] An artist of de-localisation, Boltanski was of the view that the work of art should concern neither places nor specific codes and he was also fascinated by the world of dance (including all of its traditional fantasies). To this end he used his personal ignorance of dance codes but retained his fantasies, while Bagouet deliberately let go of that knowledge which would have allowed the codes to be employed. As Boltanski, the only surviving author of this project, so marvellously said, *I didn't know and he no longer knew.* Thus the work had a double axis: it was a dance performance not coded as such where the 'stage' (plateau) which was more like a circus ring than a theatre in the cultural sense was a little displaced from the point of view of the audience. This destabilised the vision and situation of the dancers who often had to dance at the side on the pavement of the Jacques Coeur courtyard – off-stage, out of sight just as when they would sometimes appear arbitrarily in the windows of this building. Although it was made with the kind of art familiar to us in Bagouet, this work abandoned a number of choreographic pretensions. The movement language was not musicalised: like Catherine Legrand scratching Jean-Pierre Alvarez's head with small spidery hand movements or Sonia Onckelinck's headlong gallops these were in contrast to the controlled movements of previous works where the space and the movement language had been oriented towards inner enigmas and imaginations (*Le Crawl de Lucien*, 1985; *Assaï*, 1987). In *Le Saut de l'Ange* all codes were loosened (which did not prevent them from having been finely worked), for example, in the multiplicity of disparate musical references, some of which are Bagouet's responses to challenges that Boltanski thought would be insoluble (because he did not count on the extraordinary culture of choreographic ruse and invention). An example was to find a piece of music of Mozart's composed by Beethoven so Bagouet found the variations on the air of Papageno in the *Magic Flute*. The Beethoven-like piano, simultaneously allegro and melancholy returns as a lost leitmotif between the Pascal Dusapin trumpet pieces. It was the same for the costumes because the dancers were asked to 'disguise' themselves in their image of themselves as children; and thus Dominique Fabrègues created an assortment of costumes from second-hand clothes. These added to the strange dreaminess of this unidentifiable work. And like all great works *Le Saut de l'Ange* can be read in various ways: and must be seen as the fascination of two old friends with the image of childhood, which is also the image of death (the death within us of the child we have been); with the world of shadows that Bagouet entered from *Assaï* onward and which Boltanski's recent *Leçon des Ténèbres*, gradually disappearing into the night, has redoubled; and finally with an 'under story' – that of the dancers who are angels and characters, citing their own lives by means of their own movements as if it required this ruined fiction to reinvent something of the soul's truth.

Such works scattered through all the stages of the history of contemporary dance have continued to transform the criteria and tools of interpretation necessary to their apprehension. They invite a tolerance and openness of perception. They do not only make the performance but also the spectator. They invent a new kind of apprehension and a new kind of gaze, as modernity has continuously created changing definitions and counter-definitions of the choreographic work. And this involves a total availability on the part of the spectator – an acceptance that Deleuze calls 'constitutive passivity'.[15] A refusal to make an immediate judgement in order to be able to construct a truly pathic relation to the work of art. There are choreographic works as we have seen that involve no 'dance' strictly speaking. Or where other materials take precedence over or turn away from the movement itself. We are talking of course about a contemporary art's capacity, beyond dance, to make the contents of the art travel from one site to another, erasing entirely the barriers between genres: a painter like Broodthaers can produce writing, a sculptor like Takis can make sound. But well this side of these systematic ways of questioning or resignifying, the choreographic work runs its fantastic course and explores all possibilities. A work of Decouflé like *Triton* (1990) or *Petites Pièces Montées* (1994) could be thought of as an animated body-machine, like a monumental sculpture where movement incrusts the terms of a provisional question, where the body plays a reduced and decentred role – hardly surprising in a student of Nikolais. Decouflé, a light-footed but powerful dancer, has a very beautiful movement language (*gestuelle*) which only he can demonstrate. It is the same for a company like 'Castafiore' where the manipulation of objects, sound, and forms takes precedence over movement possibilities – projects where contemporary dance is affirmed as an open 'mechanism of creation' and cannot be specifically located amongst the arts. But in all cases, the work of dance has not only been part of this century's great effacing of genres but has especially proposed both its actualisation and perception through acts of *écriture*. Such acts have been very diverse but their elaboration implies a weaving, an articulation through which the body can continually re-invent its relation to the symbolic and the modes of that relation.

Corps à corps with décor

History has taught us that the first element to be eliminated was décor in the traditional sense. Because the body is what founds space, the dance avant-garde refused anything that would 'institute' a space in advance. This is why dance modernity never used a fashionable décor but questioned its role and necessity. This is what puts Diaghilev within a certain tradition which, separating the pictorial from the choreographic, makes the moving body a form on a ground which it illustrates. While Schlemmer found the décors of the painters commissioned by Diaghilev 'interesting and charming', he reproached them for doing nothing more than transpose pictures onto the stage (We know that the Ballets Russes, at least at first, succeeded in promoting Russian painters thanks to the impact of their décors).[16] Fuller's and Duncan's projects were very different as they constructed their visual universes in consonance with the sources of their movement. Duncan, as we know, overturned the norms and even the very definition of the dance work by eliminating all theatrical conventions. A dark blue curtain was her only background or, rather, absence of background, like a nocturnal thickness putting the body back into the world rather than into systems of representation (and giving movement a visible force which no longer illustrated the pictorial but involved you in it.) With the theoretical and artistic support of Appia, Dalcroze pushed this problematic further. First, by recalling that the 'living rhythm' cannot live with a fixed imagination.[17] Then by opposing two incompatible universes: a two-dimensional one (especially classical figuration with its represented depth) and the three-dimensionality of movement which carries, deports, and transfigures planes and continually produces and inhabits volumes. *Our present décors are the direct enemy of the real rhythm of the human body in three-dimensional space*.[18] The new dancer, the 'rhythmic' dancer requires a stage in which all the elements, including light, which was very important for Appia, were moving and participating in the changes in organic volume opened by movement. Here was the condemnation of classical representation and a vision of the becoming of a 'plastic' space: *real two dimensional decors with a fictional depth have no place in actual deep space: lighting which segments dark-*

ness belies plastic and movement values.[19] Thus at Hellerau, light became a
global milieu, not a source of dramatic effects. It modulated space and time.
The scenic environment had therefore to become part of 'real depth', that
which is carved and anchored in the bodies themselves as they respond to
space through rhythm and density – prefiguring Robert Rauschenberg's
work for Merce Cunningham and the work of Robert Wilson, where the
pictorial stage dissolves in order to reinvent the horizon of its own emergence elsewhere. Thenceforth the visual context is no longer contextual: it
becomes part of the *écriture* and will maintain with the danced movement
this dialectical (and neither illustrative nor fusional) aspect which founds
and furnishes the very keys to the *écriture*. According to Susan Buirge,
along with the lighting, costume and music, it will bring to the movement
propositions both meaning and counter-meaning (*sens et contresens*).

Décor has often returned under other guises, particularly by contamination with the theatre and the necessity, perhaps, of providing signposts and
visual representations when the movement alone is not sufficient. And often alas with the aim of making 'pretty pictures' (*belles images*), a problem
that marked a certain failure of dance poetics during the '80s when it gave
in to an aestheticising tendency derived from the theatre of the period. This,
however, is not how we should judge Pina Bausch's closed, sometimes naturalistic scenographies, especially all those leading up to 1980, the most
striking example being *Café Muller* with its partitions, discussed by Daniel
Dobbels.[20] It no longer frames the
dance but obstructs it, revealing, as it accumulates, a loss – with chairs and
tables as so many traps or boggy areas for movement and beings to be
caught up in. Intentionally or not, the 'return' of décor to contemporary
dance will always play more or less the same role. And it can also signal a
capitulation formulated as such by Trisha Brown when she agreed after
fifteen years or so of experimental work to return to the theatre. 'Theatricality' for her is a representational frame that enslaves action to the frames
of the visible. It is important then that visual artists (Rauschenberg, Judd)
follow her in maintaining a necessary distance from and not submitting to
the codes of spectacle or ready-made images.[21]

In all these experiences/experiments there is certainly a visual magic, an
active choice to create oneiric forms with ecstatic aesthetic force – from the
monochrome *éclat* of Rauschenberg's combines for *Astral Converted* (1991)
to Judd's coloured moving thicknesses (*Newark*, 1986). There is also an
important critical aspect, however, at least in scenographic terms: the sublime forms are there to put into question their own power to fascinate).
Beyond this singular example of resistance the question has been displaced,

if not exorcised. Usually, scenography, including that by major visual artists, involves objects or fragments, spatially speaking; there is no question of a closed, whole visual statement. Still, today experiments continue and, happily, relations between dance and scenography tend to be visual laboratories more than decorative projects.

Works and objects

On the other hand objects have been deeply integrated into choreographic *écriture*. Yvonne Rainer wrote that she loved, *the duality of props, or objects: their usefulness and obstructiveness in relation to the human body. Also the duality of the body: the body as a moving thinking, decision- and action-making entity and the body as an inert entity, object-like. Active-passive, despairing-motivated, autonomous-dependent. Analogously, the object can only symbolize these polarities; it cannot be motivated, only activated. Yet, oddly the body can become object-like; the human being can be treated as an object, dealt with as an entity without feeling or desire. The body itself can be handled and manipulated as though lacking in the capacity for self-propulsion.*[22]

Before discussing further the role of objects in the work of dancers, I must reply to (and perhaps contradict) these comments of Rainer's. Her friend Robert Morris conceived the film (*Untitled* 1972) where a large ball rolls on a wooden floor. Because of its spherical shape the object can roll of its own accord and, like any ball or balloon, this gives it a blind, powerful consciousness reminiscent of the limbs of Kleist's puppets. Beyond this illusion, however, Morris's film is powerful because the ball seems to hit and ricochet off all the obstacles that it encounters – the walls, corners, etc. It seems animated by virtue not of its power to move but to be hit, not to give an impetus but to receive one. Like a human body it is as much determined by the environment through which it moves as it is able to make its impact on that environment. It is human because it 'receives' the impact, the passing, the alterity of things. It has that quality of responsiveness which makes a living thing and which Nikolais saw in 'rebound'.

An object is another body amongst men's bodies. It is a presence and a reservoir of transformation. It is this secret relation between the object's body and the dancer's which has a primordial attraction, deeper than any theatrical exploitation of an object. Some dances and improvisations are based entirely on the manipulation of an object – the body's score is created through contact with the object, its materiality, its weight, anything that links the tactile sensations of the object's skin to the dancer's. But the object may simply be a score as in Simone Forti's 'structured improvisations' where any element of any object can be a text or pretext, as if it always already contained a movement or sense that could be deciphered. Here, it is necessary to distinguish between objects that are made artefacts with an internal 'system' and things or material elements which are not the results of a deliberate plan. All these elements are present in dance. Butoh likes to work with elemental materials: water, sand, etc. But among the constitutive elements of contemporary dance are objects in their different degrees of creation, from banal mass-produced things with no particular identity, to sculptures and artworks. The object can be functional (a chair, a cane) or it might be simply an abstract characteristic (the dances at the Bauhaus that illustrated the elementary forms of the famous Preparatory Course). Sometimes body and object are in conflict, sometimes theatrical elements serve to exalt its movement. There is also room for pure matter, like the fabric and drapes used by Jerome Andrews. The object can be re-duced to its most basic function, which was, generally speaking, the way objects were used in the so-called post-modern school and in the art gallery happenings or at the Judson Church at the beginning of the '60s: Simone Forti's dance performances used rudimentary or perhaps 'fundamental' ob-jects which were even less differentiated than objects of daily life – a plank balanced like a primitive kind of see-saw on a central support, ropes and poles. In each instance the body explores situations that are at once unto-ward and archaic: Forti's dance performance *Seesaw* at the Reuben Gallery which was part of a programme that included the work of artists like Claes Oldenburg, for example, who were gathered around the group Fluxus. In *Seesaw* the performers, Rainer and Robert Morris, initially used the plank simply to balance their weight around the fulcrum. Then they played with this. The proposition could appear simplistic if it were not for the fact that the play of the change of weight is the founding element of all movement. In *Rollers* (Reuben Gallery 1960) wooden boxes on rollers transported the performers who conversed out loud, sometimes non-sensically. They were each controlled at the end of three ropes held by members of the public and lack of co-ordination meant that their bodies were affected as they were lurched, bumped and stopped abruptly. This dance reconstitutes the ar-chaic experience of any 'transportation' and at the same time that of any 'trained' object. Of course, in this work as in the previous one, it is the unpredictable movement of the object that dictates the ongoing experiences of the bodies, in very different ways and according to different uses (like the poles the dancers meticulously join end to end in Trisha Brown's *Line up* [1970]). But in post-modern dance, whether an object is used according to what it was intended for or in some other way, it retains its neutral utility, devoid of any auratic or resonant character. Its banality, in turn, objectifies the movement to which it gives rise or which it constrains. Thus, according to schools, eras, or circumstances the object can have several simultaneous or contradictory functions. Hence, the ordinary chair which is used in a completely naturalistic way by Bausch (*Kontakthof*, 1982), half naturalistically by De Keersmaeker (in *Rosas danst Rosas*, 1982), and not at all naturalistically by Merce Cunningham in *Antic Meet* in 1954 (the chair having the quasi-status of a Rauschenberg 'ready made'). And then there are the dream objects, objects involving a supreme vision of the real, like those created by Nikolais, a sculptor-dancer who extended the body by elastic threads (*Tensile Involvement*, 1979, or *Tent)* or by appendages prolonging or displacing the body's axis and going beyond anthropomorphism to reach a universe of free physical and metaphysical movement not organised around an anatomical centre of gravity, without pre-existing paths, a world where intent has replaced relations of cause and effect. This same passion for body-objects can be found in the work of Philippe Decouflé and Philippe Guillotel, the sculptor-costumier and Decouflé's complement, in exploring a body of apparently inert matter but in fact already inhabited by an endlessly rolling and unrolling movement.

Sometimes the object is a so-called 'art' object made by a well-known artist. Indeed, the participation of a visual artist is often indicated by the presence of objects onstage (rather than as 'backdrops'), multiple objects whose role is not to define or pre-establish the space but to magnetise it (Noguchi for Graham); and sometimes to 'disarm' it (Rauschenberg), to empty it and make it available for the operations of chance. In most of the designs made for Cunningham, from Bruce Naumann's fans for *Tread* to Bob Morris's suspended rectangle in front of the stage in *Canfield*, the scenic object in itself adds nothing. It is simply a mechanism for showing the reversibility of the field opened up by the work. The same cannot be said for Warhol's found objects for *Rainforest*, for the silver helium balloons in their uncontrolled floating about are an integral part of Cunningham's aesthetic of chance and disconnection where the elements in play are allowed to *follow their own experience* as James Klosty says.[23] Thus and more so, are the detached forms of Duchamp's *Large Glass* enclosed in vinyl cubes made by Jasper Johns for *Walkaround Time*. For any work plays not only with unattainable phantoms like the flight of the bride to the unattainable height of the 'Large Glass' but it comments on them and reactivates them through the intermediary of bodily forms, sometimes literally those of the dancers (as when Douglas Dunn is lifted and carried in the image of the vaporous bride) – which gives the scenic object, the scenic work of art the sense of an active element dynamising the dance, playing with it in the evolution and construction of a dramaturgy, even of a symbolics.

In Graham's works, Noguchi's objects have a no less exemplary role: they are linked to a choreographic imaginary by their substance and form. By their substance, firstly, as they play on or evoke elementary materials: wood, bones, unpolished stone, ropes of hemp or gut; and by their form because Noguchi, being the student of Brancusi that he was, liked to make archetypal forms completely in consonance with the Jungian references of his partner choreographer: nests, plinths, steles, masts, divans, etc., that are twisted or branch out like organic forms. And there are, too, the many kinds of binding and knotting which extend the body in a stretching of ropes (*Frontier*) or else strangle it or confine it: from the tube dress of *Lamentation* to the cord of *Night Journey*. The object then becomes a support, a pivot, a bed of torture or desire, an alcove, refuge or prison according to the way the body uses it as support, spring or trap. Or more often still as an 'object' in the absolute sense of 'object of love' with all of the ambiguities of the transitional relationships that are involved here.[24] We have mentioned bones: Noguchi's stage accessories for *Cave of the Heart* are larger than life human bones, as if objects outside the body reflected the inner sculpture that we create within ourselves during our lives and which will remain after our death as ultimate witness of what had been built within us. Here is another alliance between body and object which both unifies and transcends any metaphorical exchange – even more in that one of the scenic elements is a rack on which clothes are hung like so many moulted skins whose phases of desiccation the dancer's body traverses.

And because, in fact, an object awakens movements containing within them the whole latent language to which the object's fabrication and handling have given rise, any relation of the body to materials is an infinite dance as old as the world. On the dance stage it is not a question of naturalistically miming a relationship with objects even when the latter are mundane. As we know, one only need vary the movement elements: the time, the spatial amplitude, the tonic intensity, for the relation to an ordinary object (to lift a bowl and bring to one's lips as in *1980 ein Stuck von Pina Bausch*) to take on a completely different dimension, and denature both movement and object; and to make the spectator enter a poetic universe where, as Kandinsky said, the movement's function is no longer recognisable but seems to celebrate and worship 'action'. The object itself is no longer quotidian: it becomes a sort of material enigma of ambiguous use. It is one of the beautiful things about Chopinot's *Végétal* (1995) that it worked with Andrew Goldsworthy's 'elemental' sculptures (in stone, leaves, branches) and was able to draw from them amplified movements (hitting, carrying, throwing) that tell of the body's history, at the same time as they speak of the growth and the development of the world's resources. These elements are linked to survival activities through which the dancing body finds the essential gestural ground of human communities. The body then, like an object, becomes an instrument of memory, reconstituting lost sinuosities which, through the body's dynamics, make human space an enormous storehouse of movement traces. Even before dancers like Forti and Brown investigated it in their improvisations, the object carried within it, says Laban, a great cultural score of combinations of 'effort' which have served in its elaboration. *When a dancer looks at an object, a tool... immediately an image of the movements, ideas, even feelings of the people who created this object come alive for him. It is as if the object contained an invisible score of the pressings, throwings, carryings and cuttings that gave birth to it.*[25] (Amongst the actions cited, let us not forget, are the 'actions' which in effort-shape exemplify the effort factors). But just as the object refers us back to the traces of the movements that have given it its form, its angles, its inner tensions, the dancing body can inscribe the milieu or can itself be marked by it as the recipient of an imprint of material consistencies. In *Projet de la matière* Duboc made the body an impregnated one, a site for receiving material sensations (surfaces to reflect, to soak up, surfaces of friction or sliding) which in their turn sculpted a body state in the way that the objects a Penone inserts into the root of a plant dilates or constricts, sometimes stunts its growth. We have already seen this idea of imprinting in Laban as the 'carving space' or in Nikolais's spatial imprint: but there it is the body which traces. While in certain moments of Laban's thought, in Odile Duboc's work and that of others, it is the space and its materialisation in objects that inscribes its passage in the plastic memory of the body.

In his solo *L'homme debout il...* Dominique Dupuy dances with an object as an agent of loss or instability as much as a partner able to create or launch a movement intention; and he has also explored objects based on earlier propositions. The presence of objects in his *oeuvre* relates to an approach whereby the body is constructed in and by an encounter with matter as alterity. *L'homme debout* is divided into two series of events: one is where Dupuy wanders amongst objects that are quietly brought on stage in the dark. They loom up like enigmatic, neutral characters without destination, raw objects exposed in their simple materiality but 'produced' just enough to suggest some mysterious plan. The other series of events is composed of pure dance where, moving freely like a torchlight the dancer reinvents an empty space inside and outside his own body. Artist Jean-

Pierre Schneider's objects do not have a defined identity as 'art objects'. They are both before and beyond such definition. Their presence adds nothing to the dance material: they only indicate a body frontier where its meanders, disequilibrium and mystery are engaged. The whole solo presents the relation to an object as a question: sounds made by scratching a cane on the floor for example, are also a mode of questioning. But the dance stages a still more poignant interrogation when, denuded, divested of accessories (coat and hat), the dancer's whole body trembles as he relinquishes the worldly objects whose contours and consistencies he had previously explored.

Sometimes an object is there by default. Thus Christian Bourigault's *Le chercheur dort*, in homage to his cousin Daniel Tremblay, evoked sculptures and absent forms in the way that the prematurely deceased artist had departed this world. The choreographic *écriture* sculpts like the lost moulds of Tremblay's poetic objects, evoking layers of colour on the ground, labyrinths of multiple consistencies, lunar symbols assembled apparently illogically in the way that Tremblay's strange objects were like parcels of meaning enclosed in displaced images. At the end of this evocation a star-flecked curtain appears onstage: a first and last evocation that in one gesture, but without enclosing it in a precise metaphor, tears Tremblay's universe from the invisibility where the dancing body had gone looking for it.

Music

Very early in the history of dance modernity the traditional association between dance and music became intolerable – at least in terms of the received norms as, for example, the idea of 'bending' (*plier*) dance reductively to specialised musical forms. We owe it to Isadora Duncan to have dissociated dance from so-called ballet music. For her it wasn't the 'genre' and especially the theatrical genre entailed in ballet music that was important but that which in the music speaks directly to movement and emotion. (Only the great composers can communicate with the body, she wrote in *My Life*). So she used scores that had not been written for dance but which contained the phrasing of possible movements. Witnessing Elizabeth Schwartz interpreting Duncan's choreography for Schubert's *Ave Maria* has enabled me to understand how Duncan's movement was a pure incarnation of the music. But very quickly this too came to seem like a betrayal. For Laban there was no possible or thinkable relation between the givens of music and movement. This doctrine was taken up by Mary Wigman who applied it to the mastery and measure of time common to both arts: a shared given reconsidered through theories of rhythm in which it is no longer an imposed regulatory structure but a dynamics constitutive of a 'time' that is always to be re-invented. *We need it to define the pulsations, to clarify the transitions between themes, to refine the accents, and the moments of breath and suspension.* But the musician's metre does not correspond to the dancer's because *musicians count according to the musical line and dancers count according to the rhythm of the movement.*[26] This movement rhythm, Wigman recalls a little later, depends less on time than on the very constitution of the movement (its tonic intensity, its intent) which invents its own phrasing. This is why the more 'musical' a dance is the more it must do without music and flow with an 'inner music', as Odile Duboc puts it. The great periods of radicality in dance modernity (1910-30, 1960-70) have thus given rise to works danced in silence, a practice of Wigman as well as Jooss and Leeder in Germany in Laban's wake or by Doris Humphrey and José Limón in the United States. It is notable that artists who got rid of music in certain works are also those who were passionate about it and who lived a burning 'corps à corps' with musical works. We must pay homage to Louis Horst who was able to orient dancers' attention towards what we call today the baroque repertoire. Before musicology took hold of it, modern dancers discovered the accenting of Purcell, Bach and Rameau whose irregularities are so close to dancers' own accidental and contrasting rhythms. Out of this came sumptuous and physically very sensuous works with their powerful responses to musical forms such as Humphrey's *Passacaglia* and Limón's *Choreographical Offering*, a study based on Bach's *Musical Offering* and dedicated to Humphrey. Dana Reitz too – a flautist before becoming a dancer – has returned to a silence whose fluidity is revealed by her quiet phrasing and is not 'captured' by hearing it but by felt changes in kinaesthetic sensations. Merce Cunningham's choices regarding music do not reproduce the original cleavage (even less do they initiate this break, as is often claimed). Cunningham never eschews sound in his works (except in an already very old piece called *Before Dawn*). But in an exact inverse of Wigman, he does not accept that the relation between dance and music temporalities should be made on the dynamic level – precisely where musical energy is too powerful not to dominate the dance. It is on the contrary on the notion of an absolute time – clock time – foreign to experience that he has built a possible relation to music as a pure accident of simultaneity, proving thus that from Laban to Wigman to Cunningham the breach in dance–music relation is always made through the rejection of an element judged particularly undesirable within that relation. All these strategies have aimed to liberate the dancer (and also the spectator) from emotive sources which could 'install' her/him in externally generated kinaesthetics and in ready-made emotions – which would amount to a significant sensory dispossession because movement without sound has something obscene about it in the etymological sense of the word.[27] It becomes reduced to a purely corporeal, and thus sensory, act without the emotions that are so quickly activated by music being solicited. Besides, movement is rarely truly silent: only at moments does it attain the pure, sacred silence of meditation (which Colette admired so much in the inaudible sliding of Isadora Duncan's bare feet, in contrast to the 'sound of galoshes' as she said of ballet shoes). A whole animal sonority is awakened with the sound of feet, of falling, of heightened breath. Doris Humphrey used these intelligently in *Water Study*. There, the dancers' breath, through its successive increase, becomes the metonymy rather than mimicry of the murmur of waves, the bodies' return to the sea; and accompanying their fall – the shingle sound of the dancers' fingers hitting the floor. But, beyond the use of an organicity transposed into the mineral music of the world, nothing is more unsettling than the sound of the live.

In contemporary dance, sometimes the raw sounds of the body can be heard – generating for some empathy, for most, malaise. Trisha Brown's *Glacial Decoy* (1976) orchestrates the doubly unsettling and positive character of this sound-matter: the dancers' breathlessness grows in their accelerated, freely-flowing weighted movement. Behind them, Rauschenberg's projections nudge each other across the backdrop from stage left to right where they seem to end up in the waste bin of the invisible margins. The images themselves are of nothing much: 'stuff' without meaning or aesthetic interest akin to the 'junk art' of Rauschenberg's collages. Similarly, the dancing body is engaged in its unproductive expense and the noisy breath of the dancers sounds indiscreetly visceral. Doesn't the 'glacial decoy' relate to some nocturnal dance-form caught up in a quasi-cellular agitation from which no recognisable language can emerge? It is a more-than-dance that might lead, even in the vaporous wide-sleeved costumes reminiscent of Mlle Sallé's, to the very threshold of a time out of reach.[28] Nevertheless, a precise temporality inhabits this piece in the extreme fluidity of multi-directional movements that the dancers appear to catch in the space and in their own bodies: the memory of a half-forgotten state, the weightless infant body and its first trajectories (including falling) that Brown practised in the late '70s with Bonnie Bainbridge-Cohen.[29] And the false silence, in which body sounds from the audience (coughs, scratchings, fidgeting) can usually be heard, recreates a 'primitive scene' and its prohibitions too much for the risk of an undoing (*désaississement*) in their perception of bodies, not to be evoked in the spectator. Thus can we understand only too well the meaning of music in dance: to hide all that and to cover with a sonorous layer the unbearable groanings of the working diaphragm; to cover sound with sound in order to rediscover music as a metaphor of silence. Michel Chion has said of sound in his cinema that it was there in the beginning to cover the sound of the projector.[30] But in dance the stakes are different, even if the dancing machine deserves even more to have its sounds hidden. The usually redundant or illustrative uses of music today and their superficial relation to corporeal phrasing could well be covering other anxieties: of a tonic or imaginative void; of an enervated body and perception. To which must be opposed rich and adventurous processes like those of Stephanie Aubin who looks to music for a dialectical partner and who values the encounter as a contradiction. Her pieces are often constructed around this relation and each movement, each suspension participates in phrasing's voyage through fluid and released matter/material. For Odile Duboc the 'inner music' is what engenders the whole movement and its trajectory. Here, musicality goes beyond any contingent choice of musical accompaniment. It becomes a third dimension of space and movement. For Anne Teresa de Keersmaeker music is at once a tutelary presence, an example, and an object incorporated by the dancing body. All these possibilities are often explored today by graduates of Mudra, like Keersmaeker, (who have thus been taught by Fernand Schirren). Hervé Robbe works to mirror contemporary composers like Cécile le Prado. He has always been keen to weave his diverse relations with different art media such as video, cinema and visual art, to drown perhaps or to dissolve the sensitive nerve-point of a privileged relation to musical composition. We must not forget in this brief discussion that the often ill-defined territories where contemporary dance is located allow it to encounter diverse composers, so that very interesting academic musicians, but ones who are positioned on the borders of genres and schools, often become involved – like Kaspar P. Toeplitz, Barre Philips, Steve Lacy. From avant-garde jazz to the exchange between the avant-garde and rock, these blurred zones today form fertile, if 'twilight' terrains where dance can share practices like improvisation (which is often unheard of in the major contemporary 'classical' currents) and retrace modernist paths inconceivable elsewhere. The important thing that would allow a contemporary poetics to palpitate between dance and music that is a possible silence, a double abolition of the one in the other, the one far from the other, might still be perceivable. May the secret fracture which, even in today's alliances, maintains a deep region of responsiveness and fragility, still be manifest. United more than ever in a reconciliation that had become historically unthinkable, aspirations at the limit of the possible (those, for example of Trisha Brown honing her movement according to the rigours of Bach's or Weber's 'systems'), secret or unclassifiable complicities, are those which today best guarantee the poetic sources of this instability.

Forms of language

The audible presence of language on the choreographic stage seems to go against two canonical elements of dance tradition: dancing is silent; and the authorised (and obligatory) sound must be a musical one. Contravening these two rules was one of dance modernity's first acts of rebellion. Firstly, it was necessary to overcome music's imperialism and replace it with sound from other sources, as Laban did in 1910 at his school 'Dance, Sound, Word'; and by using cries, guttural sounds and texts of individual revolt like Nietzsche's *Zarathustra* which Wigman recited while dancing at the gallery Dada in 1916.[31] After Laban, dancers danced in silence or breathed audibly or in muffled tones (Humphrey in *Water Study* or *Life of the Bee*); they read texts on stage (Graham in *Letter to the World*), etc., and they continue to experiment today. Then, because any fixed role had to be questioned and debated, they had to deny that the dancer should be mute. The ritual and sacred character attached to silent movement had to be profaned in favour of an open expressivity that no linguistic denotation would limit and whose polysemy invests it with the dreamlike aureole of an always diffuse meaning. This confers on the presence of language in current contemporary dance works a particularly unsettling role – that of an elsewhere to received codes and traditional definitions. But wilfully profaning tradition is not as important as desire for the already mentioned 'welding' (*soudure*). Speech as reparation and supplement retrieves a lost dimension and enlists contemporary dance in an anthropological continuum in which, since the work of Dalcroze and Laban, it has sought to re-connect all the pieces of the human. Words are put into the mouths of wounded beings in certain recent works which double movement with the quasi nostalgic resonance of a lost plenitude (Larrieu's *Gravures*, Dobbels's *Le ciel reste intact*; *Les Petits Poucets* by Pierre Droulers; Wim Vanderkeybus). Already, at the beginning of dance modernity, alongside Wigman's and Humphrey's aim to eschew sound, the presence of language could also have had to do with the need to refind the anthropological continuum which had been destroyed historically or fractured in the very ontogenesis of human subjects. Artaud looked for this continuum in civilisations which had not experienced our historical rupturing of language from the body. In fact, language plays very different roles on the choreographic stage according to the different values that are sought; there is the rhythm of sound, prosody, not as a soundscape but as a generative force of the movement itself (Appaix); or, by contrast, the textual, literary aspect and the connotative resonance of words joining with the resonance of movements. In fact, spoken language traverses dance either as pure emission of more or less indifferent verbal matter or as textuality that can range from vocalisations to writing, with all the in-between values from the mimesis of an acted moment to the diegesis of a story. Sometimes it accompanies movement, or takes its place. Sometimes it becomes entangled in the same process of construction as the movement (e.g. *Accumulation with talking* 1974). There is a whole catalogue of forms which it would be too fastidious to enumerate if the secret and mysterious plan to break a mutilating aphasia was not installed there as an obsession, an overturning, an appeal.

Finally there is the speech that courses through the work entangling itself in the body's movement like another stave added to the choreographic score. It is an element often found in French dance, having started in the '60s with works like Dominique Dupuy's *Visages de Femmes* in which there was montage of taped literary, political and juridical texts like the rumble of a meta-language touching and prodding the body, but transcended and deported into the energy of the dance. (Here we must remember that the spoken text, either as a voice-over or delivered onstage, paradoxically amplifies the impression of the body's silence. Here veiled, faceless more than voiceless, the dancer's mutism is doubled by her effacement, while another voice tells the history in which she will never be an actor but only the powerful, eclipsed underpinning. In Bagouet's *Meublé sommairement* (1986) an entire short story by Emmanuel Bove is read onstage. And just as actress Nelly Borgeaud's body with its perfect, limpid and musical proffering of the text is insinuated into the trajectories of the choreography, so her voice and Bove's text make a path through the middle of the movement. Sometimes she reflects the dance in her body, in her delivery with its halts and suspensions. Sometimes the dance joins in with the story, the dancers changing from pure movement to storytelling as in particular ballroom scenes where scenic action and representation of the story coincide, a strange meeting between the story in its purest inflection and a suddenly invented body mimesis. Finally, the work's time corresponds to narrated, literary time. The durations of both textualities (including their ruptures – the blanks in the story coming from hesitations in the dance) seem to be engendered by breathing the same time.

The new stages

We know that dance does not have a location. This art without fixed address
has had to explore multiple terrains of actualisation/performance. Born at
the same time as image technologies it very quickly made an alliance with
them. This often allowed it to escape the constraints of place and to investi-
gate virtual spaces where the movement might develop a greater potential
and undertake investigations forbidden in the ritual of representation. At
the dawn of dance modernity Loie Fuller overturned the relationship by
making her own body a screen for the image, receiving it, animating it with
the billowing folds of cloth whose undulating secrets her arms, deeply anchored to her body at the sacrum, alone knew. And then, by contrast, the
body entered the image. Not the image-frame but the image-matter, in the
image as the very granulation of the body: as in the exemplary work of the
Cie L'Esquisse in their choreo-film *La Chambre* (1989). Body and filmic light
work in concert the same sensible 'milieu'. We find a loom analogous to a
'milieu' where the movement gets imprinted before dispersing in clouds of
dust in Jean Gaudin and Luc Riolon's (already cited) *Summum Tempus*
(1987) danced and filmed in a plaster factory. The plaster's cloudy thickness both lifts and imprints the matter of the visible. In *Quai Bourbon*
(1987), for a series at the Musée d'Orsay, Daniel Larrieu used video to choreograph faded bursts of body memory, the child chimney-sweeps
photographed by Joseph Nègre in the 19th century. It is striking that another form of work, that of the wood-planers painted by Caillebotte, more
or less in the same period, has inspired Angelin Preljocaj in a similarly note-
worthy video work: the strong backs of the dancers become one with the
wood as they plane it, and the work movements of this miserable proletariat
give birth to the matter against which they pit themselves. And like the
plasterers, chimney-sweeps, wood-planers, the dancers with their bodies
scrape and scratch their filmic support in order to extirpate an unknown
matter. Cinema and the other film techniques then become their accom-
plice in a labour through which the body gives birth to its own 'work'
(*travail*, the work of dance as transformation of matter but also as the
birthing 'labour' of past, or still to come corporeities). *The camera must invent movements or positions corresponding to the genesis of bodies as though
they were moving through their primordial postures.* [32] Conceiving works for
film or video has become commonplace but is often more adventurous and
free than live work. Merce Cunningham, for example, liked film and video
because they avoided the problem, always conventionally resolved, of stage
entrances and exits: in *Locale* (1981) it is the camera that looks for the
dancer and brings her/him into its field. The very same dancer can escape

the field to the front – something impossible in the theatre, unless by walking over the heads of the audience. As Deleuze has said of Godard's films, *Each time he constructs a space that depends on the body.*[33] Further, for Cunningham, video in particular poses or re-poses real problems of representation that the stage space considered 'normal' for dance tends to erase from its problematics: what is the image of my own body, that by which I am localised in the world since it can travel to another space and with other characteristics? (Benjamin spoke of the landscape coming into a room; what is there to say of a body that escapes its own contours?) Is video, as 'reproduction', a distortion and reduction of the body? Certainly not. The body can make images. That is why the opposition between 'live performance' and audiovisual performance (dead performance?) is so absurd. Françoise Dupuy has often said that there is a dance as soon as there is not a form but a possible 'transformation' in an experience/experiment of movement; transformation, it goes without saying, of the dancer and the spectator. Many so-called 'live' dances transform nothing at all (because through static images or in excessive muscularity they prevent the possibility of changes in the poetics of transfer of weight). Many films or videos create from unresolved questions, body states in suspense. Even when visually distorted the body can produce weighted experience. In order to lead a distant (*différé*) audience to the corporal engagement that live performance proposes, to the mutual letting go that circulates between dancer and spectator, the performer, says Cunningham, must double her/his energy. For machines and especially electronic ones can certainly make this distant experience one of loss. In video, the body at any moment can be reduced to its pure image, a 'to-be-seen' external to its own perception and reaching the spectator only as a species of form – even if it has high definition and clarity. Both intention and tension must be maintained. But doesn't any 'representation' pose the same issues? Or more simply in this case, doesn't the body expose the problem of its own appearance? The question is important as soon as we touch upon the eternal problem of the icon and its relation to the live, especially as the waning of the latter. There, too, dance 'works' and the choreographic object undergoes singular metamorphoses. For Cunningham, as we have seen, it is an opportunity for dance to revisit its premises, its relation to narrative for example, which becomes more ambiguous. Certain dance videos play at narrative cinema: Charles Picq and Bagouet's *Tant mieux, tant mieux* with its surreal dinner scene is a surprising example. Some are filmed in Polaroid (Jean Gaudin, Marc Guerini *Les Autruches* 1985). We could also cite the films of Mourieras and Gallotta. In *Un chant presque éteint* (1987), *Ils vivaient seuls dans les villes* (1991) remnants of stage choreographies still exist but with narrative and contextual elements that were not included in the stage version. The frame of narration is displaced: urban or suburban landscapes, railway stations... but as with all Gallotta's pieces, always situations of survival – before or after an apocalypse. The dance always seeks to reclaim the vestiges that have been lost, left behind, or already there. For Gallotta, as for other choreographers like Pina Bausch, dance is already memory. Dance film examines its extent, its boundaries. But in the displacement (whether it be to a site reinvented through the camera as in the mirror double of Bouvier and Obadia's *Lampe,* 1992) film or video allow the instituted modes of production of performance/spectacle to be circumvented in order to propose other objects upon which the circuits of distribution and diffusion must work differently than on live performance. This is why companies like N+N Corsino devote themselves entirely to the technological stage. A long development has led from their first pieces (like *Le champ de Madame Carle,* 1986) recorded with analog technologies but with some use of synthetic image to their recent *Totempole* (1994) for filmic and virtual body. With the help of the 'Life Forms' software refined at Simon Fraser University they have used the computer information usually employed as compositional strategy to create a 'pictogram-dancer,' a hybrid experiment between human movement and computer animation. This surprising work takes dance into immaterial zones where the body still thinks and produces its kinesphere. It helps to perceive a 'being-body' well beyond the ontological matrix in which it is more usually confined in a whole cortege of biological definitions. The body is in the first instance a productive current. *Totempole* engages us to feel its emissions in 'the other scene', an imaginary at work in and through movement and one which can transit indefinitely. Thus is the recourse to technologies not a simple variation on the creative act, still less a prosthesis or a derivation of performance. It is another form of the choreographic work. It must lead us to think its potential as the gamut of an infinite possibility. Each work is thus invited to inaugurate its own 'exception' endlessly pushing back the limits of its own 'stage', organising between the perception of the spectator and its own, new fields of encounter, new sensations, new intelligences.

1 In 'Aperçus de la scène de la danse' in *Théâtre et Abstraction*, 1978.

2 Forti, S. *Handbook in Motion*, 1966.

3 Foster, S. in *Reading Dancing*, 1986; and Siegel, M. in *The Shapes of Change*, 1979 are examples of this.

4 A Ballet is a 'little ball'. (Transl.)

Besides, a 'ballet' is not the only important form during the historical period of Western dance. The *intermezzo* of the opera until the 19th century had a considerable role in the elaboration of stage dance as much as the court dance of the 16th and 17th centuries. At the end of the 18th century, Vigano invented the 'coreodramma' which, even in its provisional existence, is worthy of mention. As we can see, theoretical simplifications prevent an understanding of western classical dance as much if not more than contemporary dance.

5 Schlemmer, O. 'Présentation du Ballet Triadique' in *Théâtre et Abstraction*, 1978, p. 27.

6 A description and programme of *Sonnentanz* are given in Suzanne Perrottet, *Ein Bewegtes Leben*, 1990.

7 Audiovisual source: filmed interview reproduced in *Mein Leben ist Tanz*, production Internationes, 1987.

8 Audiovisual source: *Gert's Faces*, undated, uncredited. Held in the collections of the Cinémathèque de la danse at the Cinémathèque Française. See also F.M. Peter, *Valeska Gert, Tanzerin, Schauespielin*. Berlin: Hentrich, 1987.

9 Cf. the text of the theatre critic Georges Banu, 'De la présence' in *Art Press*, #182.

10 Rainer *Work*, 1973, p.9.

11 Kraus, Rosalind 'Notes on the Index: Seventies Art in America' in *October*, Autumn 1976.

12 The text is reproduced in Banes, S. *Terpsichore in Sneakers*, 1980, pp.92-95.

13 Cf Michael Kirby's study of this concept in 'La non-danse'. *Le corps en jeu*. Paris: éditions du CNRS, 1992, pp.209-217.

14 Audiovisual source: Interview with Christian Boltanski by Charles Picq. Collections de la vidéothèque de la Maison de la Danse (Lyon), 1993.

15 Deleuze, G. *The Logic of Sensation*, 2003, chapter 3, 'Couples and triptyques'.

16 Schlemmer, O. 'La scène de la danse' in *Théâtre et Abstraction*, 1978, p.88.

17 Jacques-Dalcroze, E. *Le rythme, la musique et l'éducation*, 1984, p.129.

18 Ibid.

19 Ibid.

20 Dobbels, D. 'La cloison' in *Théâtre Public*, No. 58/59, 1984.

21 *Bulletin of the CNDC Angers*, No. 9, Spring 1990 (articles by Bernard Blistène, Marianne Goldberg, Laurence Louppe).

22 Rainer. *Work*, 1973, p.134.

23 Klosty, J. *Cunningham*, 1975, p. 15.

24 Cf. *Qu'est-ce que la sculpture moderne*. Dir. Margot Rowet, exhibition catalogue. MNAM. Paris: Centre Georges Pompidou, 1988.

25 Laban, R. *Die Welt der Tanzer*. Stuttgart: Seifert Verlag, 1920, cited in Bartenieff, 1976, op.cit.

26 Wigman, Mary *The Language of Dance*, 1966, p.15.

27 Latin *obscaenus*: ill-omened or abominable. (Transl.)

28 Mlle Sallé, a soloist at the Academy Royale de Danse in the 18th century, was famous for her clothing reforms which prescribed light muslin dresses instead of 'paniers' and baroque 'barrels'.

29 Interview with Yvonne Rainer in Brunel, L. *Trisha Brown*, 1986, pp.44-46.

30 Chion, M. *Le son au cinéma*, 1985.

31 The dances at the gallery Dada have been described by several witnesses, artists and dada poets from Tzara to Art and Ball. Huelsenbeck's descriptions of Wigman appear in *Memories of a Dada Drummer*, 1974.

32 Deleuze, G. *The Time-Image*, 1989.

33 Ibid.

Memory and Identity

It is only the work that matters but, finally, the work is only there to lead us in search of it.
Blanchot[1]

In our era a double poetics of artistic creation has developed around the concept of the 'work' or *oeuvre*. If the study of structure in the field of semiology, for example, has allowed us to identify symbolic constructions as autonomous systems of organised elements, another tendency (either complementary or opposed) has been to put the idea of the work of art into crisis. The prime motives of this crisis are ideological or even political: the work or *oeuvre* is that which offers itself as an identifiable object for cultural strategies to manipulate. A work is at the same time a negotiable entity and, legitimately bearing the rights to an artistic paternity, it can be regarded as a kind of 'goods'. *The author is reputed the father and the owner of his work,* remarks Roland Barthes, after noting the implications and the historical and philosophical consequences of this engendering. *The work is caught up in a process of filiation. One can postulate: a* determination *of the work by the world (by race and then by History), a* consecution *of works amongst themselves, and a* conformity *of the work to the author.*[2]

Now, continues Barthes, if the notion of 'the work' locates creative activity in this determinist frame, it is also that which propels art matter onto the market. A work, as consumer item, returns in surplus a judgment of 'taste' which, amongst the confused evaluative criteria that are as impoverished and arbitrary as the ill-defined socio-economic context where the notion of the work functions, renders it all the more fragile. We know that Barthes opposes to the work as an item of consumption the 'text,' and even the 'intertext', as an ongoing process of construction working through the very matter/material of art and consciousness, shattering the juridical terms of 'proper' filiations: the text, *decants the work (the work permitting) from its consumption and gathers it up as play, work, production, practice.*[3] (We will return to the very important ideas for contemporary dance of work [*travail*] and practice). In the meantime, these lines written in 1971 deserve our attention. By introducing the fertile notion of 'intertext', they contributed historically to the major task of desacralising the work of art as an object of the market and of (financial or ideological) capitalisation. This task has continued to make its impact throughout the century and contemporary dance has been particularly touched by it. Indeed, everything that we have just said applies even more to the choreographic work. In the preceding pages it will have been understood that, through the wealth and diversity of its processes, the choreographic work constitutes an ideal site to observe the changing state and identity of the work of art in our era. The contemporary dance work has neither a specific frame nor fixed references that must be respected. If, today, it sometimes appears limited or confined by its canonical models, this is because of the institutional modes of distribution and the schemas that these impose on the creator as well as on audiences. It is thus essential to recall how close avant-garde choreographic currents were, historically, to dada or post-dada movements which pushed the critique of the work of art and even the creative gesture upon which it is founded so far: media images replicated ad infinitum by pop art destroyed any attempt to reconstitute an aura or market notions of an 'original'. To these artistic practices which transform or destroy authorial authority (any 'authority' coming precisely from an 'author' or whatever in the dominant ideological structures substitutes for him), critical, epistemological and literary accounts have added, indiscriminately, a further disturbance. We know all the detours, the more or less elaborate strategies of, say, Borges or Pessoa to destabilise the work as unique event and to systematically mislead the reader through ambiguous and fictional cross-references (like the famous Borgesian *Don Quixote* written in the 20th century using a simple game to redistribute words by chance.) All this witty irreverence might be sterile if it had not also inspired Nelson Goodman's reflections on the languages of art, starting with the extreme cases where art contemplates its own elusive nature in inverted mirrors. We know that dance owes to such reflections their power to reveal its own systems when the latter are approached via the symbolisation of notation systems, exposing to movement its most complex fundamentals. Along with the philosophers of art, these reflections have made of the choreographic field one of the great paradoxes where intelligence has been able to forge new paths in the understanding of human creation.[4]

Similarly, the work of art as a perfected object has been challenged by questioning its association with a traditional discipline. Rather, it is now determined not so much by its engendering as by its external form (*contours*), its characteristics, where it locates itself (which takes us back to an origin). The most interesting realisations of contemporary art (often immaterial objects) frequently exist only in terms of their slipperiness with respect to defined genres. This plurality and statutory liberty of the work relates not only to its internal transformations, but, usefully recalling Barthes, to the heterogenous ways of looking at it. In the case of the literary work, for example, the renewal of criticism through developments in linguistics and in psychoanalytic literary criticism have unmoored classical definitions in literature. In dance, we have the same or nearly the same situation: the different kinesiological or aesthetic approaches and dance's contiguity with avant-garde artistic processes in the visual arts or theatre have modified, oriented or disoriented approaches to the work and by extension the work itself. Here, we return to the intertext, but as the shaping of art by the perceptions that it engages. Sensations, mirrors, resonances (exceeding explanation), are less the fact of an artistic decision than of a general becoming of symbolic horizons.

The choreographic work: fortunes and misfortunes

But contemporary dance is constrained, even today, to follow another altogether different route. In fact, the notion of a work (*oeuvre*) as an 'opus' bearing the marks of a singular imaginary has been contested (if not scorned) for too long in the tradition of this art. That is why, before reflecting upon the transformations and extraordinary developments of choreographic *oeuvre* which have been so fertile in the period of its modernity, we first must follow the narrow and somewhat painful path of the limitations that have been imposed upon it. Currently: the notion of 'work' (*oeuvre*) as confused too readily with spectacle, dance's only market value and that on which cultural consumption (already denounced by Barthes) can 'speculate' and thus subdue and impoverish. Because 'the work' is directly assimilated to the reductive and shallow notion of spectacle (spectacle as consumer item, not as a thinking of the 'event' which by definition would escape any appropriation), it happens that we tend, sometimes wrongly, to privilege it as the dancer's only 'production'. This 'work' offers a concrete object upon which the cultural system can fix its attention (and thus exercise its power – in particular its evaluative power) and to such an extent that, for numerous observers and participants in choreographic culture, the freedom, the breathing spaces and even a significant part of dance's inventiveness, exist in the margins of spectacle, before or behind the scenes, in an off-stage (of studio practices, workshops, and other occasions) which become the real field where the important issues and concerns are formulated.

During the 1980s in France, we witnessed an inflated use of the notion of *oeuvre* (in a meta-language that is ill-defined and difficult to circumscribe because it has founded neither references nor theory) linked to another equally nebulous idea – that of '*auteur*'. And this, surprisingly, at the moment when the authorial activity of the choreographer was becoming reduced to putting together purely spectacular ingredients as a substitute for the deep work that made the artist of the '*grande modernité*' an inventor of a body, a technique and an aesthetic, and who organised all these factors in a coherent language. While everywhere else the notion of author had been complicated or contested, we witnessed choreography, on the contrary, take hold of this notion enthusiastically and make a banner of it. Was this a continuation of the interesting notion of choreauteur developed and asserted by Serge Lifar in his *Manifesto of the Choreographer* (1933)? Probably not, since the contemporary French dancer draws her/his references very little from the history of dance. It is probably more likely to be the integration, several decades later, of the notion of *auteur* developed in the cinema by André Bazin. This idea opposed *what the director has to say to the world* to the crushing power of the commercial and industrial aspects of film.[5] Nevertheless, it is uncertain whether the concept of *auteur* carried over to choreography has freed the dance creator from the economic and ideological pressures of the modes of production (as *auteur* cinema was supposed to in relation to the cinematic industry). On the contrary, the notion of choreographic *auteur* upholds a certain over-valuation of choreographic signature, and, even more, of a tag that signals (more than signs) the importance of a label: the name of the choreographer and her/his presence justifying only to itself the functioning of a company. Thus, more seriously, comes the disarray, the wounds, the grieving and rupture in the continuity of the dancer's work when (as happens only too often) the choreographer is no more. It no longer seems possible, as in the important American companies, to pursue a 'work' tied to bodies and practices beyond any simply nominal identification. Although this assessment will need to be revisited.

The strength of the work of grieving in and through dance can make of loss a resource. Pain and loss, commitment and memory bind together projects and dreams, reconstituting communities of bodies beyond any anticipated frame or organisation, and newly engaged in an eternal becoming. Companies like those of Régis Huvier (L'arrache-coeur) and, even more, of Dominique Bagouet (les Carnets Bagouet) have been able to show, in an inventive and unexpected way, how much work (*travail*) survives the civil presence of the choreographer. How much the bodies marked by him were still at work in the space where his gaze had held them in a poetic engagement that death could not dissipate. The dancer alone is the inventor of the mechanism which s/he herself puts in place as if transforming the order of disappearance into a rebirth of inspiration and desire. For the body of the choreographer, much more than her/his name as a label, is what has made the dancer, in the same way that the dancer has constructed the choreographic signature out of her/his own body. *They've finally no more need of us, the early departed ones... But we, that have need of such mighty secrets, we for whom sorrow's so often source of blessedest progress, could we exist without them?*[6]

The misfortunes and the heavy responsibility that weigh on the activity of the dancer mean that the notion of *oeuvre* in dance is still too precious to be made the object of the slightest intellectual restriction. It is too precise, in any case, to be able to confront with impunity the kinds of desacralisation staged by the art and thought of the century. We will see that it is only by her/his own account that the choreographer has been able to be considered a genuine creator and respected as such. Indeed the act of choreography, considered as a simple spectacle, has inherited a traditional foundation whose law and ideology we must examine. There is the archaic image of the *maitre de ballet* who, in the 19th century, directed or oversaw 'a show', that is, put in place a mechanism allowing the *danseurs* or rather the *danseuses* to be seen: a mechanism of exposability or 'exhibition value' to use Walter Benjamin's term. Now, this exhibition value of the ballet stage preceded (was it the anticipatory shadow?) the technical invention of apparatuses of reproduction (cinema, photography) which for Benjamin were vehicles for the exhibition value of art to the detriment of its ritual or 'cult' value.[7] And in the same way that any photograph of a human face reveals for Benjamin the fugitive and faded glint of a lost aura, at the same time, strangely, the dancing body remains the 'ultimate retrenchment' of a ritual that can no longer be performed.[8] This has for a long time prevented the dance work from being seen as the elaboration of an organic unity putting into play a complex symbolic system where several layers (movement, composition, *écriture*) interconnect.

Of course, dance analysis does not start with the *oeuvre*: the perception of the 'corporal signature' and of 'the style' acts before, or this side of, any articulation in a completed totality. Indeed, valorisation of the *oeuvre* responds initially perhaps to a more trenchant necessity which has to do with the painful dispute experienced in dance's past: that of making the choreographic work recognised as a fully fledged artistic act, which it was refused for a long time and is to a certain extent still today. That is why the demystification of respect for the art work that has occurred in all other artistic fields, the crisis brought about by unsettling or playful depersonalisation of the author, by pseudo authorings from those of Duchamp's *Rrose Selavy* to Borges' *Pierre Menard*, would not be very amusing in dance and probably not very transgressive because this could just as well be confused with what is normal. On the other hand, identification of the dance work as inalienable is most certainly one of the conquests of modernity as is, in historical or aesthetic research, the identification of an original choreographic text. Why? Because it goes against the perspectives maintained by tradition, and the presumption that the text is 'ephemeral' based on the fact that it depends for its actualisation uniquely upon a situation of spectacle (not so much on an immediate situation, but on the economic and institutional modes of production). It can be seen that what is involved is an amalgam of ideas, encountered in significant ideological ignorance and confusion, which have their most significant impact on the choreographic field and whose first victim is the dancer. The reasons for this are mysterious and very unclear and we will refrain from making any hypothesis on the subject here. Let us simply recall the classification of the arts according to Goodman.[9] Thus: 'autographic' when their existence is bound up with the materiality of a unique item (what Gerard Genette calls 'immanent'); and 'allographic' when the existence of the work, 'transcendent' for Genette, exists outside of any materiality (as concept, proposition, process, or score).[10] In the category of allographic arts, dance is the only one to be regarded as fragile and inconsistent, while the other arts, linked to actualisation by the performance/expedient of a text or score (poetry, theatre, music), are not, at least not to the same degree.

The habit of confusing 'the work' (*oeuvre*) and 'spectacle' is far from negligible in relation to the loss of choreographic works – which is loss of artistic identity but also of memory. For one loss does not happen without the other, and it is this which makes the conservation of works so crucial. Only such conservation bears witness to a singular artistic practice.

Many classical ballets of the 19th century at least in France are lost. Only their shadows remain (one romantic ballet, forgotten like all the others, deals with this theme of the shade or shadow...). Sometimes only the title remains. Usually the elements that endure are the libretto and the musical score. Sometimes a more or less precise and abundant iconography can evoke visual aspects, which can contribute in part to an imaginary of the body. But of course what is most important for us is what is destined to oblivion: the work's flesh, its text, the danced movement whose substance tends to be the first to be forgotten. Which proves how little valued as a creative act choreography has been in a whole part of our tradition and even within the profession. At best, certain ballets (*Giselle, Coppélia*) have survived by conserving that which for us is most important — the text of the danced movement. Later, and in other historical circumstances, the works of Petipa, for example, have been conserved simultaneously by notation and oral transmission. However they are all too rarely redone with faithfulness to their integrity. This disconnects their meaning from the architectural whole with which it is so closely bound up.

The fact that works have been lost, or even changed, is in itself not so serious. What is serious, in terms of the respect that the identity of a work should inspire, is that its name is retained across a series of unreflective and inauthentic (particularly from an aesthetic point of view) 'remakes'. In an artistic field other than dance where there has traditionally been respect for the author, the notion of remake can exercise a salutary irony. Its aim is precisely to destroy the authorial sacredness or the emphatic vision of the origin of a work that numerous discourses have put in question. In theo-

retically refined fields such as literature such ransacking is healthy, intelligent and necessarily provocative. But such is not the case for choreography
with its absence of any theory bearing on the history of its works, and
where the principle of the remake proceeds from a simple suspension of
artistic awareness or taste or from an unreflective search for the spectacular
equal to that seen in mainstream cinema – a desire to reinvigorate a cultural product by using a readymade prestigious title and theme. Of course
such activities form part of what Genette calls, without any pejorative overtones, 'recastings'. For, in the case of disciplines other than dance, far from
indicating transgressions, they evoke the intertextual slidings through
which the plurality of layers and functions of existence give to the text the
range of all its possible modalities of actualisation. Such manipulations
exist equally in the theatrical and lyrical domains. But there, long established texts constituting the standard of artistic existence maintain the
integrity of the work which the 'ruptures' of a director of Shakespeare or
Marlowe might authorise without significantly compromising the identity
of the work. In dance, this absolute reference of the corpus of published
texts does not exist. And in the recastings the errant materiality of the
dance work, more than in any other art, risks dissolving or losing its gestures. A revealing symptom is that, in the art of choreography, the notion
of spectacle prevails over the notion of the work which remains indistinct
and deprived of the identity that would circumscribe it within its own artistic prerogatives.

Happily, in classical ballet, we are today witnessing the development of a
conscious and reflective current where the quest for singular and intact
works (historical or contemporary) has become, simultaneously, an objective of practice, research, conviction and thought. For Jean-Paul Gravier,
following in the wake, one could say, of the Joffrey Ballet in the United
States but with a greater poetic sensibility, the quest for the work begins
with the integration of body states, with work on the movement and its
sense in the body of the dancer. There, in effect, the establishment of the
'text' begins and is pursued right throughout the whole choreographic construction. The issue is not so much an archaeological quest for authenticity,
but respect for an artistic act that can found a work, define it and make it
figure as such amongst the creations of the human spirit. Amongst such
artists the notion of work prevails over that of spectacle. Which makes the
act of performance itself more credible, more stimulating, more moving
and more beautiful.

Certain modern choreographers have been able to play on the notion of
'remake' by updating emblematic ballets of the past. This usually involves a

self-conscious transformation where, starting from a theme already used in the ballet, the contemporary creator conceives a completely different work: like Mats Ek's *Giselle*, Andy de Groat's *Lac des Cygnes* or *Bayadère*, or the *Coppélia* or *Les Noces* of Maguy Marin or Angelin Preljocaj. Extant ballets are involved in both cases, but the 'remake' works on them in an indirect way, as though it were another danced interpretation. Ek and Marin retain the libretto and the musical score, whereas de Groat only keeps the ambience and the title which are emblematic of a vague nostalgia. It will be noted, not without a certain bitterness, that what links the choreographic work to its identity is... the musical score: a strange substitution of identity in an artistic community that no longer even recognises the true site of its accomplishments. But in spite of these reservations, this kind of undertaking is interesting if its processes are informed and explicit and where the re-interpretation really works as such. Nevertheless, it is important to note that these re-makes, even if modern in their processes, only work on the classical repertoire. It is strange that so-called contemporary choreographers only work on a repertoire that is not theirs – a way perhaps that they disavow or deny a history of the body within modernity. Unless they need this 'elsewhere' in order to change, appropriate, blaspheme without risking the fundamental values of their movement. To start with there is much that might be said: these works are not part of the choreographer's real history but of a sort of mythology, of a repertoire of forms which can be innocuously mined. This fund of references can also be treated in different ways: in a cheeky, off-hand way or as though paying homage to some archetype of choreographic memory. One looks in vain for contemporary versions of modern works – such as the *Moor's Pavane* or *Cave of the Heart*. A taboo, an absence of memory perhaps (which amounts to the same thing), prevents the moderns from touching their own roots. And besides, if today's choreographers would have the audacity (sacrilege?) to take this on, the rights-holders or companies maintaining the repertoire would oppose it. For here, the idea of the choreographic oeuvre can no longer be questioned. The value of authorship in dance affirms itself as one of the great conquests of our epoch. At least as a re-conquest, if one takes into account the concern over attributing authorship in the Renaissance and Baroque periods. Only extraordinary works, but ones abandoned to the very chaos that engendered them, like Mary Wigman's magnificent *Abshied und Danke*, can be redone based on film images. Like the fragments of memory that the Company La Ronde has gathered in the touching interpretation by Dominique Brunet. Wigman did not seek to transmit her works: they were so many 'shifting landscapes' to use the title of one of her series of solos which remain now only as film images. Contingent upon these reflected bodies, a contemporary dancer can glean states or movements that can be ignited from across incredible corporal disparities. The enterprise is audacious. It has the pure quality of extreme transgressions, which adds beauty and emotion to the undertaking.

Equal in its fervour but different in its process is the project of Jean-Christophe Paré. His *Faune dévoilé* ('The faun unveiled') moves between the sketch, the text and his multiple readings of parts of the famous 1913 solo, *Après-midi d'un Faune*, by Nijinsky, another no less interesting figure in the 'institution of the text'. Here, the question of a repertoire (whether classical or not) cannot be posed: Nijinsky did not belong to any school. He was outside all reference points and invented a modernity with the (individual) decision to create his own language, but not – and in this he did not, either, belong to contemporary dance – a system of the body, where the one would legitimate the other. But the question posed by Jean-Christophe Paré arises in particular out of precise written sources – Nijinsky's notations and the joint work of Anne Hutchison-Guest and Millicent Hodgson concretised by the Joffrey Ballet. In these reconstructions we can discern an intertextual character recognisable from the practice of contemporary dance: a field of layers and superimposed borrowings where authorial value fades before the resonances it inspires. For this 'Faun unveiled' plays with its own veils and stirs up ghostly matter. The poetry of the undertaking goes beyond any question of respect and awareness. But it can only work from this profound and infinite awareness of the work and the choreographic language. 'The work' as an unbreachable identity is as evident in modern and contemporary choreography as it is in painting, the literary text and the musical score. Any alteration in the work alters its signature: that by which, since the Renaissance, both the original act of creation and the inalienable name of the author have always been identified. In addition, in modern art the signature has assumed a new importance, sometimes coming to substitute for the work itself. Beyond the simple regulation of artistic ownership, then, it is a question of a movement's vision and the *oeuvre* that it engenders. This politics of authorial legality may seem a little dogmatic, even tyrannical. But this authority is a timid one in the face of the constricting powers that are imposed on both the artistic act and on the dancer's body. Such authority only defends a small, fragile right to exist as an artist in a gigantic ideological machine where, at any moment, a movement might see its mark erased, and sometimes simply stolen, from its location in the human community and from the artistic project where it was born.

Certain periods, however, are well-known for having manifested a con-

sciousness of the existence of choreographic articulation as *'oeuvre'* and
'invention' (if only in the classical sense of the word), as an authored object
which, like other works of art, answers to an indelible 'signature'. But you
have to go way back in our culture to find something, if not equivalent, at
least analogous: to the Renaissance, to Quatrocento and late Cinquecento
Italy and Spain where the ballet masters archived compositions signed in
their name. Then to 18th century Europe, where we find compositions in
Feuillet notation which, because of this notation, benefited from the same
control over artistic ownership. Notwithstanding that in a *'basse danse'* by
Ebreo or Domenico da Piacenza, in a pavane of Caroso, to change a step or
an ordering poses the question of the definition of 'the work'. Similarly for
the Pecour, Isaac, Ballon and the other dance composers at the beginning
of the 18th century: even if the frequent copies with their variations and
transpositions, the adjustments introduced as a result of the dances' passage from the theatre to the scene/stage of the ballroom, often through the
intervention of the author himself, means that today we are faced with
several versions. But this very plurality becomes the occasion for an extremely interesting work on what Jean-Noel Laurenti calls 'establishing the
text' (*l'etablissement du texte*)[11] – whether in the verbal mode of archiving of
the Renaissance or using a system, as when the idea of notation became
common at the end of the 17th century – making the notion of identity
only more pointed and dynamic. Thus and thenceforth fixed in its spatial
and temporal parameters, the work can affirm itself as an original creation
and as an invention, and can come down to us today perfectly clear in the
particularities that define it. The historical, political and normalising motives which have led to the production and application of systems of
notation, then, are of little importance. What we inherit is an astonishing
semiological adventure, and alphabets of the body able to transmit to us
mobile forms, poetics of space, and as apparently intimate elements as shifts
of support, suspensions of weight, the balancing of the gravitational axis, a
whole play of the body's interior inscribed in a practice of the self;[12] and
which appears today in the freshness of a thinking not afraid to explore the
sensory realm, and able to communicate, across the centuries, the infinite
charm of its emergence. This parallel should not be pushed too far, however,
because the recognition of a master work in the archaic context of the craft
guilds or even in the academicism of the classical age, where the status of
the artist was more clearly defined, have nothing to do with the importance
that contemporary culture attaches to the notion of 'signature'. We are not
seeking to establish a resemblance or heritage between this earlier situation, where the work and the author were recognised in the most inviolable

aspects of an artistic proposition, and the modern consciousness of the choreographic work (*oeuvre*). To underline the paradox: those periods in which authorial rights were unknown and where the work of copying, borrowing, the circulation of forms or themes from one work to another was the rule in all domains, are nevertheless able to teach us lessons regarding the respect due to the existence of danced movement or perhaps to corporal action in general – however much these corporal states may have been manipulated ideologically. For it is important to discern here which, out the imposition of a model or the loss of movements, is more deadly.

However, in such paradoxical situations, the conservation of works creates distortions or entails risks which unmoor both thought and perception. Then, the work can only be defined in terms of the document that fixes it and becomes materially confused with it. Thus do certain ruins gain their sole notoriety from the privilege of being vestiges. A perfectly secondary and contingent work, *Le marriage de la grosse Cathos*, for example, a masquerade preserved in the notation of Favier and accompanied by exceptional musical and other documentation is only a simple *bouffonnerie de carnaval* from the court of Louis XIV.[13] It exists, however, as an entire 'choreographic work'; and because of being defined or identified as a work it moves into other symbolic states where it becomes charged with an aura having little to do with its real substance. It benefits, for example, from the interest accorded the system in which it has been recorded: Favier's writing which is marginal with respect to the royally sanctioned Feuillet system disseminated and adopted throughout Europe (where libraries are full of examples of it). By contrast, its rarity and the attention conferred on this exceptional document by two renowned researchers give it a prestige which elevates the danced contents culturally and in the order of knowledge. While the *Ballet de la Nuit*, considered at the time as the most defining of court ballets by the great baroque theoretician Menestrier, only survives as a dreamlike, evocative libretto, with its poetic content and its interpretive instructions by Isaac de Benserade, but amputated of all body poetics.

Celebration of loss: rituals of disappearance

In dance one cannot talk of memory without coming up against (or without skirting around, which amounts to the same thing) the spectre of an ancient taboo. A pervasive law – usually echoed in the doxa – condemns dance to a prohibition on remembering. At the opening of an important symposium on 'Memory and Forgetting' (at the Festival of Arles) Dominique Dupuy took the expression 'a hole in memory' literally as a kind of fireplace where ashes gradually bury and extinguish the living force of the fire.[14] As Michel de Certeau reminds us, it is wrong to regard memory as an entity in itself, and forgetting simply as a negative moment that breaches memory's integrity. Rather, it is forgetting that has the upper hand, exploiting the passage of time for its own purposes. As de Certeau says, *memory is only the return of the forgotten*.[15] Dance is not for nothing the privileged site of an impossible return, in the sense that movement continually re-opens to the immediacy of its own presence.

The beautiful word 'ephemeral' (*epi-hemera*: that which lasts only a day, *Que du matin jusques au soir* ['only from morning to night'] as Ronsard said of roses) is continually misused. Applied to dance in superficial discourses of the doxa, it becomes nauseatingly banal. Tied to the idea of forgetting, it floats about in a field of vague connotations. Then, fatalistically, we assume that it means impotence and the inability to withstand the ravages of time. But ephemeral arts are always willingly so – they contain within them the mechanisms or the programming that will send them back to the void: the provisional architectures of the baroque age, Merz's and Schwitters' perishing, crumbling pillars of rubbish and, later, the works of Jochen Gerz which he deliberately designed to become progressively invisible as they slowly effaced or inhumed themselves. In fact, in the work of Gerz (as in dance?) it was always a matter of *making the invisible space more visible*.[16] The passage from the visible to the invisible (in the work of art, in danced movement), the moment of disappearance, is essential. This doesn't mean that it is a moment of annihilation. On the contrary. For Gerz these projects of disappearance are at the same time memory projects: monuments that bury themselves, the names of concentration camps drawn in chalk on the ground that are rubbed out by the feet of the visitors, these are essentially acts of memory. For the basis of memory is not the permanence of the object but the recording itself, the value of the mark made in the collective conscience and in the bodies of the generations. Anything can be recalled, even the passage of a meteor. Forgetting strikes at what is discredited. It does not fall within the scope of our approach here to talk of 'repression', but we might well talk of the processes of negation that are useful for the survival of the ideology of a social group or of cultural institutions or institutionalised systems of production which conspire to maintain dance at the level of a saleable product, that of a pure 'exhibition' at the expense of an experience/experiment that nurtures the power of the instant. Such exposure leads to a double eclipse. Discussing Geneviève Stephenson's photographs, Daniel Dobbels has reflected upon what tempts us to consider the instant, negatively, as only ephemeral.[17] For the quality of the instant does not depend on its ephemeral character but on the instantaneous per-

ception of the sensuous intensity that inhabits it; and whose bodily emanation, in this case the photo, can capture (and keep as a secret
consummation).

A discourse of the ephemeral is usually confined to what Christophe
Wavelet aptly calls a *celebration of loss*. This celebration is not only a function of public perception nor even of the mediatised discourses that
maintain it, for dancers themselves value the notion of the ephemeral for
all sorts of complex reasons. Some of these lack, a priori, neither pertinence
nor poetic force. Thus, the feeling of ephemerality can be found in the discourse of the dancer but displaced (even ennobled). It could be said that
there is a 'bright mourning' that dancers willingly associate with their
practice, a desire for the magical things of the body to be tied to their disappearance, like an eternal sacrifice in which their bodies are engaged
through their '*travail*'. Perhaps this is a way to give back to movement the
supreme sacredness that the proximity of death confers on any becoming
(*événement*) and which the communication society, in its banality, tends to
evacuate. 'Expenditure' (*dépense*) then becomes that act of immolation in
excess that the dancer dedicates to her art and to her audience – even if s/he
draws from it on both sides not an experience of death but of entropy. Regarding the sacrifice of persons and objects in sacrificial rites, George
Bataille has noted that sacrifice returns to the sacred what servitude has
degraded and profaned.[18] Perhaps the celebration of loss is indispensable
to a ritual whereby the body of the dancer and that of the spectator escape
the 'higher' (*ultérieur*) economies where Derrida (in *Writing and Difference*),
after Bataille, has detected the acquisitive ruses of capitalist ideologies. Consequently, 'the icon', more even than 'the sign' figures vividly, even if only
momentarily, what should by definition always remain at the threshold of
figuration and, as is essential in dance, only make available to the other's
perception its force of becoming: namely, the point of an extreme tension at
the heart of the reciprocal transformation of both perception and the material. Of course, in order to retain its value, this moment must divest itself of
any notion of a founding and continuous operation reminiscent of work
not as a process of symbolic production but of capitalisation. *The introduction of work into the world substituted for intimacy and for deep and unchained
desire a rational sequence where the truth of the present moment no longer exists...*[19]

Bataille's vision which is linked to a critique of Western capitalism, resonates curiously for us with the whole early 20th century rebellion by the
pioneers of the *Frei Tanz* and their therapist friends against industrial society and the servility it imposed upon the body and its impulses. This

servility serves the 'higher result' which makes of the 'instant' a moment amongst others in the chain of movement. To revalue the instant because, there, one can escape operational constructions is clearly to return to time the indeterminate flux that certain dancers place at the centre of their artistic quest: Merce Cunningham, for example, for whom the instant is the unique form of a pure 'accident', outside of any determination; Odile Duboc, a poetess of the fleeting, who captures corporeal moments bursting free of all bonds. And while lauding her poetic orientation towards the instantaneous, we can also commend its political dimension as a resistance to the economy of the arrested image, itself generating the 'ulterior' of symbolic accumulation. But in order to manifest itself, the 'accursed share' in the case of these artists does not need to exalt the ephemeral as such. When in their art they 'capture' an accident or contingency which irregularises the sequence of things (or their simultaneity) and uncovers the unforseeable, they do not really need this crutch to compensate for the menace of a frozen instant. Often those artists whose art creates inert eternities, is centred on a 'nuclear' image, and generates a grandiose aesthetics of fixed and petrified forms, themselves, appeal to the ephemeral.

Knowledge of the works, journey through the non-verbal library

Observing works at the moment of their creation, but also maintaining the permanence of the work in the corpus of dance knowledge are both essential. You cannot have one without the other. The American-style dance concert, which restages an artist's older works alongside recent ones serves to contextualise the work in terms of a choreographic language that is evolving and forming itself into a philosophy of the body. Analysis of its components, understanding the evolutions it is undergoing, become the measure by which a new departure or a continuity can be gauged. Works cannot establish their position, much less innovate, except insofar as artists are permeable to a context and can identify a terrain and have at their disposal an observable and analysable material. A work only exists by the tear or spacing it creates in the fabric of a context – which is the way that Bartenieff understands movement itself. To void the context is to take away the very possibility of this aesthetics of spacing (*écart*) and thus to render a proposition banal or to over evaluate it (which is the same thing) by reducing it to a purely contingent initiative instead of inscribing it in a process of work (*travail*); and to see contemporary dance production endlessly identified only in terms of its stereotyped difference from ballet instead of in terms of how different contemporary schools themselves diverge or converge. Besides, the preservation of work responds to a relatively recent desire – at least one that has been articulated as such. We are indebted to Laban for the idea of founding a non-verbal library for dancers' use. This would be an immense intertext bringing choreographic works together in a network of approaches and multiple perspectives, like a storehouse where one would be able to decipher, not the resources or well-springs of the art which, as we have seen function elsewhere, but its end points. That the preservation of works, beyond the need to maintain a repertoire (a reductive term which is tainted by corporatism), might sustain an infinite dialogue between co-presences, between the stages of the body's work and also of its dreams, such are the stakes and such is for us the poetics of what could be called a 'works' memory' (*une mémoire des oeuvres*) preserving, especially, body languages and states in order, more than to perpetuate them, to know and analyse them.

The work (*l'oeuvre*), of course, constitutes a primordial pole like a collection of facts, or the elaboration of a 'system' where the articulations of an artistic project, an imaginary and a body poetics can be read more clearly and in a more structured form (in its different combinations). As Forestine Paulay notes, it is from the work and from the treatment in the work of the four (effort) factors and its different 'drives' that the dominant characteristic (tendencies or preferences according to the Laban categories of 'style') of a language emerge; and they continue to be repeated in privileged combinations – repeated, maintained, etc. (remembering that these categories have to do with qualitative material).[20] Obviously, Paulay knows only too well that, strictly, a work's actual authenticity cannot be looked for in this kind of exploration: the material is never brut nor originary. What is in play will always be the sum of the 'preferences' of the performer as the corporal 'reader' of the 'preferences' of the choreographer. For the performer, as 'medium' in all senses of the word, is as much part of the work as the rather fantasmatic concept of a 'pure' originary plan that can be disfigured, or contaminated by an interpretation. This is why the work must be the object of a filtered reading that superimposes several types of documents (live performance, notation, etc.). With the aid of such multiple methods the choreographic work can transcend the risk of its impoverishment and, thus, especially in the most inspired periods, escape (by finding indirect or roundabout ways) systems seeking to homogenise the work according to the models of cultural distribution. All the means evoked will permit movement to come closer to the coherence and visibility of a finished work. In finished works we include of course pieces whose quality of being unfinished constitutes one of the founding givens, as 'works in progress' or

performances. The work is that which mixes all these instances in one precipitation bearing a unique 'sense' and necessity, because it alone summons
up the mark of the creator in manifesting at all its levels the permanence of
or the changes in a signature (from the bodily signature of Laban to its
expansion in a construction which, in the best case, carries to the end the
marks of that signature). That is why, initially, it has seemed necessary to
look for where and how the identity of the choreographic work reveals
itself.

But why seek to define the identity of the work by relying on, if not
processes of conservation, at least on the problematics that these generate?
It is because the relations between dance and its conservation are reciprocal. On one hand, the corporeal contents of a work, its constituents, its
aesthetic and philosophical investments will determine in varied fashion
the paths along which it can be remembered. And on another, as we have
seen, the modes of recording are themselves effective in defining the work,
whether by revealing in the notation or through the transmissions that
occur within companies, the danced movement – transmissions not only of
movement but of a mode of performance to which a number of objects or
mechanisms external to the body are linked. The transmissions/transitions
governing the nature of the work and its 'projection', its substance and
trace, take us quite naturally back to Goodman's categories: an autographic
work is inseparable from the mechanism which gives it permanent
materiality, the allographic is a work whose existence depends on a system
of notation and whose materialisation requires the intervention of performers or 'interpreters' who will give it body, space, sound or voice. The
contemporary choreographic work, however, which is undeniably de-
scended from the *Gesamtkunstwerk* and from all dreams of a synthetic work,
is half-way between these two forms. On the one hand, the pivotal importance of the danced movement which constitutes its absolute foundation
refers contemporary dance inevitably back to Goodman's allographic text.
On the other, its visual aspect, even though 'intermittent', is given in an
ensemble of parameters too complete not to be likened to an art object, one
from which only a permanent 'showing' is lacking and going far beyond the
notion of 'spectacle' (both spectacle and performance) as an entity where
all of the elements (kinaesthetic, sonorous and visual) form an inseparable
unity. The work moves thus equivocally between the two extremities of this
chiasm. In most cases, the contemporary work is defined by the totality of
its musical, sonorous and visual elements. A Martha Graham work is inconceivable without the costumes, the scenic design, the music and of
course the original choreography. But the choreographic *écriture* is tangled

with the presence of objects, especially those of Noguchi which are integrated (pushed, pulled or resisted) with the dynamics and the meanings of
the movement. For Merce Cunningham it is important to insist on the different pictorial frames such as the lighting by famous collaborating artists
like Rauschenberg. And still more with Alwin Nikolais for whom the lighting is the spatial fabric which founds the piece, the 'track' like that of a
musical recording on which variations of intensity will engrave themselves
in realms where the choreographic *écriture* makes space and light move
(which is the case of the cloth in *Tent* and the ropes in *Tensile Involvement*).
Sometimes, the body is only the screen across which a projected choreography of a series of slides passes. There are pieces which, like *Somniloquy* and
Scenario with their events in light and colour, create a choreographic text
around as much as within the body. (We know the reason: choreography
for Nikolais is a metaphor of the world: man is not its central subject but a
dispersed one). The work, therefore, cannot but include the immense theatre of the world's operations with the visual or acoustic material, always
created by the master himself, an intimate part of it. A limit case is that of
Philippe Decouflé each of whose creations is an immense sculpture, whatever the nature of the event framing it (outside for the Olympic Games, or
on stage for this renowned, passionate creator who is baroque in his creation of a magical, illusionistic theatrical machine of platforms, ropes and
moving arches). It seems to us that a piece of Decouflé's is completely
'autographic,' that it is almost indistinguishable from its 'machinery'
(*dispositif*). The iterations of a performance several years after a work's creation are interesting when they bring to light the hinges and the outlines
that are indispensable to the ways in which the identity of a work is established and defined. In a recent revival of *Assaï* by the Carnets Bagouet we
could see how the strange lighting moving about the stage and auditorium,
the costumes of Dominique Fabrègues, and the scenic design of lateral rows
conceived by Bagouet himself, were essential and contributed to defining
the work. We could go even further: in a fragment of *Walkaround Time*
which was part of Cunningham's *Arles Event* in 1989, Jasper Johns's vinyl
cubes containing elements of Duchamp's *Large Glass* were carried on stage
for an extract of only several minutes. The idea is not, as Christian Boltanski
has rightly noted, to produce in the revival a 'facsimile' of the work which
would only restore an appearance, but on the contrary to search for what
Anne Abeille calls the path of the intention (*propos*): an eminently 'transcendent' notion, to use Genette's category, the score of an 'idea' which the
dancer embodies as much as does the dance's whole subject matter.[21] [22]

There are more complex approaches to a work. Elements can be suppressed or displaced. This has really nothing to do with an aesthetics of the 'remake' but rather of intentionally fragmenting, appropriating or deliberately cutting – an aesthetic of the '*pièce détachée*' which affirms and presents itself as such. (An inspired treatment of this concept can be found in Cunningham's Events with their random dismemberment of sections of works.) Dancers of the Quatuor Knust approach the works that they reconstruct using Laban cinetography by limiting themselves to considering only the 'text'. For certain works, for example of Doris Humphrey, they could (or should?) use the music (to which it is known Doris was very sensitive, including the music of silence) and the original costumes especially since they were designed by Pauline Lawrence, Humphrey's eminent collaborator and her close colleague from their youth. But in their desire to set aside anything that was not the pure reading of an inscribed text, the Knust have deliberately changed the costumes in favour of those by Sylvie Skinazi and music commissioned from Alain Bonardi. The identity of the choreographic text, too often occluded or lost in the course of history, thus appears more radically, is more exposed. This is legally possible in the case of Humphrey's work because the custodian of her work has the same openness and good humour as his mother. Of course we are dealing here with a deliberate plan where the Quatuor Knust want to devote themselves to a pure revelation of signs that no corporeal pre-requisite or imaginary frame would colour, still less determine. This treatment which is both radical and non-conformist is only possible insofar as an important theoretical reflection (particularly in France in the heritage of Labanotation) has more or less explicitly been undertaken with respect to the notion of 'the dance work'. In fact, if I have noted above the weight of what is recorded, it is not at all because it materialises and valorises as a 'sign' or 'monument' (the etymology of sign being the statue or 'signum' in Latin?) a poetic work which after all only requires its own rapture to exist. It is because the movement score, written or notated or not, is primordially that which makes a choreographic work. This score does not have a generalised or specialised archival place. Laban's non-verbal library is for the present an extremely rich library of all the movements in the world, but a largely imaginary one, containing here and there a few collections lost amongst the whirlwind of invisible but nonetheless existent scores. Gerard Genette has explained, drawing on the ideas of Goodman, that a score does not need to be a material one to make a work. It belongs in the domain of possible objects which only a performance or interpretation, will bring to life. This gives it not a fragility but, on the contrary, the inalterable nature of an ideal which no material deterioration can touch or destroy. To demonstrate the resistance of the scored to the ravages of time, Genette ironically recalls Leonardo da Vinci's rather unfortunate comments on the ephemeral character of music which dissolves in time in contrast to painting: *Poor music evaporates as soon as it is played: painting, fixed in time by the varnish, endures.*[23] The traditional power of varnish to conserve or fix is here rendered strangely uncertain by the poor state of da Vinci's celebrated *Last Supper*. While the musical score, even one from an earlier period and in a system of notation now obsolete, escapes the contingencies that might destroy it (if it weren't precisely for its only fault: the materiality of the document which is subject to the effects of use and time). For Umberto Eco, any art object, even when it has a concrete material unity, can only be a permanent imitation of itself because of the inevitable chemical or physical alterations that time brings with it.[24] We arrive at the threshold of a 'history' of autographic works which in its immanence can only be a long procession of 'remakes', shadows of original pieces, disfigured or recast by time. (It goes without saying that we ought not discredit the work itself but rather the discourse that founds its 'authenticity'.) The passage of time, a degrading, wearing out or amputation, does not constitute an aesthetic deficit for the viewer. On the contrary, unfinished, broken, dilapidated or simply old monuments arouse an inexpressible tenderness which restores to the work *as it is* an originary power. A poetic vision would consist in approaching them, not in terms of what René Passeron calls a 'global entity' but in terms of a concept tied firstly to man's work (*travail*) in his present experience.[25] This takes us back to the 'making' (*le faire*) which, even in the autographic work as a material entity, produces that scored dimension which for Genette represents, if not the nature of every work, at least the secret vocation which leads it towards its own transcendence. From the period of Dada to the present, by multiplying the interfaces between an intention and its realisation, experience and the object, contemporary art seems to respond to this call from the very heart of its own investigations.

Once more, dance constitutes a limit-point. It is the field of both the observation and the discovery of creative means, even if it has had to rethink all the vicissitudes of its own history in order to understand and thus divest itself of the judgments and valuations that have destined the symbolic productions of the body to oblivion. For, in its modernity, dance has taken the score further and has enlarged and diversified its possibilities. If a score, in the usual sense of a notation, fixes the contents, dimensions and boundaries of a work, a score as the plan for an open transcendence escapes both time and any territorialisation which would confine or reduce it: hence the scores that are designed/drawn or conceived as a set of conditions of possibility (the cube of Trisha Brown for *Locus* and the infinite exploitation that it enables as a set of directions). It is the same for improvisations with objects (enigmatic scores contained in the contours and imprints of matter, and which only the body can interpret because the object is a 'text' to be deciphered this side of any writing), the improvisation themes often proposed by Trisha Brown and, before her, by Simone Forti (they predated her structured improvisations). But it is also possible that, in a still more mysterious form, the score, by the intervention of the hand which draws it and becomes a hand-body, is only the intermediary between the world and the body, both writing and interpreting a form that it does not yet know. Regarding one of her pieces (*To be continued*, 1991) which involved an open, unfinished score, Simone Forti has written that, *working from objects, making drawing as a bridge to embodying. The eye moves, the hand moves. The body embodies, the hand moves and the body's embodiment shows in the drawn line.*[26] This exchange between body, drawing, and their 'projection' makes of the score a dynamic process joining several poles; and the inscription itself is the result of a continual adjustment between multiple layers of incarnation. Thus, there is not only one 'state' of the choreographic work as its final representational form, but there are all sorts of choreographic moments in its elaboration and rememoration, its intention, its momentary silence, its reprise. The notated score of a work already contains its own somatic resonance. In itself, Laban cinetography constitutes a text founded on the transfer of weight: its vicissitudes, instabilities, projections, and it both sets off and registers these shifts. It is a body text which describes in its most literal materiality the very texture of the act as a poetic project. What is there to say then of the second 'effort-shape' notation system elaborated by Laban at the end of his life, as a simple qualitative score where only the disposition of the subject and the ensemble of preferred qualities or 'colours' appear there before the mention of any form? These systematic notations (alert as they are to internal coherence) never deny, in the name of systematicity, the bodily charge to which they are witness. Even though they are articulated in a code, they do not stray far from the private choreographic drawings, those intimate scores where, in Forti's description, the choreographer her/himself creates the protocol which supports the relation between the body and its mark. Drawing, particularly with Brown, involves the whole body working to support the hand drawing with one stroke a line whose completion at the end of a great tangled trajectory is equivalent to the end of a phrase. The whole body is in the hand as the dance, with its phrasing, its accents, its distributions, its breath, is in the line. Even the art of drawing a self-portrait, according to the classical definition, encourages this kind of rapprochement between the body of the artist and her/his drawing. Derrida, too, describes a body already melting away from its own face as it traces itself upon the page.[27] In dance, the 'plan' even if only a sketch which may or may not have a material form, suspended in a sort of emotional margin to thought (what Susan Buirge calls the 'vague desire'), or inscribed in the line's reverie, moves between the sketch and its eventual later deposition in a sign. Between the two folds of this multiple temporality the danced work will develop, between its birth and its completion, an uninterrupted chain of intermediate stages. Mallarmé: *By an effective action, the stage illustrates only an idea...between desire and accomplishment, its perpetration and its memory...*'[28] But from one pole to another the body is always at work (*travail*) ('the work of dance'). The work's transcendence which is, as Genette notes, more on the side of making and acting than of being, gives to the choreographic work its true dimension: an opening to multiple imprints of which the body is less the reader than the agent, at once the author, performer and agent of revelation. A traveller on a line of flight which he/she never stops re-inventing.[29]

Sometimes in these half-deserted strata of 20th century history works lost their materiality but not their light. It is this light, a beam whose angle of incidence cuts across the dark edge of disappearance that Gerard Bohner sought to question in his work on the dances of the Bauhaus, including those of Oskar Schlemmer at Dessau. The solitary drift of a body which in its very movement poses questions without resolving them by a reconstruction, Bohner's dance opened a space inhabited by vanished movements. He set off in search of them through a body experience/experiment which questioned in turn planes, levels, and directions, as Schlemmer and his pupils would have done. This was a monochromatic space where the primary values of white and black alternated (*Schwarz, Weiss, Zeigen*, 1983). Schlemmer had left very precise details regarding the structure of his dances, the dancers' moves and a whole system of representations in remarkable and visually very beautiful diagrams.[30] It is from these instructions that American universities or art schools like the Academia der Kunst in Berlin have sought to reconstruct entire works, often with very interesting results. Bohner himself, as an astute dancer, has said that as soon as the dynamics and qualities of the movement phrases – the infamous question of how they are to be done – fails to be posed in any act of restitution, the essentials will be lacking. Especially where it concerns the transition between two discernible movements or the intermediary moment, that is, according to Laban, where the whole qualitative complexity of 'style' is revealed.[31] Bohner therefore chose to remain on a threshold of movement, sometimes remaining immobile as if he were waiting for a blind spot to be revealed to him, or making angular movements as though to clothe the space of this absence. Contact with objects, wooden shapes, and even a jointed mannequin evoking the anatomical models of the painting studio or the *Kunstfigur*, an inanimate dancer dear to Schlemmer, seemed to awaken latent memories in his body. Another German dancer, Susanne Linke, has made one of the most beautiful explorations of lost memory with *Affectos Humanos* (1988) in which she pays homage to a dancer she had seen while she was still an adolescent and who had inspired her to dance. This was Dore Hoyer, a student of Wigman and, in her vision and movement, one of the most radical dancers of the century, whose body could in turn shrink, expand, become planar or volumetric, be a trunk, a blade, a torch. Here, as is so often the case in dance, there is the search for a lost being (for a 'corporal signature' but also for an affective memory) as Hoyer, misunderstood by the German public, committed suicide at the beginning of the '70s. In '94 Linke again honoured her with *GB*, dedicated to her friend Bohner who had also died. The long trajectories of loss explored by Linke are inscribed in the same problematic on both sides of the Rhine but in completely different contexts. New teaching and a consciousness in younger dancers have lifted this strange prohibition on memory. Contemporary dance as an 'explosion' needed to define itself as a catastrophe without anteriority – and said so in its very aggravation of movements wholly identified with their own erupting. But even if this quality of instantaneousness remains in the movement, precisely in order to remain there without being reproduced in congealed forms, it is nevertheless indispensable that the dancing body stop denying its history. Indispensable that it be re-inscribed in history. Including its own history which, as we have seen in France, it has tried to evade as if this history were a mine-field of questions too risky to bear. We will retain, then, for memory, for the call to be co-present, the function of 'resourcing'; above all a critical function in which (historical) reference does not legitimate but on the contrary interrogates, destabilises and displaces. This is one of the aspects of the work of the Quatuor Knust in that, through the 'reprise' of small choreographic forms from the '20s, '30s or '60s, they lay forth the important choices of a modernity which they judge indispensable to revisit – and whose stakes merit ongoing consideration and circulation. Memory, then, whether or not it is supported by specific sources, far from being routine study in a course or the orderly administration of the heritage, becomes something defiant, a plan, a question asked of the bodies that have given birth to ruptures. Instead of dictating models, remembering helps us to go further. This implies that contemporary dance interrogates its memory within its own corpus. It is here that strong, necessary works share its urgencies and its questions. And the work is more profound and more artistic, too, when it begins by deciphering only half-discernible traces. Aside from the Quatuor Knust there is also the company, Icosaèdre whose name makes reference to the work and thought of Laban. With the project, *Instants d'Europe*, and using different media (films, recreations with the choreographers or their dancers, notations) this group revisits the works of Hanya Holm, Harald Kreutzberg and closer to home, Jacqueline Robinson, Karin Waehner and Dominique Dupuy.

In the margins of the non-verbal library there is a rich and fertile reservoir of tools for iconographic reproduction, especially tools which in their own kinetics can represent the flux of movement as it is experienced (and not only reproduce its image). But as soon as a 'combine' (namely, a choreographic composition), in other words a 'text' articulated on several levels, is involved, video and the cinema can no longer be trustees of the creative project. As in the case of compact discs the recording is, in the first instance, the sonorous or visual image of an interpretation. Goodman and Genette, those keen observers of the status and functions of the work of art, speak of the reproduction of a 'performance' as that which is 'unique and unrepeatable'.[32] A video-recording contains the essence of a work no more than a disc contains that of a musical score. They are the reflection (in other respects inestimable) of a 'moment' of the work to which a performance corresponds. However, both are indispensable when it comes to the public coming to know a work of the allographic type because, as far as a score is concerned, this public would not know how to give it body or perform it in their minds. I am speaking here of course of video used as a documentary tool and not as an autonomous work in itself. A movement's icon, considered as a mode of representation and approached appropriately, can reveal untold riches, but it is still important not to look there for an illusory originary perfection, (always held dear in the world of dance) or a moment complete in itself which successive manifestations through time can only spoil. The value of the 'first act' as Trisha Brown conceives it is that it can escape from itself. It does not produce any image of itself: it is barely identifiable (except by the choreographer), and still less named. No iconographic process can capture it there where it slips from representation's grasp.

Earlier, I evoked the first photographic experiments and the work that was done to exhume the body's invisibility (*le non vu du corps*) from under the weight of the so-called 'naturalistic' representations of Western art; how these techniques focused on the phases between the more usually registered key shapes; and how, because of this, the perception of a movement dynamic could be valued instead of just its form. Again, in his discussion of Geneviève Stephenson's photos, Daniel Dobbels has been able to perceive there a continuity in the photographic act up to the present, *the black spot of this gaze won over the body and wrested – since when? – from the blind, deaf things that dance fears more than any violence.*[33] Doubtless, what is visible of dance is what eludes blindness, in the same way that its memory is wrested, more painfully than elsewhere, from the menace of forgetting; and the first wound in this memory occurs in the dancer's awareness of her/his own body so that s/he can better exorcise the power of what has been done before. However, technologies of reproduction, which have created singular paths towards the poetic and which have, themselves, their own kind of 'aura,' have been able to serve contemporary dance, doubling it with a significant imaginary corpus. But dance's accompanying image has also had its destructive effects. For example, excessive 'exposability'. In exposing and overexposing itself art can make a target, as well as an epiphany, of itself – even more when it is the body's appearing which is at stake. I am thinking of the dancer's leotard hanging at the edge of one of Jasper Johns's famous targets. This is not just a question of playing with mixed (media) codes. From the contours of whose body has this unwashed leotard been cast off? What is it the emblem of? The dancing body or its loss? Because they have been so badly and so over-used and because inflated images of dance have devalued its text and its reflection, technologies of reproduction used in dance, finding body states too difficult to articulate, have been somewhat discredited. Cinema, video and photography can destroy by oc-cluding the processes – by definition invisible – which have created the tensional values. Nevertheless when a true reflection does take place (some-thing which is happening now as numerous choreographers and dancers are deciding to take their own knowledge and resources in hand) a real importance will be given to photographic iconography, and its identity will be better defined. Especially its immense poetic power as a thesaurus of the imagination. Because it has been used in dance stu-dios since the seventies, imaging technology has gradually become part of processes through which choreography itself is lost, or if not lost, is at least shaken. Its aura or absence of aura has shared the same history's afflictions (choreography having long been considered simply the means of organising a spectacle); over-exposure and the impoverishment of matter have been intertwined risks for imaging technologies. Until the joint discov-ery by Nam June Paik and Merce Cunningham that this dissipation of matter in favour of appearance and its over-valuation was precisely the knot that tied the art of video to dance: the dislocation of criteria of the visible, interrogating the body's presence always at the edge of its own disappearance in blurred zones of movement. In their work, video became the memory of a still possible dissolution of the screen as a surface of absorption, as a field upon which the dancing body and its shadows faced one another.

The work and (is?) the performative act

The performance ('spectacle'): the moment when the work of dance takes on a public dimension, when a 'work' or at least an artistic proposition encounters not only the gaze of the other (that can happen at other moments) but the moment when the dancer, in a singular and concerted fashion, creates the conditions of this encounter.

In addition, the choreographic work possesses an element that determines the very definition of dance as an art: the actualisation of a unique body-experience, the materialisation of time and space in relation to a witness-perception, and the body to body relationship instituted in a shared duration. This actualisation is not simply circumstantial with respect to the work: it partly defines it, even if it provokes a rupture in the continuum of the experience of the work, for it brings forth a whole other state of the 'choreographic material.' The score (*l'état partionnel*) itself contains in suspension the whole poetics of the performative act. Any dance can be viewed in terms of the title of Erick Hawkins's famous work *Here and now with watchers* (1957). Much more than does this concept, Hawkins developed the transparency of 'being there' which the simplicity and ease of a 'release' uncoloured by superfluous messages can give the dancer. Thanks to such processes, the performative can (finally) become what it is: a mass (bloc) of sensations, to use the Deleuzian definition of the 'percept,' shared between the actors and witnesses (actor-witnesses) of an experience. It is in this quasi cataclysmic precipitation of corporeal experience that intersecting presences (the dancers amongst them) can 'discover' the state of a choreographic work. In the mobilisation of the whole being and the whole company through the force of their wonder, presence and multiplied intensity, there lives a unique, supreme and feverish moment of creation; and the dancer has a particularly important role in this irreproducible act which is textured with all the dynamic variations of the moment and the pregnant look of the other. Something essential crystallises or is deposited. One could say, then, that amongst all of the states and stages of the work of dance, the presentation of the work (*l'oeuvre*) can be distinguished essentially as the 'maximum of tension'. If performance is privileged this is because as the

work's 'showing' it provokes in the body of dancer and spectator that intensity of mobilisation and perceptive activity which constitutes the excess of
the performative.

We must now revisit the notion of 'performance' (spectacle) in order to
wrest it from the reductive frameworks which make it, not the temporal
experience/experiment of an open gaze but simply a category of ordinary
culture. Two experiences intersect on the occasion of a performance (spectacle): that which Genette and Goodman qualify as 'performance' or as
'event'; and the experience of the spectator who is drawn into close 'liaison'
with a ritual of becoming. Susan Buirge speaks of the performative state as
a fault line (*faille*): it is this fault line that gives the work (more importantly
than its essence) its existence.[34] The force of this notion of fault line doubtless lies in the fact that the explosive state of what is mobilised in
performance is not lived as a 'positivity', as an accumulation of intensities
but, on the contrary, as the always uncertain edge of risk, or a throwing
into question. And, especially, because finally the moment of performance
'cuts' from the poetic continuum of dance activities an irremediable slice of
visibility – the seductive moment when everything stops in a finished
proposition. This is a decisive moment not only because the other's judgement is called up (and we know how powerfully critical evaluation mediates
and authorises, for its own survival, a choreographic project). But because
in contemporary dance even if, as is often the case, it has been prepared for
with the greatest care, this moment is always a visible cataclysm fallen from
an unsatisfied desire, an incomplete journey, an unfinished project which is
still being born. The brutal turn from studio rehearsals to performance involves something which is at once intoxicating and deadly. In their very
matter/material, most choreographic works carry the stigmata of these
rapid turnarounds. The risk is always to affirm too much, to frame or define
the choices too much. In a dance performance it is necessary to 'give' enor-
mously but this can also go with holding back. In the French school, a
permanent shift to a minor mode is to be admired. It avoids not the gift of
the self (which only remains more generous and real), but (over)emphasis,
and overstatement of intention (*propos*), maintaining not only a presence
and investment in the experience of the unfolding present, but giving equal
weight to 'not doing', to the empty or uncertain spaces of a moment of
suspension that is not there just to be filled up.

The intense sensations, an untoward sharing of relations, and the diffuse
feedback from the presence of the spectator in Buirge's 'fault line' conspire
to uncover the essence, contours and nature (even if it remains enigmatic)
of the poetic charge proper. It is also the moment when a general mobilisa-

tion of the choreographic actors reinforce one another and make this feverish moment of performance a unique and irreversible experience. It is also
the moment when the choreographic community feels itself most clearly.
The multiple person who gives birth to the work (in the case of a group
work) through diverse bodies is the most aware of this ensemble being. It is
even this ensemble being which is deposited like the intense charge of a
poetic desire overflowing individual awareness (even while giving back
more strongly to it its own intentions.) This comes, no doubt, from a kind of
rapture in making/transforming but also from a sharpened awareness of
participating in this making. Nor is the dance spectator so far from this
making, but is in 'liaison' (Barthes), not with what is shown, but with what
is at work, what grapples with the limits of the visible, what of body and
thought is being brought from the banks of the invisible, what is lost, con-
quered, questioned, and finally responds across the black hole of the
invisible public behind the footlights. This is much more difficult to manage
than the will to seduce or to take too great a hold on the spectator's perception thus weakening the play of sensuous experience that contemporary
dance seeks particularly to share. And it is probably out of this actualisation as event, to use a concept of Cunningham's, that in the spectator's as
much as the dancer's perception it fractures that limit of the known which
for Susan Buirge, again, is simply the threshold of her journey.[35]

The force and potential of the performative experience/experiment of
which the spectator is the privileged witness (and, because of this, participant in the creation of a relational texture) mean that for the dancer, this
experience sums up the work. It is at once its manifestation and substance.
Amongst certain French choreographers, it is the actual performance of a
work which generates its text and identity: in this case, the work depends
entirely on a sort of founding ritual of fulfilment which releases it into the
corpus of works as a scorching, chaotic theatrical experience (Fin de partie,
La maison de carton by Francois Verret; Instances by Diverrès-Montet, Les
porteuses de mauvaises nouvelles by Vandekeybus...). Once their first performances are over, some of these works can only be redone with great difficulty.
Even if an eventual reprise involving other performers puts into circulation
the concrete existence of an allographic text, for the dancer it is the performative act of creation, the work invested therein and its incarnation as a
performance that alone remains the guardian of its identity – and consequently of its memory. Each repetition will be for her/him a loss, a faded
clone in which s/he will no longer recognise either the marks or the effervescence of her/his experience. For the dancer, the work is not born at the
origin of a foundational 'text' but in the lived experience that makes the

text. Conversations with dancers from different periods and schools (Limón, Cunningham, etc.) have always given us the most evocative testimonies. These, too, can help us reflect on the essence of a choreographic work: not as a concept to elucidate but as a situation whose extreme complexity we must continually assess, a complexity which cannot be grasped but must be relived over and over at all of its levels and stages. This makes even more important the gesture of the Carnets Bagouet who give, along with the choreography of a work, their own experience as 'text', offering as one offers a slice of life this 'experience-as-text' to younger dancers or to outsiders.

Dance as an intertext

We owe to Mark Franko, perhaps more than anyone else, the idea which he has applied so effectively of a dance intertext. Inspired by a whole critical current represented by Roland Barthes, he has brought together all of the surviving landmarks that illuminate our historical knowledge of choreography into one corpus. And, more particularly, since this dancer is also an historian of *la danse ancienne*, his study of Renaissance dance, for example, passes through an 'inter-corps' which is evident in both his direct and indirect sources: in treatises on dance, descriptive literature, or even contextual elements brought together non-hierarchically and implying bodily experience.[36] This methodology in assembling the objects for consideration is completely consistent with the continuum of practices and knowledges in dance: before creation, during creation, in the aftermath of creation – all these phases share the same thread linking the layers of heterogenous experiences and all share an equal importance with regard to the poetics of movement. In a diffuse way, the intertext or inter-corps of dance thus takes on a poetic aspect that is often superior to that of the work itself as an isolated entity. Concerning contemporary dance, it is important to invoke recent artistic practices where often, as in the case of Beuys, for example, ongoing public and private activities take the place of producing an object or finished entity. It is here that contemporary dance as a 'continuum' (which the work manifests but neither resolves nor consumes) corresponds to an extremely important form of 20th-century art in which visible activities and their identification matter less than the (sometimes mediated) activity itself (from body art to the circulation of representative activities as in the work of Pierre Huyghe, for example). It is important to stress, further, that such activities, even when only framed temporarily for public visibility, are circumscribed by the time of their showing and do not exist outside these protocols of completion, whereas the dancer lives in the permanent continuum of her/his experiences, whether or not they produce acts that can be clearly identified (but this too should raise questions) as 'creative'. In fact the 'production' of the dancer is the limit case of the productive activity of the artist since her/his acts operate within the frame of experience and only emerge intermittently into a choreographic material identified as such.

Even if it has been necessary for strategic and auto-defensive reasons (and in order to know the dancer as an artist) to re-value in dance the concept of the work, it is time today to distance ourselves from a too focused vision and return to the intertextual margins. For among the elements that comprise the whole activity of the dancer, the choreographic work is only one part. Of course, the latter is evidence of the work of the body and movement, but only along with other materials which together constitute the different sites of what we call 'the work of dance' and which we have tried to evoke in all of the complex processes of making: a work that is at once corporal, theoretical, philosophical, ceaselessly transforming perception. This work is, above all, a long term project. A large part of it will not leave the dance studio: there, what will never appear in a public event lives and is pursued through creating, hesitating, rejecting. Out of this endures, much more than as a backcloth, a living poetic texture. In fact, 'the work of dance' never stops weaving an interface between continuous, intimate activities which belong to the 'practice of the self' (even if this self is multiplied in a group work) and the work of art as an isolatable, artistic element identifiable by the broader cultural collectivity. As with literary or other artistic activity, the work of dance doesn't appear in fixed blocks even if the situation of performance has inserted its grand moments, like a sudden hallucination, into the continuum of practices and the body's awareness. Writing, says Deleuze *is always a matter of becoming, always unfinished, always in the process of making oneself and overreaching any visible or lived matter.*[37] This continuum between an ongoing experience of the body giving meaning and stability to a life project, and different manifestations of the work of art is essential to life in dance. Advances (or losses which are just as important) and new knowledge of the body through techniques, group or individual research like that of Martha Graham at the beginning of her career, or of Merce Cunningham at Black Mountain College during the summer which gave birth to *Untitled Solo*, are moments of extreme importance even if no act of representation seals them in a visible way. One of the major concerns of the Judson Church and the Grand Union was to retain the openness of moments, not giving them a precise performative identity, but where the experience of the studio is prolonged and makes the work in its turn: thus Yvonne Rainer included in her work *Continuous Project Altered Daily* (1972) moments of rehearsal where the dancers were still in the process of producing and memorising movement material.

Generally speaking, even outside of the major periods of questioning, one of the great preoccupations of contemporary dance is to maintain on stage the value of an experience/experiment in process – an experience which of course concerns the spectator as much as the performer – without which the dance is lost. But what is most enigmatic is always to be found in the interstice (barely) separating the luminosity of a composition workshop or even of a 'course' and what, in being crystallised out of the gamut of choices in so-called moments of creation, stops or blocks the process. We are familiar, for example, with the miraculous studio events that an artist tries for better or worse to work into the performance; or how can the artistic hierarchy between an improvised moment between dancers, and a performance-spectacle be decided? In which of these two moments is the corporal charge or poetic intensity more alive? The work, says Barthes is a fragment of matter (*substance*).[38] In contemporary dance, the birth of its substance, its life, its evolution only inform the work at certain moments which the performance ritualises but whose plan it never completely fulfills still less does it appease the desire to pursue a journey that the actualisation of the work renders more burningly insistent. And it is the same for the corpus of works: what gamut of intensities play amongst the variations of the contemporary body? At what moment will a facet catch the light and make it shimmer even more? For the intertext of dance is prismatic, and any fixed or convergent vision must, at any moment, be re-oriented towards another threshold of appearance. Dance is woven out of its own multiple nature: each flash represents a singular quest and, as such, needs to be witnessed from out of the experiences it causes in an observer's corporal perception. All the movements engaged in the weft of an unknown must be perceived and ceaselessly deciphered, and this very deciphering must lead elsewhere, towards other enigmas. Hence, the need to see many performances whether or not they are classified as major works by the media (as, superficially, they may sometimes be). I am certainly not suggesting we should abandon strong, serious criteria of artistic judgement which allow us to distinguish an academic or derivative proposition from a real contribution to the symbolic becoming of the body. But I want to de-hierarchise the event by which the creative act is manifested and return to it its force beyond established classifications; and, as far as possible, to stir up the transitional zones of awareness where the choreographic work, its 'becoming' between the body of the dancer and that of the spectator can become an experience and not always an object. This is a work in common in which, in an encounter with action, and as a web of subtle relations, the 'choreographic material' is created.

Is this performative act which is so alive and pulsating in its 'eventful becoming,' then, the whole of the work? I do not believe so. The choreographic work is above all a poem of existence. It exists nowhere and everywhere. The 'stages' (*scènes*) of dance are states and phases and all their intermediate layers. And the mystery of the danced event is that one does not know what moment of completion or non-completion the moment of the performance actually represents. This has nothing to do with the material quality of the staging (*mis en oeuvre*) which is usually exemplary in performances of contemporary dance. Everyone knows that the work of the group will, if allowed, go on beyond the limits imposed by the performance actualisation of the act which it supports. In fact, it is not dance which is ephemeral, it is the spectator who traverses with her/his own body and history the space of an evening. It is up to her/him to hear the rustle of an ongoing effervescence of body and spirit which an experience of the work will have enabled her/him to share. The important thing concerning a work is to perceive how perception can follow a body project from one of its 'organisations' to another. And whether or not this project can give meaning to a trajectory of which the work must remain as a sign along a poetico-corporeal path.

This other distribution of events in dance also requires another type of memory which would, itself, overwhelm any recording, would be the memory of a becoming, a continuum of corporal practice inventing itself at each moment in the presence of the present – that which links bodies to one another across the convulsions of history. This memory would be capillary: a sequential touching not distributed so much in space as in time. It would be a memory that reactivated movements and beings, a sharing of body experience beyond death, all the deeper for being able to move between this life and the beyond. Dance deals with this very circulation. Every movement is a body memory and passes through two complementary forms: what is inscribed and what opens onto the unknown of a moment of experience/experiment. *As with breathing*, says Merce Cunningham, the dancer's awareness moves continuously between the diaphragmatic phases of time, caught up in the reversible exchange between the dimension of the past and that of the future *daily renewing old experiences and searching for new ones. Each new movement experience, engendered by a previous one, or an initial impress of the action of the body upon time, must be discovered, felt and made meaningful to its fullest in order to enrich the dance memory.*[39] This dance memory gives the lie to or transfigures our Occidental vision of linear time. Distanced from a causalist vision by the double influence of a post-dadaist philosophy of the accidental and the zen idea of an indeterminate time ('impermanent' as he calls it using terminology of the I-Ching), Cunningham is better able than anyone to guide us towards this future memory. Eliot Kaplan's film *Changing Steps*, based on a choreography from 1973, admirably emblematises this option. After a series of images linked to an heraclitean vision of time experienced as the continuousness-discontinuousness of fleeting sensations (flowers opening, the babbling of water, moving shadows on sunlit pavement), the film presents the work in its non-chronological choreographic unfolding. The first brightly coloured and technologically pure images shot in real time are traversed by ghostly fantasms which are the shreds of an old studio tape and the barely discernable shadows of dancers' silhouettes executing the same movements and haunting the recent images as if, before existing, they had already engendered their own ruins. In these images movement distends, slows, hesitates on the point of dilution, and the bright and implacably regular lights of the recent version give way to a monochrome half-light that comes from some other or beyond of time. Daniel Charles has written in relation to John Cage of *a suspended time out of which the three dimensions of past, present and future are manifest equally, without one stepping on the other.*[40] Hence, the mesostiche used by Cage in a 'transversal' reading of *Finnegan's Wake* using spatialised acrostiches (*use of a vertical word, supression and contraction of syllables and letters*) indicates the possible migration of elements reversibly in all directions across a non-linear textuality. This nomadic textuality founds incalculable temporalities within his own field as in Cunningham's. Memory and, in a singular way, dance memory is turned around. The movement in effect develops its sparse shreds of time where the traditional relation of the memorable (the past returning in the present) dissolves. Then another thought of history is born: particularly a history of the body. Body states can intersect and traverse zones of ellipsis and dilatation. This history can be packaged or fixed (in the over-exposed stratification of spectacle, here, sometimes menacing in its excessively static light). But at each instant of such a history the 'labour of dance' can reinvent, much more than forms, the processes of departure or exception in contemporary dance – what Foucault called the revealed or unveiled space (*espace mis à découvert*) in literary modernism (Kafka, Bataille, Blanchot) which *posited itself as experience of death, of unthinkable throught (and in its inaccessible presence), of repetition (of original innocence which is always there in the most intimate and most distant limit of language) as an experience of finitude.*[41] The innocence of the first act discussed by Trisha Brown is no longer of the order of a 'before' which would resonate in a 'now': it is, says the Derrida of 'La double séance' (and after Mallarmé), *to imitate nothing which in any way pre-existed its operation*.[42] Of the first act there is only the residual magnetism of the innocence that founded it. There is a long and laborious path to this innocence, and to the landscape (more than condition) of the possible birth of a movement. May this labour pass through the complex strategies (the protocols of certain techniques for analysing movement) the failures, dead-ends, the distorting images to be divested of, the interior mirrors to be confronted, without the specular *éclat* taking hold of a body state and enslaving it.

The tools are there. They must be worked with and visited in depth so that 'the dance work' can continue; so that, faithful to its heritage which is always to be rediscovered, other processes can emerge which will lead the dancer's body and the opening of perception that it proposes still further. For the dancing body, just like the body of the choreographic text, is what could be called the 'material'. Of this material, the whole modern dance heritage beginning with Laban gave us, not a definitive theory, but the luminous first fruits. The text of a work, as we have seen, is borne firstly in the body of the performer. If there is an authorial 'signature' this passes above all through a body signature which, by means of its own qualitative and preferential palette, not only reads but ceaselessly displaces the 'travelling focus' (according to Trisha Brown's expression – and she herself continues to pursue its unforseeable trajectory) which makes dance present. In the dancer's body, alone, can the work and the intertext, the movement material and its materiality as thought and intention approach each other. It is here that the very stuff (*pâte*) of the material is born. And in the same way that the whole theory of dance accumulated throughout the century opened perhaps only onto the hope of catching an unidentified 'grain' (which hides as much in our movements as in our words), isn't the work too only a trace? Elsewhere, between dancing bodies, between spectators' bodies and perceptions, a mysterious text is woven and never ceases to renew itself. And doubtless the thought of contemporary dance which is so sensitive and so poetically productive will no longer be satisfied with simply deciphering the beginnings.

I have invented nothing in these pages, have perhaps not even opened a new threshold of perception through which contemporary dance might discover its unknown faces. I have done nothing but collect and gather together the fragments of body experiences carried along by the flow of its extraordinary resources. In being set forth here, I hope they will not be taken as laying down a law or model, nor as creating the weight of an instituted heritage, something contemporary dance has never sought. I hope to have simply retraced, on the horizon of contemporary dance, that shadow-line which continually dissolves as it gives way to a dawn.

1 Blanchot, M. *The Book to Come*, 2003.
2 Barthes, Roland 'From work to text' in *Image Music Text*, 1977, p. 160.
3 Ibid. p. 162.
4 See Louppe's discussion of dance notation in 'Imperfections of Papers' in *Traces of Dance*, 1994, pp. 9-34. (Transl)
5 Bazin, Andre *Qu'est-ce que le cinéma?* 1956.
6 Rilke, R. 'The First Elegy' from *Duino Elegies*, 1967, pp.125–127.
7 Benjamin, W. 'The Work of Art in the Age of Mechanical Reproduction' in *Illuminations*, 1969.
8 Ibid., p.225.
9 Goodman, Nelson *Languages of Art: an approach to a theory of symbols*, 1969.
10 Genette, Gerard *L'oeuvre de l'art, immanence et transcendance*, 1995.
11 Laurenti, Jean-Noel 'Feuillet's thinking' in *Traces of Dance*, 1994.
12 Foucault, M. *The History of Sexuality. Part I.*,1990.
13 Harris-Warwick, R. & Marsh, C.G. *Musical Theatre at the Court of Louis XIV: Le Mariage de la Grosse Cathos*, 1994.
14 See Enriquez, Micheline 'The memory envelope and its holes'. Chapter Four of *Psychic Envelopes* edited by Didier Anzieu, 1990, pp.95-120. (Transl.)
15 de Certeau, M. *Histoire et Psychanalyse entre science et fiction*, 1987.
16 Gerz, Jochen *Sur l'art*, texts from 1969, 1994.
17 Dobbels, D. 'A la tombée du Jour'. Exhibition Catalogue: *Photographies de la Danse* by Geneviève Stephenson, 1995.
18 Bataille. *The Accursed Share*, 1988.
19 Ibid.
20 Paulay, Forestine, in Bartenieff et al. *Four Adaptations of Effort Theory*, 1972.
21 Boltanski, C. *Christian Boltanski à propos du 'Saut de l'Ange' de Dominique Bagouet*. Video directed by Charles Picq, in the Collection: Vidéothèque de la Maison de la Danse (Lyon), 1993
22 Abeille, A. *Planète Bagouet*. Video. Dir. Charles Picq, 1993.
23 Da Vinci, Leonardo. *Notebooks* cited by Gerard Genette in *L'oeuvre de l'art*, 1995.
24 Eco, Umberto. *The Limits of Interpretation*, 1990.
25 Passeron, René. *La naissance d'Icare, éléments d'une poétique générale*, 1996.
26 Forti, S. 'Thoughts on "To be continued"'. *Contact Quarterly*, Winter/Spring, 1994, pp.13-21.
27 *The movement with which a drawer tries desperately to capture himself is already, in the present, an act of memory.* In Derrida, J. *Mémoire d'aveugle*. Réunion des Musées Nationaux, 1990.
28 Mallarmé, S. 'Crayonné au théâtre' in *Oeuvres Complètes*, 1945.
29 Genette. *L'oeuvre d'art*, 1995.
30 Schlemmer. *Théâtre et Abstraction*, 1978.
31 Bohner, G. Conversation with the author. Lyon, 1986.
32 Genette. 1995.
33 Dobbels, D. *A la tombée du jour*, 1995.
34 Buirge, Susan. Colloquium : 'L'écriture chorégraphique'. Poitiers, 1992, (oral source).
35 Ibid.
36 Franko, Mark. The idea of an 'intertext' applied to choreographic objects is presented in the Introduction to *The Body in Renaissance Choreography*, 1987.
37 Deleuze, G. *Critique et clinique*, 1995.
38 Barthes, R. *The Rustle of Language*, 1986.

39 Cunningham, M. 'The function of a technique for dance' in *The Dance has Many Faces*, 1952.

40 John Cage cited by Daniel Charles in 'Poétique de la Simultanéité', 1987-88.

41 Foucault, M. *The Order of Things: An Archaeology of the Human Sciences*, 1973, pp.383-4.

42 Derrida, J. 'La double séance' in *Dissemination*, 1981.

Bibliography

Please note that where possible the English translations of French works are cited below and have been quoted in the body of the text.

Adolphe, J-M. 'La source et la destination. La danse en France, la mémoire, le mouvement et la perception.' *Ballett International*, January, 1991.

Adshead, Janet (ed.) *Dance Analysis: Theory and Practice*. London: Dance Books, 1988.

Adshead, J. and Layson, J. (eds.) *Dance History: An Introduction*. London: Routledge, 1984.

Agamben, Georgio 'Notes on Gesture' in *Theory out of bounds, volume 20. Means without ends: notes on Politics*, edited by S. Buckley, M. Hardt, B. Massumi. Minneapolis: University of Minnesota Press, 2000.

_____ *Le langage et la mort*. (Fr. translation) Paris: Christian Bourgois, 1990

Alexander, F. M. *The Use of the Self*. London: Methuen, 1931.

Andrews, Jerome 'Le rayonnement de l'instant' in *Marsyas*, no. 26, June 1993.

Angenot, Marc. 'Traités de l'éloquence du corps' in *Semiotica*, No. 8, 1973.

Anzieu, D. *The skin ego*. New Haven and London: Yale UP, 1989.

_____ *Le corps de l'oeuvre*. Paris: Gallimard, 1981.

Appia, Adolphe. *Oeuvres Complètes*, vol.III ('Les écrits dalcroziens'). Paris: L'Arche, 1990.

Arguel, M. (ed.) *Le corps enjeu*. Paris: PUF, 1991.

Aristotle. *Poetics*, translated and with an Introduction by G.F. Else. Ann Arbor: University of Michigan Press, 1967.

Armitage, Merle *Martha Graham*. Los Angeles: M. Armitage Publ., 1937.

Arnheim, R. *La pensée visuelle*. (Fr. translation) Paris: Flammarion, Nouvelle Bibliothèque Scientifique, 1976.

Artaud, A. *Oeuvres Complètes*. Paris: Gallimard, 1971.

Aslan, O. (ed.) *Le corps en jeu*. Paris: Editions du CRNS, 1992.

Atlani, Catherine. *Corps spirale, corps sonore*. Paris: Corps sonore, 1991.

Bachelard, G. *The Poetics of Space*. Boston: Beacon Press, 1964.

Bachelard, Gaston, *La dialectique de la durée*. PUF, collection. Quadrige.

Bainbridge-Cohen, Bonnie. *Sensing, Feeling and Action*. Northhampton, MA, Contact Editions, 1993.

Banes, Sally *Writing Dancing in the Age of Post-modernism*. Wesleyan UP, 1994.

_____ *Democracy's Body*. Ann Arbor: University of Michigan Press, 1983.

_____ *Terpsichore in Sneakers*. Boston: Houghton Mifflin, 1980.

Bartenieff, Irmgard & Lewis, Dori *Body Movement: coping with the environment*. New York: Gordon & Breach, 1980.

Bartenieff, I., Davis, M. et al *Four Adaptations of the Effort Theory*. New York: Dance Notation Bureau, 1972.

Barthes, R. *Writing degree zero*. New York: Hill & Wang, 1968.

_____ *Essais critiques*. Paris: Seuil, 1967.

_____ *The Rustle of Language*, translated by Richard Howard. New York: Hill & Wang, 1986.

_____ *Image, Music, Text*. Essays selected and translated by Stephen Heath. Fontana/Collins, 1977.

Bastin, Christine. *Mon Oeil*, No. 11, publication of the Compagnie Christine Bastin. Paris: Printemps, 1996.

Bataille, G. *The Accursed Share: an essay in general economy*. Translated by Robert Henley. New York: Zone Books, 1988.

_____ 'L'expérience intérieure' in *Oeuvres Complètes, vol. III*. Paris: Gallimard, 1976.

Baxandall, Michael *Patterns of Intention: On the Historical Explanation of Pictures*. New Haven: Yale UP, 1985.

_____ *L'oeil du Quattrocento*. Gallimard, 1973.

Bazin, André. *Qu'est-ce que le cinéma?* Paris: Cerf, 1956.

Benjamin, Walter 'The Work of Art in the Age of Mechanical Reproduction' in *Illuminations*. New York: Schocken Books, 1969.

_____ *Ecrits Francais*, edited by J.-M. Monnoyer. Paris: Gallimard, 1991.

Benveniste, E. 'The Notion of "Rhythm" in its Linguistic Expression'. *Problems in General Linguistics*. Florida: University of Miami Press, 1971, pp.281-288.

Bernard, Michel 'A propos de trois chiasmes sensoriels' in *Nouvelles de Danse*, no.18, 1993, pp.56-64.

_____ 'Esthétique et théâtralité du corps: interview with J.-M. Brohm' in *Corps Symbolique*. St Mande: Quel Corps?, 1989.

_____ *Le corps*. Paris: Editions Universitaires, 1978.

_____ *L'expressivité du corps, recherche sur les fondements de la théâtralité*. Paris: J-P. Elarge, 1976.

Blanchot, M. *The Book to Come*, translated by Charlotte Mandell. Stanford CA: University of California Press, 2003.

_____ *The Infinite Conversation*, translated by Susan Hanson. Minneapolis: University of Minnesota Press, 1993.

_____ *Le pas au-delà*. Paris: Gallimard, 1996.

Bremmer, Jan & Roodenburg, Hermann. (eds.) *A Cultural History of Gesture*. Ithaca: New York, Cornell Univ. Press, 1992.

Brook, P. *The Empty Space*. Harmondsworth: Penguin, 1972.

Brown, Carolyn. 'Carolyn Brown' in *Merce Cunningham*, edited by James Klosty. New York: Limelights, 1986.

_____ 'Time to walk in space' in *Dance Perspective*, no. 34, (special issue on Merce Cunningham), 1968.

Brown, Farber, Vaughan et al. 'Cunningham and his dancers' in *Merce*

Cunningham: Dancing in Space and Time, edited by Richard Kostelanetz. Chicago: a cappella books, 1992.

Brown, J.Morrison *The Vision of Modern Dance.* London: Dance Books, 1980.

Brunel, L. (ed.) *Trisha Brown.* Editions Bougé, 1986.

Buirge, S. 'La composition: long voyage vers l'inconnu' in *Marsyas,* no. 26, June 1993.

_____ 'Allers-retours' in *Cahiers du Renard,* no. 14, 1993.

_____ 'Conversation' (with Hanya Holm) in ibid.

Cage, J. 'Black Mountain's Untitled Event', interview with Michael Kirby. *Tulane Drama Review,* no. 21, 1966.

_____*Silence.* Cambridge MA: MIT Press, 1966.

Caplan, D. 'The Alexander Technique' in *Contact Quarterly,* no. 10, vol. 3, 1985.

Casini-Ropa, Eugenia. *La danza e l'agitprop.* Bologna : Il Mulino, 1981.

Certeau, M. de. *Histoire et psychanalyse: entre science et fiction.* Paris: Seuil, 1987.

_____ 'Histoire de Corps' in *Esprit,* no. 62, Winter 1992.

Charles, Daniel. 'Poétique de la Simultanéité', *Revue d'Esthétique,* Nos. 13-14-15 (Special John Cage), Paris, 1987-88.

Charlip, Remy. 'Composing by chance' *Merce Cunningham: Dancing in Space and Time.* Edited by Richard Kostelanetz. Chicago: a cappella books, 1992, pp. 40-43.

Chion, M. *Le son au cinéma.* Paris: Editions de l'Etoile, 1985.

Cohen, Selma-Jean. (ed.) *Modern Dance: Seven Statements of Belief.* New York: Dance Horizons, 1969.

_____ *Dance as a Theatre Art: Source Readings in Dance History from 1581 to the Present.* Dodd, Mead & Co., 1974.

_____ *Next Week Swan Lake.* Hanover and London: Wesleyan UP, 1982.

Copeland, R. 'Beyond Expressionism, Merce Cunningham's Critique of the Natural' in *Dance History: an Introduction,* edited by Janet Adshead et June Layson. London: Routledge, 1983.

Copeland, R. & Cohen, M. *What is Dance? Readings in Theory and Criticism.* Oxford UP, 1983.

Cosnier, J., Berendonnet, A., Orechionni, C. *Les voies du langage, communication verbale, gestuelle et animale.* (Preface by Didier Anzieu). Paris: Dunod, 1982.

Cunningham, M. 'A Collaborative Process between Music and Dance (1982)' and 'Space, Time and Dance' in *Merce Cunningham: Dancing in Space and Time,* Edited by Richard Kostelanetz. Chicago: a cappella books, 1992.

_____ *The Dancer and the Dance.* Interviews with J. Leschaeve. Paris: Belfond, 1980.

_____ 'An Impermanent Art' in *Esthetics Contemporary,* edited by Richard Kostelanetz. Buffalo, NY: Prometheus, 1978.

_____*Changes: notes on Choreography.* New York : Something Elses's Press, 1969.

_____ 'The Function of a Technique for Dance' in Walter Sorrell, *The Dance has Many Faces,* New York: Dance Horizons, 1952.

Damisch, Hubert. *Origine de la Perspective.* Flammarion, 1989.

Davis, M. *Toward Understanding the intrinsic in Body Movement.* New York: Arno Press, 1973.

de M'Uzan, Michel. *De l'art à la mort.* Paris: Payot, 1972.

De Spain, K. 'A Moving Decision: Notes on the improvising mind' in *Contact Quarterly,* vol.20, no.1, 1995.

De Spain, K. 'Creating chaos. Chaos Theory and Improvisational Dance' in *Contact Quarterly,* Winter-Spring, 1993, Vol. XVIII, No.1, pp21-27.

_____ 'More Thoughts on Science and the Improvising Mind' in *Contact Quarterly,* Winter-Spring, 1994.

Deleuze, Gilles   *Francis Bacon: The Logic of Sensation.* Translated by Daniel Smith. London & NY: Continuum, 2003.

_____ *Critique et clinique.* Paris: Minuit, 1995.

_____ *Difference and Repetition,* translated by Paul Patton. New York: Columbia UP, 1994.

_____ *The Fold: Leibnitz and the baroque,* translated by Tom Conley. London: Athlone, 1993.

_____ *The Time-Image.* Minneapolis: University of Minnesota Press, 1989.

_____ *The Movement-Image,* translated by Hugh Tomlinson and Barbara Habberjam. London: Athlone, 1986.

_____ *Nietzsche and Philosophy,* translated by Hugh Tomlinson. London: Athlone, 1983.

Deleuze, Gilles & Guattari, Felix *What is philosophy?,* translated by Hugh Tomlinson & Graham Burchell. New York: Columbia UP, 1994.

_____ Preface to Daney, S. *Ciné-journal.* Paris: Editions de l'Etoile, 1991.

_____ *Anti-Oedipus: Capitalism and Schizophrenia.* London: Athlone, 1984.

Dell, C. *A Primer for Movement Description (using Effort Shape and Supplementary Concepts).* New York: Dance Notation Bureau, 1970.

Denby, E. *Dancers, Buildings and People in the Street.* New York: Horizon Press, 1973

_____ *Writings on Dance.* New York: Dance Horizons, 1968.

Derrida, Jacques. *Memoirs of the Blind: The Self-Portrait and Other Ruins.* University of Chicago Press, 1993.

_____ *Margins of Philosophy,* translated by Alan Bass. Chicago: Chicago UP, 1982.

_____ *Dissemination,* translated by Barbara Hohnson. Chicago: University of Chicago Press, 1981

_____ *Writing and Difference,* translated by Alan Bass. Chicago: University of Chicago Press, 1978.

_____ *Of Grammatology*, translated by Gayatri Spivak. Baltimore: John Hopkins University Press, 1976.

Dobbels, Daniel 'Entretien avec Betty Jones and Fritz Ludin' in *Nouvelles de Danse*, special issue 'L'Héritage Humphrey Limon', July 1995.

_____ 'A la tombée du jour' in the catalogue for the exhibition of Geneviève Stephenson. AFAA, 1995

_____ 'Danse et arts plastiques au bord des épreuves' in *Io: Revue internationale de psychanalyse*, no.5, 1994.

_____'Présence de Robert Antelme' in *Lignes*, no. 21, Paris: Hazan, 1994.

_____ 'Le sous-sol' in *Le corps en jeu*. Paris: Publication of the CNRS, under the direction of Odette Aslan, 1992, pp. 205-207.

_____ *Martha Graham*. Arles: Coutaz, 1990.

_____'Le politique inaperçu' in *La danse au défi*, edited by Michèle Febvre. Montreal: Parachute, 1987

_____ 'La cloison' in *Théâtre Public*, No. 58/59, 1984.

Dominique, François. *Aseroë, figures de l'oubli*. Paris: POL, 1994.

Dowd, Irene. 'Ideokinesis: the nine lines of movement' in *Contact Quarterly*, Vol. 8, No. 2, 1983.

_____ *Taking Root to Fly: ten articles on functional anatomy*. I. Down publ., 1981. Re-ed., *Articles on Functional Anatomy*. Contact Editions, 1995.

Duboc, Odile. 'L'épreuve du temps'. *Les Cahiers du renard*, No 15, Autumn,1993.

Dubois, Kitsou. 'Pédagogie de la danse appliquée au personnel soignant, aux malades mentaux, aux astronautes' in *Marsyas* no. 18, June 1991, pp. 42-51.

Dufresne, M. *Phénoménologie de l'expérience esthétique*. Paris: PUF, 1953.

_____ *Esthétique et Philosophie*. Paris: Kincksieck, 1953.

Duncan, Isadora *The Art of the Dance*. New York: Theatre Arts, 1928.

Dupuy, Dominique 'Danser outre' in *Etats de corps, Io: international revue of psychoanalysis*, No.5, Levallois, 1994.

_____ 'L'alchimie du souffle' in *Marsyas*, No. 32, December 1994.

_____ 'Eloge du studio' in *Lettre d'Information de l'IMPC*, April, 1994.

_____ 'Le temps et l'instant' in *Marsyas*, No.28, December, 1993.

_____ 'La mesure des choses' in *Marsyas*, No. 26, Juin 1993, pp. 59-60.

_____ 'Le Maître et la Mémoire' in *Saisons de la danse*, No. 241, December 1992.

_____ 'Scènes d'une histoire dansée, ou les danses de la vie' in the Catalogue for the Wigman-Perrotet exhibition, Kunsthalle de Zurich-Musées de Marseille, 1991.

_____ 'Le corps émerveillée' in *Marsyas*, No. 16, December 1990, p.32.

_____ 'La danse contemporaine, hérésie et tradition, institution et marginalite' in *Marsyas*, No.15, September, 1990.

_____ 'Le corps émerveillée' in *Marsyas*, No. 16, December 1990.

_____ 'La danse du dedans' in *La danse, naissance d'un mouvement de pensée*, edited by L. Niklas. Paris : Armand Colin, 1989.

Dupuy, F. 'Pas de danse' in *Marsyas*, No. 18, Paris, IPMC, June 1991.

Durand, Gilbert. *Structure anthropologique de l'imaginaire*. Paris, Bordas, 1982, pp. 127-146.

Eco, Umberto. *The Limits of Interpretation*. Bloomington: Indian UP, 1990.

Ehrenzweig, A. *The Hidden Order of Art: a study in the psychology of artistic imagination*. Berkeley: University of California Press, 1967.

Enriquez, Micheline. 'The memory envelope and its holes'. Chapter Four of *Psychic Envelopes* edited by Didier Anzieu. London: Karnac Books, 1990.

Faure, E. *L'esprit des formes*. Paris: Gallimard, 1922, republished by Folio, 1991.

Febvre, Michèle *Danse Contemporaine et Théâtralité*. *La Librarie de la Danse* collection, Paris: Chiron, 1995.

_____ 'Les paradoxes de la Danse Théâtre' in *La Danse au Défi*. Montréal: Parachute, 1987.

Fedidà, P. *L'absence*. *Connaissance de l'inconscient* collection, Paris: Gallimard, 1978.

Feldenkrais, M. *Awareness through movement*. New York: Harper and Row, 1972.

Forti, Simone 'Thoughts on "To be continued"'. *Contact Quarterly*, Winter/Spring, 1994, pp. 13-21.

_____ *Handbook in Motion*. Halifax: Nova Scotia Press, 1966.

Fossen, M. (ed.) 'Valeska Gert' in *Empreintes* No. 5, March, 1983.

Foster, Susan Leigh *Corporealities: Dancing, Knowledge, Culture and Power*. London: Routledge, 1996.

_____ 'Textual Evidances' (sic) in *Bodies of the Text*, edited by Ellen Goellner and Jacqueline Shea Murphy. Rutgers University Press, 1995.

_____ *Reading Dancing: Bodies and Subjects in American Modern Dance*. University of California Press: Los Angeles, Berkeley, 1986.

Foucault, Michel *The History of Sexuality*. London: Penguin, 1990.

_____ *Discipline and Punish: the birth of the prison*. London: Allen Lane, 1977.

_____ *The Order of Things: An Archaeology of the Human Sciences*. New York: Vintage Books, 1973.

_____ *The Archaeology of Knowledge*, translated by Sheridan Smith. New York: Pantheon Books, 1972

Franko, Mark. *The Body in Renaissance Choreography*. Illinois University Press, 1987.

Fumaroli, Marc. *L'école de silence*. Paris: Flammarion, 1993.

Gagnebin, M. *L'irreprésentable*. Paris: PUF, 1984.

Gardner, Sally 'Hermeneutics and Dancing' in *Writings on Dance*, No.10, Autumn 1994, pp.37-39.

Garros, J. 'L'acte respiratoire est le chemin' in *Marsyas*, No.32, 1994.

Genette, Gerard *L'œuvre d'art, immanence et transcendance*. Paris : Seuil, 1995.

_____ *Esthétique et poétique* (Introduction), Paris, Seuil, 1992.

_____ *Nouveau discours du récit*. Paris: Seuil, 1983.

Gerard, Christine 'Enseigner l'improvisation et la composition'. Interview with Particia Kuypers in *Nouvelles de Danse*, No. 22, Winter 1995.

Gerz, Jochen. *Sur l'art*, texts from 1969. Collection: *Ecrits d'Artistes*, Paris: Ecole Supérieure des Beaux-Arts, 1994.

Ginot, Isabelle 'Fissures, petites fissures' in *La danse, naissance d'un mouvement de pensée*. Paris: Armand Colin, 1989, pp.152-3.

Giron, Sylvie, in *L'oeil dansant*, edited by Laurent Barré. Centre National Choréographique de Tours, 1995.

Gleizes & Metzinger. *Du Cubisme*. Paris: 1913, republished by Flammarion.

Godard, Hubert 'The Missing Gesture' in *Writings on Dance*, volume 15, 'The French Issue', 1995.

_____ 'Le geste inouï' in *Dansons*, January, 1993.

_____ 'Singular Moving Geographies: an interview with Hubert Godard' in *Writings on Dance*, 15, Winter 1996, pp.12-21. Originally published as 'Le déséquilibre fondateur' in *Artpress*, #Hors Serie, 'Les vingt ans d'Artpress', Autumn, 1992.

_____ 'A propos des théories d'analyse du mouvement' in *Marsyas*, No. 16, December, 1990, pp.19-23.

_____ 'Le souffle, le lien' in *Marsyas*, No.32, 1994

_____ 'La Peau et les Os', *Bulletin of the CNDC*, No. 4, July, 1989.

Goellner, E. & Shea Murphy, J. (eds.) *Bodies of the Text: Dance as Theory, Literature as Dance*. Berkeley: Rutgers University Press, 1995.

Goldberg, Marianne. 'Interview with Trisha Brown' in *The Drama Review*, Vol. 30, issue 1, 1986.

Goldberg, Rose Lee. *Performance, Live Art: 1909 to the Present*. New York: Harry N. Abrams, 1979.

Goodman, Nelson. *Languages of Art: an approach to a theory of symbols*. London: Oxford UP, 1969.

Gordon, D. 'It's about time' in *TDR*, 19, no. 1 (T-5), March, 1975.

Graham, M. *Martha Graham: her theory and training*, edited by Marianne Horosko. New York: a capella books, 1989.

_____ *The Notebooks of Martha Graham*. New York: Harcourt Brace Jovanovitch, 1973.

_____ 'A Dancer's World' in *Dance Observer*, no. 5, January, 1958.

_____ *Blood Memory: An Autobiography*. Pan Macmillan, 1992.

Greimas, A.J. (ed.) 'Langages et pratiques gestuelles' in *Langages*, Winter, 1968.

Hanna, Judith Lynne *Dance, Sex and Gender*. New York: Dance Horizons, 1990.

_____ *The Performance-Audience Connection*. Austin: University of Texas Press, 1983.

_____*To Dance is Human: A Theory of Non-Verbal Communication.* Austin: University of Texas Press, 1979.

Harris-Warwick, R. & Marsh, C.G. *Musical Theatre at the Court of Louis XIV: Le Mariage de la Grosse Cathos.* Cambridge: Cambridge UP, 1994.

Hawkins, E. *The Body is a Clear Place.* Dance Horizons, 1991.

Hay, D. *Tasting the Blaze.* Austin, Texas: Futura Press, 1985.

H'Doubler, M.N. *Dance.* Madison: University of Wisconsin Press, 1962.

Holm, Hanya. 'Hanya Speaks' in *The Vision of Modern Dance*, edited by Brown, Midlin, Woodford. London: Dance Books, 1998 (second edition), p.81.

Horosko, M. (ed.). *Martha Graham: the Evolution of her Dance Theory.* New York: a cappella books, 1982.

Horst, L. & Russell, C. *Modern Dance Forms in Relation to The Other Modern Arts.* Princeton: Dance Horizons, 1987.

Huelsenbeck, *Memories of a Dada Drummer.* New York: Viking Press, 1974.

Humphrey, Doris. *An Artist First,* with Selma Jeanne Cohen. Middletown: Wesleyan University Press, 1972.

_____ *The Art of Making Dances.* New York: Grove Press, 1959.

Hutchinson-Guest, Anne 'Nijinsky's Faune' in *Choreography and Dance*, Vol.1, part 3, 1991.

Huynh, Emmanuelle. 'Duo' in *Nouvelles de Danse*, no. 28, 1996.

_____ 'Anatomie d'Insurrection', Mémoire for the DEA de Philosophie. Université de Paris I (unpublished), 1991.

_____ 'Réflexions sur l'interprète' in *L'écriture du corps.* Lille: Le Marietta Secret, 1992.

Jakobson, R. 'Linguistics and Poetics' in *Style in Language* edited by T.A. Sebeok. Cambridge MA: The MIT Press, 1960.

Jaques-Dalcroze, Emile *La musique et nous.* Geneva: Slatkine, 1981

_____ *Le rythme, la musique et l'éducation.* Neufchatel : La Baconnière, 1984.

Johns, Jasper *Cage, Cunningham, Johns, Dancers in the Plane.* London: Thames and Hudson, 1990

Jowitt, Deborah *The Dance in Mind: Profiles and Reviews 1976-83.* Boston: David R. Godine Publ.,1985.

Jullien, François. *La Propension des Choses: pour une historie de l'efficacité en Chine.* Paris: Seuil, 1992.

Kandinsky, W. *Complete Writings on Art,* edited by Kenneth Lindsay and Peter Vergo. Boston: G.K. Hall, 1982.

Kaufmann, P. *L'expérience émotionnelle de l'espace.* Paris: Vrin, 1967.

Kestenberg, Judith 'The Role of Movement Patterns in Development. Part One: Rhythms of Movement', *New York Psychoanalytical Quarterly* No. 34, 1964, pp. 1-36.

Kirby, Michael 'La non-danse'. *Le corps en jeu.* Paris: éditions du CNRS, 1992, pp.209-217.

_____ 'The New Theatre, Performance Documentation', in *The Drama Review*, in T. 55, Sept. 1972, pp. 135-141.

Kleist, H. von. *Essai sur le Théâtre de Marionnettes.* (Fr. translation), la Traversière, 1961.

Klosty, James (ed.) *Merce Cunningham.* New York: Saturday Review Press and E.P. Dutton and Co., 1975.

Kostelanetz, R. (ed.) *Merce Cunningham: dancing in space and time.* New York: a capella books, 1989.

_____ *The New American Arts.* New York: Horizon Press, 1965.

Kraus, Rosalind 'Notes on the Index: Seventies Art in America' in *October*, Autumn 1976.

Kristeva, Julia *Revolution in Poetic Language.* Translated by Margaret Waller. New York: Columbia UP, 1984.

_____ *Polylogue.* Paris: Seuil, 1977.

_____ *Semeiotike, éléments de sémanalyse.* Collection *Tel Quel*, Paris: Seuil, 1966.

Laban, Rudolf *A Vision of dynamic space*, text and drawings edited by L. Ullmann and J. Hodgson. Surrey: Laban Art of Movement Centre, 1963.

_____ *A Life for Dance.* London: Macdonald and Evans, 1975.

_____ *The Mastery of Movement on the Stage.* MacDonald and Evans, 1971.

_____ *Rudolf Laban Speaks about Movement and Dance*, texts selected by L. Ullmann-Addelston. Surrey: Laban Art of Movement Centre, 1971.

_____ *Choreutics*, posthumous publication by Lisa Ullmann. London: MacDonald and Evans, 1966.

_____ *Principles of Dance and movement Notations.* London: MacDonald and Evans, 1956.

_____ *Effort* (with F.C. Lawrence). London, MacDonald and Evans, 1947.

_____ *Choreographie.* Iena: E. Diederichs V., 1926.

_____ *Die Welt der Tanzer, fünf Gedankenreigen.* Stuttgart: W.Seifert, 1920.

Lamb, Warren. *Posture and Gesture: an Introduction to the Study of Human Behaviour.* London: Duckworth & Co., 1965.

Lange, R. *The Nature of Dance.* London: MacDonald & Evans, 1975.

Langer, Susan. *Feeling and Form: a theory of art.* New York : Scribner, 1953.

Launay, Isabelle. 'Laban et l'expérience de danse' in *Revue d'Esthétique: 'Et la danse'*, Autumn 1992.

_____ 'La danse entre geste et mouvement' in *La danse, art du XXe siècle.* (Actes du colloque), Lausanne, Payot, 1990

Laurenti, Jean-Noel. 'Feuillet's thinking' in *Traces of Dance.* Paris: Editions Dis Voir, 1994.

Lawton, Marc 'Alwin Nikolais: le creuset' in *Nouvelles de Danse*, No. 22, 1995.

_____ 'Inventer la danse tout le temps' in *Marsyas*, No.26, June 1993.

Leroi-Gourhan, A. *Le geste et la parole.* Paris: Editions Albin Michel, 1964.

Leschaeve, J. *The dancer and the dance.* New York: M. Boyars, 1985.

Lewis, D. *The Illustrated Technique of José Limón.* New York: Harper and Row, 1989.

Livet, A. (ed.) *Contemporary Dance.* New York: Abbeville, 1978.

Lomax, Bartenieff & Paulay. 'Dance, Style, and Culture' in *Folk Song Style and Culture.* New York: AAS Publications, 1968.

Louis, M. *Inside Dance.* New York: St Martin's Press, 1981.

Louppe, Laurence 'Imperfections in the Paper' in *Traces of Dance.* Paris: Editions Dis Voir, 1994.

_____ 'Le danseur et le temps' in *L'art en scène/première*, Paris: Cie Larsen, 1994.

_____ *Hervé Robbe – Richard Deacon, voyage dans l'usine des corps.* Noisiel, La Ferme du Buisson: Collection De l'Ange, 1993.

_____ 'Piège pour un espoir', *Art Press*, No.163, April 1992.

_____ with Bourigault and Gelly. *Que dit le corps?* Alès: le Cratère Théâtre, 1995.

Maldiney, Henri *L'Art, l'éclair de l'être.* Paris: Comp'act, 1993.

_____ *Art et Existence.* Paris: Klincksieck, 1985.

_____ *Regard, espace, parole.* Lausanne: L'Age d'Homme, 1973.

Maletic, Vera. *Body Space Expression.* La Haye, Mouton de Gruyter, 1987.

_____ *On the aesthetic dimensions of the Dance, a Methodology for researching Dance style.* Ohio State University PhD. Unpublished. 1980.

Mallarmé, S. 'Crayonné au théâtre' in *Oeuvres Complètes.* Paris : Gallimard, collection La Pléiade, 1945.

Marey, E-J. *Le mouvement.* 1894, republished by Nimes: J. Chambon, 1994.

Martin, John. *The Modern Dance*, New York: A. S. Barnes, 1933.

Matisse, H. *Ecrits et propos sur l'art.* Paris: Hermann, 1972, p. 154.

Mauss, Marcel. *Sociology and Psychology: essays.* Translation of Mauss's *Sociologie et Anthropologie* by Ben Brewster. London and Boston: Routledge and Kegan Paul, 1979.

McDonagh, D. *The Rise and Fall and Rise of Modern Dance.* New York: Mentor Publishers, 1970.

McGehee, H. 'Helen McGehee' in *Martha Graham: The evolution of her dance theory and training*, edited by M. Horosko. New York: a cappella books, 1982.

Merleau-Ponty, M. *The Merleau-Ponty aesthetics reader: philosophy and painting.* G.A. Johnson (ed.) & M.B. Smith (Trans). Evanston:Northwestern UP, 1994, pp. 21-149.

_____ *Phenomenology of Perception*, Translated by Colin Smith. New York: Humanities Press, 1962.

Meschonnic, Henri. *Les états de la poétique.* Collection *Ecrits*, Paris, PUF, 1985.

_____ *Pour la poétique.*, Paris: Gallimard, 1970.

Metz, Christian. *Le signifiant imaginaire.* Paris: Christian Bourgois, 1984.

Monk, Meredith. 'Notes on the Voice' in Banes, S. *Terpsichore in Sneakers*. Boston: Houghton Mifflin, 1980, re-ed. Wesleyan UP, 1987.

Monsieur, J. (ed.) *Danser maintenant*. Bruxelles: CFC Editions, 1990.

Morris, Gay *Moving Words: Re-writing Dance*. London: Routledge, 1996.

Morris, R. 'Notes on Dance' in *Tulane Drama Review*, No.10, T-30, Winter, 1965.

Muller, H. *Mary Wigman: Leben und Werk der grossen Tanzerin*. Berlin: Quadriga-Verlag, 1986.

Nancy, J-L.*Le poids du corps*. Ecole des Beaux-Arts du Mans, 1995.

_____ *Corpus*. Paris: Métailié, 1989.

Nietzsche, F. *Thus Spake Zarathustra*. New York: Dutton, 1958.

_____ *The Birth of Tragedy: out of the spirit of music*. London: Penguin, 1993.

Nijinsky, W. *Cahiers*. Publ. intégrale. Arles: Actes Sud, 1992.

Niklas, L. (ed.) *La danse, naissance d'un mouvement de pensée*. Paris: Armand Colin, 1989.

Nikolais, Alwin 'No Man from Mars' in Selma Jeanne Cohen: *Modern Dance: Seven Statements of Belief*. Wesleyan UP, 1965.

_____ 'Nik, a documentary' in *Dance Perspective*, No.48, 1970.

Novack, Cynthia J. *Sharing the Dance: Contact Improvisation and American Culture*. Madison: University of Wisconsin Press, 1990.

Odom, Maggie. 'Mary Wigman: the early years, 1915-25'. *The Drama Review*, 24-IV, December 1980.

Passeron, René *La naissance d'Icare, éléments d'une poétique générale*. Paris: Delog, 1996.

Pavis, P. *Voix et images de la scène*. Villeneuve d'Ascq: Presses de l'Université Lille III, 1985.

Paxton, Steve 'Contact Improvisation' in *Dance as a Theatre Art* edited by Selma Jeanne Cohen. New York: Dodd-Mead, 1974.

_____ 'Improvisation is a word for something that can't keep a name', *Contact Quarterly*, Spring/Summer 1987, pp.15-19.

_____ 'The Grand Union Improvisational Dance' in *TDR*, T-55, Winter, 1972.

Perrottet, S. *Ein Bewegtes Leben*. Berne: Benteli Verlag, 1990.

Pidoux, J.Y. (ed.) *La danse: art du XXe siècle*. Lausanne : Payot, 1990.

Pleynet, M. *Les Etats-Unis de la peinture*. Collection *Fiction and Co*, Paris: Seuil, 1989.

Pomarès, Jean 'De la formation à la création' in *Positions*, notes published by the Direction Régionale des Affaires Culturelles, Provence Alpes Côte d'Azur, 1995.

Porte, Alain. *François Delsarte, une anthologie*. Paris : IPCM, 1992.

Pradier, Jean-Marie. 'Le théâtre des émotions' in *Evolutions Psychanalytiques*, No.7, 1990.

Preston-Dunlop, V. 'Laban, Schönberg, Kandinsky' in *Traces of Dance*. Paris: Editions Dis Voir, 1994.

_____ (selection, translation, annotation) *Shrifttanz*. London: Dance Books, 1989.

_____ (with Hodgson, J.) *Rudolf Laban: An Extraordinary Life*. London: Dance Books, 1998.

Rabant, Claude. *Inventer le réel, le déni entre perversion et psychose*. Paris: Denoël. Collection: *L'espace analytique*, 1992.

_____ *L'invention du réel*. Paris: Dunod, 1991.

Rainer, Yvonne 'Yvonne Rainer interviews Anna Halprin' in *Tulane Drama Review*, 10-2, Winter, 1965.

_____ *Work: 1961-72*. New York: Press of the Nova Scotia College of Art and Design & NYU Press, 1973.

Remy, Bernard 'Visions de danse' in *Nouvelles de Danse*, No. 26, Winter, 1996, pp. 18-25.

_____ 'Danse et Cinéma' in *Corps provisoire*. Paris: Armand Colin, 1992.

_____ In 'Adage'. *Biennale Nationale de Val-de-Marne*, No.1, 1985.

Rilke, R. 'The First Elegy' from *Duino Elegies* translated by J. Leishman and S. Spender. New York & London: Norton, 1967, pp.125–127.

Robinson, Jacqueline *L'aventure de la danse moderne en France, 1930-1970*. Paris: Bougé, 1990.

_____ *Eléments du langage chorégraphique*. Paris: Vigot, 1981.

Rouquet, Odile. *La tête aux pieds*, Paris: Recherche en Mouvement, 1991.

_____ *Les techniques d'analyse du mouvement et le danseur*. Paris: Editions de la Fédération française de la danse, 1985.

Ruiz, Raul *Poétique du Cinéma*. Paris: Dis Voir, 1994.

Ruyter, Nancy Lee Chalfa. 'American Longings: Genevieve Stebbins and Delsartean Performance' in *Corporealities* edited by Susan Leigh Foster. London: Routledge, 1996.

_____ *Reformers and Visionaries: the Americanization of the Art of Dance*. New York: Dance Horizons, 1978.

Scarpetta, Guy *L'impureté*. Paris: Grasset, 1985.

Schefer, Jean-Louis. *Sur un Fil de la Mémoire*. Cercle d'Etudes Philosophiques de l'Université de Strasbourg, 1991.

_____ 'Figures de mutants' in *Traffic*, No.1, 1989.

Scheflen, A. *Body Language and Social Order*. Englewood Cliffs: Prentice-Hall, 1972.

Serres, Michel, *Le contrat naturel*. Paris: Grasset, 1990

Sheyer, E. 'The Shapes of Space: the Art of Mary Wigman and Oskar Schlemmer' in *Dance Perspective*, No. 41, 1970.

Schlemmer, O. *Théâtre et Abstraction*, edited and translated by Eric Michaud. Lausanne: L'Age d'Homme, 1978.

Schlicher, S. 'The West German Dance Theatre' in *Choreography and Dance*, Vol.2, No.3, 1993.

Schulmann, Nathalie. 'Réflexion sur l'Histoire de la Danse', dossier pour l'UV Histoire de la Danse, Univ. Paris VIII, 1991-92 (unpublished).

Schwarz, Elizabeth *L'expressivité de la main en danse contemporaine*. Mémoire for the Diplôme d'Etat in Kinesiology, IFEDEM, 1994 (unpublished).

Sergeant-Wooster, A. 'Elaine Summers: Moving to Dance' in *The Drama Review*, No. 24, Dec. 1980.

Serres, Michel *Le contrat naturel*. Paris: Grasset, 1990

Shawn, Ted *Every Little Movement: a Book about Delsarte*. Pittsfield, Mass.: Eagle Printing, 1954, republished, New York: Dance Horizons, 1974.

Siegel, Marcia 'Visible Secrets' in *Moving Words* edited by Gay Morris. London: Routledge, 1996.

_____ *The Shapes of Change*. Boston: Houghton Mifflin, 1979.

_____ *Watching the Dance Go By*. Boston: Houghton Mifflin, 1977.

_____ *At The Vanishing Point*. New York: Saturday Review Press, 1972.

Sommer, S. R. 'Reflection on an afternoon' in *Choreography and Dance*, Vol. 1, part 3, special issue on Nijinsky's *Afternoon of a Faune*.

_____ 'Equipment dances: Trisha Brown' in *TDR*, T-55, September, 1972.

Sorell, Walter. *Dance in its Time*. New York: Dance Horizons, 1975.

_____ (ed.) *The Mary Wigman Book*. Middleton: Wesleyan UP, 1975.

_____ *The Dance Has Many Faces*. New York: World Publishing, 1951

Stebbins, Genevieve *Delsarte's System of Expression* (1885), republished by New York: Dance Horizons, 1977.

Steinman, L. *The Knowing Body: elements of contemporary performance and dance*. Boston: Shambhala, 1986.

Stodelle, E. *The Dance Technique of Doris Humphrey and its Creative Potential*. Princeton: Princeton Book Co., 1978.

Straus, E. *Du sens des Sens*. Bruxelles: le Moulin, 1981.

Sweigard, L. *Human Movement Potential. Its Ideokinetic Facilitation*. Lamban MD: University Press of America, 1968.

Taffanel, J. *L'atelier du Chorégraphe*. Unpublished Doctoral Thesis. Université de Paris VIII, 1994.

Terpis, M. *Tanz und Tanzer*. Zurich: Atlantis Verlag, 1946.

Terry, W. *Isadora Duncan: Her Life, Her Art, Her Legacy*. New York: Dodd Mead Publishers, 1963.

Thom, R. *L'Apologie du Logos*. Paris: Hachette, 1990.

Thomas, C. 'Le hasard dans la danse contemporaine'. Unpublished Doctoral Thesis, Université de Paris VIII, 1991

Todd, M. *The Thinking Body*. New York: Dance Horizons, 1937.

Turner, M.J. *New Dance: approach to non-literal choreography.* University of Pitts-burgh Press, 1971.

Valéry, Paul. *Œuvres Complètes.* Paris: Gallimard, 1957.
Valéry, Paul. *Variété II.* Paris: Gallimard, 1928, re-edited with an Introduction by Dominique Dupuy entitled 'La mesure des choses', p. 61.
Virilio, Paul 'Gravitational Space' in *Traces of Dance.* Paris: Editions Dis Voir, 1994.
_____ *L'inertie polaire.* Paris: Galilée, 1992.

Waehner, Karin *Outillage Chorégraphique.* Paris: Vigot, 1995.
Wagner, Richard. *The art-work of the future, and other works,* translated by William Ashton Ellis. Lincoln: University of Nebraska Press, 1993.
Walsh, Nicole 'Eric Hawkins, signification du geste dansé' in *Danse, le corps en jeu.* Edited by Mireille Arguel. Paris: PUF, 1992.
Walther, S. 'The Dance Theatre of Kurt Jooss' in *Choreography and Dance,* vol. III. Harwood Academic Publishers, 1993.
Warren, L. *Sokolow Anna : The Rebellious Spirit.* Princeton NJ: Princeton Books Company, 1991.
Wavelet, C. 'Quel corps, quelle transmission, quel enseignement?' in *Marsyas,* No. 34, Summer 1995, pp. 39-44.
Weaver, John. 'The History of the Mimes and Pantomimes' (1727), in *The life and works of John Weaver,* facsimile edition edited by Richard Ralph. London: Dance Books, 1985.
Wigman, Mary *The Language of Dance.* translated by Walter Sorell. Middletown, Connecticut: Wesleyan UP, 1966.
_____ 'Philosophy of Dance' in *Dance as a Theatre Art: Source Readings in Dance History from 1581 to the Present.* Dodd, Mead & Co., 1974.
_____ 'Composition in pure movement' in *Modern Music 8,* no.2, 1931.
Winearls, Jane. *Modern Dance, the Jooss-Leeder Method.* London: Adam & Charles Black, 1978.

Yates, Frances. *The Art of Memory.* London: Warburg Institute, 1974.

Zeami. *La tradition secrète du No.* French translation by R. Siffert. Paris: Gallimard, 1970.

Index

Lightning Source UK Ltd.
Milton Keynes UK
12 November 2010

162754UK00001B/10/P